THE CARS OF
BMC

THE CARS OF
BMC

GRAHAM ROBSON

MRP

MOTOR RACING PUBLICATIONS LTD
Unit 6, The Pilton Estate, 46 Pitlake, Croydon CRO 3RY, England

ISBN 0 947981 14 4
First published 1987

The author and publishers are grateful to The Austin Rover
Group Limited for supplying the majority of colour and
black and white pictures reproduced in this book.

Photosetting by Tek-Art Ltd, West Wickham, Kent
Printed in Great Britain by Netherwood, Dalton & Co Ltd
Bradley Mills, Huddersfield, West Yorkshire

Contents

Introduction

To all but a few insiders, this announcement, made on Friday, November 23, 1951, came as a great shock:

'For some time past the boards of Morris Motors Ltd, and the Austin Motor Co Ltd, have had under consideration the desirability of amalgamating the two companies. In the result they have arrived at the conclusion that unified control would not only lead to more efficient and economic production, but would also further the export drive, and be particularly beneficial to manufacturing and assembly abroad.

'They have formed the opinion, therefore, that amalgamation would be both in the national interest and to the advantage of the shareholders of both companies. Accordingly they propose a merger of interests . . .'

So there it was – Britain's two largest motor-manufacturing businesses were getting together to form an enormous conglomerate. Although the name of the new group had not even been invented at that time, *this* was the conception, if not the actual birthday, of the British Motor Corporation. Officially, it came into existence on March 31, 1952 (April 1 would have been tempting fate too much!), and it was much the most important British motor industry business until 1968, when Leyland Motors came along, another merger took place, and BMC became a member of the even larger British Leyland concern.

In those 16 years, the British Motor Corporation – BMC – grew mightily, in the process turning itself from a colossus into a dinosaur. I *think* I am using the word 'dinosaur' advisedly, because that great unwieldy beast had its brain at one end of a huge body, and little apparent control over its extremities; there were many occasions, even after a decade or more of so-called rationalization, when the pundits accused BMC of behaving in the same way! The other side of the argument is that the dinosaurs were very successful *at the time*, and so was BMC.

To be fair, the Corporation was to provide both good news and bad news. BMC production soared from about 236,000 cars a year in 1951-52 to a peak of 730,862 in the mid-1960s, yet in the process the group's share of UK car production fell from 53% to 40%. Even so, how could one complain about a group which produced cars as exciting as the Mini, as pleasurable as the Sprite and the MGB, and as practical as the Morris Minor? And were the enthusiasts *really* justified in deriding cars like the B-Series Farina saloons when they sold in such large quantities? As one of their aims in life, BMC's directors tried to provide something for everyone, and you only have to look at the annual profit figures to see that the policy worked.

In the 'BMC years', so many models, carrying so many marque badges and built in such variety (and in so many different factories) were sold that it was often difficult to relate one to the other. Although many books have been written about the sporting or the 'classic' BMC cars, some marques, and the cars involved, have been ignored completely.

You can see, I hope, why I felt that I *had* to write this book. Before the records were finally dispersed, and before interest in some of the less worthy cars was lost for ever, I thought it essential to write everything down.

In other words, I intend this book to be nothing less than a complete Buyers' Guide, or Directory, to the cars of BMC.

To do the job properly, however, I have had to widen the scope considerably, for no corporation and its products comes into existence by immaculate conception, or leaves no trace when it dies. On the one hand, I have surveyed the Austin and Nuffield cars which existed immediately before the merger was announced – in effect I have considered the 'dowry' which each brought to the marriage – and on the other I have described those British Leyland products which were directly descended from BMC models, or were designed by BMC before the British Leyland Motor Corporation (BLMC) was formed.

This explains why there is mention of cars like the Morris Six and the Riley RM-Series (which were both pure Nuffield), and why I have included the Austin Maxi (which was designed by BMC in the mid-1960s as the follow-on project from the 1800 'Land-crab').

I also took great interest in detailing the history and usage of the three BMC 'corporate' engines – A-Series, B-Series and C-Series – to show that here, at least, Leonard Lord's 'Grand Design' was actually successful, and I have also tried to list all the special, often very different, BMC cars built overseas.

The BMC period has always been of particular interest to me, for I was at Oxford University (and therefore close to Cowley and Abingdon) in its formative years, I took a job in the motor industry in Coventry when the 'Farina' phase was beginning, I became a BMC car owner soon after that (first with an A35, then with a carpet-floating Mini, followed by a tuned-up Austin-Healey 'frog-eye' Sprite), and I began to write about cars when the Mini-Cooper craze was at its height and the MG Abingdon factory was at its most famous. I have, in short, been a BMC-watcher all my adult life.

This does not mean, unfortunately, that the story which unfolds in the following pages is encyclopaedic. Without the existence of completely detailed archives it cannot be so. In the mid-1960s, perhaps, everything about the BMC years was known, and probably written down at Longbridge, but by the mid-1970s, when the Leyland hierarchy and swept through the factories, a lot of automobile history had unceremoniously been thrown out. There were already, in any case, yawning gaps in the archive kept by Morris Motors, and especially by Pressed Steel – unless, that is, someone out there knows better!

As far as possible, however, I hope that this book is a complete guide to The Cars of BMC, their characteristics and their relationship to each other. Maybe, when you have read it, you will understand more of Leonard Lord's 'Grand Design', and you might even have changed your mind about the Corporation's strategy. In compiling the book, I certainly did.

Autumn 1986   GRAHAM ROBSON

Acknowledgements

It would have been impossible to produce all the facts and figures quoted in this book without the help of one particular expert – Anders Clausager – who is the esteemed archivist of the British Motor Industry Heritage Trust. Not only did Anders allow me to grub around in his archive – a real privilege, as I understand it – but he checked the manuscript for mistakes, offered his opinion about *my* opinions, and helped me find a goodly proportion of the black-and-white and colour illustrations. A simple 'Thank You' is really not good enough in this case – but perhaps the book may even be of some use to BMIHT in years to come!

Then, of course, I had to check manufacturers' publicity material against the information put out when each car was launched – and that meant that I had to make repeated reference to the two most reliable motoring magazines of record – *(The) Autocar* and *(The) Motor*. These are two massive collections and I could never do without them.

There was also the pleasure of consulting back numbers of *Classic and Sportscar*, a magazine which has always been ready to feature and detail the careers of some BMC cars which other publications haughtily ignore. Editor Mark Hughes, and his archivist Jon Pressnell, must now be delighted that this job is over! For my part, I am extremely grateful for their help.

I must also acknowledge the help, mainly in being able to double-check my facts and figures, which came from all the individual marque books which have been published about BMC cars. Then, of course, there were all those unknown heroes at BMC and its component companies who produced lists, statistics and records which have survived to delight number-crunchers like myself in later years.

When it came to collecting all the illustrations, quite a number of people were helpful:

I started from my own collection, which has grown over the years, and then enlisted my publisher, John Blunsden, and his associate, Ray Hutton, to raid their own comprehensive stocks of pictures. Then it was time to call in the specialists, and I'd like to thank the following: Michael Allen, Phil Ansell, Dave Barry, Jeff Daniels, Chris Harvey, Kim Henson, Mark Hughes, Dave Kennard, David Knowles, Wilson McComb, Ray Newell, Lindsay Porter, Jon Pressnell and Paul Skilleter.

Thank you, one and all.

GRAHAM ROBSON

Chapter 1

Building an empire

The founding of BMC

All big businesses start as small businesses, and most small businesses start as the love-child of just one person; the Austin Motor Company and the Nuffield Organisation were no exception to this rule. The roots of the BMC story really took shape, way back in Victorian times, when two ambitious men – Herbert Austin and William Morris – started their careers; BMC was a long time a-coming. By the time BMC was formed, one of the two had been dead for a decade, and the other had become a Viscount. In 1952, the founding fathers of BMC were Lord Nuffield (for that is the title William Morris had adopted when ennobled in the 1930s) and Leonard Lord.

Many specialist histories have been written about the Austin and Morris marques, and as this is a book about relatively modern cars, concerning a group which only existed between 1952 and 1968, there is no need to dwell at length on the early development of the two companies. At this stage, though, it is worth recalling that the Austin Motor Company was founded in 1905, and sold only 31 cars in its first full year, while W.R.M. Motors (the predecessor of Morris Motors) started trading in 1912, and sold just 393 cars in the whole of 1913. Austin was still called Austin in the early 1950s, while W.R.M. Motors had become Morris Motors in 1919 and was to be the most important constituent part of the larger Nuffield Organisation from 1936.

To an economist, a merger between the two companies might have seemed desirable for many years, but to the companies themselves there always seemed to be good commercial reasons – or a clash of formidable personalities – to get in the way of the marriage. One of the most surprising facts about BMC, therefore, was that it took so long to be created. There had, after all, been plenty of motor industry precedents to encourage it to happen – for in the USA the giant General Motors

Corporation had been founded before the First World War, while the Rootes Group of Great Britain had been built up in the early 1930s.

Both companies, of course, had already received plenty of offers, and both Austin and Morris had previously been involved in mergers, takeovers, or potential deals on several occasions in their long histories.

The Austin company – to 1938

Herbert Austin was a farmer's son, born in Great Missenden, Buckinghamshire, in November 1866. He began work in Australia at 17 years of age, working in his uncle's engineering firm, moved on through two other jobs, then joined the Wolseley Sheep Shearing Machine Co Ltd. This Sydney-based firm transferred its head offices to Great Britain in 1889, and Herbert Austin became its manager in 1893.

He soon turned the company to making machine tools, and in 1895 (or 1896, depending on which historian is telling the story), he went ahead with the design of the original Wolseley tri-car, which was unashamedly based on the layout of the French Leon Bollée model. Threats of legal action killed that one, but a second, less contentious, tri-car was ready for the 1896 Crystal Palace Show. Production of Wolseleys began in 1900, and in the same year the tools and motor car side of the business was bought by Vickers, the large engineering and armaments combine, after which production of the range began in earnest.

It is a matter of well-known history that Austin quarrelled with his co-directors over future design (they wanted him to use vertical engines, while he wanted to stick to horizontal engines) and that they parted very acrimoniously in 1905.

During and after the dispute, you might have expected Vickers to try to stop Herbert Austin designing cars for

This was Longbridge's old Trentham assembly building in 1948, with Austin A40 Devons being built. In those days, most of the cars went for export.

another company, but perhaps someone made a mistake and forgot all about this because within weeks Austin had taken over a disused factory at Longbridge, on the southern outskirts of Birmingham, with a road frontage of a mere 200 feet on a 2½-acre site. The deal he struck included the purchase of a further 5½ acres, and there he set up his own company and prepared to build Austin cars. The first Austin car design was shown at Olympia in November 1905 – but only as a set of drawings – and deliveries of 25-30hp models began in the middle of 1906. Herbert Austin was already 39 years old.

Production – and profits – expanded mightily in the next 10 years, and Austin became a public company in 1914. It then made the big mistake of deciding to run a one-model policy at the end of the First World War, based on the 3.6-litre 20hp car. Munitions work had

encouraged him to expand his factory site to become one of the largest in Birmingham – by 1919 it covered 203½ acres, of which 58 acres was factory buildings. At this point, though, the postwar slump in demand, and a sharp rise in inflation, saw the company tumble crazily from profitability in 1919 to making huge losses in 1920 and 1921. By the spring of 1921 the Receiver had been called in. Herbert Austin's personal wealth had been decimated, and as part of the recovery programme he was even ousted from the managing director's chair for a time. In the whole of 1921, total production of Austin cars was only 2,246.

The blessing of being ousted from the guv'nor's chair was that it gave Austin the time to think and plan the new models which his company needed to survive and prosper. Two new cars did the trick – the 12/4, which

By 1962 Longbridge had expanded and been modernized. This shot, taken from the north, shows the new Car Assembly Building (CAB for short). CAB2 is closest to the camera, CAB1 to the far right, and the multi-storey building is for the temporary parking of new cars.

Longbridge in the mid-1960s, at the height of BMC's power and influence, taken from the north and looking almost due south. The large CABs (Car Assembly Buildings) are furthest from the camera, with the multi-storey park to their right. The building surrounded by lawns is 'The Kremlin' (the main administrative building), with the engineering design building to the left of the lawns and the engineering development workshops along the frontage of the dual carriageway in the foreground.

went on sale in 1922, and the legendary Seven, which followed it a year later. It wasn't long before he was back in command!

The result was an amazing turnaround. By 1926 the company was making 25,000 cars a year, the accumulated losses were paid off a few months after that, and by 1933 more than 50,000 cars a year were being produced. That year Austin made more cars than Morris – which was the pinnacle at which Sir Herbert Austin had been aiming for some years.

In the meantime, there had already been two sets of merger talks. That distinguished Austin historian, Bob Wyatt, eloquently sums up the first in his marque history *The Austin, 1905-52:*

'In 1924 there was negotiation between the Austin and Morris companies. Sir Herbert Austin and William Morris did not like each other very much. They were both products of the late Victorian era, and "captains of industry", but there the similarity ended except, perhaps, in that they were both obstinate. Austin was an engineer, but not a financier in the expansionist sense; Morris was neither an engineer nor such a financier. Austin wanted to stay in business and was not bothered about wealth because he loved engineering more than money. Morris did not bother about engineering at all, but he wanted to make as much money as he could.'

It was Sir Herbert Austin, apparently, who wanted to make a big business even larger, and he was certainly the driving force in setting up a tripartite meeting between himself, William Morris and Dudley Docker of Vickers (who still owned Wolseley). Whatever his hopes, they were soon dashed, for Morris listened politely but was clearly unimpressed as his own company profits were much more impressive than those of the companies

Morris Motors, Cowley, in the late 1920s/early 1930s period, looking east from Cowley. There was more expansion to come before 1939, after Leonard Lord had produced his rationalized production policy. The separate buildings at the top of the picture housed the then-new Pressed Steel Company.

By the 1970s, the Cowley complex had changed considerably. This shot is from the north, with Pressed Steel Company buildings in the foreground, the Oxford eastern bypass passing through the foreground, and the much expanded Morris factory with buildings on both sides of the Oxford road behind it. The overhead conveyor carried bodyshells direct from the Pressed Steel building to the paint shop in the Morris factory.

The Cowley complex, 1939-style, looking towards the north-east, with the much enlarged Pressed Steel Company buildings at the top of the picture. 'South Works' (not used for final assembly at that time) is on the right, and of course there is still no sign of the Oxford eastern bypass, which eventually threaded its way between the Cowley 'North Works' and the Pressed Steel Company buildings.

trying to merge with him. They might need him, but he certainly did not need them! Within days, it seems, the merger proposal was abandoned.

Within a year, Austin had been talking mergers with a far more formidable concern – the mighty General Motors Corporation from the USA. GM offered a firm takeover proposal, but Austin eventually turned it down because the directors thought that GM were not offering anything like enough money for the business. Many years later, GM's famous president, Alfred Sloan, wrote that he had thought Austin's factory to be in poor condition and its management weak, but that might just have been an old man's face-saving excuse. Shortly afterwards, his negotiators bought Vauxhall instead.

Austin also put in several bids for Wolseley, when Vickers allowed its car-making subsidiary to drift into bankruptcy in 1926, but was outbid by William Morris himself. [I give more details of this important event later in the chapter.] After that, Sir Herbert himself and his directors seemed to lose interest in mergers or takeovers, and the company continued to grow and remain profitable throughout the 1930s. Sir Herbert became Lord Austin of Longbridge in 1936.

By this time the company's founder was in his 70th year, growing tired of business, and actively looking around for a successor. In spite of the jibes from his detractors, it became clear that he was not going to promote his son-in-law Arthur Waite any further, and there was no obvious successor among his fellow directors. His financial 'guru' Ernest Payton was too old (and had too many outside business interests), while his production director C.R. Englebach was not only an old

Morris Motors, Cowley, in the mid-1930s, after Leonard Lord had finished with it. Those are Morris Eights in the foreground, with Series II 10s and 12s next to them.

The Morris 8 Series E was launched in 1938, and was the predecessor to the Morris Minor. Its basic bodyshell was used in the MG YA saloon of 1947, and its side-valve engine in the Minor Series MM.

man, but rapidly losing his eyesight.

In February 1938, to the astonishment of nearly everyone in the motoring industry, he chose Leonard Lord! From the moment that 'LPL' (as he was sometimes known) took up his job, the whole atmosphere at Longbridge changed. Before then it had been a traditional, almost backward-looking business; afterwards there was a forward-looking 'buzz' everywhere.

Morris and Nuffield – the between-wars phenomenon

For many years, William Richard Morris, the founder of Morris Motors who became Lord Nuffield in 1934, was always seen as the wise and benign father-figure at the head of a large and very personal business empire. Not until years after his retirement, nor particularly until after his death in 1963, did the full story emerge. The fact is that Lord Nuffield, who undoubtedly used pragmatic genius in turning a tiny car-assembling business of 1913

into Britain's largest car maker by the mid-1920s, most certainly had 'feet of clay'.

Looking back soberly, and with the considerable benefit of hindsight, I have to ask if his empire might have been more successful (perhaps, even, lastingly so, without the need for mergers) if he could ever have brought himself to ask for advice, and then to act on it. If he had, might there not have been a possibility of Leonard Lord staying at Cowley and making the Nuffield Organisation so dominant that a merger with Austin might not have been needed?

Like many small men who grow and develop into big men, Nuffield could never bring himself to have much trust in his colleagues. If not at first, then certainly in the last 20 years of his business life, the story of Morris Motors and the Nuffield Organisation is one of Lord Nuffield distrusting, arguing with, ignoring, splitting with and sometimes sacking his closest advisers.

He battled publicly, and ultimately successfully, with Sir Herbert Austin over the fate of Wolseley in 1926, and had a series of towering disagreements with the British Government over aero engine design and production policy in the 1930s. It is significant that Nuffield, alone of the major car-making concerns in Britain, was not involved in the first of the Air Ministry's 'shadow factory' schemes in the late 1930s.

My opinion is that he was at his best in the 1910s and 1920s, when he still understood the scope of his business, but out of his depth by the 1930s, when first Leonard Lord, then Miles Thomas, had to make commercial sense out of a ramshackle organization.

Morris himself was originally an artisan, of what might patronizingly be known as 'yeoman stock', born in Worcester in October 1877, though his father was a bailiff on the family farm at Headington, near Oxford. The family finally moved to Oxford in 1880, and when young Morris reached 14 years of age he became apprenticed to a bicycle repairer in the city.

In 1892, having amassed the princely sum of £4, he set himself up in the bicycle repairing business in Cowley, and from then it was a short step to start building bicycles. Business premises in High Street, Oxford were soon supplemented by workshops at Holywell Street, on the corner of Longwall, and in the next 10 years the cycle business was wound down to make way for work on cars. By 1910 The Morris Garages had been founded.

At about this time the 33-year-old Morris was shrewd enough to see the opportunity for going into motor car manufacture, and he decided to produce a popularly-priced machine. He also perceived a way to achieve this without spending a fortune in tooling and equipment. At a time when firms like Wolseley, Rover and Riley were building cars essentially by hand methods, Morris proposed to follow Henry Ford's mass-production philosophies.

To do this (and this was perhaps the most important decision of all), he decided to produce an 'assembled' car rather than manufacture most of it himself. Instead of using self-designed chassis, engines, transmissions and bodywork, all of which cost a fair fortune to design, develop and tool up for production, Morris decided to persuade components manufacturers to take those risks instead, and to concentrate all his own efforts on assembly.

In spite of initial problems over engine supply – White & Poppe of Coventry were first, Continental (of the USA) were chosen for the second model, and Hotchkiss & Cie produced 'copied-Continentals' immediately after the First World War – it was a remarkably successful strategy. Much of the design of the original 'bullnose' Morris was done by 'Pop' Landstad, who was White & Poppe's chief draughtsman in Coventry.

The first Morris car was built in 1913, in an old and disused military training college at Temple Cowley, which was right on the edge of the built-up area of Cowley, itself a suburb of Oxford. Almost at once, however, the new company needed more space, buildings were erected at the other edge of the side road, and in the next 20 years the Cowley complex grew, in a somewhat haphazard manner, along what is now the B480, away from the city centre. By the end of the 1920s, Pressed Steel had also been established close by, and before the end of the 1930s the Morris Motors/Pressed Steel complex was as large as that at Longbridge, and just as higgledy-piggledy in layout.

Except for the hiccup of 1921, when Morris had to slash his prices repeatedly to keep his factories working, production shot rapidly upwards. From 387 cars in 1919, sales leapt to 20,048 in 1923 and to 55,582 in 1925, and all were based on the same 'bullnose' design. Morris Motors went 'public' in 1926. Then, in the next few years, something seemed to go wrong at Cowley, for although several new models, including the little Morris Minor of 1928, were introduced, sales fell away, and it was not until Leonard Lord arrived in the early 1930s to sort out the mess that sales began to perk up again. By the late 1930s, production was up to between 90,000 and 100,000 cars a year, and Morris was once again ahead of Austin. The two big advances made by a company that was very conservative in its designs was that the first chassisless model (the Morris 10 Series M) was introduced in 1938, and more and more overhead-valve engine designs were used.

In the meantime, not only had William Morris become Sir William in 1928 and Lord Nuffield in 1934, but he had become involved in a whole series of agreed acquisitions, takeovers and new business ventures. Since some of these (bought after 1926) were originally financed from his personal fortune, and some by Morris Motors, it was all very confusing until 1935, when one of Leonard Lord's most important moves was to see that the 'personal' companies were absorbed by Morris Motors. All these moves are important to the BMC story, for they illustrate the sprawling empire that had to be rationalized in the 1950s and 1960s.

The first flourish of buys included Osberton Radiators, Hotchkiss & Cie, Hollick and Pratt, E.G. Wrigley & Co, and the SU carburettor company – all of which were major suppliers to Morris Motors. The first four soon became Morris Radiators, Morris Engines, Morris Bodies and Morris Commercial Cars.

Then, in 1926, came the rumoured approach for his business from General Motors, which was supposed to have offered £11 million for the Morris empire. I have been careful to use the word 'rumoured', because references to this bid are usually based on the opening

The MG factory at Abingdon was always an assembly, rather than a manufacturing, centre. Early in the 1950s, when BMC was formed, MG TD sports cars and YB saloons were built on the same lines – and pushed from station to station.

words of a highly dramatized life of Lord Nuffield (*The Nuffield Story,* by Robert Jackson – long out of print). It may be more significant that *no mention* of this approach from a team headed by GM's president Alfred Sloan, which would have been of the utmost importance to the development of the Morris business, is made either in the official biography, or by Sloan in his memoirs!

At the end of 1926, however, Vickers allowed the Wolseley car-making business to go into liquidation, and Morris fought to buy the business, against Austin and one other un-named foreign company. After an unprecedented courtroom auction, in which Morris was quite determined to outbid everyone else, he personally acquired the company for £730,000. Not only was Wolseley speedily revived by Morris managers (which included the young Leonard Lord, whose reputation as a production planner was already booming), but it soon began to provide overhead-camshaft engines for use in new Morris and MG models.

In the meantime, Cecil Kimber, of Morris Garages (which was Morris' *original* concern and still his personal property), had been developing sporting Morris cars which he soon titled 'MG'. By the end of the 1920s the MG Car Company had been set up, installed in a factory at Abingdon, just a few miles south of Oxford, and was selling more and more sports cars which used engines and transmissions built by Wolseley.

Not that all Morris ventures were successful. In 1924, it had been decided to set up a car-making plant at Le Mans, in France, but the Société Française des Automobiles Morris Leon Bollée (which made Morris cars of British design) staggered from crisis to crisis. The French did not take to the cars in the way that the British had done, and the business was finally closed down in 1931.

In 1932, Leonard Lord, who had made such an impact in Birmingham, at Wolseley, was brought in to Cowley as managing director of Morris Motors. He masterminded the complete rejuvenation of the product line, saw the assembly process finally brought up to date, oversaw the financial integration of MG and Wolseley into Morris Motors – then abruptly stormed out of his job in August 1936 when Lord Nuffield refused to grant him a share of the increased profits that his genius had generated.

According to his then-colleague, Miles Thomas (who had become Wolseley's managing director by that time): 'His rupture with Nuffield in 1936 hurt him deeply. He sat in my office one afternoon in Birmingham while the strain and the anger of the split were still heavy on him and, suddenly blowing the ash off the inevitable cigarette between his lips, said, "Tommy, I'm going to take that business at Cowley apart brick by bloody brick". Later events proved that, if he didn't do just that, he became its dominating force in no uncertain way.'

We should not forget those words, nor the events leading up to them, for it was one of the principal influences behind the birth of the BMC combine in the early 1950s.

Before the outbreak of the Second World War, however, there were two more significant pieces of corporate action. Riley, that proud family-owned car-making business from Coventry, spent far too much of its money on motor racing and a plethora of unnecessary new models, and fell into the hands of the Receiver early in 1938. In the autumn, Lord Nuffield personally bought Riley – for £143,000 – then promptly re-sold it to Morris Motors for a mere £100. There was little time to rationalize Riley in the next year or so, only to get things moving again; the big changes would have to wait until postwar days. In the same period, and to make Nuffield progressively less dependent on outside suppliers of bodies, the company set up Nuffield Metal Products on land adjacent to Wolseley, in Birmingham – its first major product being the Morris Eight Series E shell.

Austin and Leonard Lord, 1938 to 1952 – the build-up to BMC

Having sworn revenge on Lord Nuffield and taken a round-the-world trip in the meantime, Leonard Lord popped up again at Austin in February 1938 as works director in succession to C.R. Englebach. Almost at once it became clear that he was Lord Austin's heir-apparent, and at whirlwind speed he began to evolve a radical new-model policy which not only included several entirely new cars, but the introduction of Austin trucks as well.

Four weeks after joining the company, Lord presented his master plan at a board meeting. It was to involve new 8, 10 and 12hp cars with side-valve engines, 14, 18 and 25hp cars with overhead-valve engines, and a line of trucks which would share their 3½-litre six-cylinder engine with the largest of the proposed cars.

Although Austin had had a diesel-engined truck under development at Longbridge since 1935, this was immediately scrapped by the decisive Leonard Lord, who took the very simple alternative of buying in some Bedford trucks, having them copied, and putting his new 'Birmingham Bedfords' on sale at the beginning of 1939. Even allowing for the urgency of the situation, this was fast going indeed! As far as the cars of the future were concerned, the *real* significance of the 'Birmingham Bedford' was that the six-cylinder engine became the postwar D-Series used in the Princess range, while the four-cylinder derivative of it was used in cars like the A70, A90 and Austin-Healey 100.

The new 8hp, 10hp and 12hp cars were all revealed during 1939, but the outbreak of war killed off the rest of the programme. During the war, Austin continued to build military versions of the 8hp (until 1942) and the 10hp (throughout the six years), the 2.2-litre overhead-valve 'four' was developed in that period, and the 16hp car was announced before the end of 1944.

In the meantime, Lord Austin gradually withdrew from his business, attended his last board meeting in November 1940, and died on May 23, 1941, aged 75. Unlike Lord Nuffield, he had not amassed a huge fortune, for his will totalled a mere £509,712. At this time, E.L. Payton took over as chairman and managing director, while Leonard Lord (who had been the *de facto* boss of Austin for three years already) officially became joint managing director in 1942. A year later Lord also became deputy chairman, and when Payton's health suddenly collapsed in November 1945, 'LPL' became Austin's chairman and chief executive. It was a position

The MG factory in 1956 was assembling MGAs (foreground), ZA Magnettes (centre) and Riley Pathfinders (behind the steel pillars). No sign, yet, of any Austin-Healeys, of course.

of great power and influence that he was to occupy for the next 16 years.

The postwar Austin company went from strength to strength under Lord. As part of the re-armament programme and the shadow factory scheme the company had built two massive new plants at Cofton Hackett, which was about a mile further south of the old Longbridge buildings, standing alongside the Birmingham-Bristol railway line. Impressive numbers of complete aeroplane engines and – later – complete aircraft had been built there in the 1939-45 period, the 'planes having been flown out by way of the airfield on top of the hill which has since been submerged by the CAB assembly buildings. Clearly the company would not be short of space in which to build its postwar vehicles,

though Cofton Hackett was not available right away, as the last Lancaster aircraft was not finished off and delivered until 1946.

Leonard Lord's first priority was to get the assembly lines moving again, and by the end of 1945 the prewar-style 8hp, 10hp, 12hp and 16hp cars were all in production again. The first true postwar models to appear were the very large A110 Sheerline/A120 Princess saloons and limousines – the Princess being built in North London by Vanden Plas, the specialist coachbuilding company which was absorbed by Austin in 1946. Almost immediately, the engines of these cars were enlarged to 4 litres, their names becoming A125 and A135, respectively.

Then came the A40 Devon and Dorset models later in

By the mid-1960s, the MG factory had changed very little, but the cars were completely different. MGB GTs are on the closest assembly line, Sprites and Midgets in the centre and MGB tourers behind the pillars.

1947, which not only were the first postwar mass-production Austins, but used an all-new 1.2-litre overhead-valve four-cylinder engine. Although this unit was different in many ways from the BMC B-Series engine which followed in the early 1950s, it was a definite and obvious ancestor to that famous 'building block'.

A year later Austin also launched the A70 Hampshire and A90 Atlantic models, which shared the same chassis and different versions of the larger four-cylinder engine developed from the truck unit, but had entirely different styling; the A70 looked like an overgrown A40, but the A90 looked . . . different!

The postwar product line, therefore, was now complete, and Austin could get on with yet more exciting developments. Some of them were bricks-and-mortar – the erection of an all-new car-assembly building (which

explains its title of CAB) on top of the hill, filling in the gap between the old Longbridge plant and the Cofton Hackett building and obliterating the airfield site (now surplus to requirements) as well as new administrative and design engineering blocks – but another was the evolution of a completely new small car. The new CAB was ready in summer 1951, in time to accept the next wave of new Austin models.

Austin wanted to call their new design the 'Austin Seven' (nostalgia was alive and well in the sales department), but eventually they had to settle for A30 instead; this new model was to have a great deal of influence on the small cars of BMC which followed it. Not only did it have a small and narrow monocoque (with styling helped along by the Loewy Studio, no less), but it had a brand-new small four-cylinder engine with

Austin-Healey 3000 bodies were painted and trimmed by Jensen at West Bromwich, but finally assembled at Abingdon.

overhead valves, which looked for all the world like a shrunken A40 unit but was different in almost every detail; this was the A-Series design, which would still be built at Longbridge in the late 1980s! Design commenced in the late 1940s, and the first derivative – a four-door saloon priced at £507 – was unveiled in the autumn of 1951.

With car production rushing up to more than 130,000 units a year; and profits to £8.3 millions by 1951, the stage was set for the next phase in Leonard Lord's master plan – the merger with the Nuffield Organisation.

Indian summer – Nuffield's last 10 years
During the Second World War, the Nuffield Organisation contributed a lot to the war effort, and produced thousands of military vehicles and trucks,

though it made virtually no passenger cars. Lord Nuffield took ever fewer executive decisions as the years passed by, his vice-chairman Oliver Boden died suddenly due to overwork, and the result was that Miles Thomas (soon to become Sir Miles) was called back to Cowley from Wolseley in Birmingham to become Nuffield's vice-chairman and effectively, if not actually, its chief executive. As Sir Miles later wrote in his autobiography:

'Nuffield characteristically said that he was going to "leave it all" to me, that I should be paid £10,000 a year, but that he "would like to know what was going on".'

As Sir Miles later found out, what that *actually* meant was that although Lord Nuffield spent more and more time away from his factories, often on long sea voyages, he seemed to be jealous of every decision taken in his absence, destructively interfered on many other occasions, and eventually made life very difficult for his staff. Perhaps it was not surprising that Sir Miles later considered an offer to join Austin, at Longbridge, to work in harness with Leonard Lord, nor that in November 1947 the two parted company, Reg Hanks (who had accompanied Nuffield on his last sea trip) becoming vice-chairman in his place.

At almost the same time, Lord Nuffield peremptorily 'retired' nine of his fellow board directors, including 'Pop' Landstad, H.A. Ryder, H. Seaward and Victor Riley. From that time, in my opinion, the Nuffield Organisation was living on borrowed time, and its policies gradually seemed to slip into limbo. The only obvious rationalizations made (in 1949) were to bring Wolseley car assembly into Cowley from Birmingham,

and to locate Riley car assembly at the MG factory at Abingdon instead of in Coventry.

From 1945 to 1948, the only truly new car to be announced by a Nuffield company was the graceful RM-Series Riley model, for the Wolseley 8 and the MG Y-Type saloons were both prewar designs whose announcements had been deferred by the six years of war. Lord Nuffield, it is said, did not like the look of any of the new designs put up for approval by his engineers. Even so, postwar demand for *anything* that moved was such that Morris production increased to 68,772 in 1947-48, which was a higher figure than that being achieved by Austin.

At the Earls Court Motor Show of October 1948, there was a positive spate of new models from the group. In

Final pass-off of a whole variety of BMC sports cars at Abingdon in 1959 includes Austin-Healey 3000s, MGAs and MGA Twin-Cams and 'frog-eye' Austin-Healey Sprites.

Vanden Plas, Kingsbury, in 1974 (after the end of the BMC era), with Austin-based Allegros becoming Vanden Plas models.

addition to the new Morris Oxford and Six saloons, and their closely related Wolseley 4/50 and 6/80 derivatives, the famous Morris Minor was launched. However, the good news also had to be tempered by disappointment in parts of the new cars' specifications.

While the Morris Minor had splendid roadholding and a modern style, it was inflicted with an ancient (mid-1930s) side-valve engine design. In the bigger cars, there was a nice-sounding but none too efficient line of overhead-camshaft engines – except for the Morris Oxford, for which a newly-designed but old-fashioned side-valve engine had been chosen.

For the time being, however, these new cars were good enough to propel Nuffield sales – at home and overseas – to their highest levels. By 1951, the group was making up to 120,000 cars a year (nearly as many as Austin) and nearly £9 million in annual profits. But Lord Nuffield was an old man of 74 who seemed to have lost his appetite for innovation. Perhaps the approach from Leonard Lord and Austin came in the very nick of time.

Austin and Nuffield join forces – the BMC merger of 1951–52

We now know that Leonard Lord wanted to merge Austin with the Nuffield Organisation several years before it actually happened, and that Lord Nuffield could never see any advantage in this. As Graham Turner later wrote in *The Leyland Papers*:

'Lord once remarked that they [Austin and Morris] were like two Second Division teams trying to play in the First Division. Altogether, there seemed a good deal of logic in a merger: the only trouble was that Nuffield and Lord had not been on speaking terms for a long time.'

In spite of everything, however, the two companies tentatively got together – at arm's length, as it were – in October 1948. The official statement put out by both companies was that:

'Lord Nuffield and Mr L.P. Lord have recently had a series of talks which have resulted in an arrangement whereby there is to be a constant interchange of information on production methods, costs, purchases, design and research, patents and all other items which would be likely to result in manufacturing economies.

The object is to effect maximum standardization, coupled with the most efficient manufacture, and by the pooling of all factory resources, a consequent reduction of costs.'

Although the media – in particular the motoring press – indulged themselves in a positive orgy of speculation about this move, the truth behind it all was that very little indeed was achieved before the accord was dissolved nine months later, in July 1949. The 'engagement' was broken off with the aid of a very bald uninformative statement, and Lord Nuffield's official biographies rather smugly summarized that: 'It was, however, decided that the time was not ripe for the merger.' The fact of the matter, almost certainly, is that the two chairmen were no more likely to agree in 1948–49 than they had in 1936, when they had parted so acrimoniously.

This, of course, was never imparted to the shareholders, and if it had not been for the resource shown by Lord Nuffield's personal secretary, Charles (Carl) Kingerlee, the impasse might have persisted for some time. First of all, on the pretext of sending birthday wishes to Lord Nuffield in October 1950, Leonard Lord spoke to him on the telephone, shortly afterwards Kingerlee visited Leonard Lord at his home to discuss the merger which he now believed to be inevitable, and eventually LPL paid a visit, unannounced, to Lord Nuffield at his home.

With the ice broken, the Austin chairman then made a clandestine visit to see Lord Nuffield at Cowley, the two rapidly agreed that a merger *should* take place, and that the two boards of directors should be briefed and asked for their approval. Leonard Lord had no trouble with his own board, but Lord Nuffield's directors (as the obvious 'underdogs' in such a corporate move) were strongly against a merger, and Lord Nuffield had to tell Leonard Lord that the tentative agreement was to be put off once again.

Lord's retort was immediately to commission all the tooling for the new A30 model and to tell Carl Kingerlee about this. It rapidly became clear that the competition, rather than the co-operation, between the two companies might get even more intense, so within a year Leonard Lord made yet another approach to Lord Nuffield, and this time there was no last-minute breakdown. Lord Nuffield decided to sell his company, whatever his board might think.

The major opposition came from Reg Hanks (who nevertheless joined the BMC board and served on it for several years), who thought that: '. . . if Nuffield wanted to lose prestige and standing, he was certainly going the right way about it. Lord would keep him out of the factory just as he had kept Lord Austin out of the Longbridge plant'.

That was the last flourish of resistance, and the merger went ahead, at last. On March 31, 1952, the British Motor Corporation officially came into existence – and Britain had a 'First Division' motor manufacturer for the first time.

A well-known, but historic, picture. This is Lord Nuffield (left) with Leonard Lord (in glasses), his managing director at Cowley for a time. Later, the two became rivals, but from 1952 they were back in harness, if not always in agreement.

Chapter 2

In the driving seat

Sir Leonard Lord, Sir George Harriman
and their senior colleagues

In less than 20 years, BMC produced many new models and several important managers, but the Grand Design was all to the credit and restless energy of one man – Leonard Lord. Without Len Lord there would have been no Austin-Nuffield merger in the first place, and without Len Lord the Corporation would not have developed and expanded in such a remarkable manner.

Such was Lord's unmistakable personality and his remarkable character that there were times when the pundits, particularly Fleet Street journalists, were tempted to call BMC a 'one-man band'. But it was never as simple as that. For sure, Lord was a thrusting and aggressive manager, an expert production engineer and a compulsive designer, but he could not do it all alone. Behind the scenes, BMC's fortunes were refined by other, often unsung heroes.

Marriage partners
When the Austin-Nuffield merger was proposed in November 1951, Leonard Lord was chairman and managing director of Austin, while Lord Nuffield was chairman of the Nuffield Organisation, with Reg Hanks as his vice-chairman. There had been no nonsense involving negotiation by committee. Lord and Nuffield had done the deed between them, and their respective managements eventually approved the deal when there was little more to discuss.

The irony of all this was that Leonard Lord came into BMC as a conqueror, rather than as a civilized partner, for he had spent many formative years working for companies owned by William Morris (before he became Lord Nuffield), had been Lord Nuffield's managing director at Morris Motors for a short and turbulent period in the 1930s, had stormed out of Cowley after a blazing row in 1936, and had never forgiven Lord Nuffield for his attitude at that time. He was instantly to

become the dominant partner in BMC in 1952.

My description of the personalities involved must begin with the observation that Leonard Lord, aged 55 at the time of the merger, was still reaching the height of his powers, while Lord Nuffield, at 74, was really slipping towards retirement. In psychological terms, Leonard Lord was the aggressor, while Lord Nuffield was the defendant.

'LPL', Len Lord, Sir Leonard, or Lord Lambury?
Like many successful business tycoons, honours were heaped on Leonard Lord's shoulders once his genius had become obvious. He might not have been an 'establishment' figure, but his services to the motor industry were enormous. From being plain Leonard Lord, or 'LPL' as he was often called by his colleagues, he was knighted in 1954, and took the title of Lord Lambury in 1962 following his retirement. ('Lord Lord would sound bloody stupid', was LPL's typically trenchant remark when the peerage was announced!)

Leonard Percy Lord was born in Coventry in 1896, and was originally educated at Coventry's famous Bablake school. All his early career was in the 'motoring city', for an apprenticeship at Courtaulds was followed by a period at the Coventry Ordnance factory, then a short time at Daimler, until he joined Hotchkiss & Cie (which was shortly to become the Morris Motors Engines Branch) in 1921. His first links with Morris Motors and the future Lord Nuffield were really forged at that time.

In his autobiography, Sir Miles Thomas describes LPL as working in the production planning office at that time, and being a 'sharp-faced young ginger-haired Yorkshire lad of about the same age as myself, a tough, farsighted character named Len Lord . . .'. LPL, in fact, was not a Yorkshire lad (he *may* have had Yorkshire-born parents, although we do not know this for certain), but he

Leonard Lord (right) was not only a formidable businessman, but a compulsive designer. Here he is inspecting a model of the proposed Austin A90 Atlantic; Austin's chief stylist, Dick Burzi, is with him.

had all the blunt and forceful Yorkshire habits in his manner.

LPL worked well with Frank Woollard, general manager of Morris Engines from 1923, who was really the father of mass-production and transfer machining in the British motor industry; he was soon a marked man, with promotion prospects ahead of him. It was while he was at the Morris Motors Engines Branch that he came to know the works manager, George (later nicknamed 'Old George') Harriman, and his son 'Young George'. 'Young' George Harriman and Leonard Lord struck up a friendship at the time which they were to retain for more than 40 years, and 'Young George' eventually succeeded Sir Leonard as BMC's chairman in 1961.

In 1927, William Morris transferred Leonard Lord to Wolseley, in Birmingham, to reorganize the production facilities of what was a very run-down business; he was so successful in this that when it became time for the Morris Motors Cowley complex to be modernized Leonard Lord was drafted in as managing director.

During the next four years Leonard Lord not only cemented his reputation in the British motor industry, but he became irrevocably unable to get on with Lord Nuffield. It must have been an exciting, if traumatic, period for all concerned, for the factory was re-equipped from end to end. The work involved the introduction of flow-line assembly and moving assembly lines (previously, all Morris cars had been pushed from station to station), the design of a number of successful new cars, and the introduction of the Morris 'Series' philosophy,

where new models were not introduced immediately before the Olympia motor show, but when the tooling and facilities were ready.

It was at this time, too, that Lord ditched the Morris Minor's small (Wolseley-designed) overhead-cam engine in favour of a simple and rugged side-valve unit designed quite simply by buying examples of the new Ford Model Y 933cc units and copying them! It might not have been ethical, but it worked – and it was something Lord was to do again at Longbridge in future years.

The same period saw Nuffield's rambling business and financial affairs knocked into shape, with both the personally-owned car companies, MG and Wolseley, brought into the Morris Motors net. For Lord Nuffield it was all too much. Although Lord had originally been given a free hand, Lord Nuffield felt compelled to interfere at every stage, not always successfully and usually against Lord's wishes. Neither was a tolerant man, and when Leonard Lord demanded a substantial share of the profits which his work had begun to generate there was an immediate and bitter quarrel. Lord stormed out of Cowley, not to return for 15 years, and although there was a partial reconciliation in 1937, when Lord agreed to manage Lord Nuffield's £2 million Special Areas Trust (set up to alleviate unemployment in 'hard core' problem areas) it was a fragile peace.

It was inevitable that Leonard Lord would soon re-enter the motor industry, but everyone – especially Lord Nuffield – was surprised when he joined the Austin Motor Company at Longbridge as their works director. That, of course, was only the start of things, for Lord Austin had already settled on Leonard Lord as his successor, gave him a completely free hand to do whatever was necessary to the business, and began to withdraw from the scene.

The scene was set, therefore, for Leonard Lord's next great surge forward and the further enhancement of his already high reputation. As I have already recorded in the previous chapter, he swept through the Longbridge workshops, design offices and corridors of power like a whirlwind, scattering cigarette ash at every turn, inspiring many of his subordinates to greater things, and infuriating as many others.

The staid old Austin company of the mid-1930s was turned into an amazingly productive wartime machine, then modernized and hurled at the beckoning export opportunities which opened up in the late 1940s. Mistakes were made – some of them substantial ones – but one could never again accuse Austin of being a backward company, or one which was merely ticking over. Wherever you looked or listened at Longbridge there was a hum of activity.

One of the mistakes, which took some years to resolve, was that Austin's own in-house body-making facilities were not built up fast enough, and until the mid-1950s the company would have to rely on independent concerns like Fisher & Ludlow and Pressed Steel for most of its bodies.

The other, which cost a great deal of money, was that Leonard Lord was convinced that Austin could make a big impression in North America. First of all he bounced breezily into that continent with the A40 Devon, which was not nearly flashy enough, or large enough, to interest the Americans and Canadians, and then he produced a monumentally vulgar car in the A90 Atlantic, whose styling was nothing like that of *any* previous Austin (thank goodness . . .), and whose endurance record exploits at the Indianapolis race track did nothing to build up sales. The Americans, quite obviously, did not like what Austins had on offer, and the company had to withdraw across the Atlantic, humiliated. From 1945 to 1954 Austin exported 83,393 vehicles to Canada, but only 49,537 to the USA.

There was, however, nothing to stop Leonard Lord's march towards a bigger, more prestigious and more profitable Austin Motor Company, and there never seems to have been much doubt in his mind that the merger with the Nuffield Organisation was really a takeover, with all the muscle on Austin's side. For 'BMC', therefore, read 'Austin' in Leonard Lord's mind; he might never have admitted it in so many words, but all his actions made that intention quite clear.

After two rebuffs – in 1948 and again in 1950 – he finally forced through the Austin-Nuffield merger in the winter of 1951-52, and from March 31, 1952 he became the British Motor Corporation's deputy chairman and managing director. Lord Nuffield was BMC's chairman, but was soon pushed out of the decision-making process and he resigned before the end of the year. From this point on, Leonard Lord was chairman, the supremo of BMC, and the most powerful personality in the British motor industry.

At this time his deputy managing director was George ['Young George'] Harriman and the only other directors on the main board were Reg Hanks (ex-Nuffield vice-chairman) and the two financial specialists, Major A.C. Herring and Wilfred Hobbs. The Austin Motor Company and the Nuffield Organisation continued to exist, to trade and even to compete with each other for sales all over the world. Most British towns and cities had Austin *and* Morris dealerships which, in later years, sold virtually the same cars against each other! There was really no dealer rationalization until after the British Leyland merger of 1968.

The chairman became Sir Leonard in the New Year's

George Harriman, later Sir George, was Sir Leonard Lord's right-hand-man for many years and succeeded him as BMC's chairman. It was Sir George who negotiated the merger of BMC with Jaguar, then of BMH with Leyland.

Alec Issigonis at the wheel of an early-model BMC Mini. The two made each other famous.

John Cooper (right) was not only a famous racing car constructor, he also inspired the birth of the BMC Mini-Cooper. Here he is presenting a trophy to Jack and Betty Brabham.

honours list in January 1954, and continued to mastermind all the changes and major investments at BMC for the next decade. His only concession to age was gradually, but obviously, to prepare George Harriman to take over from him when he chose to retire, but this most certainly was not done in a hurry.

He chose to go into partial retirement in 1956, when he reached his 60th birthday, whereupon George Harriman became his joint managing director, but he was still the driving force behind the whole operation until his retirement from executive duties on his 65th birthday when, according to the official company statement: 'He has agreed to remain on the board as a non-executive director, and to become vice-president of the Corporation, of which Lord Nuffield is president.' Within weeks, he received a peerage and took the title of Lord Lambury of Northfield.

At this point I must recall Sir Leonard's well-known character, as it became obvious to many of his colleagues. He was, above all, an entrepreneur, a self-made man and a do-everything businessman, who was very widely respected by his workforce, the world at business, and the public at large. He was, on the other hand, a real rough diamond, whose overriding genius was as a get-things-done production engineer. He was never likely to stop at calling a spade a spade when 'bloody shovel' would do instead, and to receive the rough edge of his tongue was an experience not to be wished. His longtime friend and colleague, Frank Woollard, wrote of him at the time of the Austin Motor Company's Golden Jubilee in 1955 that:

'Sir Leonard Lord is a profound man but also a man of quick decision and prompt action. He has that supreme gift of reducing difficult situations and involved problems to elementary terms without falling into the trap of over-simplification. He is frank and direct in all his dealings . . . He is completely honest in thought, he does not deceive others and, more important perhaps, he does not deceive himself.'

Unlike Lord Nuffield, he does not seem ever to have been a petty man, and sometimes he surprised everyone by his unpublicized kindnesses, but he could be very abrasive with senior colleagues who displeased him, or stood up against his abrupt decision-making. Joe Edwards, for instance, was sacked in 1956 when he was already BMC's much-liked manufacturing director, so it must have been galling for Lord Lambury in 1965, when BMC took over Pressed Steel, for its managing director at the time was – Joe Edwards.

In every way, of course, Leonard, Sir Leonard, or Lord Lambury completely dominated the BMC scene as long as he was around. Even though he effectively retired in 1961, to concentrate on his farming in Worcestershire, he still served in 1963 after Lord Nuffield died, and did not finally cut his links with the Corporation until reaching his 70th birthday, in November 1966.

When he died, in September 1967, he had been involved with Morris, Austin or BMC for most of his working life. In every way, he was greatly missed, and the 750,000 annual vehicle sales the Corporation had already achieved were his legacy to the nation.

Lord Nuffield – the past master

The founder of the Morris marque, and the governor of everything connected with the Nuffield Organisation in more recent times, had very little indeed to do with BMC. As I have already made clear, he was an old man before the mergers were ever proposed and by 1951, when Leonard Lord finally persuaded him to join forces with Austin, it was high time that he had found a successor to run his businesses.

In many ways Lord Nuffield was a very lonely man as he grew old, for he had no sons or daughters and few personal friends, so he spent many of his later years systematically giving away the great fortune that he had amassed by the 1930s, for good and charitable purposes.

Although Lord Nuffield and Leonard Lord negotiated the BMC merger as equals (and their shareholders did, indeed, get equal rights under the terms agreed), there was never any doubt that Leonard Lord was going to be the dominant partner. History, they say, has a habit of repeating itself, and the same personal situation arose in 1968 when BMC was absorbed into British Leyland – although on that occasion George Harriman and Sir

Donald Stokes negotiated as equals, but Sir Donald soon emerged as the Big Boss, when BMC's worsening trading position became obvious.

From the spring of 1952, Leonard Lord spent more and more of his time at Cowley, where he continued to have clashes with Lord Nuffield, and at one time threatened to walk out on him for the second time in 16 years; he sent a resignation letter round to Nuffield Place.

For Lord Nuffield this was the final straw. He realized that he personally could no longer stand up to Lord, so he backed down, and at BMC's first Annual General Meeting on December 17, 1952 he announced his resignation from the chair. Thereafter he would be the company's president, a purely honorary position, and although he kept his small, old-fashioned office in the original military academy building at Cowley, and still tried to keep office hours to deal with his correspondence, he was never again involved in the business-making decisions of the company which had absorbed his business.

He died in August 1963, at the great old age of 85 years, leaving behind the 'Morris' marque, which was to live on, way beyond the BMC years, into the early 1980s.

'Young George' – Sir George Harriman, BMC's third chairman

By the time Leonard Lord become BMC's absolute supremo, it was quite clear that his successor, one day, would be George Harriman. 'Young George', who had been born in Coventry in 1908, began his working life as an apprentice at Morris Engines, where he soon befriended Leonard Lord. After making his name in the city as a rising businessman and a fine sportsman (he captained the Coventry and Warwickshire rugger teams, and had an England trial in 1933), he left Morris Motors in 1940 to join Leonard Lord at Longbridge as machine-shop superintendent.

Thereafter, his promotion was swift, for he became Longbridge's production manager from 1944, and joined the board of directors as general works manager in September 1945. After Austin's chairman, E.L. Payton, died early in 1946, Leonard Lord leaned more and more heavily on Harriman, and the two ex-Coventry men began to run the Austin empire as their own fiefdom.

Yet George Harriman was a completely different character from Leonard Lord. Where Lord was rough and ready, Harriman was smooth and gentlemanly, and where Lord was impulsive, aggressive and quick to make his move, Harriman was a more gradual, reasoning and cautious businessman. The dichotomy was clear – if a top man had to deal with the workforce, then Leonard Lord was ideal, but if a top man had to talk to politicians, or to the money men in the city, then George Harriman was the perfect choice.

George Harriman was a handsome man, and always impeccably dressed, who came to run BMC in a very different way from his predecessor – and perhaps that was one of the reasons why it eventually had to merge with Leyland. Compared with Leonard Lord, Harriman was not at all as ruthless, and perhaps far too mindful of other people's feelings. More recently, the point has been made that Sir George could never have done the surgical reduction of British Leyland's size and losses which Sir Michael Edwardes carried out at the end of the 1970s.

In postwar years, George Harriman continued to rise within the Austin, and later the BMC, hierarchy. He became deputy managing director to Leonard Lord in 1950, and on the formation of BMC became deputy managing director of the Corporation as well. From the autumn of 1956, when Sir Leonard went into semi-retirement, George Harriman not only became deputy chairman, but also joint managing director, then in 1958 he became the Corporation's sole managing director as Sir Leonard continued merely as the executive chairman. When Sir Leonard retired, George Harriman also took on the mantle of chairman, and he held both posts until the British Leyland merger in 1968. On the way, too, there were honours – the OBE in 1943, the CBE in 1951 and, finally, the well-deserved knighthood in 1965.

Sir George's lasting achievements were to manage BMC on his own, in its final 10 years, when annual production rose from 448,000 vehicles to a peak of 731,000 and post-tax profits soared from £9.4 million to £16.3 million. These were also the years in which the company's links with Pininfarina became obvious, when 'badge engineering' was so strongly (cynically?) applied, and the front-wheel-drive revolution heralded by the 1959 Mini took place.

He also saw BMC successfully take over Pressed Steel in 1965, merge happily with the Jaguar-Daimler group in 1966, and sell itself (for a very good price) to Leyland at the beginning of 1968. The new company resulting from the BMC-Jaguar merger of 1966 was British Motor Holdings, and after Sir George had merged this combine with Leyland at the beginning of 1968, he became the first chairman of British Leyland itself.

Like Lord Nuffield before him, however, Sir George did not last long thereafter. Even before the first BLMC board meeting took place, Sir Donald Stokes and his Leyland colleagues had established a dominant position on the new board, and Sir George agreed to stand down after a decent interval. That 'decent interval' ended in September 1968, after which the Leyland directors were in complete control. Sir George became BLMC's honorary president, but took no further executive part in the business. He died in May 1973, no doubt unhappy with the way things had turned out. He was only 65.

... also featuring ...

In a business this large, there were many able managers, some of whom were more obviously 'visible' than others. It would be possible, of course, to fill the book with details of many careers, but I only have space to mention these few:

First of all, I should consider the designers. During the

Second World War, Jules Haefeli took over as chief designer from A.J.W. Hancock, but he fell from favour when his Austin A125 Sheerline was such a flop, and he was replaced by Johnny Rix in the late 1940s. Over at Cowley, Morris' chief engineer at the time of the Morris Minor/Oxford/Wolseley 6/80 development period was Vic Oak.

From 1949, Gerald Palmer arrived at Cowley, first to head up the MG/Riley/Wolseley design teams, but from 1954 to become BMC's group chassis and body designer; Bill Appleby was still running all engine design at Longbridge, with Dick Burzi as chief stylist. Except, of course, that Sir Leonard Lord was the *de facto* chief engineer, bubbling over with ideas, interfering like mad, and generally managing to have an intuitive and authoritative finger in every possible pie! The group's engineering co-ordinator (which was more of an administrative position than a design post) was S.V. Smith, and for a time Austin's chief designer was Arthur Moore, Charles Griffin being his opposite number at Cowley.

In the meantime, a rising star had appeared at Cowley, disappeared to Alvis in the early 1950s, only to be attracted back to BMC's design headquarters at Longbridge in 1956 – he was Alec Issigonis. The brilliant Turkish-born (but British-nationality) designer came to England in 1922, completed his education in London, and started work in the motor industry a few years later. At the age of 30, having worked for a period at Humber-Hillman in Coventry, Issigonis joined Morris Motors at Cowley, and immediately started working on independent front suspension designs for a new generation of Morris cars. The MG Y-Series IFS, which was used in modified form on many sports cars including the long-running MGB, was originally to his credit.

During and after the Second World War, in close consultation with Nuffield's Sir Miles Thomas, Issigonis designed and developed the 'Mosquito', which saw the light of day in 1948 as the Morris Minor. He then spent a further four frustrating years working on improvements to the design – and building a front-wheel-drive version of the car! – before moving to Alvis, in Coventry, to design a completely new 3½-litre V8-engined car, which just happened to have Moulton-developed hydraulic connection between the front and rear suspension.

After three years of hard work on this project, Issigonis was told that the Alvis company could not afford to put his complex design into production, so almost immediately he accepted an offer from Sir Leonard Lord to move to Longbridge and open up a new advanced design department. It is now a matter of well-documented history that Issigonis, who was later awarded the CBE for his efforts in 1964 and was knighted in 1969, used that

Donald Healey, a real live wire, sold his Healey 100 project to BMC, whereupon it became the Austin-Healey 100. His family business later designed the first of the Austin-Healey Sprites. Right, the 100,000th MGA to be built, in 1962, with general manager John Thornley leaning on the screen, 'Cec' Cousins standing behind it and chief engineer Syd Enever at the wheel.

springboard to evolve the phenomenally successful front-wheel-drive Mini, the 1100/1300s and 1800s which followed, and even to take the rather dubious credit for the Austin Maxi of 1969, which BMC were developing at the time of the merger with Leyland. He joined the main board of BMC in 1963, and held that position until the company was wound up in 1968.

For more than a decade, before he retired in 1971 to become a technical consultant to British Leyland, Sir Alec kept himself in the motor industry's limelight, not only as a superb self-promoting PR man for his own work and for the new series of advanced cars from BMC, but through his frequent and often outrageous statements. Can he really have been serious when he suggested that the original Mini's driving position was so obviously 'sit-up-and-beg' because: 'A driver needs to be uncomfortable to stay alert.'?

I should make it clear that Sir Alec had nothing at all to do with the engineering of the late 1950s and 1960s conventional BMC cars such as the B-Series Farinas, the A40 Farina and the Austin A99/A110 generation. Much of the credit for these crs, and for the ADO 61 Austin 3-litre which came at the end of the BMC period, goes to Charles Griffin.

Of the senior managers who rose to the top of BMC during this period, two names stand out, one being Jim Woodcock and the other Joe Edwards. Jim Woodcock, like Leonard Lord, was a long-serving Morris Motors man, though he was 10 years younger, and had started his career as a craft apprentice at Wolseley in 1922. Clearly,

Leonard Lord spotted his promise during his sojourn at Wolseley, for in 1935 he was transferred to Cowley as supplies supervisor, later became assistant works manager, took over as works manager of the Cars Branch in 1945, then became production manager in 1947. Ever the production expert, he became vice-chairman Reg Hanks' personal assistant in 1953, deputy chairman (to

Joe Edwards, who later became BMC's managing director under Sir George Harriman, welcoming the Tory party leader, Edward Heath, MP, to Cowley in 1967.

31

Sir Leonard Lord) of Morris Motors in 1955, and joined the main board of BMC to become George Harriman's deputy in the autumn of 1956.

For the next eight years Jim Woodcock virtually ran the Cowley end of things for Sir Leonard Lord and George Harriman before rather unexpectedly deciding to retire in 1964, when he was still only 58 years of age. As this book was being written in 1986, Jim Woodcock was still hale and hearty, but had not worked again in the motor industry after his resignation.

Joe Edwards had first joined the Austin Motor Company in 1929 and was a very able and respected manufacturing specialist who, by the 1950s, had become BMC's manufacturing director. In *The Leyland Papers*, Graham Turner tells us that: 'When Harriman, whom Lord was grooming as his successor, fell seriously ill with an ulcer in 1952 and Edwards stood in for him, Lord was apparently impressed enough to wonder for a time whether he had found another candidate for the job.'

It was in 1956, however, that the typical explosive row which Sir Leonard had with so many people, blew up between Joe Edwards and himself; the flash point was over suggested new responsibilities, and the result was that Edwards was sacked, after 27 years' continuous service.

Within a matter of days Joe Edwards had joined the Pressed Steel Company, at Cowley, in a similarly high position, and by 1965, when his company was approached by BMC, he was once again in a very strong position as the managing director of that company. Following the merger, he joined the BMC board as one of the four deputy managing directors (to Sir George Harriman), but as soon as Lord Lambury finally left the board he became BMC's sole managing director in June 1966; when British Motor Holdings (BMH) was formed in December 1966, Joe Edwards was the conglomerate's chief executive, second only to Sir George Harriman.

Poor Joe Edwards was still in that important post when the BMH-Leyland merger saw the formation of British Leyland at the beginning of 1968, and he found himself in an iniquitous position. He expected nothing less than to work alongside Sir Donald Stokes and for Sir George Harriman, not *under* Sir Donald, and when it became obvious that the Leyland management would be dominant, he decided to resign. He left the company in April 1968, just before BMH was wound up.

As I indicated at the beginning of this section, however, it has been impossible to mention everyone of significance, so I can only conclude this chapter by saying that many more people had much to offer, and that without them BMC might not have had such a successful existence for so long.

Gerald Palmer arrived at Cowley in 1949 to look after Riley and Wolseley new-model design, but also produced the MG Magnette ZA and several stillborn projects with which Len Lord did not agree!

Jim Woodcock, right, welcoming the President of Finland, Mr Kekkonen (left) to the Cowley factory in 1961.

A bold idea that backfired. Austin applied American-influenced styling to the A90 Atlantic in the hope that the car would attract a strong North American market, but reaction was disappointing. The Atlantic was also offered in convertible form with the option of a power-operated top.

Replacing the earlier A40 Devon saloon, the Somerset offered more bulbous styling on a broadly similar mechanical base. There was a strong family resemblance to the larger Austin A70 Hereford saloon.

A leaner look returned to the A40 range when the Somerset gave way to the Cambridge, which was also offered with a 1.5-litre engine as the A50. White-wall tyres and an external sun visor were by no means uncommon on home-market Austins in the 1950s.

The Farina styling as first applied to the A55 Cambridge was distinguished by pronounced tail-fins, which would subsequently be remodelled into a less obtrusive shape as part of an overall facelift.

The A40 designation returned to the Austin range in 1958 with this neat Farina-styled body, which covered essentially A35 running gear. Deservedly popular, this car could be said to have been the forerunner of the modern hatchback.

The Farina-styled A40 in its original form with characteristic Austin wavy-mesh grille confined to a rectangular shape. On the Mk II version introduced in 1961 the grille was widened to blend in with the light units and in 1962 this 948cc A-Series engine was replaced with a 1,098cc derivative. The engine in this particular car is highly modified, with twin SU carburettors. The brake servo is also non-standard.

The design which proved the validity of the concept of a universal small car. This is a 1961 Mini in its Mk I form, its grille identifying it as being badged as an Austin rather than as a Morris.

John Cooper was quick to identify the sporting potential of the Mini, and the result was the Mini-Cooper, which in turn led to this even more sporting Mini-Cooper S. The 970cc engine of this example was one of three alternative power units offered, the others being of 1,071cc and 1,275cc.

An immaculately preserved Austin Mini-Cooper, a car which won much of its acclaim on the race tracks and rally routes of the world, but which more recently has become a significant sight at concours gatherings.

Often referred to irreverently as the Land-crab, the Austin 1800 and its Morris and Wolseley equivalents nevertheless offered almost unrivalled passenger space within moderate overall dimensions, thanks to the transverse engine and front-wheel drive layout.

The original Austin-Healey 'frog-eye' Sprite, a sports car of stark simplicity but immense charm, which earned itself many friends and achieved considerable success in sporting circles.

This view of an immaculately restored early Sprite is a reminder that any luggage had to be stowed away through the cockpit and that body protection at the rear was confined to a pair of overriders.

The production life of the 'Big Healey' spanned 15 years from the introduction of the original 100 model in 1953. The other car in this picture is a 1966 3000 Mark III Convertible, the final version of the series, which had been introduced two years earlier.

The man who started it all. Donald Healey with one of the last of the 'Big Healeys', with the Cornish coast, close to his home, in the background.

The 3000 Mark II, the first model to be given the vertical-bar grille, was only available in 1961/2 as either an open two-seater (BN7) or a two-plus-two (BT7); the BJ7 Convertible was still a year away, but would quickly become the most popular version.

Although built by Austin and incorporating A30 and A40 running gear, the Metropolitan was inspired by and produced for Nash and its unusual styling had much in common with that of the American company's early Rambler model. The horizontal-bar grille of the first cars was later replaced by this considerably neater design.

The Metropolitan was sold in both convertible and hardtop forms, and although initially produced with the 'American market in mind, it became available in the UK after it had been uprated into the Metropolitan 1500 with the aid of the larger BMC B-Series engine.

Longest-lived car in the Vanden Plas catalogue was the Princess 4-Litre Limousine, which was inherited from the Austin range in 1957 and was only dropped 11 years later following the merger of BMC with Jaguar, when it was considered to be obstructing the market for the new Daimler limousine which Vanden Plas was to assemble.

Vanden Plas became the producer of upmarket versions of mainstream BMC models from the late 1950s, and one of the most attractive of these was the Princess 3-Litre, based on the Farina-styled C-Series saloons. The availability of a 4-litre engine from Rolls-Royce later enabled this car to be upgraded into a Princess 4-Litre R.

The Princess 1300 was the prestige version of the Issigonis-designed 1100/1300 family of four-door saloons and was considered to be a much more successful adaptation than the Princess version of the Austin Allegro which would eventually replace it in the post-BMC period.

One of the rarest of 1957 Morris Oxford Series III saloons, this car, fitted with Manumatic transmission (which allows the driver to make gear-changes through a conventional steering column-mounted gear-lever but without a clutch pedal), was discovered by Colin Goldsworthy in 1984 when it had covered less than 17,500 miles from new.

Long before his Mini came on the scene, (Sir) Alec Issigonis' reputation as a car designer had been firmly established with his Morris Minor, over 1.6 million of which were to be produced in various forms between 1948 and 1971. This immaculate two-door Minor 1000 typifies the care with which so many owners of these thoroughly practical cars maintain and treasure them today.

Like its smaller stablemate, the Minor, the Oxford was also offered as a timber-decorated Traveller estate. The unfluted bonnet top and different exterior brightwork identify this as a Series II rather than a Series III model.

The Morris Isis was effectively a longer-wheelbase version of the Oxford with a 2.6-litre C-Series engine in place of the 1.5-litre B-Series unit. This is the Series II version, which was a contemporary of the Oxford Series III and sold in limited quantities from 1956 to 1958.

A Mk II version of the Mini-Cooper, identified by the enlarged grille. The additional quarter-bumper bars which were a feature of the earlier Mk I cars had disappeared by this time. The wide-rim wheels of this immaculately turned-out example emphasize the car's competition pedigree.

The last of the Oxfords from the pre-Farina period was this Series IV Traveller, with four-door bodywork devoid of any external wood decoration. It remained in production for some months after the Oxford saloon had appeared in Series V form with Farina styling.

An MG inherited by BMC on its formation was this traditional YB saloon, based on a prewar design and powered by the 1,250cc engine shared with the TD Midget at the time of its launch in 1951. It was withdrawn from production two years later.

The MG marque had to accept its share of badge-engineering during the BMC years. The Magnette Mk III, above left, had its equivalents in the contemporary Austin, Morris, Riley and Wolseley ranges, as did the MG 1100, above right, although there was no mistaking the MG grille.

The MG TF, the last of the traditionally styled sports cars from Abingdon, was offered first with the 1,250cc, then with the larger-bore 1,466cc version of the four-cylinder Nuffield engine. Note the coveted registration number of this car.

The MGA, the shape of which was based on that of a design prepared for racing at Le Mans, was in due course destined to distinguish itself with its own competition glory both as a works team car and in private hands. The Targa Florio was part of the racing history of this beautifully preserved hardtop.

The MGB, which replaced the MGA in 1962, became BMC's best-selling sports car, with this open tourer accounting for a large majority of sales; it was not joined by the GT coupe until the end of 1965. The MGB was the first car to use the BMC B-Series engine in 1.8-litre form.

A direct derivative of the MGB, the MGC was distinguished by larger wheels, and beneath the bonnet was BMC's big six-cylinder engine in 2.9-litre form. It was fitted with torsion-bar front suspension in place of the MGB's wishbones and coil springs.

The elegant Riley 1½-litre saloon in its final RME form, from which the earlier model's running-boards had been deleted and to which more rounded wings had been fitted. Two-tone paintwork was a popular option on this model.

The Pathfinder, with its slab-sided bodywork, was BMC's successor to the 2½-litre version of the RM-Series Rileys. Designed prior to the formation of BMC, it retained use of the 'Big Four' engine from the earlier model.

The Riley One-Point-Five, based on a modified Morris Minor floorpan, and like the Minor equipped with torsion-bar front suspension, was born from an abandoned attempt to produce a replacement Morris or Austin saloon. Its relatively high-output engine gave the saloon a performance which a few years later might have warranted a 'GT' badge on the boot-lid.

The Riley Two-Point-Six, which replaced the Pathfinder in 1957, had its equivalent in the Wolseley range in the 6/90 Series III saloon. However, the two-tone colour scheme was a Riley feature and a different instrument layout was also designed for the Riley version of this example of badge-engineering.

The 4/68 and its later replacement the 4/72 were the Riley versions of the Farina-styled B-Series range of BMC saloons within which the five marques were distinguished by different grille designs and minor variations in exterior trim.

Largest Wolseley saloon at the time of the BMC formation was this 6/80, powered by Nuffield's 2.2-litre six-cylinder overhead-camshaft engine. There was also a four-cylinder 4/50 version, although the larger car outlasted it by a year.

The elegant lines of the Wolseley 4/44, introduced in 1952, were retained when the car was uprated into the 15/50 with the aid of the B-Series engine in place of the original 1,250cc power unit, and were also adopted in 1953 for the very attractive MG Magnette saloon.

The Wolseley 1500, which shared the same basic body structure with the Riley One-Point-Five, used the BMC B-Series engine in a more modest state of tune and was marketed as a refined family car rather than as a high performer. The exterior sun visor was, of course, an extra.

This rear view of the same Wolseley 1500 identifies it as one of the original series built from 1957 to 1960. On the Mk II version which followed it the bonnet and boot hinges were hidden from view.

This Wolseley 6/99 offered buyers an upmarket alternative to the Austin A99 on its introduction in 1959. Both cars were powered by the BMC C-Series engine in 2.9-litre form and they differed little apart from their level of trim and equipment and, of course, their radiator styling.

The Wolseley 16/60 similarly found its market as a more fully equipped alternative to the Austin Cambridge and Morris Oxford versions of the B-Series Farina-styled saloons, and a considerable number of them were supplied with a two-tone 'sandwich' paint finish.

The contrasting colour strip at waist height identifies this as the sporting Mk II 'S' version of the Wolseley 18/85. It was perhaps the most elegant of BMC's Land-crab series, although it did not reach market until after the Corporation had become part of British Motor Holdings.

Chapter 3

AUSTIN

When the BMC merger was proposed in November 1951, the Austin marque was thriving and there were big plans for the future. For the time being, production had peaked at about 132,000 cars a year, but two important new-car introductions were pending.

There were four ranges of cars in series production at that time. The true volume-assembly models were the A40 Devon (first seen in 1947), the A70 Hereford (1950) and the unsuccessful A90 Atlantic (1948), while the A125 Sheerline/A135 Princess, being very large and expensive cars, were built in rather more limited quantities. The Princesses would continue to be built until 1968, with very few mechanical changes, although inevitably there were some alterations to the styling of their coachbuilt bodies.

Two other cars were almost ready for sale. Although the 'New Austin Seven' (more familiarly and soon officially to be known as the A30) had been unveiled in October 1951, volume production was not to begin until May 1952. In addition, a completely new body was to be made available for the A40 in February 1952, this being the more rounded Somerset style, to replace the A40 Devon shape. It looked very similar to the A70 Hereford, and had obvious visual links with the new A30.

The first season's offering from Austin to BMC was therefore the A30, A40, A70, A90 and A125/A135 line-up. The only 'dud' among this lot was the A90, which had failed badly in the USA (for which market it had originally been intended), and this would be dropped in the summer of 1952.

While Leonard Lord and his planners started to sort out a corporate strategy for new BMC models, Austin stood pat for three whole seasons. However, during that time, the Austin-Healey sports car came into existence (see the Austin-Healey section), and the Nash Metropolitan (which was actually a Nash-styled body with Austin A30/A40 running gear – see the Metropolitan section) also went into production at Longbridge.

In the autumn of 1954, two new ranges of car, which had monocoque bodies and very similar styling, went on sale. The A40/A50 Cambridge replaced the A40 Somerset, while the A90 Westminster took over from the A70 Hereford and the already-defunct A90 Atlantic. Although these cars were updated and modified over the years, they were to be built until 1958–59, with new rear-end sheet-metal styles from early 1957.

The A30 became the A35 in autumn 1956, and the A50/A90/A105 cars received a tail-lift, but the next new body shape was the A40 Farina, a two-box design looking like an estate car, its unique monocoque shell being styled by Pininfarina, but hiding A35 running gear. This was to remain in production until 1967, slotting in above the smallest Austin saloons, but below the A50/A55/A60 types.

In 1958, BMC also introduced the Austin Gipsy, which was a four-wheel-drive vehicle, aimed directly at the Land-Rover market, though unsuccessful in this.

In 1959, there was a rash of new 'Farinas'. The old A50/A55 range was replaced by the new A55 Farina, which featured a new monocoque, complete with tail-fins; this was to be shared in all but badging, decoration and other minor details with four other BMC marques. Later in the year, the old A90/A95/A105 range was dropped and replaced by the Farina-styled A99, the bodyshell of which was also to be used for the Wolseley 6/99 and Vanden Plas Princess 3-litre models.

1959, however, was memorable for the launch of BMC's first transverse-engined front-wheel-drive car, the Mini (yet again, Austin tried to impose the model name 'Austin Seven' on the public, but they wouldn't have it . . .).

Two years later there was a wholesale reshuffle of models, with a lot of detail, but no fundamental changes, the A40 becoming Mk II, A55 becoming A60, and A99 becoming A110. At the same time, the Mini range was reshuffled, and the first of the extremely successful Mini-Coopers was launched.

The transverse-engined, front-wheel-drive, Austin 1100 arrived in 1963 (a year after its Morris 1100 'clone' had been introduced at Cowley), and a year after that, in the autumn of 1964, the third-generation front-wheel-drive car, the Austin 1800, was put on sale. This was the first transverse application of the B-Series engine, and was the car which eventually became known, affectionately (I think!), as the 'Land-crab'.

There was then a three-year period of consolidation, as front-wheel-drive cars gradually took over almost completely at Longbridge, cars like the Mini-Moke being launched, automatic transmission arriving as an option for the Mini, and the A40 Farina fading away; '1300' versions of the various 1100s were progressively introduced in 1967, and all-synchromesh gearboxes were promised for the coming winter. The last new Austin-badged BMC car to make its bow was the ADO61-type 3-litre, which used some of the 1800's body panels, but was nevertheless a front-engined, rear-drive car, to replace the old A110 model.

BMC was submerged into British Leyland from the first months of 1968, but it is worth noting that the Austin Maxi was well on its way by that time, having already been designed and partly developed by Alec Issigonis' team. The new overhead-cam E-Series engine was to be manufactured at the Cofton Hackett factory. This car, however, was not introduced until the spring of 1969. Alec Issigonis was also beavering away at the design of an

ohc-engined Mini replacement, which was coded 9X and also known as the 'Pininfarina Mini'. Because BMC was already strapped for cash, it could not afford to put 9X into production, nor could British Leyland afford it at the beginning of the 1970s, and like several other small-car projects of the 1960s and 1970s, it was scrapped.

Just as the British Leyland merger was being formalized, several old BMC Austins were discontinued. The A40 died in November 1967, the A35 van and the Gipsy early in 1968 along with the A110 and the ancient Vanden Plas Princess (née A135 Princess). It was all part of a rationalization programme which had rather tardily been applied by the old management.

Postscript

BMC could draw on many more trademarked names than they actually used in the 16 years of their existence. In 1968, the SMM & T *Register of Model Titles* had the following Austin Division passenger car names listed but not yet used on postwar models:

Andover	Colwyn	Marlborough	Sherborne
Arrow	Conway	Mayfair	Speedy
Ascot	Goodwood	Newbury	Twini-Mini
Burnham	Guard	Nippy	Whippet
Cambrian	Guardsman	Nomad	Whitehall
Carlton	Harley	Norfolk	Windsor
Carousel	Harrow	Open Road	York
City	Hertford	Ranelagh	
Clifton	Kempton	Ripley	
Clubman	Longbridge	Ruby	

Many of these names, of course, had been used on Austins of the pre-1939 period. I wonder if Vauxhall had to buy the 'Carlton' trademark?

The Austin A30 four-door saloon – the first user of the new BMC A-Series running gear in 1951.

Austin A30 (1951 to 1956)

In the 1920s and 1930s, Austin's prosperity had been founded on the legendary Seven, but that car had died of old age in 1938, and the new Eight was a bigger and different type of car. It took six years for Austin to get round to announcing a new small car after the Second World War, and even then it was not ready to go on sale. In those six years, Austin's big seller had been the A40 Devon, but this was a larger car and therefore not a direct rival of the Morris Minor; when Leonard Lord's merger overtures to Nuffield were rebuffed, he immediately authorized a start on the new A30 project. Because of the obvious historical connotations, the sales staff tried to call it the 'New Seven', but the public would have none of it.

Apart from the gearbox, which was a development of that introduced for the 1939 Eight, the whole design was new. The A30 was the first Austin product to have a unit-construction body/chassis structure, and the first to use a small, simple, overhead-valve engine that became known as the A-Series. In that respect, the A30 was very important indeed, for the A-Series, and the A-Plus which followed it in 1980, are still a very important feature of the Austin-Rover scene as this book is being written.

Like several other British small cars of the period, the A30 was underpowered, rather basically equipped, and really a scaled-down version of a larger car rather than a 'ground-up' concept of its own. It had quite a cramped cabin, with only 48 inches of shoulder room across the front seats, and there was quite a lot of body roll on corners, but the car had a perky and willing character. The original production car was a four-door saloon, and deliveries began in May 1952, but from the autumn of 1953 there was also a two-door version, and a year later these cars were joined by the two-door Countryman estate car version of the design, which was a *very* close relative of the van

The tiny 803cc A-Series engine looks lost even in the small engine compartment of the Austin A30. No heater on this car, incidentally!

Facia of the A30, 1953-56 variety. The later A35 looked similar, except for having a short remote-control gear-change.

Austin A30 specification

Produced: Longbridge, 1951-56. 222,823 of all types built, including 26,047 vans.

General layout: Unit-construction body/chassis unit, saloon, estate and van styles, saloons having 2 or 4 passenger doors. Front-mounted engine driving rear wheels.

Engine and transmission: A-Series, 4-cylinder, ohv, in-line. 803cc, 58 x 76.2mm, 28bhp at 4,800rpm; 40lb ft at 2,200rpm. 4-speed gearbox, no synchromesh on 1st gear; live (beam) rear axle with hypoid-bevel final drive.

Chassis: Independent front suspension, coil springs and wishbones. Worm-and-peg steering. Rear suspension by half-elliptic leaf springs. Front and rear drum brakes. 5.20-13in tyres.

Dimensions: (saloons) Wheelbase 6ft 7.5in; front track 3ft 9.25in; rear track 3ft 10.75in; length 11ft 4.4in; width 4ft 7.1in; height 4ft 10.25in. Unladen weight (approx) 1,500lb.

Typical performance: (saloon, 4-door) Maximum speed 62mph; 0-50mph 29sec; standing ¼-mile 26.5sec; overall fuel consumption 42mpg.

Derivatives: 4-door saloon 1951-56; 2-door saloon 1953-56; estate car (and van) 1954-56.

Fate: Replaced by larger-engined A35 range in autumn 1956.

BMC also produced a two-door saloon version of the A30, with the same small, kidney-shaped rear window.

A30 interiors were only *just* roomy enough for four passengers.

which appeared at the same time.

In those days, you didn't get a heater, or windscreen washers, but at £554 in 1952 not many eager customers complained. What you *did* get was up to 40mpg fuel economy and a tiny four-seater which would fit into most people's parking spaces. The A30 was different in so many ways from the Morris Minor that the two cars could, and did, co-exist for many years after the BMC merger took place. The A30, however, needed to be faster and longer-legged to cope with late 1950s performance needs, and that is why the A35 was developed.

Austin A35 (1956 to 1968 – see data table for details)
Five years after the A30 had been announced, the A35 replaced it. Basically, the new car used all the successfully established body, chassis and driveline engineering of the A30, and improved on it. In particular, the engine was enlarged and made more powerful and torquey, while the transmission was changed to suit.

The A30, in truth, had been something of a buzz-box because of its limited power and low gearing. The A35 not only had an 18% larger engine with 21% more power, but this produced 25% more torque and the unit was much more robust than before; there was more acceleration for the asking, so an entirely fresh (closer-ratio) set of transmission ratios was fitted and the axle ratio was raised from 4.875:1 to 4.556:1. The A35 was also given a remote-control gear-change with a very pleasant action.

To match the improved driveline, there were styling changes which included the use of a painted (instead of chrome-plated) radiator grille and an enlarged rear window. At the same time, BMC also introduced a very smart little A35 pick-up, whose carrying capacity was tiny, and whose attraction was very limited because of this. There was very little demand, and it was withdrawn after only 497 examples had been built in about a year.

By the end of the 1950s, the A35 had been elbowed out of the limelight at Longbridge, on the one hand by the arrival of the smart new A40 Farina, which used mainly A35 running gear, and on the other by the sensational new front-wheel-drive Minis. The A35 saloons were dropped to make way for the Minis, in any case, but the Countryman and van derivatives carried on until 1962, at which point the Countryman was

Austin A35 specification

As for Austin A30 range except for:
Produced: Longbridge, 1956-68. 353,849 of all types built, including 210,575 vans and 497 pick-ups.
General layout: Pick-up style also produced, 1956-57.
Engine and transmission: 948cc, 62.9 x 76.2mm, 34bhp at 4,750rpm; 50lb ft at 2,000rpm.
Dimensions: Height 4ft 11.25in.
Typical performance: (saloon, 4-door) Maximum speed 72mph; 0-60mph 30sec; standing ¼-mile 23.5sec; overall fuel consumption 40mpg.
Distinguishing features from previous model: Painted instead of chrome grille, wraparound rear window (saloons), remote-control gear-change.
Derivatives: 2-door and 4-door saloons 1956-59; pick-up 1956-57; estate car 1956-62; van 1956-68. Van with 1,098cc engine 1962-66, with 848cc engine 1964-68.
Fate: Saloons displaced by A40 Farinas and new front-drive Minis in 1959, derivatives eventually died off and not replaced.

The A35 was recognized, externally, by its painted (instead of chromed) grille and its larger rear window.

Austin's A30/A35 Countryman was an all-steel estate car, a little smaller and by no means as attractive as the rival Morris Minor Traveller. This was the A35 variety.

dropped, leaving the van to soldier on alone until 1968. In those final years, the vans were built with 1,098cc engines (1962 to 1966), then with 848cc engines (1966 to 1968), all of which were versions of the ubiquitous A-Series unit.

Although the A30/A35 range was important, on its own, it was also a vital 'building block' in the BMC product scheme of things in that it provided running gear for the A40 Farina, engines for almost *every* other small BMC car, and suspension items for cars as varied as the Metropolitan and the Austin-Healey Sprite.

The A35 pick-up was very rare, and had very little carrying capacity. Nevertheless, there was a certain style . . .

Austin A40 Farina (1958 to 1961)

BMC's first links with the Italian styling firm we now know as Pininfarina were forged in the mid-1950s, and for a time that concern shaped all BMC's new mass-production models, and advised on others done in-house. The first of the Farina cars was also arguably the best of all – the new-generation A40, launched in the autumn of 1958.

There had already been three generations of postwar A40 (Devon/Dorset, Somerset and Cambridge) before this one, but it was an entirely different type of car. Earlier A40s had used 1.2-litre engines of B-Series or pre-B-Series type, but the A40 Farina used the smaller, lighter, A-Series running gear.

Apart from its Italian styling, the A40 Farina's real novelty was in its packaging, for at first it was no more or less than a two-door, two-box, estate car style; there was no such thing then, or later, as an A40 saloon with a separate boot compartment. The first A40s had a fixed rear window at high level, and under it was a let-down tailgate. The luggage area was arranged, estate-car style, with a rear seat backrest which could be folded down to increase the available volume.

Up front, there was what we came to know as the typically-Austin 'wavy-mesh' radiator grille, and one interesting cost-

---

Austin A40 Farina specification

Produced: Longbridge, 1958-61. 364,064 A40s of all types built.
General layout: Unit-construction, pressed-steel body-chassis structure, in 4-seater, 2-door estate car style. Front-mounted engine driving rear wheels.
Engine and transmission: BMC A-Series engine, 4-cylinder, ohv, in-line. 948cc, 62.9 x 76.2mm, 34bhp at 4,750rpm; 50lb ft at 2,000rpm; 4-speed gearbox, no synchromesh on 1st gear; centre-floor gear-change; live (beam) rear axle with hypoid-bevel final drive.
Chassis: Independent front suspension, coil springs and wishbones. Cam-and-peg steering. Rear suspension by half-elliptic leaf springs. Front and rear drum brakes. 5.20-13in tyres.
Dimensions: Wheelbase 6ft 11.5in; front track 3ft 11.5in; rear track 3ft 11in; length 12ft 0.25in; width 4ft 11.4in; height 4ft 8.75in. Unladen weight (approx) 1,680lb.
Distinguishing features from previous model: Entirely different car compared with earlier Austin A40 – using many A35 mechanical components in new shell.
Typical performance: Maximum speed 72mph; 0-60mph 35.6sec; standing ¼-mile 24.5sec; overall fuel consumption 38mpg.
Derivatives: Estate-style saloon from 1958, Countryman version with upper and lower opening tailgates from late 1959.
Fate: Discontinued in 1961 in favour of A40 Mk II.

The new A40 of 1958 was the first Farina-styled BMC car to be announced. Most of the running gear was lifted from the A35.

54

The original A40 Farina of 1958 used the same speedometer as the A35, and there were many A35 components under the skin, too.

saver was the fitment of counterbalanced lift-up door windows, without winding mechanism. Inside the car, the front seats could be tipped forward to give access to the rear seats, and one glance at the steering wheel and simple instrument panel confirmed this car's use of A35 componentry.

Running gear was almost pure A35, for the 34bhp/948cc A-Series engine, four-speed transmission and hypoid-bevel final drive were the same, as was the coil-spring front suspension, although there were wider tracks front and rear to suit the more spacious and boxy styling. The hydraulic front/mechanical rear Lockheed braking system was also like that of the A35, though the front drums were enlarged to take care of the extra weight of the A40.

A year after the initial A40 launch, the true A40 estate car (called Countryman) arrived, different only in that the rear window and its surrounding panel was arranged to hinge up, while the tailgate continued to hinge down; this gave complete, unhindered, access to the luggage area. The two versions of the same basic shape (it was almost impossible to tell them apart unless you looked carefully for panel closing lines, for every other exterior panel was the same) then carried on until the last A40 Farina was built in 1967.

The original version (retrospectively called Mk I) was only built until 1961, when it was displaced by the much improved Mk II version.

Austin A40 Farina Mk II (1961 to 1962)

In the autumn of 1961, BMC's second orgy of facelifting took place – the first such session had occurred in 1956. In this process, every one of the Farina-styled cars came in for attention, both to chassis engineering and to the detail styling.

The A40 Farina therefore became Mk II with more power, a longer wheelbase, better suspension and improved

---

Austin A40 Farina Mk II specification

As for Austin A40 Farina except for:
Produced: Longbridge, 1961-62. 364,064 A40s of all types built.
Engine and transmission: 37bhp at 5,000rpm; 50lb ft at 2,500rpm. 4-speed gearbox, no synchromesh on 1st gear.
Chassis: Anti-roll bar on front suspension.
Dimensions: Wheelbase 7ft 3.1in. Unladen weight (approx) 1,800lb.
Distinguishing features from previous model: Longer wheelbase, new front grille, wind-up door windows, different trim style.
Typical performance: Maximum speed 75mph; 0-60mph 27.1sec; standing ¼-mile 23.7sec: overall fuel consumption 32mpg.
Derivatives: As for Mk I model.
Fate: Discontinued in 1962 in favour of 1.1-litre-engined model.

---

appointments. The wheelbase increase was achieved by moving the axle back on the leaf springs, this allowing the wheelarch pressings to be reprofiled and the rear seat to be moved back by a couple of inches. Further to improve the roadholding, a front anti-roll bar was added, along with telescopic instead of lever-arm rear dampers. This was also the point at which full hydraulic braking, by Girling, was fitted.

Engine power was increased from the original 34bhp to 37bhp, simply by ditching the original downdraught Zenith carburettor and manifold in favour of the Morris Minor 1000's SU carburettor.

Body changes included the standardization of wind-up windows, a new horizontally-slatted radiator grille and a newly-styled facia/instrument panel.

Strangely enough, this derivative was only built for one model year before the 1.1-litre-engined version took over.

The A40 became 'Mk II' in the autumn of 1961, with a longer wheelbase and a different grille, and a year later (the car illustrated) it inherited the enlarged 1.1-litre A-Series engine. It was built until the end of 1967.

Austin A40 Farina, with 1.1-litre engine (1962 to 1967)

It was in the summer/autumn of 1962 that BMC started building the new transverse-engined Morris 1100 saloon, and it was to rationalize with the engine requirements of this very important range that several other BMC models were up-engined at the same time. Thus, after only one year, the A40 Mk II's engine was increased in size from 948cc to 1,098cc.

Not only was the new engine more powerful and torquey than before, but it was matched by a substantially redesigned transmission which included baulk-ring synchromesh (but still no synchromesh on first gear).

Apart from the redesigning of the facia and control layout from the autumn of 1964, this was the last important modification made to the A40's specification. Even though its sister car, the A35, was only built as a light commercial van from 1962, the A40 went on selling steadily until November 1967, when it was quietly dropped.

Austin A40 Farina 1.1-litre specification

As for Austin A40 Mk II except for:
Produced: Longbridge, 1962-67. 364,064 A40s of all types built.
Engine and transmission: 1,098cc, 64.6 x 83.7mm, 48bhp at 5,100rpm; 60lb ft at 2,500rpm.
Typical performance: Maximum speed 79mph; 0-60mph 23.9sec; standing ¼-mile 22.9sec: overall fuel consumption 31mpg.
Fate: Discontinued in 1967 and not replaced.

Austin A40 Devon (1947 to 1956 – see table for details)

For the first two years after the end of the Second World War, Austin concentrated on building prewar designs, then the first of their new mass-production models, called the A40 Devon, was introduced in 1947. It was due to be replaced by a new model, the A40 Somerset, when the formation of BMC was announced, and by the time the merger was formalized that change had already taken place.

The A40 Devon (a four-door saloon – there was a two-door version called the Dorset which had disappeared by 1951) was new from end to end – engine, transmission, chassis and body style. In one way it was a technical step back, for the new 1939-model Ten had used a platform chassis, with the floor welded to the frame, whereas the 1947 Devon used a conventional frame and separate all-steel bodyshell.

There were two real novelties in the car – the brand-new 1.2-litre four-cylinder engine (which was the direct ancestor, but *not* the same design, as the BMC B-Series unit), and the use of independent front suspension, which was entirely new to Austin.

The engine was of an utterly conventional overhead-valve design, except that the pushrod valve gear lived on the same side of the block as the cylinder head ports and made the use of siamesed porting inevitable. It used the same cylinder stroke – 88.9 (3.5 inches in Imperial measure) – as first used in the 1932 Austin 10, and this measurement was to persist in all B-Series and C-Series engines throughout the 1950s, 1960s and 1970s. The independent front suspension featured coil springs and wishbones, but the upper wishbone arms were provided by the actuating arms of the lever-type dampers. This was a neat and technically elegant way of making one component do two

The A40 Devon was launched in 1947, and was just about to be dropped when BMC was founded. The two-door version of this style (dropped before BMC was formed) was the Dorset.

The Mk II version of the A40 Devon, as built at the end of 1951 when BMC was founded, had this facia. Much of the instrumentation was carried forward to the new A40 Somerset. The A40 Devon's 1,200cc engine was a predecessor of the B-Series design of the 1950s, but was very different in detail.

jobs, and was to feature in many Austin and BMC layouts in the future.

The chassis had cruciform bracing and looked good and strong, but the suspension was soft, and often became softer with age as the lever-arm dampers wore out. The styling of the

Austin A40 Devon specification

Produced: Longbridge, 1947-52. 273,958 A40 Devon saloons, 26,587 Countryman estates, 140,060 vans and pick-ups built.

General layout: Separate box-section steel chassis-frame with steel bodyshell. Devon model in 4-seater, 4-door saloon car style. Front-mounted engine driving rear wheels.

Engine and transmission: Austin A40-type engine (predecessor of B-Series design), 4-cylinder, ohv, in-line. 1,200cc, 65.48 x 88.9mm, 40bhp at 4,300rpm; 59lb ft at 2,200rpm; 4-speed gearbox, no synchromesh on 1st gear; centre-floor gear-change; steering-column change from August 1951; live (beam) rear axle with spiral-bevel final drive.

Chassis: Independent front suspension, coil springs and wishbones. Cam-and-peg steering. Rear suspension by half-elliptic leaf springs. Front and rear drum brakes. 5.25-16in tyres.

Dimensions: Wheelbase 7ft 8.5in; front track 4ft 0.5in; rear track 4ft 1.5in; length 12ft 9.25in; width 5ft 1in; height 5ft 5.75in. Unladen weight (approx) 2,145lb.

Typical performance: Maximum speed 70mph; 0-60mph 37.2sec; standing ¼-mile 24.7sec; overall fuel consumption 34mpg.

Derivatives: Countryman estate car (1949-52), van and pick-up (1948-56) plus A40 Sports (see separate entry); A40 Somerset (see separate entry) used the same rolling chassis with different coachwork.

Fate: Discontinued in 1952 in favour of new A40 Somerset range.

car was distinctive, and a definite but evolutionary step forward from that of the 1939-style Tens and Twelves, which the Devon replaced. It featured obvious wing lines moulded into the sides and there was a large 'alligator' bonnet, but no running-boards.

This was the car that Leonard Lord used, none too successfully, to spearhead his assault on the United States market in 1947-48, but by 1949 it was clear that it had been a failure, and some unsold cars were sent back to Longbridge for reworking. Although the A40 Devon had been facelifted in 1949, with a reduced price and simplified equipment, and improved yet again at the end of 1950, its style was dating rapidly, and the A40 Somerset of 1952 arrived during the formation of BMC.

The rare Austin A40 sports was really a convertible, and was built on a slightly-modified A40 Devon/Somerset chassis with a tuned engine. Jensen built the bodies at West Bromwich.

This was the result of a respray (off-white with red wheels and black top) carried out in the mid-1950s on the A40 Sports owned by BBC scriptwriter Alan Simpson.

Austin A40 Sports (1950 to 1953)

This model was important for BMC in that it was inspired by the first commercial links between Austin and the Jensen company of West Bromwich. In the late 1940s, Jensen had approached Austin for D-Series engine supplies to use in its PW and Interceptor models; at that stage, Austin's chairman, Leonard Lord, had seen the styling of the forthcoming Interceptor, liked its looks, and invited Jensen to produce a similar style for the A40 chassis.

The result was the A40 Sports, which was announced in October 1950 and was built in small numbers at Longbridge until 1953. Jensen not only styled, but produced the all-steel bodyshell, which was not really a sports car shape, but a two-door four-seater convertible with smooth, but not outstandingly beautiful lines. Final assembly was at the Jensen factory at West Bromwich.

The A40 Devon's rolling chassis was slightly modified for use in the A40 Sports. A modified cylinder head and the use of twin SU carburettors allowed peak power to be boosted to 50bhp, and an anti-roll bar was added to the independent front suspension. Compared with the Devon saloon, the Sports was considerably lower, but as there had been no weight-saving the performance was only slightly better.

The first cars had a conventional centre-floor gear-change, but from August 1951 a steering-column change was fitted

Austin A40 Sports specification

Produced: Longbridge, 1950-53. 4,011 cars built.
General layout: Separate box-section steel chassis-frame with all-steel bodyshell in 4-seater, 2-door sports tourer style. Front-mounted engine driving rear wheels.
Engine and transmission: Austin A40-type engine (predecessor of B-Series design), 4-cylinder, ohv, in-line. 1,200cc, 65.48 x 88.9mm, 50bhp at 5,000rpm; 61lb ft at 3,000rpm; 4-speed gearbox, no synchromesh on 1st gear; centre-floor gear-change at first, steering-column change from August 1951; live (beam) rear axle with spiral-bevel final drive.
Chassis: Independent front suspension, coil springs and wishbones. Cam-and-peg steering. Rear suspension by half-elliptic leaf springs and anti-roll bar. Front and rear drum brakes. 5.25-16in tyres.
Dimensions: Wheelbase 7ft 8.5in; front track 4ft 0.5in; rear track 4ft 1.5in; length 13ft 3.25in; width 5ft 1in; height 4ft 9.0in. Unladen weight (approx) 2,175lb.
Typical performance: Maximum speed 78mph; 0-60mph 25.6sec; standing ¼-mile 23.2sec; overall fuel consumption 29mpg.
Derivatives: None.
Fate: Discontinued in 1953 in favour of new and much faster Austin-Healey 100 sports car.

instead, this bringing the A40 Sports chassis in line with that of the last Devons and the forthcoming Somersets.

Even though Austin's PR chief, Alan Hess, took an A40 Sports around the world (flying the car for much of the distance, by the way . . .) as a publicity stunt, it made little impact in the showrooms. When the Austin-Healey 100 – which was a *real* sports car – came on the scene, Jensen gained the body assembly contract for that new model, and the A40 Sports was dropped to make space for it at West Bromwich.

Austin A40 Somerset (1952 to 1954)

Just as the rather bulbous A70 Hereford was a rebodied A70 Hampshire, the A40 Somerset of 1952 was little more than a rebodied A40 Devon. In addition, there were mechanical changes, and the option of a convertible coupe.

The Somerset (yet another of the well-liked 'Counties' series of postwar Austins) was announced in February 1952 and was either the last of the pre-BMC models, or the first BMC model, depending on how you view the corporate process. (The BMC merger had been proposed in November 1951, and the new company began operating on March 31, 1952.)

Under the skin, there was the A40 Devon's chassis, only altered by the provision of a fashionable (and not at all precise!) steering-column gear-change, and although the 1.2-litre engine had a little more horsepower (the A40 Sports cylinder head was used in this case), and the final-drive ratio had been raised slightly, the car's top speed was still just under 70mph.

The new body style was virtually an A70 Hereford lookalike, with more bulbous lines; the passenger doors, apparently, *were* the same. In overall size, the Somerset was very similar to the Devon, but there was a little more length and width inside the cabin; there was a bench-type front seat and the handbrake was an 'umbrella' handle under the facia.

In September 1952, eight months after the launch of the saloon, the Somerset drophead coupe was announced. This

retained the same chassis and general styling lines, but there were only two passenger doors. The bodyshell was constructed for Austin by Carbodies of Coventry, and included a three-position hood (fully down, fully erect, or erect with the front folded back into the 'de Ville' position.

Both these styles sold well, even though they had to fight important competition from cars like the Ford Consul and the Hillman Minx (not to mention the Morris Oxford!), but in the autumn of 1954 they were dropped to make way for the new monocoque A40/A50 Cambridge range. As far as the British customers were concerned, the Somersets were a bit too 'Transatlantic' in both their looks and their behaviour for the early 1950s – more performance and more precise handling and gear-changing were really needed.

Austin A40 Somerset specification

As for Austin A40 Devon except for:
Produced: Longbridge, 1952-54. 166,063 Somerset saloons and 7,243 Somerset convertible coupes built.
Engine and transmission: 42bhp at 4,400rpm; 62lb ft at 2,500rpm. 4-speed gearbox, no synchromesh on 1st gear; steering-column gear-change.
Chassis: Anti-roll bar on rear suspension.
Dimensions: Length 13ft 3.5in; width 5ft 3in; height 5ft 4in. Unladen weight (approx) 2,140lb.
Distinguishing features from previous model: Entirely new pressed-steel coachwork, more rounded, looking like A70 Hereford.
Typical performance: Maximum speed 69mph; 0-60mph 31.6sec; standing ¼-mile 24.3sec; overall fuel consumption 30mpg.
Derivatives: Convertible coupe (1952-54).
Fate: Discontinued in 1954 in favour of all-new monocoque A40 Cambridge model.

The A40 Somerset was a pre-BMC design which made its bow early in 1952. Strictly speaking, this car should have overriders on its bumpers.

The A40 Somerset was also offered in drophead-coupe form with a three-position hood. It cost £701 in 1954, £36 more than the saloon.

Austin A70 Hereford (1950 to 1954)

After the Second World War, Austin's first new cars were the very large Sheerline/Princess models, and their second was the A40 Devon. After a further year, in which the A40 sold very well indeed, they introduced the A70 Hampshire and A90 Atlantic models, which shared the same chassis and different versions of the same engine, but had entirely different body styles.

The A70 Hampshire, which looked very similar to the A40 Devon, was produced for only two years before an entirely new and rather more bulbous bodyshell was produced in autumn 1950. This was the A70 Hereford, which was to remain in production for four years at Longbridge and be built in three different guises.

The A70 Hereford chassis followed the same basic lines as that of the A40, but was very different in detail, for it had a 6.5in longer wheelbase (3in longer than the original) and much wider wheel tracks at front and rear. The general layout of the independent front suspension (and some components) was shared with the A40 Devon, including the lever arms of the dampers, which also doubled duty as top wishbones.

The 2,199cc overhead-valve four-cylinder engine was basically that of the postwar 16hp model first seen in 1944, and was effectively a 'four-out-of-six' cylinder version of the big A125/A135 unit which had been introduced in 1939 for use in Austin's new range of light trucks. It was, in almost every way, a Leonard Lord invention.

Like the Hampshire before it, the Hereford had a steering-column gear-change which, matched by a divided-bench front seat, allowed the maximum possible passenger accommodation. The saloons had four doors (these were the same assemblies as on the A40 Somerset) and there was a great deal of leg and elbow room for all passengers.

Two other body styles were also sold on the Hereford's chassis. The A70 coupe was shown at the same time as the new saloon was announced. This body was produced for Austin by Carbodies, and had something in common with the A40 coupe,

as it also had a two-door style using the saloon's wing lines and a three-position hood, for which power operation was an optional extra.

The third style, introduced in the summer of 1951, with deliveries starting shortly after this, was the Countryman, which was an estate car conversion of the saloon car's style, with four passenger doors and a rear shell containing sizeable chunks of wood and metal alike.

Austin A70 Hereford specification

Produced: Longbridge, 1950-54. 48,640 saloons, 1,515 estate cars and convertible coupes built.
General layout: Separate box-section steel chassis-frame with all-steel bodyshell in 4-seater, 4-door saloon style. Front-mounted engine driving rear wheels.
Engine and transmission: Austin A70-type engine (smaller predecessor of Austin-Healey 100 engine design), 4-cylinder, ohv, in-line. 2,199cc, 79.4 x 111.1mm, 68bhp at 3,800rpm; 116lb ft at 1,700rpm; 4-speed gearbox, no synchromesh on 1st gear; steering-column gear-change; live (beam) rear axle with spiral-bevel final drive.
Chassis: Independent front suspension, coil springs and wishbones. Cam-and-peg steering. Rear suspension by half-elliptic leaf springs. Front and rear drum brakes. 5.50-16in tyres.
Dimensions: Wheelbase 8ft 3.0in; front track 4ft 6in; rear track 4ft 8in; length 13ft 11.5in; width 5ft 9.6in; height 5ft 5.6in. Unladen weight (approx) 2,825lb.
Typical performance: Maximum speed 81mph; 0-60mph 21.4sec; standing ¼-mile 22.1sec; overall fuel consumption 22mpg.
Derivatives: Convertible coupe (1951-52), Countryman estate (1951-54).
Fate: Discontinued in 1954 in favour of new monocoque A90 Westminster range.

The Hereford was another pre-BMC model and was built from 1950 to 1954. It looked almost exactly like the A40 Somerset, and its engine was a smaller version of that found in the Austin-Healey 100 of 1952-56.

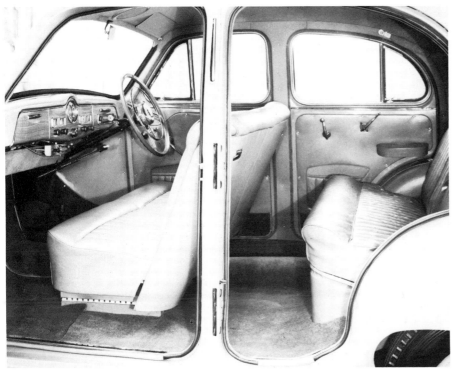

The A70 Hereford's interior, featuring a divided bench front seat, a steering-column change and an umbrella-handle handbrake.

The A70 Hereford's interior, featuring a divided bench front seat, a steering-column change and an umbrella-handle handbrake.

The Austin A90 Atlantic could be bought as a convertible or as a two-door hardtop. Neither car sold at all well, but the engine and (modified) transmission were later used in the Austin-Healey 100 four-cylinder cars.

Because none of these cars sold in very large quantities, few changes were made in the four years that they were on the market. All were discontinued in the autumn of 1954 to make way for the new A90 Westminster model.

Austin A90 Atlantic (1948 to 1952)

The A90 Atlantic was a failure by almost any standards – the styling was thought ghastly by many people, it wasn't a very fast car, and it sold very slowly indeed. Austin aimed it squarely at the car-hungry United States market, where it was decisively rejected. Its only claim to fame, today, is that its engine and (modified) transmission were used to power the Austin-Healey 100 sports car!

The A90 Atlantic was introduced at the same time as the A70 Hampshire, in the autumn of 1948, the two cars sharing the same chassis and 8ft wheelbase. The running gear, too, was the same, except that the A90's engine was a larger (2,660cc) version of that used in the A70. However, when the A70 Hampshire gave way to the longer-wheelbase Hereford in 1950, the A90 Atlantic's chassis was left unchanged. Like the A70, too, the A90 had a steering-column gear-change and a divided bench front seat.

The 2.6-litre Austin A90 engine, complete with twin SU carburettors, was also found in the Austin-Healey 100 of 1953-56.

The truly controversial feature was the styling, which is best described as 'unmistakable'. There was no conventional Austin-type radiator grille at all, but a low and wide air intake with a central 'Cyclops' driving lamp. There were *two* Flying-A Austin badges – one above and behind each headlamp – and the front wing line swept diagonally down across the door pressings to meet the rear bumper extensions.

There were only two passenger doors, but four-seater accommodation (rather cramped in the rear), and the only body available at first was a convertible, with optional power-operated hood and window lifts. On the facia, there was a rev-counter on one side of the panel display, a speedometer on the other, and a cluster of minor instruments. *The Autocar* called

The Austin A90 Atlantic's instrument panel, rather garish, but none-the-less sporting an engine rev-counter. The steering-column gear-change was quite normal for new models of the period.

the shape 'striking but not gaudy', which was making the best of a bad job.

A year after the initial launch, the A90 hardtop, or sports saloon, was launched, this really being the same bodyshell from which the hood and its mechanism had been removed and a permanent roof installed in its place, but there were still only two passenger doors, and the same restricted rear seat accommodation.

This did not help, for in spite of the car being used to set a raft of endurance speed records at the Indianapolis race track, the Americans were not at all impressed, and it flopped on both sides of the Atlantic. A full two years before the first of the large BMC cars, the A90 Westminster, was ready to go on sale, the A90 Atlantic had been dropped.

Austin A125 Sheerline (1947 to 1954)

Even though their very large cars never sold in large quantities, Austin always seemed to have at least one such model in the range. In spite of all the obvious mass-production priorities which should have been tackled first, Austin chose to introduce an all-new large car as their first postwar model.

One corporate move which helped this decision was that Austin bought the Vanden Plas coachbuilding business in 1946, which meant that they could introduce two new cars simultaneously on the same basic chassis – the Austin-assembled car being known as the Sheerline, and the Vanden Plas model as the Princess.

The new chassis, first seen in 1947, was a massive frame with a 9ft 11in wheelbase, coil-spring independent front suspension with semi-trailing wishbones and that familiar 1940s Austin feature of lever-arm dampers doubling up as top wishbones. The engine was Austin's big overhead-valve six-cylinder truck

---

Austin A125 Sheerline specification

Produced: Longbridge, 1947-54. 9,000 Sheerlines of all types built.
General layout: Separate box-section chassis-frame and steel bodyshells in 6-seater, 4-door saloon body style, or 8-seater, 4-door limousine style. Front-mounted engine driving rear wheels.
Engine and transmission: BMC D-Series engine, 6-cylinder, ohv, in-line. Original engine (A110 model), 3,460cc, 85 x 101.6mm, 110bhp at unspecified rpm; (A125 model), 3,993cc, 87.3 x 111.1mm, 125bhp at unspecified rpm. 4-speed gearbox, no synchromesh on 1st gear; steering-column gear-change; live (beam) rear axle with hypoid-bevel final drive.
Chassis: Independent front suspension, coil springs and wishbones. Cam-gear steering. Rear suspension by half-elliptic leaf springs and anti-roll bar. Front and rear drum brakes. 6.50-16in tyres.
Dimensions: (saloon) Wheelbase 9ft 11in; front track 4ft 10in; rear track 5ft 0in; length 16ft 0in; width 6ft 1in; height 5ft 7in. Unladen weight (approx) 4,340lb. (limousine) Wheelbase 11ft 0in; length 17ft 0.4in, unladen weight (approx) 5,600lb, other dimensions as saloon.
Typical performance: (saloon) Maximum speed 80mph; 0-60mph 19.4sec; standing ¼-mile 21.9sec; overall fuel consumption 14mpg.
Derivatives: Saloon came first, built 1947 to 1954 (A110 for first few cars only), limousine followed from late 1949 to 1954.
Fate: Discontinued in 1954 and not replaced, but equivalent A135 Princess carried on.

The Austin A125 Sheerline had an Austin-styled (as opposed to Vanden Plas-styled) razor-edge bodyshell, but the chassis and 4-litre engine were shared with the A135 model.

unit, which had been introduced in 1939 and may now be called the D-Series. There was a steering-column gear-change and a hypoid-bevel final drive (other new Austin passenger cars of the period had spiral-bevel axles), and an interesting suspension detail was the mounting of a rear anti-roll bar, linked to the damper arms.

Austin never officially announced the output of the engine, but clearly it was not enough at first. The original Sheerline was called A110 and had a 3,460cc engine, but after only 12 cars had been built the engine size was enlarged to 3,993cc and the model became the A125.

Styling of the all-steel bodyshell was by Austin, and was not at all as dignified and successful of that of the 'rival' Princess; it is said that Leonard Lord later sacked the executive responsible! Even so, the Sheerline sold steadily, mainly to councils for Mayoral use, or to hire car operators, for it did not have the aura of a private car. Recognizing this at an early stage, Austin announced a long-wheelbase (11ft 0in) version of the chassis, and topped it by a limousine version of the same four-door style, with an extra window behind the rear passenger door. Ambulance and hearse versions were also produced by special coachbuilders.

By the time that BMC was founded, the Sheerline was already a long-neglected model in the line-up for there were no significant improvements during the 1950s. The car was dropped in 1954, after which all cars on this vast chassis were Princesses, assembled at Kingsbury.

Austin A135 Princess Mk II (1950 to 1953)
The Vanden Plas coachbuilding business, based at Kingsbury, in North London, was taken over by Austin in 1946, and within a year this little company had started building Austin-based models. The first car was the Princess, which married a VDP-

Austin A135 Princess Mk II specification

As for Austin A125 Sheerline Mk I except for:
Produced: Kingsbury, 1950-53. 760 cars and chassis built.
Engine and transmission: 3,993cc engine, 130bhp at 3,700rpm; 212lb ft at 2,200rpm.
Dimensions: (saloon) Unladen weight (approx) 4,370lb; (limousine) Length 17ft 11in; unladen weight (approx) 4,760lb.
Distinguishing features from previous models: Different front grille and enlarged rear window, plus new badging.
Typical performance: (saloon) Maximum speed 86mph; 0-60mph 19.5sec; overall fuel consumption 16mpg. (limousine) Maximum speed 79mph; 0-60mph 23.3sec; standing ¼-mile 23.0sec; overall fuel consumption 15mpg.
Derivatives: Princess II was itself a derivative of Princess I, built 1947-50, using same rolling chassis as Sheerline models. Princess III, Princess IV and Vanden Plas Princess (see separate entries) all used same basic chassis until late 1960s.
Fate: Discontinued in 1953 in favour of Mk III model.

styled and produced body to the large new chassis also forming the basis of the Sheerline.

Compared with the Sheerline chassis, that of the Princess had a more powerful engine, which used twin carburettors instead of the single unit of the Sheerline. As with the original Sheerline, this was clearly not enough, so after 32 A120 Princesses had been built the engines became 4-litre units, and the model name A135.

The first series of Princesses was displaced by the Princess

The first Austin Princess was designated A120 in 1947 (this show), but soon became A135 when the engine was enlarged. The A110 shown here (background) was the original Sheerline, which later became the A125.

The A135 Princess Mk II was based on the Mk I, but had a different rear door window glass outline.

The Austin A135 Princess Mk I and Mk II had the same facia style, with square instrument outlines and a wood finish.

Mk II in 1950, where the visual changes were concentrated on restyling the rear quarter-window to give improved visibility for rear-seat passengers, and this was the current Princess when the BMC merger took place, running through to the autumn of 1953.

All Princess bodies took shape around the coachbuilder's traditional wooden framing, with some alloy castings also employed, though the majority of the aluminium skin panels were pressed by Austin at Longbridge. From the end of 1950 there were two distinct versions of the Princess – the saloon on the same wheelbase as the Sheerline saloon, and the touring limousine, which used the lengthened wheelbase.

Compared with the styling of the Sheerline, that of the Princess was much more delicately and expertly carried out. Perhaps the front-end style was still a little plain, but the wing line, the rear quarters (rather similar to that of the Mk VI Bentley) and the general treatment of the razor-edge shape was much more successful. The trimming and furnishing was beautifully carried out, but the whole thing was really let down by the facia panel, whose square instrument cut-outs were very obviously like those used in the Sheerline.

Even so, this car was a great success – in sales *and* financial terms – and the Princess Mk III which took over from it was merely a mildly facelifted version.

Austin A135 Princess Mk III (1953 to 1956)

For 1954, the Vanden Plas Princess range was rationalized and expanded; with relatively minor modifications it became known as the Mk III series.

The same basic body style was retained, but there was a new and altogether neater front-end styling. There was also new trim and furnishing, and a new heating and ventilation unit. This model ran on for three more successful years before being discontinued in favour of the very different Princess Mk IV.

The only styling change of note for the A135 Princess Mk III was to the radiator grille.

Austin A135 Princess Mk III specification

As for Austin A135 Princess Mk II except for:
Produced: Kingsbury, 1953-56. 350 cars and chassis built.
Distinguishing features from previous models: Different front grille and enlarged bumpers plus new trim and furnishing.
Derivatives: Princess III was itself a derivative of Princess II. Saloon and touring limousine versions were made. Princess IV and Vanden Plas Princess (see separate entries) all used same basic chassis until late 1960s.
Fate: Discontinued in 1956 in favour of Mk IV model.

Austin A135 Princess Mk IV (1956 to 1959)

After nine years it was high time that the Princess body style was changed, and the new fourth series was very different in many respects. Paradoxically, however, it was also an outright failure, for it was much more expensive than the superseded Princess III and only 200 of these cars were produced in three years.

The basis of the Princess IV was the same type of chassis-frame as that used on earlier Sheerline and Princess models

Austin A135 Princess Mk IV specification

Produced: Kingsbury, 1956-59. 200 cars built.
General layout: Separate box-section chassis-frame and coachbuilt wood-and-steel bodyshell, in 6-seater, 4-door saloon body style, or 6-seater, 4-door limousine style. Front-mounted engine driving rear wheels.
Engine and transmission: BMC D-Series engine, 6-cylinder, ohv, in-line. 3,993cc, 87.3 x 111.1mm, 150bhp at 4,100rpm; 227lb ft at 2,400rpm. GM Hydramatic automatic gearbox, four forward gears; steering-column gear-change; live (beam) rear axle with hypoid-bevel final drive.
Chassis: Independent front suspension, coil springs and wishbones. Cam-and-peg steering with power assistance. Rear suspension by half-elliptic leaf springs. Front and rear drum brakes. 6.50-16in tyres.
Dimensions: Wheelbase 10ft 1.7in; front track 4ft 10.7in; rear track 5ft 0in; length 16ft 9in; width 6ft 1in; height 5ft 5.7in. Unladen weight (approx) 4,590lb.
Distinguishing features from previous models: New body style compared with previous Princess III, plus new engine and automatic transmission.
Typical performance: (saloon) Maximum speed 99mph; 0-60mph 16.1sec; standing ¼-mile 20.6sec; overall fuel consumption 12mpg.
Derivatives: Saloon and limousine models both available on same chassis and to same basic style. Princess limousine used similar chassis, but different engine and coachwork.
Fate: Discontinued in 1959 and not replaced, but rather different Princess limousine carried on until 1968.

except that its wheelbase had been lengthened by a couple of inches. Changes to the chassis included the use of Girling power-assisted steering, and there was no anti-roll bar on the rear suspension.

The engine, though still basically D-Series, was radically different from the earlier types. On the earlier cars the cylinder head ports were on the left and the spark plugs on the right; on this, the DS7 derivative, both the block and the cylinder head were new, with ports now on the right and spark plugs on the left. There was a higher compression ratio (7.6:1 instead of 6.8:1), better breathing and a peak power output of 150bhp. This engine was also used in some versions of the Jensen 541R GT saloon and was coupled to Hydramatic automatic transmission of the type used in current Bentley and Rolls-Royce models.

The new body style was arguably nota as dignified as that which it displaced and it had more striking and obvious wing lines. As before, there were some steel and some aluminium panels, with assembly carried out at Kingsbury. Inside the car, one of the more pleasing features was the latest facia panel, which had the principal instruments ahead of the driver's (or chauffeur's) eyes.

For this chassis, there was only one wheelbase on offer, and one basic body style, which could be supplied as a conventional saloon, or as a touring limousine. This, however, was the last of the short-wheelbase Princess cars, for after the Princess IV was dropped, it was not replaced, although the long-wheelbase 4-litre limousine carried on until 1968.

In August 1957, the Princess IV theoretically lost its 'Austin' identity and became simply a Princess, but this was purely a badge-engineering exercise, and accordingly this model is not covered in the Princess/Vanden Plas section.

Austin Princess 4-litre (1952 to 1957)

Early in 1952, just as the BMC empire was beginning to take shape, Vanden Plas was invited to design an all-new body style to be built on coachbuilt lines to take over from the unsuccessful Sheerline limousine. This car was unveiled at the 1952 Earls Court motor show, and with no more than minor modifications was to remain on the market until 1968, by which time BMC had been absorbed into the new British Leyland combine. If you measure success by the time it was on the market, this was BMC's most successful car.

The basis of this car was the longer-wheelbase Sheerline/Princess chassis, and from summer 1958 that chassis was actually assembled at Kingsbury. When introduced, the 4-litre

engine either had a single Stromberg carburettor or a triple-SU carburettor installation. From late 1956, and after they became available on the Princess IV model, the long-wheelbase limousine was also offered with Hydramatic automatic transmission and power-assisted steering.

From August 1957 the Austin Princess ceased to exist, as the 'Austin' part of the title was dropped in favour of the short-lived Princess marque, which then transmuted itself into Vanden Plas in 1960.

The A135 long-wheelbase limousine's facia of the 1950s was well furnished with instruments and controls, but the minor instruments were almost lost in the veneer of the panel.

The Austin A135 Princess long-wheelbase limousine was launched in 1952 and was built in various guises until 1968.

Austin A40 Cambridge (1954 to 1957)

When it arrived, the A40 Cambridge was the third-generation Austin A40, and the first to have been designed under the umbrella of the BMC organization. Compared with the superseded A40 Somerset it was new from stem to stern, and there was neither a family likeness, nor many significant carry-over mechanical components. The Cambridge, in fact, was much more closely related to the contemporary A90 Westminster than any other car.

Like all other important new models which were to come from Austin in the future, the Cambridge was built around a chassisless, unit-construction bodyshell, one which was narrower and lower, but no less roomy, than the A40 Somerset which it replaced. It was an altogether more 'square' car than the bulbous Somerset, with a 'non-Austin' radiator grille profile, slightly hooded headlamps, a wing crown line which swept through from headlamp cowls to the tail, and those characteristic ribbed rear quarters which soon led to cynics calling them 'cow hips'. It was offered as a four-door saloon or a two-door saloon at first, but the two-door option was dropped

from the British market after a few prototypes had been built.

Although there were similarities in the chassis of the new and the old A40s, much was brand new and all was modified. The 1.2-litre engine, although having the same swept volume as before, was actually the under-bored version of the new corporate B-Series unit, but still produced 42bhp. It was backed by a brand-new B-Series four-speed transmission, which still had steering-column change control, and there was also a new hypoid-bevel B-Series back axle unit. This drive line had already been seen on the new MG Magnette ZA and the Morris Oxford SII, would soon be used in the MG MGA, and was the real foundation of BMC's 'building block' strategy for the 1950s and 1960s.

Front suspension was a slightly modified version of that previously seen on the A40 Somerset, though the lever-arm dampers were larger and therefore more resistant to fade. The doors would be shared, in toto, with the A90 Westminster bodyshell, but although the two cars looked alike there were few other shared components.

Compared with the Somerset, the new car's boot was larger, but had an awkwardly high sill, while access to the engine bay was helped by a wide 'alligator' opening bonnet panel. The facia was mostly painted metal, with an instrument pod ahead of the driver's eyes, and the heater was only standard on De Luxe models.

The A40 Cambridge of 1954, the first of the monocoque-bodied B-Series saloons. It was also available as an A50, with a 1.5-litre engine.

Although the A40 Cambridge sold well enough, it was overshadowed by the success of the larger-engined A50 version, and when the time came to restyle the shell for early 1957, the A40 itself was discontinued. The *next* A40, the Farina model of late 1958, was an entirely different type of car, based on A35 running gear.

Austin A50 Cambridge (1954 to 1957)

'A50' was a new model number at Austin in 1954, and really indicated no more than a larger-engined, more-powerful version of the A40 model. The A50 shared all the same basic design, body styling, running gear and suspension with the A40, except that a two-door body option was never offered, and the engine was enlarged.

The A50's engine was the definitive 1,489cc 50bhp version of the new B-Series design, and like the 1.2-litre version it was

> ### Austin A50 Cambridge specification
>
> As for Austin A40 Cambridge except for:
> **Produced:** Longbridge, 1954-57. 114,867 A50s of all types built.
> **Engine and transmission:** 1,489cc, 73.025 x 88.9mm, 50bhp at 4,400rpm; 74lb ft at 2,100rpm. Optional overdrive (top, 3rd and 2nd gears) from early 1956, 2-pedal Manumatic transmission optional from late 1956.
> **Chassis:** From autumn 1956, 5.90-13in tyres.
> **Typical performance:** Maximum speed 74 mph; 0-60mph 28.8sec; standing ¼-mile 23.2sec; overall fuel consumption 28mpg.
> **Fate:** Discontinued in 1957 and replaced by the facelifted version, called A55 Cambridge.

The A40/A50 Cambridge cars of 1954 used the B-Series engine, allied to Zenith carburettors.

The A40/A50 instrument display featured wide expanses of painted metal. Still no sign of a floor gear-change, either.

equipped with a downdraught Zenith carburettor. Because it was more powerful and more torquey than the smaller engine, it was allied to the higher final-drive ratio (4.875:1 instead of 5.125:1), though the gearbox itself was just the same.

All the doors were fitted with drop-glass windows at first, but this was replaced by a proper wind-down mechanism in a matter of weeks.

Among the mechanical improvements made available during the run of the A50 were the option of a Borg-Warner overdrive (from early 1956), which was allied to the 5.125:1 final drive of the A40. This was identical to that already offered for the A90 Westminster, and could be arranged to cut-in automatically when the road speed exceeded 32mph in second, third or top gears. Right at the end of the car's run, a package of changes made for the 1957 season included the option of Manumatic transmission (two-pedal control) and the use of smaller, 13in road wheels – all of which was actually paving the way for the introduction of the revised A55 model in the following year.

The A50 was dropped in 1957 to make way for the A55 model, which was a re-engineered version of the A50 itself.

Austin A55 Cambridge Mk I (1957 to 1959)

In 1956 and 1957, BMC gave a mid-term facelift to several of the best-selling models, and in this process the A50 became the A55. Although clearly still based on the design of the original A50, the car was demonstrably different and better in some respects.

The new car was announced in February 1957 and was unchanged, mechanically, from the 1957-model A50 which had been on sale for four months. The major styling change was at the rear, where the sheet metal was new, the original 'cow hips' had gone, and there was a longer and more attractive tail with a lower sill, and an even larger boot than before. To round it all off there was a slightly modified front style and an enlarged rear window, and a rather contrived duo-tone paint

---

Austin A55 Cambridge Mk I specification

As for Austin A50 Cambridge except for:
Produced: Longbridge, 1957-59. 369,616 A55 Cambridges of Mk I *and* Farina Mk II types built.
Engine and transmission: 51bhp at 4,250rpm; 81lb ft at 2,000rpm. Optional centre-floor gear-change from spring 1958.
Dimensions: Length 13ft 10.9in; unladen weight (approx) 2,325lb.
Distinguishing features from previous model: Lengthened tail and new rear style, wraparound window, Manumatic transmission option.
Typical performance: Maximum speed 75mph; 0-60mph 31.8sec; standing ¼-mile 23.3sec; overall fuel consumption 34mpg.
Derivatives: None.
Fate: Discontinued in 1959 in favour of all-new Farina A55 Cambridge model.

---

job could also be supplied. All these changes had already been seen on the rather larger bodyshell of the 1957-model A95 Westminster, so there was nothing unexpected about their appearance.

The engine, which had been slightly uprated for 1957 in the last of the A50s, produced 51bhp, and there was the choice of manual, manual plus Borg-Warner overdrive, or Manumatic transmission.

The A55 (the 'Mk I' title was applied retrospectively after the next generation of A55s arrived in 1959) was in production for two years, and in this time the only important change was that a centre-floor gear-change became optional equipment from April 1958; this, in fact, was the same linkage as planned for use in the next generation of A55s.

Early in 1957, the A50 became A55 with the aid of a restyled tail – longer, with a larger boot and more pleasing lines.

The Austin A90 Westminster of 1954 was a lookalike of the A50 Cambridge, but there were very few common parts. It was the first BMC model to use the new C-Series six-cylinder engine.

This is the facia style of the original Austin A90 Westminster. Note the gear-change pattern on the gear-lever knob.

Austin A90 Westminster (1954 to 1956)

As soon as the BMC business started to operate, two major new-model programmes got under way – Morris beginning the design of their Oxford/Isis range, and Austin starting to develop the two cars eventually announced as the A40/A50 Cambridge and the A90 Westminster. In fact, although the A40/A50 Cambridge and the new Westminster cars looked as if they had the same bodyshells on different wheelbases, only the door pressings were common.

The A90 Westminster, announced as a last-minute show surprise in October 1954, was a direct replacement for the A70

Hereford, which was dropped to make way for it at Longbridge. It was also an effective replacement for the 2.6-litre A90 Atlantic, even though that car had been phased out two years previously. Such were the illogical ways of the young BMC organization that the A90 Westminster was also a direct competitor for the soon-to-be-announced Morris Isis, with which it shared the engine, gearbox and final-drive assemblies! In BMC at this time, the economics of scale were used in one direction – running gear – but not at all in respect of bodies, for the A90 and the Westminster had entirely different shells.

That of the A90 was a conventionally engineered unit-construction style, rather long and slim, and looking very similar indeed to the A50 Cambridge, although it had a much longer wheelbase and wider wheel tracks. Although there were many common features inside the two (A50 and A90) cabins – the same stylists and engineers obviously having been at work – the actual instrument layout was unique, though the same types of steering-column gear-change, heater and radio installation were used. The rear end style was almost identical, for the same type of 'cow hip' rear quarters and high-sill boot-lid opening were in evidence. The independent front suspension was developed from that of the obsolete A70/A90 Atlantic layout, and had the characteristic lever-arm damper/

Austin A90 Westminster specification

Produced: Longbridge, 1954-56. 25,532 A90 Westminsters of all types built.

General layout: Pressed-steel unit-construction body/chassis structure, in 4-seater, 4-door saloon style. Front-mounted engine driving rear wheels.

Engine and transmission: BMC C-Series engine, 6-cylinder, ohv, in-line. 2,639cc, 79.4 x 88.9mm, 85bhp at 4,000rpm; 124lb ft at 2,000rpm; 4-speed gearbox, no synchromesh on 1st gear; steering-column gear-change; optional overdrive (top and 3rd gears) from early 1956; live (beam) rear axle with hypoid-bevel final drive.

Chassis: Independent front suspension, coil springs and wishbones. Cam-and-peg steering. Rear suspension by half-elliptic leaf springs and anti-roll bar. Front and rear drum brakes. 6.40-15in tyres.

Dimensions: Wheelbase 8ft 7.75in; front track 4ft 3.5in; rear track 4ft 3.25in; length 15ft 2.25in; width 5ft 4in; height 5ft 3.75in. Unladen weight (approx) 2,912lb.

Typical performance: Maximum speed 86mph; 0-60mph 18.9sec; standing ¼-mile 21.0sec: overall fuel consumption 20mpg.

Derivatives: A95 and A105 models (see separate entries) evolved from this design, which itself shared some panels and basic styling with the A40/A50 Cambridge models.

Fate: Discontinued in 1956 in favour of revised A95 model.

top wishbone installation. The rear suspension was stiffened up by means of an anti-roll bar.

The engine, of course, was all new, for this was the first mass-production application of the Morris-designed BMC C-Series six-cylinder unit. For the A90, it had a single downdraught Zenith carburettor and a peak power output of 85bhp, and it was matched by the new C-Series four-speed gearbox, which had baulk-ring synchromesh, and a selector mechanism mounted in the side of the casing to make the provision of a steering-column change easy.

Although the original A90 was only to remain in production for two years (it was replaced by the longer-tailed and much improved A95 in the autumn of 1956), it also gave rise to the much faster A105 derivative, and indirectly to the Vanden Plas interpretation of that theme. One important mechanical improvement, phased in from the first weeks of 1956, was the option of the Borg-Warner overdrive, which worked on top, third and second gears. Like that also offered on the A50 Cambridge, this could be engaged so as to cut in automatically when the car's speed rose above 30mph and the throttle was momentarily eased.

The A90 Westminster's C-Series engine installation of 1954 included the use of a downdraught carburettor.

Austin A95 Westminster (1956 to 1959)
In the autumn of 1956, BMC introduced no brand new models, but went in for a positive orgy of facelifting and significant re-engineering of existing cars. It was at this time that the A95 Westminster evolved from the A90.

The original A90 Westminster had only been in production for two years (and about 25,000 cars) by 1956, so there was no question of a major redesign being carried out. The basic chassis engineering was not changed, but there was a 2in longer wheelbase (achieved by redesigning the rear springs and the position of the axle fixing), and the 2.6-litre engine was made 7bhp more powerful. The Borg-Warner overdrive option was continued, and in addition Borg-Warner automatic transmission was optionally available.

For 1957, the A90 Westminster became A95 by having a new long-tail body style and an increased power output.

72

The rear of the car was restyled, along the same lines as the A50-to-A55 transformation (but months in advance of it), with a longer and smoother tail, wraparound rear window and a much reduced sill height for the boot. There was also a new grille, new wheel trims and different decorative treatment along the sides. This car, of course, was closely related to the facelifted A105 model.

At the same time, BMC introduced the A95 Countryman, which was a four-door estate car version of the saloon, incorporating a horizontally split rear door arrangement.

This model carried on, virtually unchanged except for the addition of an optional centre-floor gear-change for manual-transmission cars from spring 1958, until the spring of 1959, when it was finally phased out ahead of the launch of the new Farina-styled A99 cars.

Austin A95 Westminster specification

As for Austin A90 Westminster except for:
Produced: Longbridge, 1956-59. 28,065 A95 Westminsters of all types built.
Engine and transmission: 92bhp at 4,500rpm; 130lb ft at 2,000rpm; optional Borg-Warner automatic transmission. Optional centre-floor gear-change from spring 1958.
Dimensions: Wheelbase 8ft 9.75in; length 15ft 0.7in; unladen weight (approx) 2,975lb.
Distinguishing features from previous model: Lengthened tail and new rear style, wraparound window, automatic transmission option.
Typical performance: Maximum speed 90mph; 0-60mph 19.8sec; standing ¼-mile 21.8sec: overall fuel consumption 20mpg.
Derivatives: A95 estate car also available and A105 very closely related to this design.
Fate: Discontinued in 1959 in favour of all-new Farina A99 Westminster model.

Austin A105 (1956 to 1959)

The A90 Westminster had been in production for less than two years when BMC introduced a higher-powered derivative of it, which they called the A105 (the Westminster name was no longer used). The original A105 was the short-tail variety, built only in the 1956 model year, but most A105s were the long-wheelbase, long-tail facelift variety.

Announced in May 1956, the A105 had a twin-SU carburettor/102bhp version of the 2.6-litre C-Series engine, which was in the same tune as that fitted to the original Austin-Healey 100-Six which followed a few months later. To match this extra power, Borg-Warner overdrive (operating on top and third gears – but, unlike the A90, not on second gear) was made standard.

The whole car sat an inch lower on its suspension, and there was a great deal of extra 'comfort' equipment and special colour schemes, plus Transatlantic-style whitewall tyres.

At facelift time, in October 1956, the A105 received the longer wheelbase, optional automatic transmission and lengthened tail/wraparound rear window treatment of the

The A105's 2.6-litre C-Series engine had twin SU carburettors and a gallery-type of inlet manifold.

The Austin A105 was a tuned and better specified version of the A90 Westminster, with a two-tone colour scheme.

A95, plus duo-tone colour schemes, but no Countryman version was ever sold. As with the A95, there was optional floor-change control from spring 1958. Like the A95, the A105 was dropped in mid-1959 to make way for the A99/Wolseley 6/99 style.

Austin A105 specification

As for Austin A90 and A95 models except for:
Produced: Longbridge, 1956-59. 6,770 A105s of all types built.
Engine and transmission: 102bhp at 4,600rpm; 141lb ft at 2,600rpm; overdrive (on top and 3rd gears) standard.
Dimensions: Height 5ft 3.75in.
Typical performance: Maximum speed 96mph; 0-60mph 15.4sec; standing ¼-mile 20.2sec: overall fuel consumption 22mpg.
Derivatives: From autumn 1956, A105 inherited longer tail, wraparound rear window, 8ft 9.75in wheelbase, 15ft 0.7in overall length and optional Borg-Warner automatic transmission. Optional centre-floor gear-change from spring 1958.
Fate: Discontinued in 1959 and replaced by the new Farina-styled A99 Westminster.

Austin A105 Vanden Plas (1958 to 1959)

The first A105 Vanden Plas was produced to special order for the personal use of BMC's chairman, Sir Leonard Lord. He was so delighted with the result that he then requested Vanden Plas to produce the cars in quantity, and 500 were built in little more than a year. It was more important, however, that this was the start of Vanden Plas' expanding coversion business for BMC, which went on to encompass cars like the 3-litre Princess and the Princess 1100 models.

Mechanically, the A105 Vanden Plas was the same as that of the standard A105, for all the changes were in trim and furnishing. Cars were built at Longbridge, without trim and upholstery, then delivered to the Vanden Plas works at Kingsbury for completion. Compared with the standard product, the Vanden Plas derivative had wood (walnut) facia and door cappings, leather seat facings, thick pile carpet on the floor, and a wool cloth headlining. There were special exterior paint jobs, side flashes and badges, and right from the start the cars could be supplied with centre-floor or steering-column gear-change controls. As with the ordinary A105, Borg-Warner overdrive was standard equipment and automatic transmission was optional.

For 1957, BMC gave the A105 a new tail style, longer and smoother behind the doors, together with a new grille and a contrasting colour stripe along the flanks.

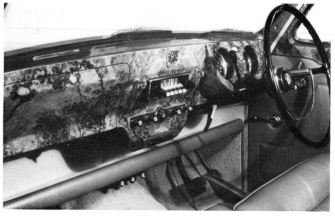

Vanden Plas refurnished the A105 to produce the A105 Vanden Plas model. New features included this sumptuously trimmed wooden facia, still with standard instruments.

Austin A105 Vanden Plas specification

As for Austin A105 facelift model except for:
Produced: Longbridge and Kingsbury, 1958-59. 500 A105 Vanden Plas models built.
Dimensions: Unladen weight 3,105lb.
Typical performance: Maximum speed 94mph; 0-60mph 17.8sec; standing ¼-mile 21.2sec: overall fuel consumption 20mpg.
Fate: Discontinued in 1959 and replaced by the new Princess model derived from the A99 Westminster.

The Farina-styled A55 Cambridge was announced in 1959, and came complete with tail-fins and a rather narrow track.

The A55 Cambridge Countryman, a four-door estate car, was announced in the autumn of 1960.

Austin A55 Cambridge Mk II (1959 to 1961)

Although the A40 of 1958 was the first Farina-styled BMC car to make its appearance, the family of B-Series cars launched progressively from December 1958 was commercially the most important of all. It was this finned design, eventually built as Austin, Morris, MG, Riley and Wolseley, which led to BMC being accused of cynical badge-engineering – yet the critics all conveniently forgot the fact that sales boomed during the 1960s when the process was at its height, so BMC must have been getting *something* right!

The first B-Series Farina car to be announced was the Wolseley 15/60 of December 1958, and the Austin-badged car, given the name of A55 Cambridge Mk II, followed it in January 1959, actually as the first Longbridge-built derivative from this family. It took over directly from the A40/A50/A55 Mk I family of 1954-58.

All five cars used the same basic body structure, with different nose treatment and sometimes different rear details to make them different, but all used the same, rather squared-up, four-door passenger cabins and one version or another of the ubiquitous B-Series engine/transmission package. As launched in 1959, the A55 had a rather severe, square, mesh front grille, very prominent fins and a body style which left the wheels well tucked in and looking a touch too small for the rest of the machine. There was a plain and simple instrument display, a split-bench front seat arrangement and a rather willowy centre-floor gear-change position (a steering-column change was optional, but few such cars appear to have been built); the handbrake lever was tucked away between the driver's seat cushion and the door sill.

Mechanically there were no surprises, except that the 1,489cc engine had adopted the 'Nuffield' type of SU carburation and gained a few horsepower in the process. There was no transmission alternative, the overdrive and Manumatic options of the obsolete A55 having been dropped when that car disappeared.

At first there was only the four-door saloon, but from the spring of 1960 a neat four-door Countryman estate car version was added to the line-up (this style also being offered for the Morris Oxford, but not the MG/Riley/Wolseley versions).

This was the BMC period in which Austin and Morris dealer chains still had a separate existence, still fought each other in thousands of high streets for individual sales, and still demanded their own versions of every range to sell. Nowadays, of course, it goes without saying that the Austin A55 Mk II was *exactly* as fast, economical and spacious as the Morris Oxford Series V, but in 1959 it was more than a dealer's reputation was worth actually to admit this!

This situation persisted throughout the 1960s, by which time the A55 had become the A60, a change which occurred in late 1961.

Austin A60 Cambridge (1961 to 1969)

In the BMC mass facelift session of autumn 1961, the A55 was transmuted into the A60, and although the same basic bodyshell and mechanical layout was retained, it became a much better car in all aspects. With that in mind, it is not at all surprising that it stayed in production for more than seven years. BMC's management themselves must have been surprised, and rather taken aback, by the continuing demand, for they had expected it to die when faced with in-house opposition from the new front-wheel-drive 1800. When they found orders *not* drying up, and Longbridge could no longer cope with the production of both types, assembly of Austin Cambridges was moved to Cowley, where the cars took shape among their Oxford, MG Magnette, Riley and Wolseley equivalents.

The A60 of late 1961 was really a thoroughly re-engineered and slightly restyled A55, with shaved-down rear fins and a different front grille.

As with the A55, there was also an A60 Countryman.

Compared with the A55, the A60 had a longer wheelbase, wider tracks, better roadholding, modified styling, a bigger engine and more performance – plus, for the first time, the option of Borg-Warner Type 35 automatic transmission. It was quite a transformation.

Visually, the A60 was recognized by a new and rather wider-mouthed front grille, while at the rear the fins had been reduced in size and aggressiveness, with new tail-lamp clusters being specified, plus different duo-tone colour schemes to extra order. There was a new facia style, with simulated wood-grain finish, modified seating and trim, and other details.

Mechanically, the big change was a corporate switch from 1,489cc to 1,622cc B-Series engine, which boosted the power and torque, with overall gearing raised to suit. Also, the car's wheelbase had been increased by 1.1 inches by the simple expedient of moving the rear axle back on its springs. The front and rear tracks were both increased, anti-roll bars were added to front and rear suspension, and the result was much better handling response than before, but still no more than adequate by modern standards.

In the next seven years, few changes were made to the A60, which continued to be built as a saloon or an estate car. However, duo-tone paintwork was standardized from the autumn of 1962, and there were further minor development changes at the end of 1964. The A60 and its sister car, the Morris Oxford Series VI, went on until 1969, when British Leyland finally killed off the Austin, but the Morris lived on until 1971.

Austin A60 Diesel (1961 to 1969)

At the same time as the A55 became the A60, it was given the option of a small diesel engine, a unit which was actually a beefed-up conversion of the B-Series petrol engine. At first this was an export-only model, but from summer 1962 it was made available on the British market.

As you might expect, the A60 Diesel was a much slower, noisier, rougher, but more economical car than the petrol-engined version, and for all the obvious reasons it sold very slowly indeed. Most of the cars built were used as taxis, or for similar commercial ventures, and very few survive to this day.

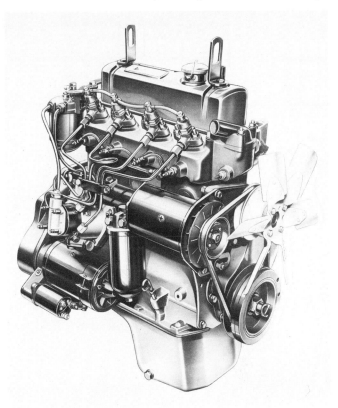

BMC developed a 1.5-litre diesel version of the B-Series engine, which became available in the A60 and Morris Oxford models.

Austin A60 Cambridge specification

As for Austin A55 except for:
Produced: Longbridge, 1961-65, then Cowley, 1965-69. 175,674 cars built at Longbridge, approximately 101,000 at Cowley. (Accurate Cowley figures are not available.)
Engine and transmission: 1,622cc, 76.2 x 88.9mm, 61bhp at 4,500rpm; 90lb ft at 2,100rpm; 4-speed gearbox, no synchromesh on 1st gear; centre-floor gear-change or steering-column change; optional automatic transmission.
Chassis: Front and rear anti-roll bars.
Dimensions: Wheelbase 8ft 4.35in; front track 4ft 2.6in; rear track 4ft 3.4in; length 14ft 6.5in.
Distinguishing features from previous model: Different front and rear bumpers, changed profile to rear fins, new grille and facia, new waistline mouldings.
Typical performance: Maximum speed 81mph; 0-60mph 21.4sec; standing ¼-mile 21.8sec; overall fuel consumption 26mpg.
Derivatives: Estate car version also available. Close mechanical and family resemblance to all other B-Series Farina models.
Fate: Both body types discontinued in 1969 in favour of the already established and entirely different Austin 1800 model.

Austin A60 Diesel specification

As for petrol engined A60 except for:
Engine and transmission: BMC B-Series diesel engine, 1,489cc. 40bhp at 4,000rpm; 64lb ft at 1,900rpm.
Dimensions: Unladen weight 2,520lb.
Typical performance: Maximum speed 66mph; 0-60mph 39.4sec; standing ¼-mile 25.9sec: overall fuel consumption 37mpg.
Distinguishing features from previous models: Diesel engine and obvious diesel 'knock' when being driven.
Fate: Discontinued in 1969 and not replaced.

Close relations – the Austin A60 (left of picture) and the Morris Oxford Series VI (right); both these are fitted with the 1.5-litre diesel engine.

Austin A99 Westminster (1959 to 1961)

The first Farina-styled Austin to be introduced was the A40 of autumn 1958, and this was followed by the new B-Series range at the beginning of 1959. The new large cars – Austin A99 and Wolseley 6/99 respectively – were the third Farina-styled cars to be launched in a matter of months.

It is important to realize that these two cars replaced a varied selection of early-BMC products in a successful rationalization move. After 1959 there was no large Riley or large Morris. But it was not all logic, for the body structure of this new Austin A99 was built at Longbridge, while the near-identical Wolseley 6/99 shell was produced at Cowley!

The A99 followed the same Farina-inspired lines as the Austin A50/Morris Oxford family, but was an altogether larger, squatter and somehow more impressive monocoque, riding on a 9ft wheelbase and using the latest version of the C-Series engine. This had been enlarged to 2,912cc (the same size as that introduced at the same time in the Austin-Healey 3000), used twin SU carburettors and produced 103 bhp. This was matched by a new transmission – an all-synchromesh, three-speed gearbox with Porsche synchromesh, and there was Borg-Warner overdrive on top and second gears; steering-column gear-change control was still standard and Borg-Warner automatic transmission was optional.

The Farina-styled A99 model was announced in the summer of 1959, complete with the obligatory tail-fins.

The A99 facia of 1959. Note the overdrive control under the parcel shelf.

Austin A99 Westminster specification

Produced: Longbridge, 1959-61. 13,410 cars built.
General layout: Unit-construction, pressed-steel body-chassis structure, in 5-seater, 4-door saloon car style. Front-mounted engine driving rear wheels.
Engine and transmission: BMC C-Series engine, 6-cylinder, ohv, in-line 2,912cc, 83.34 x 88.9mm, 103bhp at 4,500rpm; 158lb ft at 2,000rpm; 3-speed gearbox, all synchromesh; Borg-Warner overdrive standard on top and 2nd gears; optional Borg-Warner automatic transmission; live (beam) rear axle with hypoid-bevel final drive.
Chassis: Independent front suspension, coil springs, wishbones and anti-roll bar. Cam-and-peg steering. Rear suspension by half-elliptic leaf springs and anti-roll bar. Front disc and rear drum brakes. 7.00-14in tyres.
Dimensions: Wheelbase 9ft 0in; front track 4ft 6in; rear track 4ft 5.25in; length 15ft 8in; width 5ft 8.5in; height 4ft 11in. Unladen weight (approx) 3,305lb.
Distinguishing features from previous model: Entirely different monocoque and Farina body style from superseded A95/A105 models.
Typical performance: Maximum speed 98mph; 0-60mph 14.4sec; standing ¼-mile 20.4sec; overall fuel consumption 19mpg.
Derivatives: The Wolseley 6/99 was mechanically identical and shared the same monocoque, but had a different nose style and upgraded trim. Both cars were superseded by the Austin A110/Wolseley 6/110 models in autumn 1961.
Fate: Discontinued in 1961 and replaced by the A110, which used the same basic design.

Coded AD0 10 in the BMC scheme of things, the A99 and the badge-engineered Wolseley 6/99 were mechanically identical and utterly conventional in all respects. The suspension layout was similar to, but not the same as, that of the superseded A95/A105 cars, and there was a rear anti-roll bar on the original model, plus servo-assisted front wheel disc brakes. The new model provided undistinguished handling and performance, and was both heavy and bulky, but at least it was very roomy – in other words, it could not possibly have been more different, in looks or in design philosophy, from the startling Minis which were about to be launched from the same factory. Alec Issigonis was always happy to admit that he had had *nothing* to do with the design of these big cars.

The Wolseley 6/99 (see separate entry) was virtually the same car, but had a different nose with the traditional Wolseley grille, and a much more luxuriously trimmed and equipped interior.

Austin A110 Westminster (1961 to 1964)

In the autumn of 1961, as in the autumn of 1956, BMC introduced no new models, but facelifted most of them. In this process, every single one of the Farina-styled cars received attention, which included improvements to roadholding (a longer wheelbase and other attention to the chassis) and to the engines. It was in this way, only two years after introduction, that the A99 was replaced by the slightly different A110.

The new A110 retained the same basic unit-construction chassis/monocoque as the original A99, but there was a 2-inch longer wheelbase (arranged by moving the back axle rearwards on its springs) which allowed modified wheelarches to be designed and more space to be provided in the back seats. Also

In the autumn of 1961, the A99 was updated to become the A110, with a more powerful (120bhp) engine and a different grille.

The interior of the A110 Westminster, left, complete with floor gear-change and divided-bench front seat. The A110 Westminster's 3-litre C-Series engine, complete with a twin SU carburettor installation.

Austin A110 Westminster specification

As for A99 except for:

Produced: Longbridge, 1961-64. 26,105 Mk I and Mk II-type A110s built.

Engine and transmission: 120bhp at 4,750rpm; 163lb ft at 2,750rpm. Optional Borg-Warner automatic transmission.

Chassis: Rear suspension with transverse anti-sway hydraulic damper. Optional power-assisted steering from summer 1962.

Dimensions: Wheelbase 9ft 2in; height 5ft 0.5in. Weight 3,470lb.

Distinguishing features from previous model: Restyled facia, manual gear-change on centre-floor and twin exhaust system.

Typical performance: Maximum speed 102mph; 0-60mph 13.3sec; standing ¼-mile 19.4sec; overall fuel consumption 19mpg.

Derivatives: Series II model took over in spring 1964. Wolseley 6/110 was mechanically identical, but with different nose style and interior trim.

Fate: Discontinued in the spring of 1964 in favour of Mk II models.

---

at the rear was a newly-installed transverse shock absorber, between the axle casing and the bodyshell, to contain incipient axle sway due to all the rubber in the rear suspension linkage. After the first few months, power-assisted steering became optional.

The engine was significantly more powerful, with 120bhp, this being achieved by 'raiding' the experience gained with Austin-Healey 3000s and involving cylinder head changes, a different camshaft profile and a twin-bore exhaust system. For this model, too, the gear-change lever was back on the floor – the steering-column change fashion now being well-and-truly gone.

The only way to identify the A110 from the A99 was by the new horizontally-slatted grille and the wood-grain finish to the facia. At the same time as the A99 was transformed into the A110, the Wolseley 6/99 became the 6/110.

Austin A110 Westminster Mk II (1964 to 1968)
In May 1964, BMC produced the third and final version of the Farina-styled Austin A99, calling it the A110 Mk II; at the same time they also produced the parallel model, the Wolseley 6/110 Mk II. Compared with the superseded A110, the only obvious external change was to the grille, which was of

Last of the C-Series Farina-styled cars was the A110 Mk II of 1964.

The A110 Mk II Super de Luxe's interior, complete with wooden facia and picnic tables in the back of the front seats.

Austin A110 Westminster Mk II specification

As for A110 except for:

Produced: Longbridge, 1964-66. Cowley 1966-68. 26,105 Mk I and Mk II-type A110s built.

Engine and transmission: 120bhp at 4,750rpm; 163lb ft at 2,750rpm. 4-speed gearbox, no synchromesh on 1st gear; optional Borg-Warner overdrive; optional Borg-Warner automatic transmission.

Chassis: Rear suspension with transverse anti-sway hydraulic damper, no anti-roll bar. 7.50-13in tyres.

Dimensions: Wheelbase 9ft 2in; height 5ft 0.5in. Weight 3,470lb.

Distinguishing features from previous model: Restyled facia and interior and smaller road wheels.

Typical performance: Maximum speed 102mph; 0-60mph 13.3sec; standing 1/4-mile 19.4sec; overall fuel consumption 19mpg.

Derivatives: Wolseley 6/110 Mk II was mechanically identical, but with different nose style and interior trim.

Fate: Discontinued early in 1968 in favour of entirely different Austin 3-litre model.

anodized aluminium mesh on the basic (*ie* non-Super de Luxe) derivative, although the expert might also have picked up the use of 13in instead of 14in diameter road wheels. Inside the car, the basic A110 had a modified instrument layout and fixed-rake leathercloth seats, while the Super de Luxe version had wood-veneered facia and door cappings, leather seat facings and reclining front seat backs.

Under the skin, the engine was not changed, but there was a new four-speed gearbox (like that of the Austin-Healey 3000), behind which the Borg-Warner overdrive was no longer standard, but an optional extra. For this derivative the latest British-built Borg-Warner Type 35 automatic transmission became optional. Suspension changes centred around the use of larger-section tyres on smaller wheels, the lowering of the

bodyshell to produce a 0.6in lower ride height, and the use of angled telescopic rear dampers instead of the lever-arm type of previous A99/A110 models; the transverse damper of the original A110 was no longer fitted. Thicker front disc brakes, an inertia-operated pressure-limiting valve in the rear brake circuit and yet another different exhaust system were all included in the latest package, but the overall performance was little changed. This car was replaced by the Austin 3-litre in 1968.

The Austin 3-litre of 1967 was not yet in volume production at the time British Leyland was founded. It had separate seats, and the transmission selector for the optional automatic box was on the tunnel, but there was only a strip speedometer.

Austin 3-Litre specification

Produced: Cowley, 1967-71. 9,992 of all types built.
General layout: Pressed-steel unit-construction body/chassis structure, in 4-seater, 4-door saloon style. Front-mounted engine driving rear wheels.
Engine and transmission: 'New Generation' BMC C-Series engine, 6-cylinder, ohv, in-line 2,912cc, 83.34 x 88.9mm, 124bhp at 4,500rpm; 161lb ft at 3,000rpm. 4-speed gearbox, synchromesh on all forward gears; centre-floor change; optional overdrive on top gear; optional Borg-Warner automatic transmission; final drive directly mounted to monocoque with hypoid bevel.
Chassis: Independent front suspension, Hydrolastic spring/damper units and wishbones. Power-assisted rack-and-pinion steering. Independent rear suspension by Hydrolastic spring/damper units and semi-trailing arms, interconnected to front suspension; self-levelling at rear. Front discs and rear drum brakes. 185-14in tyres.
Dimensions: Wheelbase 9ft 7.5in; front track 4ft 8.25in; rear track 4ft 8in; length 15ft 5.7in; width 5ft 6.75in; height 4ft 8.75in. Unladen weight (approx) 3,290lb.
Typical performance: Maximum speed 100mph; 0-60mph 15.7sec; standing ¼-mile 20.1sec; overall fuel consumption 16mpg.
Derivatives: None.
Fate: Discontinued in 1971 and not replaced by British Leyland.

Austin 3-Litre (1967 to 1971)

One of the last major new models to be launched by BMC before the British Leyland merger was announced was the big Austin 3-litre, which took over from the long-running Austin A99/A110 family. Although the engine size of the new car was the same as before, almost every component of the new design was different from the old. Frankly, this was not a successful project, for the car had lumpy styling, uninspiring handling, an almost complete lack of character and a distinct lack of marketing effort put behind it.

Although the new car was a front-engine/rear-wheel-drive machine, its spacious cabin shared the basic dimensions and quite a number of the same panels (including the doors) with the front-wheel-drive Austin/Morris 1800 models. The long nose and simple tail section, however, were completely different.

Up front was the familiar-*sounding* 2,912cc engine, but this was a completely redesigned (shorter and lighter) version of the old C-Series unit, with few common parts, which was also used in the new MG MGC announced at the same time. Behind it there was a new all-synchromesh four-speed manual transmission with optional Laycock overdrive on top, third and second gears, along with another alternative, that of Borg-Warner Type 35 automatic transmission.

The 'chassis' included all-independent suspension, with Hydrolastic units interconnected front to rear, and self-levelling rear suspension, the front linkage being by double-wishbone geometry, the rear by trailing arms. Power-assisted rack-and-pinion steering was standard, and naturally there were front-wheel disc brakes.

The original 3-Litre, announced before production was ready to begin, had single rectangular headlamps high up and at each side of the mesh grille, but the body pressings were clearly arranged for twinned circular units to be fitted. By the time the first official deliveries were made in the late spring of 1968, BMC had become BLMC, the twin-headlamp nose had been adopted, and the final drive gearing had been raised, but even that car did not survive for long.

From October 1968, just one year after announcement (and probably only six months after deliveries began), the 3-Litre became 'De Luxe', with much better sound-deadening and quality of fittings, with a revised facia and more comfortable seats, and it was in this guise that it sold slowly, if steadily, for the next two years or so. But as a BMC, as against a British Leyland, invention, competing against rival in-house cars like the Triumph 2.5 PI at a very similar price, it could not be expected to last long, and it was quietly dropped, almost unnoticed and unmourned, in the spring of 1971.

When Sir Alec Issigonis retired in 1971, this PR picture highlighted his achievements with the Mini. The car registered 621 AOK was the very first Longbridge-built example of 1959.

This special cutaway Mini display model shows the astonishing packaging achieved with this front-wheel-drive layout.

Austin Mini [also known as Austin Seven] (1959-1967)

The concept, birth and history of the Mini project is now well known, but it is worth recalling that it was *the* first modern transverse-engined front-wheel-drive small car in the world, the first BMC car to have all-independent suspension, and the first to pack so much interior passenger space into such a small bodyshell. It was the first of a whole series of cars which Alec Issigonis' team developed for BMC in the last 10 years of its existence.

Except that the Mini's original engine was a short-stroke, 848cc version of the ubiquitous A-Series, everything else about the design was new. The styling of the tiny little two-door saloon was clearly influenced by the Morris, as opposed to the Austin end of the BMC heirachy (there are definite whiffs of Morris Oxford in the lines), and its unit-construction shell was destined to be made in several different factories, in several different types.

All the cars and light commercial vehicles, however, used the gearbox-in-sump layout, and at first all used the rubber cone spring layout which Alex Moulton had developed for BMC. There was all-independent suspension, rack-and-pinion steering, 10in diameter road wheels and astonishing grip, roadholding and response. There was also a hard, joggly ride, cramped seating for four people, and all manner of teething troubles at first, mainly connected with water leaks and water on the ignition.

In all respects except for badges and dealer networks, the Austin Seven (as BMC failed to get the new car named) was the same as the Morris Mini Minor, and both marques of saloon were soon joined by Countryman (Austin) and Traveller (Morris) estate versions on a 4-inch longer wheelbase, by vans based on those estates, and even by useful little pick-ups. At Longbridge, the Austin Mini took over at once from the A35 saloon, though the A35 estate cars and vans carried on for some time.

In the first eight years, the trim and badging line-up was reshuffled from time to time, with a Super from late 1961 and a Super de Luxe taking over in late 1962. Plain metal-bodied Countryman estates were announced as an option to the 'country cottage' wood-battened variety from late 1962. Meantime, the 'Seven' part of the title gave way to 'Mini' in January 1962 – but that was what the public had always called the car anyway! Then, from late 1964, the Hydrolastic suspension system, interconnected front to rear, took over

---

Austin Mini specification

Produced: Longbridge and Cowley, 1959-67. More than 5,000,000 of *all* types of Mini built by early 1986.
General layout: Pressed-steel unit-construction body-chassis structure, in 4-seater, 2-door saloon or estate body styles, plus vans and pick-ups. Front and transversely-mounted engine driving front wheels.
Engine and transmission: BMC A-Series engine, 4-cylinder, ohv, in-line. 848cc, 62.9 x 68.26mm, 34bhp at 5,500rpm; 44lb ft at 2,900rpm; 4-speed gearbox, no synchromesh on 1st gear; centre-floor gear-change; spur-gear final drive. Optional automatic transmission from late 1965.
Chassis: Independent front suspension, rubber cones and wishbones. Rack-and-pinion steering. Independent rear suspension by rubber cone springs and trailing arms. Front and rear drum brakes. 5.20-10in tyres. Hydrolastic suspension units, interconnected front to rear, from late 1964.
Dimensions: Wheelbase 6ft 8in; front track 3ft 11.75in; rear track 3ft 9.9in; length 10ft 0.25in; width 4ft 5in; height 4ft 7in. Unladen weight (approx) 1,290lb.
Typical performance: Maximum speed 72mph; 0-60mph 27.1sec; standing ¼-mile 23.6sec; overall fuel consumption 40mpg.
Distinguishing features from previous models: Totally different in every way from any previous Austin or other BMC models, with front-wheel drive and tiny 10in wheels.
Derivatives: Austin Mini and Morris Mini Minor were identical in all but badging. Mini-Cooper, Mini-Cooper S and Mini-Moke followed (see separate entries). 2-door saloon from 1959, longer-wheelbase estate car from 1960, plus van and pick-up light commercial vehicles.
Fate: Discontinued in 1967 in favour of Mk II models.

from the rubber cone systems, but only on the saloons, while from late 1965 the new four-speed AP automatic transmission was offered as an option on saloons only.

In the meantime, more, better and faster Minis had proliferated (see separate entries), and the foundations were laid for a long-running saga which was still not over when this book was written in the mid-1980s. However, in the autumn of 1967, just before BMC gave way to British Leyland, the original Mini was replaced by the very similar Mini Mk II.

Original Austin Seven (Mini) models looked like this in 1959.

An Austin Super Mini had slightly better trim and a different grille from the ordinary de Luxe models.

It wasn't long before the Mini saloons were joined by an estate car, which had a slightly lengthened wheelbase. This was the Austin Seven Countryman version.

Austin Mini Mk II (1967 to 1969)

In autumn 1967 the Mini range had been selling very strongly indeed for eight years (up to 250,000 a year of all types were being built by this time), but BMC thought it time to freshen up the image and expand the range, without making major style or engineering changes. The result was that the Mk II cars took over, visually little changed, but technically better than before.

All cars had a new, slightly enlarged front grille, and the saloons also had an enlarged rear window and larger tail-lamps. The standard Mini was much as before, but the Super de Luxe had a new three-instrument facia panel (that of the Mini-Cooper) and restyled seats.

The most important development was that the Mk II models were now to be offered with a choice of 848cc or 998cc engines. The larger of these had significantly more power and torque than the original, being a single-carburettor version of

The well-filled engine bay of the Austin Mini Mk II, showing the transverse engine installation and the radiator at the side, by the left-side wheelarch.

Austin Mini Mk II specification

Produced: Longbridge and Cowley, 1967-69. More than 5,000,000 of all types built by early 1986.

General layout: Pressed-steel unit-construction body-chassis structure, in 4-seater, 2-door body styles. Front and transversely-mounted engine driving front wheels.

Engine and transmission: BMC A-Series engine, 4-cylinder, ohv, in-line. 848cc, 62.9 x 68.26mm, 34bhp at 5,500rpm; 44lb ft at 2,900rpm. Alternative engine (for Mini 1000), 998cc, 64.58 x 76.2mm, 38bhp at 5,250rpm; 52lb ft at 2,700rpm. 4-speed gearbox, no synchromesh on 1st gear at first, but all-synchro from autumn 1968; optional automatic transmission; centre-floor gear-change; spur-gear final drive.

Chassis: Independent front suspension, Hydrolastic units and wishbones. Rack-and-pinion steering. Independent rear suspension by Hydrolastic units and trailing arms. Interconnection between front and rear suspensions. Front and rear drum brakes. 5.20-10in tyres.

Dimensions: (saloon) Wheelbase 6ft 8in; front track 3ft 11.4in; rear track 3ft 9.8in; length 10ft 0.25in; width 4ft 7.5in; height 4ft 5in. Unladen weight (approx) 1,400lb.

Typical performance: 850 as original Mini. (1000) Maximum speed 75mph; 0-60mph 26.2sec; standing ¼-mile 22.7sec; overall fuel consumption 34mpg.

Distinguishing features from previous models: Enlarged rear window, different front grille, tail-lamps, remote-control gear-change and trim changes, plus 998cc option.

Derivatives: As with early Minis, sold as saloon, or longer-wheelbase (7ft 0.1in) estate (Countryman) plus vans and pick-ups. Also see Mini-Cooper and Mini-Cooper S. Morris Mini was same car with different badges.

Fate: Discontinued in 1969 as marque badges were dropped; all Minis became, simply, BL Minis.

For 1968, the Austin Mini became a Mk II, with a different grille and other changes, plus a 998cc engine option.

The Austin Mini Mk II was distinguished by the use of larger tail-lamp clusters and an enlarged rear window, plus new badging.

the existing Mini-Cooper unit, and the same as the Riley Elf/ Wolseley Hornet engine; this car was also provided with a remote-control (Mini-Cooper type) gear-change. The AP automatic transmission was optional with either engine, and although the manual transmission was not changed immediately, an all-synchromesh gearbox was fitted, without fanfare, from the summer of 1968.

In this form the Austin Mini (along with Morris, Mini-Cooper, *et al*) continued to sell even better than ever as BMC was swallowed up in the new British Leyland organization. However, in October 1969, all Mini-based vehicles lost their marque badges as British Leyland began their rationalization programme, and at this juncture the *Austin* Mini died away. Thereafter all such cars were purely 'Minis', though it took years for the various licensing authorities to be convinced.

The technical changes phased in at the same time included the fitting of wind-up windows to the passenger doors, the dropping of Hydrolastic suspension in favour of the original rubber cone type, and the rejigging of the bodyshell to get rid of the external door hinges. At the same time, too, the long-nose Mini 1275GT was introduced, but this, like the non-marque-badged Minis, was a British Leyland rather than a BMC car.

Austin Mini-Moke (1964 to 1968 in UK, to date overseas)
Once the Mini phenomenon took off, BMC were persuaded to design all manner of derivatives, some for fun, some for publicity purposes, and some with a very definite commercial niche in mind. The most rugged-looking of all, a rather impractical little machine which has nevertheless lived on into

The Austin Mini-Moke, which used the Mini's front-wheel-drive power pack in a starkly-equipped open structure.

the mid-1980s, was the Mini-Moke; like other Minis of the period, this was 'Austin' or 'Morris' badged, but the engineering was always the same.

The Moke was first developed with an eye to military sales. In theory, it could have been a very light, go-almost-anywhere vehicle, a whole size smaller than the Jeep or Land-Rover. That was the theory, but the practice was that its wheels were too small, its ground clearance too low, and its front-wheel-drive traction too limiting in scope, so the British forces rejected it. Not even a twin-engined version (one at the front, one at the rear, the two being entirely unconnected!) made much sense.

BMC then sat back, considered its position, and eventually put the Mini-Moke on sale as something of a 'fun machine' for the civilian market. (It could not be classed as a 'commercial' for it had four seats and no load-carrying space.) Although it had the same wheelbase as the saloons, the same transverse engine/front-wheel-drive package, and the same front and rear chassis components, the Moke was built on an entirely different platform-style, punt-shaped, pressed-steel monocoque, with no sides, no doors, no weather protection –

in fact no anything! In fairness, a hood and some very skimpy all-weather equipment could be provided, but this was more for show than for effect (particularly in really blustery conditions), and the Mini-Moke's typical habitat was scudding up and down London's trendy King's Road, painted in psychedelic colours and overloaded with exuberant young people.

It was not enough of a success for the new British Leyland combine to keep it on, so from October 1968 its UK manufacture was closed down, and all the tooling was sent out to BLMC Australia, where it continued until the early 1980s. After this it was once again transferred to a factory in Portugal, where assembly continued in the mid-1980s. By that time the wheels had grown from 10in to 13in diameter, the engine had grown to 998cc (and on some examples to 1,275cc), and the weather protection had gradually been improved. The specification details included here, however, are for the original Longbridge-built version.

Austin Mini-Cooper (1961 to 1967)
As with the Mini, the origins of the Mini-Cooper are well-known. Grand Prix constructor John Cooper (who was already using BMC A-Series engines in his Formula Junior racing cars) got his hands on an early Mini, modified it with an eye to racing it in saloon car events, and sold the idea of building 1,000 – which the company was not at all sure could be sold – to BMC management. The rest, as they say, is history...

The productionized hot-rod, christened a Mini-Cooper, and Austin or Morris badged to suit the still-competing dealer chains, was announced in the autumn of 1961, and immediately began to sell as fast as BMC could make the cars. Compared with the mass-production Mini, the original Mini-Cooper had a long-stroke, twin-carb, 55bhp engine of 997cc, a gearbox with a remote-control gear-change, and tiny front disc brakes. The only external recognition points were different grille and badges, while inside the cockpit there was a higher standard of trim, plus the first use of the three-dial instrument panel later used on many up-market Minis.

The Mini-Cooper had an exuberant giant-killing character, for although its 85mph top speed and 0-60mph acceleration in 18sec sounds pedestrian by today's standards, it was startling for a small car in the early 1960s. Not only that, but the car's handling was quite phenomenal, and the engine could be tuned to produce very high outputs indeed. It was soon a successful racing or rallying saloon car.

The engine, however, was never used in any other BMC car, so when the opportunity came to rationalize, without a loss of performance, this was taken. From the beginning of 1964 the original, unique, 997cc engine was dropped in favour of the very different 998cc A-Series unit, which was actually a tuned version of that being fitted to the Riley Elf/Wolseley Hornet 'Minis' of the period. There was no stated change to peak power outputs, but the revised engine certainly gave the Mini-

The Austin Mini-Cooper of 1961 had a 55bhp, 997cc engine.

Austin Mini-Cooper specification

Produced: Longbridge, 1961-67. 101,242 Mini-Coopers of all types (Austin and Morris Mk I and Mk II) built.
General layout: Pressed-steel unit-construction body-chassis structure, in 4-seater, 2-door saloon body style. Front and transversely-mounted front-mounted engine driving front wheels.
Engine and transmission: BMC A-Series engine, 4-cylinder, ohv, in-line. Original engine, 997cc, 62.43 x 81.28mm, 55bhp at 6,000rpm; 54lb ft at 3,600rpm; from 1964, 998cc, 64.58 x 76.2mm, 55bhp at 5,800rpm; 57lb ft at 3,000rpm. 4-speed gearbox, no synchromesh on 1st gear; centre-floor gear-change; spur-gear final drive.
Chassis: Independent front suspension, rubber cones and wishbones. Rack-and-pinion steering. Independent rear suspension by rubber cone springs and trailing arms. Front disc and rear drum brakes. 5.20-10in tyres; 145-10in tyres from 1964. Hydrolastic suspension units, interconnected front to rear, from late 1964.
Dimensions: Wheelbase 6ft 8in; front track 3ft 11.75in; rear track 3ft 9.9in; length 10ft 0.25in; width 4ft 5in; height 4ft 7in. Unladen weight (approx) 1,400lb.
Typical performance: Maximum speed 85mph; 0-60mph 18.0sec; standing ¼-mile 20.9sec; overall fuel consumption 27mpg.
Distinguishing features from previous models: Larger, tuned engine, and remote-control gear-change, plus front disc brakes, different grille, facia and badging.
Derivatives: Morris Mini-Cooper was identical in every way but for badges and grille. Mk II models (see separate entries) followed. Mini-Cooper S had specialized engine and transmission components.
Fate: Discontinued in 1967 in favour of Mk II model.

Cooper more acceleration and a higher top speed than the original ever had.

At the same time as the mass-produced Minis were given Hydrolastic suspension, so were the Mini-Coopers, which was not too popular with most of the cars' customers (but they had no choice, so had to live with the rather queasy ride). Later, from the end of 1965, a reclining front seat option was made available, and then, in the autumn of 1967, the original Mini-Cooper was displaced by the slightly modified Mk II model.

Austin Mini-Cooper Mk II (1967 to 1969)

When the mass-production Mini became 'Mk II' in the autumn of 1967, the Mini-Cooper followed suit, with virtually no technical changes at the time. However, from the summer/autumn of 1968, an all-synchromesh gearbox was fitted, thus

Austin Mini-Cooper Mk II specification

As for Austin Mini-Cooper except for:
Produced: Longbridge, 1967-69.
Engine and transmission: All-synchromesh gearbox from autumn 1968.
Typical performance: (also for 998cc-engined Mk I model) Maximum speed 90mph; 0-60mph 16.8sec; standing ¼-mile 20.1sec; overall fuel consumption 33mpg.
Distinguishing features from previous models: Different front grille and enlarged rear window, plus new badging.
Derivatives: Austin was identical to Morris of the period, except for badging.
Fate: Discontinued in 1969 and not replaced.

When Minis became Mk II, so did the Mini-Coopers. The Austin and Morris, henceforth, shared a common slatted grille style.

improving one not-very-good aspect of a cheeky, full-of-character, little car.

Like the other Mk II Minis, the Mk II Mini-Cooper had a different, larger grille, the larger rear window, bigger tail-lamps and new badging to suit. By this time, radial-ply tyres were standard, and it was an appealing little package which continued to sell strongly until the autumn of 1969. When the Minis lost their individual marque badges, the Mini-Cooper was dropped completely.

Some British Leyland salesman tried to convince the enthusiasts that the long-nosed Mini 1275GT was its equal, if not a better car, but the customers knew better and always mourned the untimely death of the Mini-Cooper.

Austin Mini-Cooper S (1963 to 1967)

If you want to consider the Mini family's breeding in horseflesh terms, the Mini-Cooper evolved from the Mini, and the Mini-Cooper S evolved from the Mini-Cooper. In simplistic terms, the Mini-Cooper S was really the Mini-Cooper with bigger and better engines and brakes and – eventually – a bigger and better options list.

The major step forward for all the Mini-Cooper S family was the engine itself. At first for use in Formula Junior, then Formula 3 racing cars, and only later for road cars, the A-Series engine was completely rejigged, with cylinder bore centres being moved around to allow for a bigger bore, with more rigid cylinder head holding down arrangements and – eventually – a choice of three different piston strokes, all making the Mini-Cooper S ideal for one form of motor sport or another.

The new sub-family of engines had a 70.6mm cylinder bore, and the first unit to be offered used the 850 Mini's stroke, which gave a capacity of 1,071cc; thus the 1071S was born in March 1963, but was only built until August 1964 as something of an interim model.

Austin Mini-Cooper S specification

As for Austin Mini-Cooper except for:
Produced: Longbridge, 1963-67. 4,017 1071S, 972 970S and 40,449 1275S of all types (Austin and Morris, Mk I and Mk II) built.
Engine and transmission: A-Series engine, three types: 970S: 970cc, 70.6 x 61.91mm, 65bhp at 6,500rpm; 55lb ft at 3,500rpm. 1071S: 1,071cc, 70.6 x 68.26mm, 70bhp at 6,000rpm; 62lb ft at 4,500rpm. 1275S: 1,275cc, 70.6 x 81.28mm, 76bhp at 5,800rpm; 79lb ft at 3,000rpm.
Chassis: 145-10in tyres.
Dimensions: Front track 4ft 0.6in; rear track 3ft 11.3in; unladen weight (approx) 1,410lb.
Distinguishing features from previous model: Wider-rim wheels, radial-ply tyres and different badging.
Typical performance: (1071S) Maximum speed 95mph; 0-60mph 12.9sec; standing ¼-mile 18.9sec; overall fuel consumption 27mpg. (1275S) Maximum speed 97mph; 0-60mph 10.9sec; standing ¼-mile 18.2sec; overall fuel consumption 30mpg. (970S) No authentic independent figures available.
Derivatives: Austin and Morris models were identical in every way. Mk II and Mk III models followed (see separate entry).
Fate: Discontinued in 1967 in favour of Mk II models.

From the spring of 1964 the two definitive engines were slotted into place – the 970cc engine had an ultra-short stroke (it was the only over-square A-Series engine ever put into production), and the car fitted conveniently into the 1-litre competition class, while the 1,275cc unit had the 81.28mm stroke which had already been seen in the original 997cc Mini-Cooper engine of 1961, and this made the 1275S ideal for the 1.3-litre category.

The 'chassis' of the Mini-Cooper S was virtually the same as that of the Mini-Cooper, except that bigger front disc brakes with servo assistance were always standard, as were radial-ply tyres. The saloon style itself, the seating and the instrumentation were all the same as the Mini-Cooper at first, with only the 'S' badges giving the game away to some hapless motorist who had been passed at high speed!

Development changes in the next few years included the fitting of Hydrolastic suspension from autumn 1964, the building of many 1275S cars with coolers, twin fuel tanks and wide-rim wheels during 1965, and the standardization of all those components from the beginning of 1966; by that time, too, a reclining front seat option had been introduced.

Incidentally, although the 970S was only built for 11 months, in 1964 and early 1965, 230 Austins had 'wet suspension' and 262 were 'dry'. There were no 'wet' 1071Ss.

From the spring of 1965, only the 1275S remained in production, the 1071S and the 970S both having been withdrawn, but this single derivative sold better and better as time passed, and it was still a formidably successful competition car when the Mk II Mini range took over in the autumn of 1967.

Mini-Coopers and Mini-Cooper S models all used the same type of three-dial oval instrument nacelle and a remote-control gear-change.

The Austin Mini-Cooper S Mk II had twin fuel tanks, wide-rim wheels and that distinctive bonnet badge.

Austin Mini-Cooper S Mk II (1967 to 1969)

As with all the Mini family, in the autumn of 1967 the 1275S progressed from its original to the Mk II specification, mainly by the adoption of the new grille, rear window and tail-lamps and revised interior trim. There were no changes, or power boosts, to the 1,275cc engine.

An all-synchromesh gearbox was gradually, but not 'cleanly' (in production terms) phased in on the 1275S during 1968, and all the 1966 improvement package of twin tanks, oil cooler and wide-rim wheels was retained. Similarly, Hydrolastic suspension was retained, in spite of the wishes of most customers, who would have preferred the harder ride, but more precise handling, of the original rubber-suspension car.

When the Austin Mini lost its badges and became a pure 'Mini' in October 1969, it was clear that the Austin Mini-Cooper S's days were numbered. In fact it was not until March 1970 that the final, unbadged Mini-Cooper S Mk III was announced. This car, which really counts as a British Leyland model, had the same basic 'chassis' and running gear as ever, but was fitted with the winding door windows and concealed door hinges of other Mini models.

The last Mini-Cooper S of all was built in June 1971, and the only remaining high-performance Mini left was the 1275GT, which was a very poor substitute indeed.

Austin Mini-Cooper S Mk II specification

As for Austin Mini-Cooper S Mk I except for:
Produced: Longbridge, 1967-69.
Engine and transmission: Only 1,275cc engine available; all-synchromesh transmission fitted during summer 1968.
Distinguishing features from previous models: Different front grille and enlarged rear window, plus new badging.
Derivatives: Austin was identical to Morris of the period except for badging. From spring 1970, Mk II became Mini (*not* Austin) Mk III, with wind-up windows.
Fate: Discontinued in 1970 in favour of Mk III, itself discontinued in 1971 and not replaced.

The back view of a Mini-Cooper S Mk II, complete with twin fuel tank outlets and the new badges.

The Mini-Cooper S Mk II facia style was the same as that of the 1963-67 cars which preceded it.

The complete Mini range of 1968, Austins, Morrises, Rileys, Wolseleys, *et al.*

92

Austin 1100 (1963 to 1967)

To follow the huge sales success of the BMC Minis, Alec Issigonis' team produced a larger-engined, more spacious and more stylish car on the same lines. This was the famous 1100/1300 range of cars, produced in even more versions than the B-Series Farinas, which were built from 1962 to 1974 in huge numbers.

Because of the quirky way in which BMC's two main sales companies – Austin and Morris – competed with each other throughout the life of the combine, one was often given a head start over the other. On this occasion, the Morris 1100 came first, in the summer of 1962, and the launch of the mechanically-identical Austin 1100 was delayed until the autumn of 1963. Consequently, many people always called these cars 'Morris' 1100s, and the main description of the type appears under that car's heading.

The Austin, like the Morris, had a transversely-mounted A-Series engine driving the front wheels, and the clever, but not altogether successful, Hydrolastic suspension. As far as the British market was concerned, all Austin 1100 saloons had four doors, though there was a two-door version for other markets. Compared with the Morris 1100 which started it all off, the Austin had its own 'wavy mesh' grille and a neat but almost totally anonymous facia with a strip speedometer layout.

There was a rush of changes in 1965 and 1966 – the heater finally becoming standard in 1965 on the higher-priced De Luxe model, the option of AP automatic transmission from the end of that year, then the arrival of a neat and capacious two-door Countryman estate from the spring of 1966, and finally the offer of a reclining front seat option from May that year. All these improvements were faithfully mirrored in the specification of the Morris 1100.

Austin 1100 specification

Produced: Longbridge (some cars at Cowley), 1963-67. 1,052,000 cars of all 1100/1300 body types built.
General layout: Pressed-steel unit-construction body-chassis structure, in 4-seater, 4-door saloon body style. Front and transversely-mounted engine driving front wheels.
Engine and transmission: BMC A-Series engine, 4-cylinder, ohv, in-line. 1,098cc, 64.58 x 83.72mm, 48bhp at 5,100 rpm; 60lb at 2,500 rpm. 4-speed gearbox, no synchromesh on 1st gear, from 1965 optional AP automatic gearbox, 4 forward gears; centre-floor gear-change; spur-gear final drive.
Chassis: Independent front suspension, Hydrolastic units and wishbones. Rack-and-pinion steering. Independent rear suspension by Hydrolastic units, trailing arms and anti-roll bar. Interconnection between front and rear suspensions. Front disc and rear drum brakes. 5.50-12in tyres.
Dimensions: Wheelbase 7ft 9.5in; front track 4ft 3.5in; rear track 4ft 2.9in; length 12ft 2.7in; width 5ft 0.4in; height 4ft 4.7in. Unladen weight (approx) 1,800lb.
Typical performance: Maximum speed 78mph; 0-60mph 22.2sec; standing ¼-mile 22.7sec: overall fuel consumption 33mpg.
Distinguishing features from previous models: Entirely new type of Austin model with Pininfarina styling.
Derivatives: Morris 1100 was the same car, with different badges and details; MG 1100, Riley Kestrel and Wolseley 1100 models were all slightly modified versions. Countryman estate for 1966 and 1967. Mk II (see separate entry) was the same car with minor changes.
Fate: Discontinued in 1967 and replaced by Mk II models.

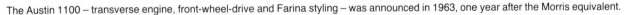

The Austin 1100 – transverse engine, front-wheel-drive and Farina styling – was announced in 1963, one year after the Morris equivalent.

The Austin 1100's instrument display was entirely different from that of the Morris 1100.

This display shows the transverse engine and transmission, plus the Hydrolastic suspension, of the Austin/Morris 1100 model.

So nearly identical were the Austin and Morris versions of the same design that it was quite easy to assemble Austins at Cowley at one period (and Morrises at Longbridge, for that matter). For once, BMC did not let one of their cars go on for too long before improving it, so the change from original 1100 to 'Mk II' came in the autumn of 1967 when the car was still at the height of its popularity.

Austin 1100 Mk II (1967 to 1971)
By 1967, BMC's product planners were at their most productive and (some would say) most cynical period, so when the 1100 became 1100 Mk II very little was expected. In fact, although the car was mechanically not changed at first, it was a better, more versatile and suitably modernized product which

The 1100s became 'Mk II' in the autumn of 1967, the obvious external changes including the cut-back tail-fins and new tail-lamps.

sold very well indeed for the next few years.

The most important changes were that henceforth there was to be a 1.3-litre version (see Austin 1300), an all-synchromesh transmission would soon become available, and the choice of two-door or four-door saloon styles was to be made available on the British market.

Visually, the Mk II cars had cropped tail-fins, with a new style of tail-lamp, and the Austin grille was very nearly the same as the Morris version – the Austin could be identified because it had a larger number of prominent horizontal bars than the Morris. There were saloons and estates, a choice of manual or automatic transmission, and de Luxe or Super de Luxe types. Under the skin, the important innovation was the fitting of new Lockheed SC (swinging caliper) front disc brakes. All-synchromesh gearboxes were not available on 1100s at first, but followed later, the change being completed in September 1968.

The 1100 Mk II was built until the autumn of 1971, when it was replaced by the final facelift, the Mk III model.

Austin 1100 Mk II specification

As for Austin 1100 Mk I, except for:
Produced: 1967-71.
General layout: 2-door and 4-door saloon bodies always available, Countryman estate only for 1967 and 1968.
Engine and transmission: All-synchromesh manual gearbox from mid-1968.
Distinguishing features from previous models: Different front grille, chopped-off tail-fins with different tail-lamps, trim and details.
Derivatives: 1100 Mk II was itself a derivative of the original 1100, similarly 1300 Mk II (see separate entry). Morris 1100/1300 was virtually the same car; also MG, Riley, Wolseley and Vanden Plas used same basic design.
Fate: Discontinued in 1971 in favour of Mk III model.

The Austin 1300 Super de Luxe models had this characteristic grille and perforated road wheels.

Austin 1300 Mk II (1967 to 1971)

The original front-drive Austin 1100 ran successfully for four years, and during 1967 something of a 'pilot' run of 1.3-litre-engined cars were sold in the more luxuriously equipped MG/Riley/Wolseley versions of this car. It was reasonable, therefore, to expect a mass-production 1300 model before long.

When BMC's planners facelifted the 1100 in the autumn of 1967 they split it into two different lines – the 1100 Mk II (see separate entry) and the new 1300 Mk II. This car took all the detail styling changes of the 1100 facelift (including the cropped tail-fins), and was built in myriad forms – two or four doors, de Luxe or Super de Luxe, saloon or estate car, manual or automatic transmission. All-synchromesh gears were available from the start, and the 1,275cc/58bhp engine was a productionized and detuned version of the original 'S' specification engine previously used only in the Mini-Cooper S.

The Mk II was replaced by the Mk III in the autumn of 1971.

Austin 1300 Mk II specification

As for original 1100 model except for:
Produced: Longbridge, 1967-71. 1,052,000 1100s and 1300s of all types (Mk I and Mk II) built.
General layout: 2-door, 4-door and estate car types available.
Engine and transmission: 1,275cc, 70.6 x 81.28mm, 58bhp at 5,250rpm; 69lb ft at 3,000rpm. All-synchromesh manual transmission from mid-1968.
Dimensions: Unladen weight (approx) 1,780lb.
Typical performance: Maximum speed 88mph; 0-60mph 17.3sec; standing ¼-mile 20.7sec; overall fuel consumption 30mpg.
Distinguishing features from previous model: Different grille, cropped-off fins, different tail-lamps and trim.
Derivatives: Austin and Morris models were identical in every way. Mk III models followed (see separate entry).
Fate: Discontinued in 1971 in favour of Mk III models.

Austin America (1968 to 1971)

The America was a brave, but not very successful, attempt to tailor the specification of a car to the USA market's special needs. Although introduced in March 1968, at which time the formation of British Leyland had already been announced but not yet formalized, it was a BMC car, inspired by BMC dealer requests from the United States, where it replaced the MG 1100 two-door 'Sportsedan'. In essence, the America was a two-door 1300 Mk II saloon, suitably badged, in which the 1,275cc engine was de-toxed and the AP four-speed automatic transmission was standard equipment.

Specially for USA sale, BMC developed the Austin America, which had its own unique badge and a two-door style.

The Austin America was always built with this unique two-spoke steering wheel and a T-handle to the automatic transmission selector.

Austin America specification

Produced: Longbridge, 1968-71. Approximately 59,000 cars built.

General layout: Pressed-steel unit-construction body-chassis structure, in 4-seater, 2-door saloon body style. Front and transversely-mounted engine driving front wheels.

Engine and transmission: BMC A-Series engine, 4-cylinder, ohv, in-line. 1,275cc, 70.6 x 81.28mm, 60bhp at 5,250rpm; 69lb ft at 2,500rpm. AP 4-speed automatic transmission; centre-floor gear-change; spur-gear final drive.

Chassis: Independent front suspension by Hydrolastic units and wishbones. Rack-and-pinion steering. Independent rear suspension by Hydrolastic units and trailing arms. Interconnection between front and rear. Front disc and rear drum brakes. 5.50-12in tyres.

Dimensions: Wheelbase 7ft 9.5in; front track 4ft 3.5in; rear track 4ft 2.9in; length 12ft 2.7in; width 5ft 0.4in; height 4ft 4.7in. Unladen weight (approx) 1,800lb.

Typical performance: No authentic independent figures available.

Distinguishing features from previous models: No previous models, but closely related to 1300, with Austin America grille badges and wing flashes, different trim and seats, automatic transmission standard and special steering wheel.

Derivatives: None, though basic chassis and structure was itself derived from Austin 1100/1300 front-wheel-drive saloon.

Fate: Discontinued in 1971 in favour of Austin Marina ('federalized' version of Morris Marina).

Other special touches included special seating, safety belts in front *and* rear seating positions, and a special alloy-spoked steering wheel. There were many detail safety features inside the car, including different switches and controls and a padded gear-lever selector knob.

The America was very definitely 'export only' and sold only in the USA, Canada and Switzerland.

Austin's 1300GT was a cheaper, but no less effective, version of the MG 1300 Mk II, complete with 70bhp engine.

The Austin 1300GT's facia and instruments were shared by the Morris 1300GT, MG 1300 Mk II and Riley 1300 Mk II models, but with different surface finishes.

Austin 1300GT (1969 to 1974)

Although this derivative of the 1100/1300 range was introduced in the autumn of 1969, by which time British Leyland had taken over from BMC as the parent company, it was still recognizably a BMC car. In effect, you could consider it as either an Austin version of the MG 1300 or an Austin 1300 with the MG 1300's engine! There was also a Morris version, identical in every way except for the Morris badging.

Austin 1300GT specification

Produced: Longbridge, 1969-74. 52,107 cars of original and Mk III-based types built.

General layout: Pressed steel unit-construction body-chassis structure, in 4-seater, 4-door saloon body style. Front and transversely-mounted engine driving front wheels.

Engine and transmission: BMC A-Series engine, 4-cylinder, ohv, in-line. 1,275cc, 70.6 x 81.28mm, 70bhp at 6,000rpm; 74lb ft at 3,250rpm. 4-speed gearbox, all synchromesh; centre-floor gear-change; spur-gear final drive.

Chassis: Independent front suspension, Hydrolastic units and wishbones. Rack-and-pinion steering. Independent rear suspension by Hydrolastic units and trailing arms. Interconnection between front and rear suspension. Front disc and rear drum brakes. 145-12in tyres.

Dimensions: Wheelbase 7ft 9.5in; front track 4ft 3.5in; rear track 4ft 2.9in; length 12ft 2.7in; width 5ft 0.4in; height 4ft 4.7in. Unladen weight (approx) 1,900lb.

Typical performance: Maximum speed 93mph; 0-60mph 15.6sec; standing ¼-mile 20.0sec; overall fuel consumption 27mpg.

Distinguishing features from previous models: Compared with other 1300s, GT had different grille, wheel trims, badging and interior, plus twin-carb engine.

Derivatives: MG 1300 Mk II and near-identical Morris 1300GT were all to same design. Mk III 1300GT was same car with face-level facia vents.

Fate: Discontinued in UK in 1974 in favour of larger-engined Austin Allegro models.

The 1300GT's structure was that of a four-door Austin/Morris 1300 Mk II, and was externally distinguished by a unique grille style and 'spoke-wheel' wheel embellisher plates, plus a long differently-coloured spear along the body sides. The facia and instrument layout was that of the MG 1300, with three circular dials, except that black vinyl, instead of wooden veneer, was the surface finish of the panel; there was an alloy-spoked, padded-rim steering wheel and reclining front seats to complete a nicely thought-out package.

The 1,275cc engine had twin SU carburettors and produced 70bhp – the identical tune to that of the MG 1300. Since the Hydrolastic suspension was slightly lowered and the handling and roadholding was the equal of the MG, the Austin's £20 lower price made it an even better bargain, especially as it offered four doors instead of the current MG's two.

When other 1300s were updated to Mk III, in the autumn of 1971, the 1300GT carried on virtually unchanged except that face-level vents were added to the facia to improve the overall ventilation. All in all this was a very successful little car, as the sales figures (which far exceeded those of the equivalent MG) prove.

The Austin 1300GT engine had its vulnerable high-tension ignition leads protected by a plastic cowl.

The Austin 1300 became 'Mk III' in 1971, but with no more than minor changes from the previous model.

Austin 1100 Mk III (1971 to 1974)

With the Morris Marina already announced in 1971, and with design of the Austin Allegro finalized, British Leyland were not likely to make any major changes to the 1100/1300 models before withdrawing them from production. The upgrading of the 1100, from Mk II to Mk III specification, was therefore an entirely cosmetic exercise.

The visual changes were to provide a new matt black grille, with a single horizontal brightwork bar and new badging, plus revised seat styling and a new facia panel with circular instruments. Under the bonnet, the engine was given a large plastic cover to protect the ignition system from water. There were no bumper overriders on these latest cars, which continued in production even after the Austin Allegro (which was the 1100/1300 models' replacement) was announced in 1973.

It is worth noting that although there was a Mk III Austin, there was no equivalent Morris saloon as this would have clashed with the Marina.

Austin 1100 Mk III specification

As for 1100 Mk II model except for:
Produced: Longbridge, 1971-74.
General layout: No estate car derivative.
Distinguishing features from previous models: New grille with matt black finish and single horizontal bar, plus badging and seat style revisions.
Fate: Discontinued in 1974 in favour of new BLMC-designed Austin Allegro model.

Austin 1300 Mk III (1971 to 1974)

At the same time as the 1100 was slightly modified and changed from Mk II to Mk III, the same changes were introduced for the 1300.

The visual differences were that 1300 Mk IIIs had a three-bar piece of brightwork across the grille, and of course there was still a Countryman estate car version. The last of these cars was built in June 1974, a full year after the car's replacement, the Austin Allegro, had been launched.

Austin 1300 Mk III specification

As for 1300 Mk II model except for:
Produced: Longbridge, 1971-74.
Distinguishing features from previous models: New grille with matt black finish and three horizontal bars, plus badging and seat style revisions.
Fate: Discontinued in 1974 in favour of new BLMC-designed Austin Allegro model.

The Mk III Austin 1300 facia had a plain wooden panel and circular instrument dials.

Mk III Austin 1100s and 1300s were easily identified by the number of horizontal grille bars – one for the 1100, three for the 1300.

This was the complete Austin/Morris 1100/1300 range in Mk III form. By this time, there were no differences between the two marques except in badging.

Austin 1800 (1964 to 1968)

Once the Mini had found its feet, BMC soon became convinced that the same basic mechanical layout should be adopted for all its future mass-production cars. The Mini was the first generation of such cars, the 1100 was the second, and the 1800 was the third. Although it was designed around the much larger B-Series engine, the general engine/transmission/suspension installation of the 1800 was very similar to that of the 1100 models. Like the 1100s, too, the 1800 was always slated to be built behind various badges.

Like Issigonis' other front-wheel-drive cars, the Austin 1800 was a miracle of packaging, for although it was a mere 13ft 8in long, it had the most spacious passenger cabin of any British mass-production car of the day. It was a bulky package, but all would have been well if the styling had been graceful. Unfortunately, it was not. Pininfarina did the concept, then BMC's own team interfered with this, the chosen shape was distinctly Plain Jane, and the car had to fight against its ungainly looks and somehow 'lumpy' reputation throughout its career. Issigonis, they say, was not interested in styling, only in

engineering; not for nothing was this car nicknamed the 'Super Land-crab'...

At one time, no doubt, it was meant as an effective replacement for the A60, but during development the front-wheel-drive 1800 grew larger, heavier and ever more different. The result was that the two types carried on, side by side, for more than four years and sold to different types of customer.

Although the 1800 was let down by its styling and stodgy behaviour, it could take credit for the huge amount of passenger space and the very rigid body-chassis unit. For those who liked Hydrolastic suspension, this was also a very well-developed system. For the Austin 1800, BMC developed the ultimate B-Series engine in which the capacity was pushed out to 1.8 litres and a five-bearing crankshaft was included for the first time. For all the usual production engineering reasons, this engine and bottom-end was also fitted to the MGB sports car, but not, strangely enough, to the B-Series Farina models which might have benefited from the extra torque and smoothness.

The 1800 was the first BMC car to have an all-synchromesh

The 'Super Land-crab' of 1964 – the original Austin 1800, with transverse engine and front-wheel drive.

The Austin 1800's facia and instrument layout was plain, almost to extremes.

Austin 1800 specification

Produced: Longbridge, 1964-68. 373,356 1800s and 2200s of all types, badges and years built.

General layout: Pressed-steel, unit-construction body-chassis structure in 5-seater, 4-door saloon body style. Front and transversely-mounted engine driving front wheels.

Engine and transmission: BMC B-Series engine, 4-cylinder, ohv, in-line. 1,798cc, 80.26 x 88.9mm, 80bhp at 5,000rpm; 100lb ft at 2,100rpm. 4-speed gearbox, all-synchromesh; centre-floor gear-change; spur-gear final drive.

Chassis: Independent front suspension, Hydrolastic units and wishbones. Rack-and-pinion steering (optional power assistance from late 1967). Independent rear suspension by Hydrolastic units, trailing arms and anti-roll bar. Interconnection between front and rear suspensions. Front disc and rear drum brakes. 175-13in tyres.

Dimensions: Wheelbase 8ft 10in; front track 4ft 8in; rear track 4ft 7.5in; length 13ft 8.2in; width 5ft 7in; height 4ft 7.5in. Unladen weight (approx) 2,645lb.

Typical performance: Maximum speed 90mph; 0-60mph 17.1sec; standing 1/4-mile 20.5sec; overall fuel consumption 24mpg.

Distinguishing features from previous models: Entirely new type of front-wheel-drive BMC model without ancestors.

Derivatives: Austin/Morris 1800 was the same car, with different badges and details. Wolseley 18/85 model was a slightly modified version. Mk II (see separate entry) was the same car with minor changes.

Fate: Discontinued in 1968 and replaced by Mk II models.

gearbox, and this had a cable linkage to the floor-mounted gear-lever. Strangely enough, few people complained about this, whereas the similar Maxi installation attracted a tirade of abuse.

The original 1800 was on the market until 1968, by which time it had been joined by the mechanically identical Morris 1800 and the very closely related Wolseley 18/85 derivatives. There were minor improvements to the facia and instrument layout in the spring of 1967 (at about the time the Wolseley 18/85 was introduced), and power-assisted steering became optional from September 1967. The Mk II model replaced it, but there were no major changes.

The Austin 1800 became 'Mk II' in 1968, with larger wheels, slight power increases and some styling retouching.

From the rear, the Austin 1800 Mk II was obvious by its vertical tail-lamp clusters and new badges.

Austin 1800 Mk II (1968 to 1972)

The front-wheel-drive 1800s became 'Mk II' in May 1968, just as BMC was about to be submerged into the new British Leyland concern, but the changes were relatively minor. As had happened with the 1100/1300s, the Mk II Austin and Morris 1800s were more nearly identical in looks than before, although the grilles were different, and each car had its own badging, front and rear.

Styling changes included slightly sharpened-up rear quarters, with incipient fins, and vertical tail-lamp clusters instead of the horizontal fittings of the original cars. Inside the car there were facia revisions, a padded roll to the under-facia shelf, a repositioned handbrake and the use of rocker switches.

Mechanically, the engine was pepped-up slightly with a higher compression ratio, better cylinder head breathing and lightweight pistons. Power-assisted steering was optional, as on the last of the Mk Is, and larger (14in diameter) wheels with narrower-section tyres were fitted.

If the 1800s had sold as well as planned, there would have

Austin 1800 Mk II specification

As for 1800 Mk I except for:
Produced: 1968-72.
Engine and transmission: 86bhp at 5,300rpm; 101lb ft at 3,000rpm. Optional AP 4-speed automatic transmission.
Chassis: 165-14in tyres.
Typical performance: Maximum speed 93mph; 0-60mph 16.3sec; standing ¼-mile 19.9sec; overall fuel consumption 27mpg.
Distinguishing features from previous models: New front grille (common with Morris), different rear wings and vertical tail-lamp clusters, different trim, facia equipment and details.
Derivatives: 1800 Mk II was itself a derivative of the original 1800. Austin 1800/Morris 1800 virtually the same car; Wolseley 18/85 used same basic design. Mk III (see separate entry) followed on.
Fate: Discontinued in 1972 in favour of Mk III derivative.

The Austin 1800 Mk II's facia had a wooden strip, but was otherwise like that of the Mk I.

The Austin 1800 Mk II engine bay (below), which had a revised air cleaner and different 'plumbing' arrangements compared with the original 1800. The Austin 1800 S (below right) had a twin-carburettor 1.8-litre engine in similar tune to the MGB sports car.

been more scope for development changes, but by this time it was clear that the car was not a great success, and it was allowed to bumble on, unimproved, until 1972, when the final derivative, the Mk III, took over.

Austin 1800 Mk II 'S' (1969 to 1972)

In the 'good old days' of BMC, this high-peformance version of the 1800 would doubtless have been called a 'Cooper', but under the new regime of British Leyland there was no chance of that. Nevertheless, it was a derivative planned by BMC before British Leyland took over and – as was still occasionally happening, to give one dealer chain a temporary advantage over their rivals – the Morris version came a full year before the Austin was put on sale.

The Austin 1800 Mk II 'S', therefore, was identical in all respects with the Morris, which is to say that it looked the same as an ordinary Mk II except for the badge on the tail, had a 96bhp version of the 1.8-litre engine (twin SU carbs, a three-branch exhaust manifold and an MGB camshaft profile did the trick), slightly revised gearbox ratios and larger Girling four-

---

Austin 1800 Mk II 'S' specification

As for 1800 Mk II except for:
Produced: 1969-72.
Engine and transmission: 96bhp at 5,700rpm; 106lb ft at 3,000rpm; automatic transmission not available.
Typical performance: Maximum speed 99mph; 0-60mph 13.7sec; standing ¼-mile 19.4sec; overall fuel consumption 22mpg.
Distinguishing features from previous models: No external changes except for 'S' badging on tail, plus twin-carb engine.
Derivatives: 1800 Mk II 'S' was itself a derivative of the original 1800 Mk II. Austin 1800/Morris 1800 was the basic car.
Fate: Discontinued in 1972 in favour of the 2200 model.

---

spot front disc calipers to cope with the 100mph performance.

In 1972 it was dropped because the smoother and even more powerful 2200 was a better sales proposition.

The final version of the Austin 1800 was the Mk III of 1972, with a new grille style, but few mechanical improvements.

A view of the Austin 1800 which emphasizes the car's unusually wide doors and the slimness of the rear pillars flanking the deep rear screen.

<table>
<tr><td colspan="2">

Austin 1800 Mk III specification

As for 1800 Mk II except for:
Produced: 1972-75.
Distinguishing features from previous models: New grille style (commonized with Morris) and slightly revised facia, with handbrake between seats.
Derivatives: 1800 Mk III was itself a derivative of the Mk II. Austin 1800/Morris 1800 was virtually the same car.
Fate: Discontinued in 1975 in favour of the new British Leyland-designed ADO 71 18/22 range.

</td></tr>
</table>

Austin 1800 Mk III (1972 to 1975)
Although the Mk III derivative of the 1800 was not announced until March 1972, four years after the BMC era was over, it was still a 'BMC' car, and still recognizably derived from the original Issigonis 1800 of 1964.

Compared with the Mk II which it displaced, the Mk III only had slight revisions to the grille and interior, a floor-mounted handbrake between the seats, a new steering wheel and a rod-operated gear-change instead of the previous cable variety. There was, of course, an identical Morris equivalent, and these cars carried on until the beginning of 1975, when they were dropped in favour of the British Leyland-designed ADO 71

18/22 series, which we later came to know as Princess models.

The Mk III was not distinguished, in itself, but it was this phase of 'Land-crab' which saw the use of a transverse six-cylinder engine in the 2200 models (see separate entry).

Austin Sprite (1971 only)

Once British Leyland took control of all the companies making up the BMC combine, their managers set about dismantling most of the existing royalty and consultancy agreements, which had led to cars like the Mini-Coopers and the Austin-Healeys. The Austin-Healey 3000 line had gone before the British Leyland formation, but the Austin-Healey Sprite carried on for another three years.

When the royalty agreement with Donald Healey was terminated at the end of 1970, the Austin-Healey Sprite was, quite simply, rebadged as an Austin Sprite, and was built alongside the MG Midget at Abingdon between January 1971 and July 1971. After only seven months, however, the Austin Sprite was dropped, for the MG Midget was exactly the same car as the obsolete Sprite and was still selling very well indeed.

If we agree that the Austin A40 Sports of the early 1950s was not a sports car, but a tourer, the short-lived Austin Sprite was, and is, the *only* Austin-badged sports car ever to be produced in postwar years.

Austin Sprite specification

Produced: Abingdon, 1971 only. 1,022 cars built.
General layout: Unit-construction body-chassis structure, in 2-seater sports car style. Some cars with removable hardtop. Front-mounted engine driving rear wheels. Identical in every way with the 1970-model Austin-Healey Sprite.
Engine and transmission: BMC A-Series, 4-cylinder, ohv, in-line. 1,275cc, 70.6 x 81.28mm; 65bhp at 6,000rpm; 72lb ft at 3,000rpm. 4-speed gearbox; no synchromesh on 1st gear; live (beam) rear axle with hypoid-bevel final drive.
Chassis: Independent front suspension, coil springs and wishbones. Rack-and-pinion steering. Rear suspension by half-elliptic leaf springs. Front disc and rear drum brakes. 5.20-13in tyres.
Dimensions: Wheelbase 6ft 8in; front track 3ft 9.25in; rear track 3ft 8.75in; length 11ft 5.5in; width 4ft 5in; height 4ft 1.75in. Unladen weight (approx) 1,575lb.
Typical performance: Maximum speed 94mph; 0-60mph 14.1sec; standing ¼-mile 19.6sec; overall fuel consumption 30mpg.
Distinguishing features from previous model: Equivalent of Austin-Healey Sprite Mk IV, but fitted with 'Austin' front badge.
Fate: Dropped in favour of MG Midget model later in 1971.

For 1971 only, there was a sports car known as the Austin Sprite, which was no more or less than the Austin-Healey Sprite of the year before.

The upswept body line behind the front wheels, derived from the original 'frog-eye' Sprite and its one-piece lift-up front bodywork, remained a styling feature throughout the life of the Sprite.

The interior of the Austin Sprite in its 1971 specification, with additional bolstering of the seat cushions. By this stage the MG Midget was identical apart from the different badges on the facia and the steering wheel boss.

Chapter 4

AUSTIN-HEALEY

The story of the meeting which led to the foundation of the Austin-Healey marque has been told many times. Donald Healey started to build Healey cars, at Warwick, in 1946, with one basic chassis design, but with Riley, Nash (USA) or Alvis engines and transmissions. Then, in 1952, and with the encouragement of Leonard Lord, he started a new project as a private venture, using Austin A90 Atlantic running gear. The one-and-only prototype, which he called the Healey 100, was shown at Earls Court in October 1952, where BMC's managing director saw it, liked it, and did an historic deal with the Cornishman – the Healey company would be responsible for car design (and for future designs) while BMC would look after production, sales and marketing of what would become an Austin-Healey.

The first Longbridge-built 2.6-litre Austin-Healey 100 BN1 was delivered in 1953, and the special racing 100S models (assembled at Warwick) were announced in the autumn of 1954. The BN2 derivative of the BN1 came along in 1955, and quite a number of these cars were further modified by the Healey Company to become 100Ms. The body-chassis of all these cars was produced for BMC by Jensen, of West Bromwich.

From the autumn of 1956, the car's wheelbase was slightly lengthened so that 2+2 seating could be installed, the C-Series six-cylinder engine took over from the obsolete A90 unit, and the car became the 100-Six. Just over a year later, final assembly of Austin-Healeys was removed to the MG factory at Abingdon, and it remained there until the marque was dropped at the end of 1970.

From then on, the 'Big-Healey' progressed through a series of sub-derivatives, the last being the 3000 Mk III, which was dropped at the end of 1967, *before* the formation of British Leyland.

In the meantime, Healey was invited to design a new small sports car, using Austin A35 or Morris Minor 1000 parts as required. The result was the Austin-Healey Sprite of 1958, which was always known as the 'frog-eye' because of the location of the headlamps in the sloping bonnet; as with the 'Big Healey' by this time, final assembly was at Abingdon.

From mid-1961, the Sprite became Mk II, with more conventional styling and an opening boot-lid, and at the same time it was also badge-engineered into the MG Midget. For the rest of its career, for every Sprite there was an equivalent Midget.

Throughout the 1960s, there were no basic styling changes, but several important updates – 1,098cc engine from 1962, winding windows and a half-elliptic rear suspension from mid-1964, and a 1,275cc engine from late 1966.

Following the formation of British Leyland, the Healey franchise was rapidly run down, the last Austin-Healey was built at the end of 1970, and in 1971 only there was a short run of Austin Sprites. The MG Midget, on the other hand, carried on until 1979, having been defaced by big energy-absorbing black bumpers in the autumn of 1974 and given the transplant of a Triumph Spitfire 1.5-litre engine and gearbox.

Austin-Healey 100 BN1 (1952 to 1955)
Although the Healey 100 was originally a piece of private enterprise by Donald Healey, when Leonard Lord inspected the original prototype he decided that his factories could produce and sell the cars in tens of thousands, and so he instantly bought up the design for BMC's use. The single prototype Healey 100 of 1952 became a production reality as the Austin-Healey 100 in the spring of 1953.

The new sports car also helped BMC solve one of its early problems – that whereas the Longbridge engine facilities were tooled up to make a lot of 2.6-litre four-cylinder engines for the

Donald Healey (in the car) and Sir Leonard Lord (chairman of BMC) with one of the very first Austin-Healey 100 BN1s at the BMC factory at Longbridge.

The Austin-Healey 100 BN1 had sleek lines at the rear, with only two small tail-lamps to break up the contours.

A90 Atlantic, the A90 was proving a commercial failure and was not selling. The Healey 100 design was drawn up around the A90 engine, a modified version of its gearbox, its rear axle and most of its front suspension, steering gear and brakes.

Once sorted out for production, the car's chassis was built by a supplier, the bodyshell was added to it by Jensen, at West Bromwich, who also painted and trimmed it before it was sent to Longbridge for final assembly. Incidentally, Jensen got the structural build contract because it had done a good job in producing the bodies for the Austin A40 Sports. Jensen had also proposed its own version of a BMC-engined sports car, but had lost out in the head-to-head contest with Donald Healey.

Mechanically, therefore, the Austin-Healey had a lot in common with the A90 Atlantic. The engine was virtually the same 2,660cc unit, as was the gearbox and its internals, but the gear linkage was arranged so that first gear could not be used, and the A90's second gear became the Austin-Healey's first gear. The sports car also had an overdrive as standard, arranged to work on top and second gears, thus giving a five-speed transmission.

The main attraction of the new car, of course, was in its styling, for the lines were truly elegant, and were to be used by BMC, with only minor modifications, for the next 15 years on all the 'Big Healeys'. Among the many characteristic features were the windscreen, which could be folded flat (by sliding the base of the pillars forward), the use of centre-lock wire wheels as standard, and the very restricted ground clearance, which could lead to embarrassing noises (and damage!) as the exhaust system hit the ground.

In its original form, which became affectionately known as the BN1 after the chassis identifying sequence used by BMC, the Austin-Healey 100 was built for more than three years on a special assembly line remote from the main mass-production cars at Longbridge. A gradual series of improvements resulted in more and more of the shell being built from pressed steel instead of aluminium, and the new BMC C-Series hypoid-bevel back axle replaced the A90 unit for 1955.

The BN2, which took over in 1955, was the same basic model, but with further significant improvements.

Austin-Healey 100S (1955 only)

Throughout his long and distinguished career, Donald Healey was always interested in motor sport, so once the Austin-Healey 100 was launched it was not at all surprising that faster versions were developed for racing and record-breaking. The 'Special Test Cars' of 1953 and 1954 eventually matured into the 100S model, which was announced in 1954, but only delivered during 1955.

The production car (only 50 were built, some with individual modifications requested by customers) was based on the standard body-chassis structure of the BN1 model, but with many important improvements for competition purposes. Most importantly, the engine was treated to an entirely new light-alloy head casting (designed by Weslake) in which the carburettors were on the right, rather than the left of the engine bay, and peak power was 132bhp, compared with 90bhp for the standard road car. Behind the race-developed engine was a

---

Austin-Healey 100 BN1 specification

Produced: Longbridge, 1953-55. 10,688 cars built.
General layout: Chassis welded to bodyshell on assembly, in 2-seater sports car style. Some cars with removable hardtop. Front-mounted engine driving rear wheels.
Engine and transmission: Austin A90 type, 4-cylinder, ohv, in-line. 2,660cc, 87.3 x 111.1mm, 90bhp at 4,000rpm; 144lb ft at 2,500rpm. 3-speed gearbox with overdrive on top and 2nd gears, all synchromesh; live (beam) rear axle with spiral-bevel final drive at first, hypoid-bevel for 1955.
Chassis: Independent front suspension, coil springs, wishbones and anti-roll bar. Cam-and-peg steering. Rear suspension by half-elliptic leaf springs and Panhard rod. Front disc and rear drum brakes. 5.90-15in tyres.
Dimensions: Wheelbase 7ft 6in; front track 4ft 1in; rear track 4ft 2.75in; length 12ft 7in; width 5ft 0.5in; height 4ft 1in. Unladen weight (approx) 2,015lb (with later steel-skinned body 2,150lb).
Typical performance: Maximum speed 103mph; 0-60mph 10.3sec; standing ¼-mile 17.5sec; overall fuel consumption 25mpg.
Derivatives: 100S model (see separate entry).
Fate: Replaced by BN2 model in autumn 1955.

Austin-Healey 100S specification

Produced: Warwick, 1955. 50 cars built.
General layout: Chassis welded to bodyshell on assembly, in 2-seater sports car style. Front-mounted engine driving rear wheels. Lightweight racing version of BN1.
Engine and transmission: Austin A90 type, much modified, 4-cylinder, ohv, in-line. 2,660cc, 87.3 x 111.1mm, 132bhp at 4,700rpm; 168lb ft at 2,500rpm. 4-speed gearbox without overdrive; no synchromesh on 1st gear; live (beam) rear axle with hypoid-bevel final drive.
Chassis: Independent front suspension, coil springs, wishbones and anti-roll bar. Cam-and-peg steering. Rear suspension by half-elliptic leaf springs and Panhard rod. Front and rear disc brakes. 5.50-15in racing tyres.
Dimensions: Wheelbase 7ft 6in; front track 4ft 1.6in; rear track 4ft 2.75in; length 12ft 4in; width 5ft 0.5in; height 3ft 6in. Unladen weight (approx) 1,924lb.
Typical performance: Maximum speed 119mph; 0-60mph 7.8sec; standing ¼-mile 16.1sec; overall fuel consumption 20mpg.
Fate: Dropped at end of 1955 racing season and not replaced.

The Austin-Healey 100S was a 50-off 'homologation special' built at Warwick, with a 132bhp engine, different front grille, no bumpers and a much-lightened structure.

Below right, this was the Austin-Healey 100 BN2 fitted with a 100M conversion. The louvred bonnet and the bonnet strap are obvious identification points.

BN2-type four-speed gearbox (but there was no overdrive) and there was a choice of final-drive ratios.

To keep all this power in check, Dunlop disc brakes were fitted to all four wheels, there was an engine oil cooler and a louvred bonnet panel. Most cars were fitted with Dunlop racing tyres. In addition, there was a new 20-gallon fuel tank.

Jensen produced light-alloy skin panels for the body, and there was no provision for bumpers, windscreen, sidescreens, or hood. The front grille aperture was oval, and smaller than that of the standard car. Most cars were delivered with a smart white-and-blue colour scheme – the darker colour being on the lower half of the shell and the wing crease line providing the junction between the two shades.

All the 50 cars were built by the Donald Healey Motor Company at Warwick, and only six of them were originally delivered to British customers; naturally, these are the rarest of all 'Big Healeys' – and the fastest, too! The Weslake-derived engine was never used on any other BMC car, in spite of being much more powerful and efficient than the original variant. It had been developed far too late to be of any interest to BMC.

Austin-Healey 100 BN2 (1955 to 1956)
From the late summer of 1955, the Austin-Healey 100 progressed from BN1 to BN2 chassis specification. The only visual change to the styling (which was still not all *that* obvious) was that the front wheelarch cut-outs were slightly enlarged.

The engine was the same as before, but behind it there was a brand-new C-Series four-speed gearbox (as fitted to the new Austin A90 Westminster, for instance) with altogether more sensible ratios, and overdrive was retained on top and third gears. The hypoid-bevel back axle was retained, and there were more effective drum brakes with a greater swept area.

There was one important derivative of this car, the 100M. In this case, the M stood for Modified: standard BN2s were delivered to the Donald Healey Motor Company premises in Warwick, where they were given a 110bhp (Le Mans-spec) engine, stiffened suspension, including the use of a front anti-roll bar. A louvred bonnet panel with leather strap, and a duo-tone paint job (which not all examples seemed to have) were added at Longbridge before the cars were delivered to

---

Austin-Healey 100 BN2 specification

As for Austin-Healey 100 BN1 except for:
Produced: Longbridge, 1955-56. 3,924 cars built, of which 1,159 were converted to 100M tune by the Donald Healey Motor Company.
Engine and transmission: 4-speed gearbox with overdrive on top and 3rd gears, no synchromesh on 1st gear; hypoid-bevel final drive.
Distinguishing features from previous model: Larger front wing wheelarch cut-outs and different gear-lever knob markings.
Derivatives: 100M, with 110bhp at 4,500rpm; 143lb ft at 2,600rpm; unladen weight 2,168lb.
Fate: Replaced by six-cylinder 100-Six BN4 model in autumn 1956.

Warwick. The 100M tune-up kit was also applied to older cars, at customers' requests, and the 1,159 production total includes these cars.

Both the 100 BN2 and 100M were only built for a single model year, for by 1956 the A90 engine was considered to be obsolete. The next 'Big Healey', the 100-Six, was a very different type of car.

Austin-Healey 100-Six BN4 (1956 to 1959)

By the mid-1950s, BMC's long-term engineering strategy was becoming clear. Among their many rationalization proposals was one to concentrate on a newly-designed C-Series six-cylinder engine for their medium-to-large series production cars. Almost as soon as this engine made its bow, in the autumn of 1954, it was clear that the old 2.6-litre engine of the Austin-Healey 100 was living on borrowed time. In the autumn of 1956 it was declared obsolete, and the C-Series found a home in the latest 'Big Healey', which became the 100-Six and carried the BN4 chassis code.

The 100-Six, however, was much more than an engine-transplanted BN2. The most important chassis change was to increase the wheelbase by nearly 2 inches; there were longer doors and very cramped 2+2 seating accommodation. However, I reckon that the '+2' seating was much better for carrying parcels than people because there was absolutely no legroom. The seating reshuffle meant that the spare wheel had had to be relocated, and this meant there was considerably less luggage space in the boot than before.

Austin-Healey 100-Six BN4 specification

Produced: Longbridge, 1956-57, Abingdon, 1957-59. 6,045 cars built at Longbridge, 4,241 built at Abingdon.
General Layout: Chassis welded to bodyshell on assembly, in 2+2 seater sports car style. Some cars with removable hardtop. Front-mounted engine driving rear wheels.
Engine and transmission: BMC C-Series, 6-cylinder, ohv, in-line. 2,639cc, 79.4 x 88.9mm, 102bhp at 4,600rpm; 142lb ft at 2,400rpm. 4-speed gearbox with optional overdrive on top and 3rd gears; no synchromesh on 1st gear; live (beam) rear axle with hypoid-bevel final drive.
Chassis: Independent front suspension, coil springs, wishbones and anti-roll bar. Cam-and-peg steering. Rear suspension by half-elliptic leaf springs and Panhard rod. Front and rear drum brakes. 5.90-15in tyres.
Dimensions: Wheelbase 7ft 8in; front track 4ft 0.75in; rear track 4ft 2in; length 13ft 1.5in; width 5ft 0.5in; height 4ft 1in. Unladen weight (approx) 2,435lb.
Typical performance: Maximum speed 103mph; 0-60mph 12.9sec; standing ¼-mile 18.8sec; overall fuel consumption 26mpg.
Distinguishing features from previous model: Longer wheelbase, disc wheels on some cars, air intake in bonnet panel, different grille, 2+2 seating.
Derivatives: From autumn 1957, and consequent on assembly move to Abingdon, engine performance was increased to 117bhp at 4,750rpm, 149lb ft at 3,000rpm.
Fate: Dropped in favour of new 3000 model in 1959.

The Austin-Healey 100-Six BN4 was the first six-cylinder-engined Austin-Healey; it was launched in 1956, and these disc wheels were standard.

The 2.6-litre C-Series engine developed 102bhp, and was somehow shoehorned into the original engine bay, backed by the C-Series gearbox and axle assemblies from the BN2. Compared with the BN2, however, the 100-Six had disc wheels as standard (and wires as optional extras), and the overdrive had also become an optional extra. As before, there was an optional, removable, hardtop which turned the sports car into a snug little saloon. However, there was no denying the fact that BMC had achieved a very considerable price increase for the model without actually making it any faster.

The 100-Six could be recognized, not only by its disc wheels (where fitted), but by the new bonnet panel air intake, the typically Austin 'wavy-mesh' radiator grille, and the two-tone colour scheme which many customers chose. Like all the previous 'Big Healeys', most BN4s went to North America, where customers presumably did not mind having a car that was 270lb heavier, a little slower *and* less fuel efficient than the old BN2 model.

The original 100-Six, in other words, was a triumph of production engineering over character, and most media pundits were disappointed in its behaviour at the time. The 2+2 seating layout, somehow, could not make up for its less gainly behaviour.

As before, Jensen produced painted and trimmed body-chassis units, and until the autumn of 1957 final assembly was at Longbridge. From that time, however, BMC concentrated

The Austin-Healey 100-Six had a 2.6-litre C-Series engine and a four-speed gearbox. Note the offset selector arrangements.

all corporate sports car assembly at the MG Abingdon factory, where Austin-Healey assembly began in November 1957. It was at this time that the BN4 received a much-needed power boost – from 102 to 117bhp – with the aid of a new cylinder head casting and manifolds, and it ran on in this form until 1959. During this time, too, it was joined by the BN6 derivative (see separate entry), and both sales and reputation noticeably improved.

The Austin-Healey 100-Six BN6 could also be purchased with this smart detachable hardtop. Drum brakes were still fitted all round.

Austin-Healey 100-Six BN6 (1958 to 1959)

The BN6 derivative of the 'Big Healey' design was, in effect, a BMC second guess of the revised six-cylinder car theme, and it sold very well. The original theory behind the launch of the six-cylinder car was that the market really wanted 2+2 seating – the arrival of the BN6 *two*-seater meant that BMC had been wrong – or, at least, partly wrong!

All the BN6 derivatives were built at Abingdon, and all had the upgraded 117bhp 2.6-litre engine. All, too, were based on the basic longer-wheelbase/six-cylinder engine theme announced in 1956. The difference, however, was that the '+2' seating had been discarded to return the format to that of the original Austin-Healey 100, and the metal tonneau panel surrounding the cockpit was therefore made longer to cover the unused space. The spare wheel and battery mountings reverted to their original positions, luggage space was restored, and all in all the BT6 was a more desirable car. The standard mechanical equipment and the optional extras were the same on both cars.

Austin-Healey 100-Six BN6 specification

As for 100-Six BN4 except for:
Produced: Abingdon, 1958-59. 4,150 cars built.
General layout: 2-seater accommodation.
Engine and transmission: 117bhp engine of late-model BN4 fitted to all cars.
Typical Performance: Maximum speed 111mph; 0-60mph 11.2sec; standing ¼-mile 18.1sec; overall fuel consumption 21mpg.
Distinguishing features from BN4: 2-seater accommodation and shorter cockpit cut-out.
Fate: Dropped in favour of new 3000 model in 1959.

The Austin-Healey 100-Six BN6 was the two-seater version of the BN4.

Austin-Healey 3000 Mk I (1959 to 1961)

For BMC, 1959 was a year of major new-model activity, not only because of the birth of the Mini, the B-Series Farinas and the C-Series Farinas, but because there were two new sports car developments announced from Abingdon. It was in the spring of 1959 that the 100-Six models were phased out in favour of the 3000s.

Structurally, and in their styling, there was virtually no difference between the old and the updated types except for the new badging on the grille and the boot-lid. Mechanically, there was the enlargement of the six-cylinder engine from 2.6 to 2.9 litres (124bhp against 117bhp, with no increase in vehicle weight), a revised transmission with more suitable gearbox ratios, and the adoption of Girling disc brakes for the front wheels in place of the previous drums.

The new 3000, like the 100-Six, was available either as a two-seater (BN7), or a 2+2-seater (BT7), with the same range of options as before. Because it had a more torquey engine, and very reassuring brakes, it sold very well indeed – although the vogue for two-seaters seemed to be on the wane at last, for only one in five of all 3000s had that seating layout. Very few, too, seem to have had hardtops, though the majority were equipped with wire-spoke wheels and overdrive.

BMC, however, were into their most 'fidgety' period, and did not leave the car alone for long; the Mk II version took over in 1961 and the original became retrospectively known as the Mk I.

Austin-Healey 3000 Mk I specification

As for 100-Six BN4/BN6 except for:
Produced: Abingdon, 1959-61. 2,825 2-seaters, 10,825 2+2 seaters built.
General layout: 2-seater (BN7) or 2+2 seater (BT7) accommodation.
Engine and transmission: 2,912cc, 83.36 x 88.9mm, 124bhp at 4,600rpm; 162lb ft at 2,700rpm.
Chassis: Front disc brakes, rear drum brakes.
Typical Performance: Maximum speed 114mph; 0-60mph 11.4sec; standing ¼-mile 17.9sec; overall fuel consumption 20mpg.
Distinguishing features from BN4: '3000' badges at front and rear; front discs visible through wire-spoke wheels.
Fate: Dropped in favour of 3000 Mk II model in 1961.

The original Austin-Healey 3000 of 1959 had a 2.9-litre engine and front disc brakes.

The Austin-Healey 3000 Mk I and Mk II had this facia and instrument layout, with the offset and cranked gear-lever. A remote-control lever arrived in 1961.

The Austin-Healey 3000 Mk II's engine/gearbox assembly, showing the triple-SU carburettor installation and the original type of gear-change mechanism.

Austin-Healey 3000 Mk II (1961 to 1962)

Looking back from a quarter of a century later, the 3000 Mk II seems to be something of an anomaly, for there was a short-lived move to a triple-carburettor engine that was abandoned in the following year. However, since 1961 was another 'all change' year for BMC's sports cars (there were new-model Sprites, Midgets *and* MGAs in that year), perhaps this can be excused.

The 3000 Mk II (still coded BN7 and BT7 – with only 355 two-seaters being sold) was very similar indeed to the Mk I which it replaced, except for the 132bhp three-SU engine. The visual clues identifying the Mk II were the use of a grille and

bonnet air-intake with vertical bars instead of wavy slats, and an appropriate front badge.

A little heralded improvement, too, came in the autumn of 1961 when an entirely new gearbox casing was fitted, this incorporating a new and more positive linkage to the gear-lever, which now had a remote-control mechanism from the top of the box and a short stubby vertical lever, much more in keeping with the sports car character than the previous type.

The Mk II soon proved to have an engine which needed a lot of finicky attention to keep it in tune, so when the time came to make a futher improvement, BMC were happy to abandon triple-carbs.

Austin-Healey 3000 Mk II specification

As for 3000 Mk I except for:
Produced: Abingdon, 1961-62. 355 2-seaters, 5,095 2+2 seaters built.
Engine and transmission: 2,912cc, 83.36 x 88.9mm, 132bhp at 4,750rpm; 167lb ft at 3,000rpm.
Typical Performance: Maximum speed 112mph; 0-60mph 11.5sec; standing ¼-mile 18.8sec; overall fuel consumption 18mpg.
Distinguishing features from BN4: '3000' Mk II' badge at front and new vertically-barred grille and air intake.
Fate: Dropped in favour of 3000 Mk II convertible model in 1962.

From the summer of 1962, the 'Big Healey' became the 3000 Mk II Convertible, complete with a wraparound screen and wind-up windows.

This was the driving compartment of the Austin-Healey 3000 Mk II Convertible, showing the remote-control gear-change and the wind-up windows in the doors.

Austin-Healey 3000 Mk II Convertible specification

As for 3000 Mk II except for:
Produced: Abingdon, 1962-63. 6,113 cars built.
General layout: All cars built as 2+2 seaters, with wind-up door windows and foldaway hood.
Engine and transmission: 2,912cc, 83.36 x 88.9mm, 131bhp at 4,750rpm; 158lb ft at 3,000rpm.
Dimensions: Unladen weight 2,460lb.
Typical performance: Maximum speed 117mph; 0-60mph 10.4sec; standing ¼-mile 17.8sec; overall fuel consumption 17mpg.
Distinguishing features from BN4: Wind-up windows in doors, foldaway hood, wraparound windscreen.
Fate: Dropped in favour of 3000 Mk III Convertible model in 1964.

Austin-Healey 3000 Mk II Convertible (1962 to 1963)

By mid-1962, the 'Big Healey' had been on sale for more than nine years, but it continued to sell remarkably well, especially in North America. By this time there had already been six derivatives, but the seventh was the most radical change so far.

The title – Mk II Convertible – tells its own story. Although the same basic structure, layout and style was retained, to send this car into the second decade of its life there had been a major carve-up and improvement of the passenger cabin and the weather protection.

Instead of a near-flat screen, there was a new, larger and slightly wraparound screen. Instead of detachable sidescreens, there were now winding windows in the doors. Instead of a build-up 'DIY' soft-top, there was a proper foldaway hood. It was at this juncture, too, that the original two-seater layout was abandoned, for every Convertible had 2+2 seating.

Mechanically, this was the time for the 2.9-litre engine to revert to twin SU carburettors, but with the aid of different details and efficient manifolding the peak power was virtually the same as before. The overdrive was still optional, though the vast majority of cars seemed to have it fitted.

There was still one 'Big Healey' change to come, for the Mk II Convertible was made obsolete for the 1964 season.

The Austin-Healey 3000 Mk II Convertible had this 2.9-litre engine, complete with twin semi-downdraught SU carburettors.

Austin-Healey 3000 Mk III (1964 to 1967/68)

The last change to the larger Austin-Healey format came early in 1964 when the Mk III derivative was announced. Although the smooth exterior lines of the 1962-63 Convertible were retained, there was a considerable power boost to make this the fastest Austin-Healey of all, and a complete refit to the interior.

Up until 1963, the facia and seating of all 'Big Healeys' had been based on the same design, but the Mk III was all new. There was a smooth new facia, with wooden veneer to the panel, there was a centre console surrounding the gear-lever (with a storage box between the seats), a new seat style and a neat fold-down luggage support panel which could cover over the '+2' seating.

The engine, still of 2.9 litres and with twin SU carburettors, was boosted to no less than 148bhp, this partly being due to a more efficient exhaust system whose main silencers were under the left-side sill, with extra silencers below the back bumper.

That was Phase I, but Phase II cars, produced after the first 1,390 Mk IIIs had been built, were provided with revised rear chassis and suspension. The chassis side members on this last derivative dipped deeper below the rear axle to allow for more wheel movement, and instead of being located by a Panhard rod, the axle was located by twin trailing arms, which were mounted above and in parallel with the leaf springs.

It was in these final years that the racing and rallying Austin-Healeys became truly formidable machines. In fully-modified form they had light-alloy skin panels, four-wheel disc brakes and engines producing more than 200bhp – they were, without

The final derivative of the 'Big Healey' was the 3000 Mk III, built between 1964 and 1967; visually, this type was much like the Mk II Convertible.

A completely revised facia display and a centre console between the seats identify this as a Mk III Convertible.

Austin-Healey 3000 Mk III specification

As for 3000 Mk II Convertible except for:
Produced: Abingdon, 1964-67/68. 17,712 cars built.
General layout: Phase I cars as Mk II Convertible; Phase II cars with different rear suspension.
Engine and transmission: 2,912cc, 83.36 x 88.9mm, 148bhp at 5,250rpm; 165lb ft at 3,500rpm.
Chassis: Phase II cars had rear suspension by half-elliptic springs and twin radius-arms.
Dimensions: Unladen weight 2,548lb.
Typical performance: Maximum speed 121mph; 0-60mph 9.8sec; standing ¼-mile 17.2sec; overall fuel consumption 20mpg.
Distinguishing features from previous model: Mk III badge at front of car, new facia style, restyled seating, centre console.
Fate: Dropped in favour of MG MGC, which was introduced in 1967.

doubt, the best rally cars in the world.

Production of Mk IIIs ran down in the autumn of 1967, not only to make way for the MG MGC, with which it might have had to compete head-to-head, but also because there was no intention to sell it in the USA in 1968, where the cost and complication of meeting new safety and emissions legislation was no longer justified.

The last series-production Mk IIIs were built in December 1967, though one final car (for the UK market) was produced in March 1968. It is important, I feel, to point out that the 3000 was *not* killed off by British Leyland, for production had effectively ceased before the merger took place.

The first type of Austin-Healey Sprite was always nicknamed 'frog-eye' – you can see why from the position of the headlamps.

Austin-Healey Sprite Mk I (1958 to 1961)

For BMC, the Sprite was a very important car – not only because of its own success in a 13-year run, but because the design was also transmuted into that of an MG (the Midget), which sold for 18 years. The directors certainly got their money's worth out of one design, which was updated many times over the years.

The original Sprite was designed by Donald Healey Motor Company engineers, at the invitation of BMC, to use as many as possible of the Austin A35 and Morris Minor 1000 mechanical components. The Sprite, in fact, used modified A-Series engine, gearbox and back axle assemblies, Morris Minor rack-and-pinion steering and A35 front suspension.

The little car featured a pressed-steel body-chassis unit, which was quite unorthodox in many ways. For one thing, back axle location was by cantilever quarter-elliptic leaf springs and radius-arms (which could encourage roll oversteer of a very sharp, if ultimately harmless, nature); for another, there was no exterior access to the luggage space in the tail; and for another, the whole of the front bodywork (bonnet, nose and wings) was hinged from the scuttle and opened wide to give access to the engine bay.

More than anything, however, the car got its cheeky character from the styling. In the first design, Healey had wanted to put lay-back headlamps in the bonnet (Lamborghini-style), but the cost-accountants knocked that on the head. Instead, the headlamps were mounted in pods in the bonnet, rather than in the front wings, and this inevitably led to the car getting its nickname of 'Frog-eye' (or 'Bug-eye', as an alternative).

The 'frog-eye' Sprite had no exterior boot-lid access – luggage had to be stowed through a hole behind the seats.

Design and development was completed by MG, at Abingdon, and the Sprite (this was an old Riley trademark, incidentally) went into production at Abingdon in 1958, alongside the MGA and the Austin-Healey 100-Six models. In its original form it was not considered very pretty, and it was certainly not very fast (look at those performance figures and compare them with those of a 1980s super-economy saloon), but it was remarkable value for money – and it was alone in its class. Quite simply, there were *no* other budget-priced small-engined sports cars like this in the world, and as a result it sold like hot cakes.

The Sprite's defects were many and various in detail, but the concept was triumphantly right. One forgave the over-eager steering, the bumpy ride and the rubber-matted floor coverings because it had such a cheerful character and such amazing agility. It says much for the Sprite that with each succeeding model change (and there were several) a bit of character seemed to be lost, and a bit more 'corporate rationalization' seemed to come in instead.

More than anything else, the original Sprite, which some still consider to be plain ugly (or, at best, *jolie laide*), was the foundation on which more conventional, and even more successful, Sprites and Midgets of the 1960s and 1970s were designed. The 'Frog-eye' was displaced by the first of these more conventional machines in 1961.

Austin-Healey Sprite Mk II (1961 to 1964)

After three years, the Sprite was redesigned, and in the process many of its original recognition points were lost. The original Mk II of 1961 (which was also produced as the badge-engineered MG Midget) was a much more conventional car than before.

Although the Mk II retained the same basic body-chassis

Austin-Healey Sprite Mk I specification

Produced: Abingdon, 1958-61. 48,999 cars built.
General layout: Unit-construction body-chassis structure, in 2-seater sports car style. Some cars with removable hardtop. Front-mounted engine driving rear wheels.
Engine and transmission: BMC A-Series, 4-cylinder, ohv, in-line. 948cc, 62.9 x 76.2mm, 43bhp at 5,200rpm; 52lb ft at 3,300rpm. 4-speed gearbox; no synchromesh on 1st gear; live (beam) rear axle with hypoid-bevel final drive.
Chassis: Independent front suspension, coil springs and wishbones. Rack-and-pinion steering. Rear suspension by cantilever quarter-elliptic leaf springs and radius-arms. Front and rear drum brakes. 5.20-13in tyres.
Dimensions: Wheelbase 6ft 8in; front track 3ft 9.75in; rear track 3ft 8.75in; length 11ft 5.25in; width 4ft 5in; height 4ft 1.75in. Unladen weight (approx) 1,328lb.
Typical performance: Maximum speed 86mph; 0-60mph 20.5sec; standing ¼-mile 21.8sec; overall fuel consumption 34mpg.
Fate: Dropped in favour of restyled Mk II model in 1961.

'tub' and an unchanged centre-section, there were big changes fore and aft. It is said that the front end was designed by one team and the rear end by another, but if that is so, a remarkably harmonious job was made of it.

At the front, the Mk II had conventional headlamps in the wings, and a normal-width lift-up bonnet, with a square letter-box style front grille. At the rear, the lines were squared-up, and the luggage compartment was given an ordinary lockable boot-lid. The engine had 46bhp, instead of the 'Frog-eye's' 43bhp, which allowed top speed to be pushed up to more than 85mph.

In October 1962, however, a good little car was made even better. Along with several other BMC models of the period, the Sprite's 948cc engine was discarded, and the long-stroke 1,098cc unit was fitted instead. At the same time, front-wheel disc brakes were added to the specification, and a baulk-ring synchromesh gearbox was also standardized. This allowed top speed to be nearer to 90mph, and the changes came only just in time as Triumph announced their pretty little Spitfire, a direct competitor, at exactly the same time. For the next few years, these cars would compete against each other for sales in the North American market.

There was much more to come from the Sprite, however, and the next derivative was announced in 1964.

Austin-Healey Sprite Mk II specification

As for Sprite Mk I except for:

Produced: Abingdon, 1961-64. 20,450 cars built with 948cc engine, 11,215 with 1,098cc engine.

General layout: As original 'Frog-eye' model, except for restyle and external opening boot-lid.

Engine and transmission: 948cc engine, 46bhp at 5,500rpm; 53lb ft at 3,000rpm.

Dimensions: Length 11ft 5.9in; unladen weight 1,525lb.

Typical performance: Maximum speed 86mph; 0-60mph 20.0sec; standing 1/4-mile 22.0sec; overall fuel consumption 39mpg.

Distinguishing features from previous model: Restyled bodyshell with headlamps in wings and external boot-lid.

Derivatives: From autumn 1962 to 1964, 11,215 cars produced with 1,098cc, 64.58 x 83.72mm engine, 56bhp at 5,500 rpm; 62lb ft at 3,250rpm. Front disc brakes and rear drums. Styling unchanged. 89mph top speed, 0-60mph 16.9sec, standing 1/4-mile 21.0sec, overall fuel consumption 30mpg.

Fate: Dropped in favour of Mk III model in 1964.

In mid-1961, the Sprite became 'Mk II', with new front and rear styling and a conventional external boot-lid and access. The MG Midget Mk I was the same car with different badges.

The Sprite Mk III was launched in 1964, and had a larger windscreen, wind-up windows and half-elliptic leaf-spring rear suspension.

Austin-Healey Sprite Mk III (1964 to 1966)

The third species of Austin-Healey Sprite was announced in March 1964, and it was easy to see that competition from Standard-Triumph had forced further changes. The basic styling of the car (which was also produced as the MG Midget Mk II) was much as before, but there had been a great deal of improvement to the equipment.

The running gear benefited from a more robust and deeper-breathing 1,098cc engine, which was rated at 59bhp, and there was a new rear suspension layout in which the axle beam was suspended on half-elliptic leaf springs; this meant that the last of the 'Frog-eye' car's idiosyncracies had been dropped.

There were significant body improvements. Not only was there a new and more stylistic facia layout, but winding windows were fitted to new doors, and there was a deeper windscreen to suit. The three-spoke steering wheel looked much like that of the MGB, but there was still scope for improvement, on the next model, in the soft-top layout.

Nevertheless, it was a better car than the previous model, and it sold well until replaced by the Mk IV version of 1966.

Austin-Healey Sprite Mk IV (1966 to 1970)

In October 1966, BMC announced what many people consider to be the best Sprite of all; this was the Mk IV model, in which there was not only an engine worthy of the model, but a neat foldaway soft-top which improved the little car's looks. The equivalent MG Midget was the Mk III.

The Mk IV's engine was still one of the A-Series family, but this time it was a detuned version of the Mini-Cooper S's 1,275cc unit, and produced 65bhp with a great deal of lusty mid-range torque. It made the Sprite faster than its bitter rival, the Spitfire III, and somehow it felt right, without strain or fuss, perhaps for the first time in its career.

All previous Sprites had needed to have their soft-tops built-up from separate sticks and a separate plastic hood, but the Mk IV's soft-top was all of a piece, and there was a neat pouch to cover it when stowed.

For the next four years, the Sprite carried on, mechanically little changed, and always flanked by the equivalent MG Midget at Abingdon. Because there was a lot of pressure from the sales force for this car to be kept abreast of burgeoning legislation from the USA, there was little time to make major changes to the design. Accordingly, it was not until the autumn of 1969 that the Sprite next received attention from the stylists. There was a new grille, badging, crackle-finish facia and the fitment of cast-alloy road wheels – all these changes being faithfully mirrored on the MG Midget.

Austin-Healey Sprite Mk III specification

As for Sprite Mk II except for:
Produced: Abingdon, 1964-66. 25,905 cars built.
Engine and transmission: 1,098cc engine, 59bhp at 5,750rpm; 65lb ft at 3,500rpm.
Chassis: Rear suspension by half-elliptic leaf springs.
Dimensions: Front track 3ft 9.25in; length 11ft 5.9in; unladen weight 1,566lb.
Typical performance: Maximum speed 92mph; 0-60mph 14.7sec; standing ¼-mile 19.8sec; overall fuel consumption 30mpg.
Distinguishing features from previous model: Wind-up windows in doors, larger screen, new facia and instrument panel.
Fate: Dropped in favour of Mk IV model in 1966.

In the autumn of 1966, the Sprite became 'Mk IV', complete with a detuned version of the Mini-Cooper S's 1,275cc engine.

From this view, the re-engineered soft-top of the new Sprite Mk IV is obvious. This car was almost identical with the Midget Mk III.

Austin-Healey Sprite Mk IV specification

As for Sprite Mk III except for:
Produced: Abingdon, 1966-70. 21,768 cars built.
Engine and transmission: 1,275cc engine, 70.6 x 81.28mm, 65bhp at 6,000rpm; 72lb ft at 3,000rpm.
Dimensions: Unladen weight 1,575lb.
Typical performance: Maximum speed 94mph; 0-60mph 14.1sec; standing ¼-mile 19.6sec; overall fuel consumption 30mpg.
Distinguishing features from previous model: Foldaway hood instead of build-up variety.
Derivatives: For 1970 model year, the grille was standardized with the MG Midget and cast-alloy wheels were fitted.
Fate: Austin-Healey marque dropped in favour of Austin model, which was produced only in 1971. Note: The badge-engineered MG Midget carried on until the end of 1979.

However, British Leyland had been formed by this time, and it became known that the new management wanted to get rid of all royalty agreements. The 'Healey' name was an obvious target for assassination, and at the end of calendar year 1970 the Austin-Healey Sprite was killed off. For 1971 only, the car was re-badged and sold as an Austin Sprite. The Midget, however, lived on until 1979.

Chapter 5

METROPOLITAN

I have purposely headed this chapter 'Metropolitan' because the car concerned was *originally* called a Nash (for USA sale), was badge-engineered into a Hudson (also USA sale) for a time, and became a Metropolitan (it was never badged, externally, as an Austin, even though it then carried Austin chassis numbers and chassis plates) when sold in the UK and elsewhere.

The original Metropolitan was the NXI prototype of Nash of the USA, who assessed Standard-Triumph and Fiat components and expertise before settling on BMC to do the manufacturing job for them. Structures were by Fisher and Ludlow, running gear was pure Austin, and final assembly was at Longbridge.

The car's launch was early in 1954, when it still had the A40-type of 1.2-litre engine, but this was soon displaced in favour of a BMC B-Series engine of the same dimensions. The car's only major facelift came in April 1956, at which point the 1.5-litre BMC engine was fitted instead of the A40.

From the spring of 1957, the Metropolitan became available outside the USA, it was finally given an external boot-lid access in 1959, and the last Metropolitan of all was built in 1961. Some cars certainly remained unsold, especially in the USA, until 1962.

In those seven years, only the one basic type of Metropolitan was ever built, and a restyle was never even contemplated. Because of its unique styling and 'marketing platform', the car never really had any competition among its fellow models at Longbridge during its production life.

The original Metropolitan was built for Nash of the USA by BMC, but not sold in Europe at first. There were closed or convertible two-door types.

Every Metropolitan had this type of facia, instrument display and interior. Note the steering-column gear-change, the bench front seat and the almost complete lack of space behind that bench.

Metropolitan (badged Nash or Hudson – 1954 to 1956)

Although the Metropolitan could never have been classed as a pretty car, it was certainly a commercial success for BMC, and was a most intriguing 'cookoo in the nest' at Longbridge for seven years. The styling was pure Detroit, from the Nash Corporation, but almost all the engineering was by the Austin designers.

Nash wanted to market cars much smaller than those their own factories could build, so they evolved the NXI prototype and hawked it round Europe, asking various manufacturers to consider inserting their own running gear and assembling it on Nash's behalf in their own factories, purely for sale in the United States. Fiat and Standard-Triumph were both interested, but BMC finally took up the option in 1952.

The monocoque structure, styled by Nash to include a dropped 'elbow rail' along the top of the doors, and having very restricted front and rear wheelarch cut-outs, was a very close-coupled two-door four-seater on a 7ft 1in wheelbase, and was available as either a convertible or a hardtop. The spare wheel was carried on the tail, under a cover, and there was no external access to the boot compartment. The shell itself, which was produced for BMC by Fisher and Ludlow, had nothing in common with any other Austin, Nash, or BMC product – yet the running gear was almost pure BMC.

The first cars had the old-type Austin A40 Somerset 1.2-litre engine, but from mid-1954 the new BMC B-Series unit was standardized. Behind this sturdy engine there was a three-speed transmission whose gear-change lever stuck out of the junction of the steering column and facia panel, and the back axle unit was an Austin A30 A-Series unit.

Metropolitan specification

Produced: Longbridge, 1954-56. 104,377 of *all* types of Metropolitan built.

General layout: Pressed-steel unit-construction body-chassis structure, in 4-seater, 2-door hardtop or convertible body styles. Front-mounted engine driving rear wheels.

Engine and transmission: Austin A40-type engine at first, BMC B-Series engine from mid-1954, 4-cylinder, ohv, in-line. 1,200cc, 65.48 x 88.9mm, 42bhp at 4,500rpm; 58lb ft at 2,400rpm; 3-speed gearbox, no synchromesh on 1st gear; steering-column gear-change; live (beam) rear axle with hypoid-bevel final drive.

Chassis: Independent front suspension, coil springs and wishbones. Cam-and-roller steering. Rear suspension by half-elliptic leaf springs. Front and rear drum brakes. 5.20-13in tyres.

Dimensions: Wheelbase 7ft 1in; front track 3ft 9.25in; rear track 3ft 8.8in; length 12ft 5.4in; width 5ft 1.5in; height 4ft 8.75in. Unladen weight (approx) 1,850lb.

Typical performance: Maximum speed 72mph; 0-60mph 27.0sec; standing ¼-mile 23.8sec: overall fuel consumption 34mpg.

Distinguishing features from previous models: Totally different from any previous Austin or US-built Nash models, but using many engine, transmission and suspension parts as fitted to current A30 and A40 models.

Derivatives: Nash and Hudson badged versions were sold in the USA, but none were officially sold in the UK.

Fate: Discontinued in 1956 in favour of Metropolitan 1500 model and UK market derivative.

Although much of the coil-spring independent front suspension was from the A30, there was a typically-Nash installation of the coil spring *above* the top wishbone, and supported on the structure rather like a MacPherson strut. The roadholding capabilities of this car were usually derided by motoring writers (or perhaps ignored by the more diplomatic of them in the hope that the readers would then make up their own minds).

Nash merged with Hudson soon after the new car was launched, so the Metropolitan, as it was to be called, was marketed in the USA first as a Nash, then as a Hudson for a time. Although it was a well-known car to the British motoring enthusiasts, they could not buy it, even if they wanted to, for all deliveries went straight to North America.

However, even though it had a willing performance, and quite an engaging character, Nash did not consider the original

car fast enough for their roads, so the opportunity for an engine change was also matched with a facelift – and the Metropolitan 1500 of 1956 was the result.

Metropolitan 1500 (badged Nash, Hudson or Metropolitan, 1956 to 1961)

In April 1956, the Metropolitan received its only major facelift, for not only were there important styling changes, but the engine was made larger and more powerful. The new version, which was quite logically known as the Metropolitan 1500, had a new and neater front grille, whereas the original bonnet air intake had been removed. There was a new chrome strip along the body sides so that the car could be supplied in duo-tone colour schemes.

The original 1.2-litre engine was dropped, and the 1500 was equipped with a 47bhp version of the 1,489cc B-Series unit, as

The facelift Metropolitan was eventually sold in Britain and Europe, but never badged as an Austin. Note that although these cars have British registrations, they are left-hand-drive models.

already found in several other BMC models. Thus equipped, the Metropolitan soldiered on until 1961, by which time the Americans had got bored with it, Nash were not interested in tooling up for a new style, and so it was discontinued.

There were a few Hudsons, but mainly Nashes, before BMC were encouraged to start selling the car outside North America. The right-hand-drive car, announced in April 1957, was to be called simply a Metropolitan 1500. As far as is known, it was *never* badged as an Austin (even though there were Austin chassis plates and engine markings), although most people came to call it by that name.

Between 1957 and 1961, the only major packaging change was to include an opening boot-lid to give direct access to the stowage area, and to mount the spare wheel internally – this was introduced on export cars in 1959 and became available in the UK from the summer of 1960.

Metropolitan 1500 specification

As for Metropolitan except for:

Produced: Longbridge, 1956-61. 104,377 of *all* types built.

Engine and transmission: B-Series engine, 1,489cc, 73.02 x 88.9mm, 47bhp at 4,100rpm; 74lb ft at 2,100rpm.

Distinguishing features from previous model: Bonnet scoop deleted, new mesh grille, new colour schemes.

Typical performance: Maximum speed 75mph; 0-60mph 24.8sec; standing ¼-mile 22.5sec: overall fuel consumption 29mpg.

Derivatives: As for 1.2-litre model, but Hudson only until 1957. Also sold as Metropolitan (*not* Austin) from spring 1957.

Fate: Discontinued in 1961 and not replaced.

Chapter 6

VANDEN PLAS

Here is a name which started out as that of a respected coachbuilder, became the 'top of the line' label for a range of Austins (rather like it became later for various Austin-Rover products), then became a fully-fledged marque in its own right. Confusing? Not really, for it all happened in a gradual and logical way.

Vanden Plas was a great name among British coachbuilders between the wars, with a factory at Kingsbury, most notable for producing a range of styles on Bentley and Alvis chassis. The business was taken over by Austin in 1946, and was immediately set to work producing the very large A135 range of Princesses; the Princess shells were assembled *in toto* by Vanden Plas.

For at least a decade, however, the name Vanden Plas was not applied to the title of any Austin or BMC car. Then, in 1958, the Austin A105 Vanden Plas was announced (see Chapter 3 for more details) – which was an A105 supplied untrimmed to Kingsbury and completed to Vanden Plas' own high standards.

From the summer of 1959, however, there was a further change. To replace the A105, there was the new Austin A99, and the up-market luxury version of this car came along in October 1959. At first it was called the Princess 3-Litre, but from May 1960, when only a few cars had been built, it was rebadged as a Vanden Plas Princess 3-Litre. This car was a great success, of its type, and was built until the summer of 1964.

At this point the car's concept was changed, and although it retained basically the same monocoque and styling, it was fitted with a 4-litre six-cylinder Rolls-Royce engine and Borg-Warner automatic transmission and given the name Princess 4-Litre R. The initial public response flattered, to deceive, and it sold very slowly after the first two years, finally being dropped in 1968 at the very end of the life-span of the BMC combine.

In the meantime, another Vanden Plas success story

had begun. The front-wheel-drive transverse-engined 1100 model (first badged as a Morris, then an Austin) had been launched in 1962, and from the end of 1963 there was a beautifully trimmed and furnished version of the same car, completed at Kingsbury, and known as the Vanden Plas Princess 1100. This sold well, was given the larger 1,275cc engine from 1967, and outlived the British Leyland merger by six years until 1974. At this point it was replaced by the British Leyland-inspired and Allegro-based 1500 model, which was neither as nice, nor as nice-looking.

No other BMC-based Vanden Plas cars were ever put on sale, though prototypes based on other ranges were often produced for appraisal. The Vanden Plas factory at Kingsbury closed down in 1979, the last Vanden Plas car was produced at Abingdon in 1980, and more recently the name has been applied by Austin-Rover to versions of Austin and Rover cars.

Princess 3-Litre (1959 to 1960)
– rebadged Vanden Plas Princess 3-Litre (1960 to 1961)
The story really starts with the Austin A105 Vanden Plas, which was a specially trimmed and furnished version of the A105, personally inspired by Leonard Lord and produced in 1958 and 1959. It was such a publicity success, for absolutely minimal investment, that when the time came to launch a new large BMC car, the up-market Vanden Plas version was clearly desirable.

First, however, I must clear up the question of marque badging. From 1946 to summer 1957, every car produced for Austin by Vanden Plas, at Kingsbury, was badged as an Austin. Then, without changing the cars in any way, the Austin

When the C-Series Farina-styled Austin A99 was announced in 1959, a luxuriously trimmed Princess 3-Litre version of it was developed. This car did not *officially* become a Vanden Plas Princess until the summer of 1960.

Princess IV of the period was 'de-badged', and officially became known simply as the Princess. This was the situation in the autumn of 1959, when the new large Farina-styled saloons were born. Officially, the Vanden Plas version was to be known as a Princess 3-Litre, even though the general public still tended to call it an Austin Princess 3-Litre.

It was so confusing and unsatisfactory that BMC changed everything around again, so that from May 1960 the same cars became known as Vanden Plas Princess 3-Litre. All clear now?

Whatever the title, the Vanden Plas-produced 3-Litre was structurally and mechanically identical to the new Austin A99 and Wolseley 6/99 saloons. The cars took shape at Cowley, alongside the Wolseley 6/99 model, but were still incomplete when delivered to Kingsbury, in North London, for furnishing and completion to Vanden Plas standards.

Compared with the Wolseley 6/99, therefore, the Princess 3-Litre had a prominent special grille and an overhanging bonnet panel, and there were special wheel nave plates and paint schemes to add to the air of exclusivity.

The interior was entirely special, with a fine-grain walnut veneer instrument board, special instruments, specially trimmed and padded seating, and a great deal of extra sound-deadening to help make the passenger compartment as quiet as possible. Because of the type of clientele these cars attracted, a higher proportion of them were fitted with automatic transmission than was found in the Austin or Wolseley equivalents.

Even though the 3-Litre was obviously developed from a more mundane machine, it still exuded a general air of added quality, was carefully assembled, and it sold well. The Mk II which followed was an even better car.

Vanden Plas Princess 3-Litre specification

Produced: Kingsbury, 1959-61. 4,719 cars built.
General layout: Pressed-steel unit-construction body-chassis structure, in 5-seater, 4-door saloon body style. Front-mounted engine driving rear wheels.
Engine and transmission: BMC C-Series, 6-cylinder, ohv, in-line. 2,912cc, 83.34 x 88.9mm, 103bhp at 4,750rpm; 157lb ft at 2,300rpm. 3-speed gearbox, all synchromesh, with Borg-Warner overdrive on top and 2nd gears; Optional Borg-Warner 3-speed automatic transmission; steering-column gear-change; live (beam) rear axle with hypoid-bevel final drive.
Chassis: Independent front suspension, coil springs, wishbones and anti-roll bar. Cam-and-peg steering. Rear suspension by half-elliptic leaf springs. Front disc and rear drum brakes. 7.00-14in tyres.
Dimensions: Wheelbase 9ft 0in; front track 4ft 6in; rear track 4ft 5.25in; length 15ft 8in; width 5ft 8.5in; height 4ft 11in. Unladen weight (approx) 3,465lb.
Typical performance: (Automatic-transmission version) Maximum speed 97mph; 0-60mph 17.9sec; standing ¼-mile 21.4sec; overall fuel consumption 17mpg.
Distinguishing features from previous models: Entirely new monocoque with unique styling, not connected with previous Vanden Plas-trimmed Austin A105 model.
Derivatives: Originally car was badged as a Princess, but became Vanden Plas Princess from May 1960. Mk II model followed in late 1961, and Princess R derived from this in 1964. Car was itself derived from Austin A99/Wolseley 6/99 design of same period.
Fate: Discontinued in 1961 in favour of Mk II model.

Vanden Plas Princess 3-Litre Mk II (1961 to 1964)

When BMC facelifted their Austin A99/Wolseley 6/99 models in the autumn of 1961 (at which time they became Austin A110/Wolseley 6/110 respectively), they handed on the same mechanical improvements to the Vanden Plas derivative.

Visually, therefore, the Vanden Plas was virtually unchanged from the original, but because it had significantly more power than before it had become a genuine 100mph car. Road-testers suggested that it offered 'luxury at a very competitive price', which was exactly the right sort of image which BMC had hoped to develop for the car.

Like the Austins and Wolseleys, the Mk II version of the Princess 3-Litre had 120bhp from its retuned 2.9-litre engine, a longer wheelbase and suspension changes to add to the stability, and it was made even better from mid-1962 when power-assisted steering became optional.

The way to pick the Mk II from its ancestor, incidentally, was to observe that the rear bumper overriders had been moved outboard to be in line with the tail-fins.

From the autumn of 1961, the Vanden Plas Princess 3-Litre became 'Mk II', although visual changes were not noticeable.

Vanden Plas Princess 3-Litre Mk II specification

As for original 3-Litre model except for:

Produced: Kingsbury, 1961-64. 7,984 cars built.

Engine and transmission: 120bhp at 4,750rpm; 163lb ft at 2,750rpm. Centre-floor change for manual-transmission car; optional power-assisted steering from mid-1962.

Chassis: Rear suspension with transverse anti-sway hydraulic damper, no anti-roll bar.

Dimensions: Wheelbase 9ft 2in; height 5ft 0.5in. Unladen weight (approx) 3,660lb.

Typical performance: (Automatic-transmission version) Maximum speed 105mph; 0-60mph 16.9sec; standing ¼-mile 21.4sec; overall fuel consumption 18mpg.

Distinguishing features from previous models: Longer wheelbase, rear suspension changes, centre-floor change for manual-transmission car and facia changes.

Derivatives: Car itself was derived from Austin A110/Wolseley 6/110 design. Princess R of 1964-68 was derived from the 3-Litre Mk II.

Fate: Discontinued in summer 1964 in favour of Princess R model.

Vanden Plas Princess 4-Litre R (1964 to 1968)

Although BMC had high hopes of the Princess R, and public reaction was favourable at first, its attraction soon faded away, production fell to a trickle in the latter years, and it eventually died away, a commercial and marketing gamble which failed.

In the early 1960s, BMC was in a very expansionary mood and spent some time talking to Rolls-Royce in general terms about merging some interests. Although these talks were eventually abandoned, the single concrete result was that the prestigious Rolls-Royce company developed a special version of their six-cylinder engine, which they called the FB60 type, and this was then offered by BMC in a much revised Princess saloon. Because it was a 3,909cc unit, the new car's title was 4-Litre Princess R, and rumours persist that the R was meant to stand for Royal, but that the use of this adjective was frowned on in court circles.

The basic design, style and structure of the Princess R was still that of the Princess 3-Litre (which meant that it was still related to the Austin A110), but the design had been reworked from stem to stern to justify a much higher price and to make it more exclusive and worthy of the Rolls-Royce engine.

The engine itself was an alloy-block, short-stroke version of the familiar six-cylinder Rolls-Royce unit, which was used not only in Rolls-Royce and Bentley passenger cars up to 1959, but in many military vehicles. With a quoted peak of 175bhp it was much more powerful than the superseded 3-litre BMC C-Series engine, though this was never backed up by flashing acceleration figures or a dramatically higher top speed.

Vanden Plas Princess 4-Litre R specification

Produced: Kingsbury, 1964-68. 6,555 cars built.
General layout: Pressed-steel unit-construction body-chassis structure, in 5-seater 4-door saloon body style. Front-mounted engine driving rear wheels.
Engine and transmission: Rolls-Royce FB60 engine, 6-cylinder, ioev, in-line. 3,909cc, 95.25 x 91.44mm, 175bhp at 4,800rpm; 218lb ft at 3,000rpm. Borg-Warner 3-speed automatic transmission; steering-column gear-change; live (beam) rear axle with hypoid-bevel final drive.
Chassis: Independent front suspension, coil springs, wishbones and anti-roll bar. Cam-type steering, with power assistance. Rear suspension by half-elliptic leaf springs. Front disc and rear drum brakes. 7.50-13in tyres.
Dimensions: Wheelbase 9ft 2in; front track 4ft 6.9in; rear track 4ft 5.25in; length 15ft 8in; width 5ft 8.5in; height 4ft 11in. Unladen weight (approx) 3,530lb.
Typical performance: Maximum speed 106mph; 0-60mph 12.7sec; standing ¼-mile 18.9sec; overall fuel consumption 15mpg.
Distinguishing features from previous models: Modified monocoque, with different front and rear styling, no rear fins and smoother roof-line, plus Rolls-Royce engine, compared with obsolete Mk II model.
Derivatives: None, though basic chassis and structure was itself derived from Austin A110 Mk II/Wolseley 6/110 Mk II model.
Fate: Discontinued in 1968 and not replaced.

From the summer of 1964, the Vanden Plas Princess became the 4-Litre R, with a six-cylinder Rolls Royce engine and automatic transmission as standard. Visual identification included pared-down tail-fins and a restyled roof panel, along with built-in auxiliary lamps.

Automatic transmission was standard, the suspension was virtually the same as before except for a massive new front cross-member, and there was even more attention to sound-deadening.

The bodyshell was changed, in detail, in many ways. Compared with the A110, there was a new roof panel (offering more headroom), no peaks over the front and rear windows, a more upright rear window in any case, and the rear end was smoothed out by eliminating the fins and providing horizontal tail-lamp clusters. However, the most important change of all was to the price – which was £1,994, compared with £1,474 for the 3-Litre in the UK market.

Sales took off with a rush, but once the word got around that the engine was wasted on the rest of the car, demand slumped. Even with Vanden Plas trying all they knew to ensure top build quality, BMC could not sustain interest in the car. Sales had been expected to exceed 100 cars a week, but such figures were not realized and production was down to 200 cars *a year* by 1967. The Princess R was quietly withdrawn from production at the beginning of 1968, just before British Leyland would surely have killed it off.

The Austin Princess 4-Litre limousine of the 1950s became 'Princess' in 1957 and finally 'Vanden Plas Princess' in 1960. It was then built in this form until 1968.

Vanden Plas Princess 4-Litre Limousine (1957 to 1968)

The *Austin* Princess long-wheelbase limousine had originally been introduced by the fledgling BMC organization in the autumn of 1952, had been fitted with the later Princess IV model's automatic transmission and power-assisted steering in 1956, but was otherwise still the same car when it was 'de-badged' in August 1957.

For the next decade, the stately Princess Limousine carried on in production at Kingsbury, with very few mechanical or styling changes, and few improvements to the equipment for BMC to boast about. The most significant change, indeed, was that the anonymous Princess was re-badged yet again, to become the Vanden Plas Princess, in mid-1960.

By the mid-1960s, this massive machine had nothing in common with any other BMC car, and it was only because it was effectively a hand-assembled machine, in which the other, age-old, tooling costs had been amortized years earlier, that BMC kept it on the market. There was virtually no private sale for this near-5,000lb limousine, with all sales going to local councils for their mayors to use, or to hire-car concerns for use at weddings and funerals.

Production was down to 250-300 cars a year by this time, and Vanden Plas were actually developing its successor when the British Motor Holdings group (controlling BMC and

Vanden Plas Princess 4-Litre Limousine specification

Produced: Kingsbury, 1957-68. 3,344 cars of all types (Austin, Princess or Vanden Plas) built between 1952 and 1968.

General layout: Separate box-section chassis-frame and coachbuilt wood-and-aluminium-and-steel bodyshell, in 8-seater, 4-door limousine style. Front-mounted engine driving rear wheels.

Engine and transmission: BMC D-Series engine, 6-cylinder, ohv, in-line. 3,993cc, 87.3 x 111.1mm, 120bhp at 4,000rpm; 185lb ft at 2,000rpm. 4-speed gearbox, no synchromesh on 1st gear; optional GM Hydramatic automatic gearbox, 4 forward gears; steering-column gear-change; live (beam) rear axle with hypoid-bevel final drive.

Chassis: Independent front suspension, coil springs and wishbones. Cam-and-peg steering, with power assistance from 1956. Rear suspension by half-elliptic leaf springs. Front and rear drum brakes. 7.00-16in tyres.

Dimensions: Wheelbase 11ft 0in; front track 4ft 10.5in; rear track 5ft 2.5in; length 17ft 11in; width 6ft 2.5in; height 5ft 10in. Unladen weight (approx) 4,810lb.

Typical performance: Maximum speed 75mph; 0-60mph 26.0sec; standing ¼-mile 23.1sec: overall fuel consumption 14mpg.

Distinguishing features from previous models: New body style compared with earlier Princess limousines, with permanent 8-seater accommodation.

Derivatives: Original Austin became Princess in 1957, then Vanden Plas Princess in mid-1960, with no other significant changes.

Fate: Discontinued in 1968 and replaced by Jaguar Mk 10-based Daimler Limousine, still in production in mid-1980s.

Jaguar) was founded in 1966. Since Jaguar-Daimler were also developing a large new limousine, it obviously made sense to pool resources. The result was that no large new Vanden Plas Princess was produced to replace the old 4-litre limousine, but the Kingsbury concern at least got the job of assembling the new Daimler DS420 limousine which took its place in 1968. That car, of course, is still being made, latterly at the Jaguar factory, in the mid-1980s.

Vanden Plas Princess 1100 (1963 to 1967)

The endearing little Princess 1100 was not a carefully thought out car, product-planned by BMC, but really came into existence by chance. It was in 1962, immediately after the introduction of the new front-wheel-drive Morris 1100, that Fred Connolly, of the famous firm of curriers, asked Vanden Plas to make a special luxury version of that car for his personal use. The result was such an appealing machine, complete with all the finest hides and wood veneer finish of the larger BMC-based Princess models, that BMC then decided to put such a car into production. The prototype, complete with Princess-style grille, was shown at Earls Court in 1963, and deliveries began during the winter of 1963-64.

Mechanically, the Princess 1100, as it became called, was identical to the MG 1100 of the period, but every Princess was fitted with four passenger doors, and the majority were sold in the UK. The rather soft Hydrolastic suspension and the spacious interior (relative to the overall size of the car) were exactly right for the character of the car, which sold very well indeed. Some observers, in fact, christened this car as an ideal model for those retiring from business, and certainly many of the first owners were elderly.

At first, cars were partly built at Longbridge, with final assembly, trim and decoration at VDP's Kingsbury factory, but

The Vanden Plas Princess 1100 was a nicely-equipped special version of the MG 1100, with leather seating, a wooden facia, pile carpets and a special gront grille flanked by matching auxiliary lights.

The Vanden Plas Princess 1100/1300 models always used this unique wood-veneer facia and instrument display, which was not shared by any other front-drive BMC car.

between January 1966 and March 1967 a considerable number were completely built at Longbridge; this was at the time when the Kingsbury plant was full of other Vanden Plas models.

Like other front-drive 1100s, this model was updated and superseded in the autumn of 1967. Incidentally, two prototype 'MG' Princesses were built and exported to the USA.

Vanden Plas Princess 1300 (1967 to 1968)

In the summer of 1967, a very few Princess 1100s were fitted with the newly-developed 58bhp single-carburettor 1,275cc engine and badged 'Princess 1275', but the properly-titled Princess 1300 was not put on sale until the autumn of 1967. This model had the lightly restyled rear bodywork of the Mk II Austin/Morris 1100s and new 1300s, and retained the same 58bhp engine, like the interim MG 1275 and 1300 saloons.

It was on this strictly interim Princess 1300 that automatic transmission became optional, and on which the new BMC all-synchromesh manual transmission became available.

After only one year, the Princess 1300 was once again updated, becoming Mk II, with a more powerful engine.

Vanden Plas Princess 1100 specification

Produced: Kingsbury, 1963-67 (also Longbridge, 1966-67). 16,007 1100s of Mk I *and* Mk II types built.
General layout: Pressed-steel unit-construction body-chassis structure, in 4-seater, 4-door saloon body style. Front engine, transversely-mounted engine driving front wheels.
Engine and transmission: BMC A-Series engine, 4-cylinder, ohv, in-line. 1,098cc, 64.58 x 83.72mm, 55bhp at 5,500 rpm; 61lb ft at 2,500rpm. During summer-autumn 1967, some cars sold with 1,275cc engine, 70.6 x 81.28mm, 58bhp at 5,250rpm; 69lb ft at 3,500rpm. 4-speed gearbox, no synchromesh on 1st gear; centre-floor gear-change; spur-gear final drive.
Chassis: Independent front suspension, Hydrolastic units and wishbones. Rack-and-pinion steering. Independent rear suspension by Hydrolastic units, trailing arms and anti-roll bar. Interconnection between front and rear suspensions. Front disc and rear drum brakes. 5.50-12in tyres.
Dimensions: Wheelbase 7ft 9.5in; front track 4ft 3.5in; rear track 4ft 2.9in; length 12ft 2.7in; width 5ft 0.4in; height 4ft 4.7in. Unladen weight (approx) 1,950lb.
Typical performance: (1,098cc version) Maximum speed 85mph; 0-60mph 21.1sec; standing ¼-mile 21.7sec: overall fuel consumption 31mpg.
Distinguishing features from previous models: Entirely new type of Vanden Plas model with Pininfarina styling.
Derivatives: Austin/Morris 1100 was the same car with different badges, details and engine tune. MG 1100, Riley Kestrel and Wolseley 1100 models were all slightly modified versions, too. Mk II (see separate entry) was same car with minor changes.
Fate: Discontinued in 1967 and replaced by Mk II models.

Vanden Plas Princess 1300 specification

As for original 1100 model except for:
Produced: Kingsbury, 1967-68, 27,734 of all Princess 1300 types built.
Engine and transmission: 1,275cc, 58bhp at 5,250rpm; 69lb ft at 3,000rpm. All-synchromesh manual transmission fitted during 1968; optional automatic transmission available.
Dimensions: Unladen weight (approx) 2,015lb.
Typical performance: As for 1.3-litre version of original 1100.
Distinguishing features from previous model: Changes as for Princess 1100 Mk II model.
Fate: Discontinued in autumn 1968 in favour of Mk II model.

The Vanden Plas Princess 1300 was trimmed and furnished like the 1100 had been, and the car displayed an elegance which would not be repeated in the Princess version of the Allegro which was to follow it during the Leyland era.

The Vanden Plas Princess 1300 could be identified from the rear by different badging and trim details.

Vanden Plas Princess 1100 Mk II (1967 to 1968)

For a very short interim period (autumn 1967 to spring 1968), Vanden Plas produced a Mk II version of the Princess 1100. Like other such interim front-drive BMC cars, this incorporated the slightly-restyled bodyshell (with cut-back fins) with the original 1,098cc engine.

A very few of these cars were built with optional automatic transmission. Their equipment and fittings were otherwise identical to those of the new 1300s.

Vanden Plas Princess 1100 Mk II specification

As for Princess 1100 Mk I except for:
Produced: 1967-68.
Engine and transmission: Optional AP 4-speed automatic transmission.
Distinguishing features from previous models: Chopped-off tail-fins with different tail-lamps, trim and details.
Derivatives: 1100 Mk II was itself a derivative of original 1100. Also 1300 (see separate entry). Austin 1100/1300 was same car; also MG, Riley and Wolseley all used same basic design.
Fate: Discontinued in 1968 and not replaced.

Vanden Plas Princess 1300 Mk II (1968 to 1974)

As with the MG 1300, BMC took time to arrive at a definitive Princess 1300 specification. The definitive 1300 was the Mk II, which was quietly phased into production in the autumn of 1968, and differed from the original in having a twin-carburettor, 65bhp engine on manual-transmission models and a less highly-tuned (60bhp) engine where automatic transmission was specified. The car still looked almost exactly like the original 1100 of 1963, except of course for badging and the cropped fins and different tail-lamps of the Mk II body style.

This was a highly successful model which made many

friends for BMC, and a goodly number of cars have survived into the 1980s. It was during this period that BMC's successors, British Leyland, moved mechanical assembly of the Princess models from Longbridge to Cowley, though final assembly continued to be at Kingsbury.

The Princess 1300 Mk II continued to sell steadily after the mainstream 1100/1300 models were dropped, and it was not until May 1974 that it was dropped in favour of the much less appealing Allegro-based 1500 model.

Vanden Plas Princess 1300 Mk II specification

As for Princess 1300 Mk I except for:
Produced: 1968-74.
Engine and transmission: 65bhp at 5,750rpm; 71lb ft at 3,000rpm. With automatic transmission, 60bhp at 5,250rpm; 69lb ft at 2,500rpm.
Typical performance: No authentic independent figures published.
Fate: Discontinued in spring 1974 in favour of new Austin Allegro-based 1500 model.

Chapter 7

MORRIS

In any merger there is a dominant partner and a subservient partner. At the time of the formation of the British Motor Corporation there was never any doubt that Nuffield was going to be the underdog. Although the company's profits were high, equal to those of Austin, it was not producing as many cars. Worse, its management was ageing rapidly and so, too (except for the amazing little Morris Minor) were its models.

Morris' postwar range had been inspired by the driving force of the Nuffield Corporation, Sir Miles Thomas, before he was ousted by Lord Nuffield in 1947. Thereafter, Nuffield himself (who had been a rather remote chairman for some years) had to become more of the 'hands-on' boss again, and his deputy, Reg Hanks, did not have the flair of his predecessor.

This was soon to show up in the very boring range of cars which were coming forward for the mid-1950s. In 1951-52, Morris relied on the Morris Minor for the vast majority of its sales, for the only other private cars in the range were the closely-related Morris Oxford (Series MO) and the longer-wheelbase Morris Six. The Cowley factory, of course, was extremely busy, not only building these Morris models, but also producing Wolseleys (4/50 and 6/80) and a number of light commercial vehicles.

Once the merger had been formalized, BMC began to formulate its medium-term strategy, and while this envisaged the production of a very few rationalized engines and transmissions, it did not immediately envisage shared bodyshells. Morris Motors, therefore, was encouraged to produce the next generation of Morris cars from its own design and development staffs – though the new BMC engines had to be used to power them.

[It is worth noting that although Austin engineers already had the A-Series engines, and were about to design the B-Series, it was the Morris Engines Branch which was entrusted with the design, tooling and production of the new six-cylinder C-Series engines, which were first used in the autumn of 1954.]

Immediately after the foundation of BMC, Morris' cars were the Morris Minor (Series MM), which had an ancient-design four-cylinder side-valve engine, the Morris Oxford (Series MO), with an engine which, although new in 1948, was an old-fashioned side-valve design, and the Morris Six, whose passenger cabin was the same as that of the Oxford, but which had a Wolseley-influenced but Morris-designed overhead-cam 'six' up front; this, incidentally, sounded fine, but was rather gutless *and* thirsty. In 1951, all had been retouched – the Minor with high-mounted headlamps for all markets and glass side windows for the convertible, the Oxford with seating changes but no change to the sheet metal (there was a different grille in 1952), and the Six with a pressurized engine cooling system and a more powerful heater.

Nothing major could be done for the next couple of years, except that the light, modern little A-Series BMC engine and gearbox were swiftly slotted into the Morris Minor's monocoque, it therefore becoming Series II instead of MM. The Six was always overshadowed by the Wolseley 6/80, on which it was based, and it faded away during 1953, which left the Oxford MO (whose styling was really that of the Morris Minor on a more bulky scale) to struggle on against formidable opposition from Austin (the A40 Somerset) and Ford (the Consul).

Then, in 1954, came the first big change when the old Oxford was killed off, and a new monocoque body-chassis unit, which eventually gave birth to new Oxford Series II *and* Cowley derivatives, was launched. Whereas Austin was going for 'cow-hips' and slim lines in its new Cambridges and Westminsters, the Oxford/Cowley was a bulbous beast, with a spacious interior and rounded exterior lines. The Oxford was the up-market 1.5-litre derivative, the Cowley the stripped-out 1.2-litre version. Then, as later, the public showed that they did not really like 'hand-me-down' models, for the Cowley was not a great success.

The Oxford's styling was pure Cowley, and if you look carefully you can certainly see some lines and shapes which went into the styling of the first Mini of 1959, for there was a definite Cowley input into this machine as well. We must also remember that Alec Issigonis was involved in both designs.

The BMC influence in this car was, of course, the use of new, standardized, B-Series engines, transmissions and back axles, so when the new Isis was launched in 1955 it was no surprise to see how BMC and Nuffield had begun to co-operate even more closely. This Isis, in effect, was a rather ungainly long-wheelbase version of the Oxford Series II, where the lengthy front-end concealed the new six-cylinder C-Series engine and transmission.

Then, in the autumn of 1956, it was time for a reshuffle, and for a facelift to all existing Morris cars. The Minor became Minor 1000 by using the latest 948cc engine and transmission, the Oxford became Series III with a fluted bonnet, rear fins grafted on and very unsuitable duo-tone colour schemes, and the Isis became Series II with similar changes to the Oxford.

This, however, was nearly the end of Morris as a separate company. Although its development facility would be retained right into the 1970s (the Marina and the 18/22 'Princess' cars were both developed from Cowley, but not designed there), the next generation of Morris models would all be BMC corporate designs, inspired from Longbridge (and Italy!).

Although there was to be no Morris equivalent of the A40 Farina, and there would be no new six-cylinder car to succeed the lumbering Isis, there was a Morris version of the B-Series Farina car (which, although built by Pressed Steel and assembled at Cowley, was an A55 'clone'), a Morris Mini-Minor, a Morris 1100/1300 and a Morris 1800/2200.

The front-wheel-drive cars were all corporate designs, with corporate engines, and their absolute interchangeability with Austin equivalents was proved by the fact that Morris cars were sometimes assembled at Longbridge and Austins at Cowley. It all depended on where the pressure on production was greater at the time.

Just as BMC was giving way to British Leyland, this philosophy of interchangeability was being carried a stage further, for although production of Austin Maxi engines and transmissions was carried out at Longbridge, the body structures were built by Pressed Steel, at Cowley, and final assembly was also at Cowley. By this time, for sure, all traces of Morris individuality had been lost.

Postscript:
These were the Morris Division trademarks noted in the 1968 edition of the SMM & T's *Register of Model Titles*, which had not been used on postwar cars:
Captain
Carousel
Major (used on Australian BMC models)
Maxi (this, of course, was later used for the Austin)

The first of the Morris Minors, the MM, had low headlamps, but this type had been discontinued before the BMC merger.

The Morris Minor's style barely altered in a 23-year life from this early MM except for headlamp position, different badging and tail-lamps and, from late 1956, a larger rear window.

The Morris Minor MM's facia style, clearly produced with right-hand or left-hand steering in mind.

Morris Minor Series MM (1948 to 1953)

Although the famous Morris Minor did not make its debut until the autumn of 1948, it was conceived in the dark days of the Second World War by Alec Issigonis, who was encouraged and supported by Nuffield's then vice-chairman, Sir Miles Thomas. For a time the project was kept secret from Lord Nuffield himself, and for a long time after he *was* told he did not approve of it!

The charm of the Morris Minor, in austerity Britain in 1948,

was not only that it *was* new, but that it was a spacious small car with distinctive styling, crisp handling and steering, and a remarkably endearing character. Even though it was not helped by having to use the ancient 1930s-design side-valve four-cylinder engine, the rest of the Minor's design was up to date, and it soon became a best seller.

Technically, the new Minor was a great step forward from the old Eight Series E, which had a separate chassis and very backward-looking styling; the new Minor had a stiff unit-construction bodyshell (with several different styles planned), torsion-bar independent front suspension and rack-and-pinion steering gear. There were certainly ways in which the looks could be improved – the low-mounted headlamp position was neither attractive nor efficient in illumination, and the split screen was certainly cheap, rather than good looking, for instance – but the package was nonetheless very appealing. Issigonis had wanted to use an all-new flat-four engine, but one must never forget that this was an unadventurous side-valve design. Thank goodness the overall width of the car (and

---

Morris Minor Series MM specification

Produced: Cowley, 1948-53, 176,002 of all types built.
General layout: Pressed-steel unit-construction body-chassis structure, in 4-seater style and various derivatives. Front-mounted engine, driving rear wheels.
Engine and transmission: Nuffield-designed engine, 4-cylinder, sv, in-line. 918cc, 57 x 90mm, 27bhp at 4,400rpm; 39lb ft at 2,400rpm; 4-speed gearbox, no synchromesh on 1st gear; centre-floor gear-change; live (beam) rear axle with hypoid-bevel final drive.
Chassis: Independent front suspension, torsion bars and wishbones. Rack-and-pinion steering. Rear suspension by half-elliptic leaf springs. Front and rear drum brakes. 5.00-14in tyres.
Dimensions: Wheelbase 7ft 2in; front track 4ft 2.6in; rear track 4ft 2.3in; length 12ft 4in; width 5ft 1in; height 5ft 0in. Unladen weight (2-door saloon, approx) 1,735lb.
Typical performance: Maximum speed 62mph; 0-50mph 24.2sec; standing ¼-mile 26.3sec: overall fuel consumption 40mpg.
Derivatives: 2-door saloon (1948-53), 4-door saloon (1950-53), tourer (convertible) (1948-53) and SII was a re-engined version of the original Minor MM.
Fate: Discontinued in 1953 and replaced by Series II models, which had A-Series ohv engine.

The 'high headlight' Minor MM was in production when BMC was formed, but was dropped in favour of the Series II in 1953.

also the wheel tracks) had been increased by a full 4 inches at a late prototype stage, for this transformed the looks and the car's handling.

At first, only the two-door saloon and tourer (convertible) types were on offer, but a four-door saloon joined the range two years later. Nuffield was already considering a Traveller (estate car) derivative and a light van, but neither type was introduced on the original MM chassis. One important styling change, introduced in January 1949 on North American export models and from early 1951 on all models, was the 'high-headlamp' nose, which placed 7-inch lamps in a much more useful place *and* improved the car's overall looks.

Apart from renaming the tourer as a convertible in mid-1951, the Series MM Minor received no major modifications in the last two years of its life. Once the BMC merger had taken place it became clear that a major engine rationalization programme was planned, and this soon led to the use of the new BMC A-Series engine in the Minor. In this way the Series II Minor was born, but both types were built together, at Cowley, until February 1953. The Series II was 'export only' at first.

Morris Minor Series II (1952 to 1956)
The Minor Series II appeared in the autumn of 1952, less than a year after the BMC merger had been proposed, and only seven months after the new company began operating. In that brief period, BMC's planners settled their engine and transmission rationalization plan, decided to ditch the Minor MM's side-valve units in favour of the newly-designed overhead-valve A-Series engine and gearbox, built prototypes, tested the new combination and prepared the car to go on sale!

The four-door Series II was launched in October 1952, and although the original side-valve MM continued for a time, it was finally made obsolete in February 1953. According to all the figures, the Series II was more powerful and should have

<table>
<tr><td>

Morris Minor Series II specification

As for Morris Minor Series MM except for:
Produced: Cowley, 1952-56, 269,838 Minor SIIs of all types built.
Engine and transmission: BMC A-Series with ohv. 803cc, 58 x 76.2mm, 30bhp at 4,800rpm; 40lb ft at 2,400rpm.
Distinguishing features from previous model: All SIIs had high-mounted headlamps (also fitted to some MMs) plus extra body styles, plus new grille from late 1954. All SIIs had a bonnet mascot, never used on MM type.
Typical performance: Maximum speed 62mph; 0-50mph 25.7sec; standing ¼-mile 26.9sec; overall fuel consumption 36mpg.
Derivatives: As for Series MM, plus Traveller (estate) from 1953-56 and vans and pick-ups from 1953-56.
Fate: Discontinued in 1956 in favour of larger-engined Minor 1000 range of models.

</td></tr>
</table>

had better performance than the Series MM, but in practice it was no better, and because it was also lower-geared the Series II soon got a reputation as an under-powered buzz-box.

Compared with the late-model Series MM, the styling of the Series II was unchanged, and except for the adoption of a horizontal-bar radiator grille and a restyled facia from October 1954, would not be changed throughout its four-year career. The existing range of body styles was continued, while new Traveller estate, van and pick-up derivatives were all added from 1953. At the beginning of 1954, the original Nuffield type of back axle (as shared with the MG YB and the TD) was dropped in favour of the Austin A30-type A-Series axle – this was another rationalization move.

The Series II was displaced by the Minor 1000 in the autumn of 1956.

Visually, the Series II Minor was little different from the MMs, except that later models had this horizontal grille style. The Traveller, with its wood battens, was a popular derivative.

From late 1956, the Minor became the Minor 1000, complete with 948cc engine, one-piece screen, larger rear window and better gear ratios. It was a much improved car.

Morris Minor 1000 (1956 to 1962)

When the Minor Series II gave way to the Minor 1000 in 1956, more than a mere power increase and enlarged engine was involved. There were styling changes, the character of the whole car was altered and pointed up-market, the handling balance felt even better than before, the overall gearing was raised and the gear ratios themselves were much improved.

The '1000' part of the title gave the clue, for the A-Series engine had been opened out from 803cc to 948cc and made more powerful and torquey in the process. The new gear ratios also made it much easier to push the car along fast – on this, and on the equivalent Austin A35, the effect was to produce what some people saw as budget-price sports saloons which could be used effectively in club races and rallies.

The styling changes centred around a curved, one-piece windscreen and an enlarged rear window, while inside the car there was a stubby, remote-control gear-change, a dished

Morris Minor 1000 specification

As for Morris Minor Series II except for:
Produced: Cowley, 1956-62 (and Abingdon, 1960-62), 554,048 Minor 1000s of all this type built.
Engine and transmission: 948cc, 62.9 x 76.2mm, 37bhp at 4,750rpm; 50lb ft at 2,500rpm.
Distinguishing features from previous model: One-piece instead of vee windscreen, enlarged rear window on saloons, plus badge details.
Typical performance: Maximum speed 73mph; 0-60mph 25.9sec; standing ¼-mile 23.4sec; overall fuel consumption 38mpg.
Derivatives: As for Series II.
Fate: Discontinued in 1962 in favour of larger-engined (1.1-litre) Minor 1000 range of models.

steering wheel, lids for the glove lockers and other details. A larger fuel tank was phased in five months later.

Until the Minor 1000 was upstaged by the sensational new Mini of 1959, it was BMC's most charismatic small car, and it sold so well that in January 1961 BMC was able to celebrate production of the millionth Morris Minor with a run of 350 lilac-coloured Minor Million two-door saloons.

The Minor 1000's character also included a hilarious tendency to axle tramp if all of its torque was used in hard cornering, a quite characteristic exhaust boom on the over-run, and a hard ride which was one of the reasons for its sensational smooth surface handling. This was definitely the most successful Morris Minor of its day, for the derivative which took over in the autumn of 1962 was overshadowed by more modern BMC machinery.

Morris Minor 1000 (1.1-litre engine) (1962 to 1971)

In the autumn of 1962, BMC introduced the first of their Pininfarina-styled front-wheel-drive cars, the Morris 1100, and at the same time they also fitted the newly-developed 1,098cc A-Series engine to several other BMC cars. It was in this process that the Morris Minor 1000 was upgraded, and at the same time a baulk-ring synchomesh gearbox was specified.

This was the last important change made to the Morris Minor range in what would eventually be a 23-year career. By this time it had slipped into a BMC backwater, where it was rarely touched by the engineers and rarely promoted by the advertising staffs or the dealers, but continued to sell (and sell, and sell!) on its long-established reputation. Even by the early 1960s it had become known as the archetypal 'District Nurse's car', or the car for the retired family, and its fine handling

The Minor 1000 Traveller sold in large numbers, for it had a very practical estate car rear end, and with its wood trim it looked very smart, too.

The Minor 1000 was always available with this convertible body style, which had permanent hood rails.

Glove locker lids came . . .

Morris Minor 1000 (1.1-litre) specification

As for Morris Minor 1000 (948cc) except for:
Produced: Cowley, 1962-71 (and Abingdon, 1962-64), 303,443 Minor 1000s of this type built. (Vans and pick-ups built at Adderley Park from 1964-71.)
Engine and transmission: 1,098cc, 64.58 x 83.72mm, 48bhp at 5,100rpm; 60lb ft at 2,500rpm.
Distinguishing features from previous model: Detail changes only over the years.
Typical performance: Maximum speed 74mph; 0-60mph 24.8sec; standing ¼-mile 22.8sec; overall fuel consumption 31mpg.
Derivatives: As for Series II. Tourer/convertible discontinued 1969, saloons discontinued at end of 1970, Traveller estate discontinued 1971, and light commercial versions by end of 1971.
Fate: Discontinued in 1971 and not replaced.

. . . and went on Minor 1000s, usually to suit the whims of the marketing departments or the cost controllers.

qualities had become outdated by front-wheel drive, all-independent suspension and other new-fangled developments. Glove box lids came and went, but this was about the height of the changes made.

Soon after British Leyland was formed, the specialized Minor production facility (which included a unique body plant in Birmingham) began to be run down. The convertible was dropped in June 1969, the saloons were discontinued in November 1970, and the last Traveller was built in April 1971. At least one 'new' Minor 1000 was built by a dealer, from parts, a few years later, and soon these cars were to figure strongly in the restoration world.

The Morris Oxford MO, complete with side-valve 1.5-litre engine, was announced in 1948 and built with this grille style until 1952.

The Morris Oxford MO's side-valve engine, tucked well down in a wide engine bay. This was the 1952 model, with revised battery position to suit the heater installation.

Morris Oxford Series MO specification

Produced: Cowley, 1948-54, 159,960 of all types built.
General layout: Pressed-steel unit-construction body-chassis structure in 4-seater, 4-door body style and various derivations. Front-mounted engine driving rear wheels.
Engine and transmission: Nuffield-designed Type VS15M engine, 4-cylinder, sv, in-line. 1,476cc, 73.5 x 87mm, 41bhp at 4,200rpm; 65lb ft at 1,800rpm; 4-speed gearbox, no synchromesh on 1st gear; steering-column gear-change; live (beam) rear axle with hypoid-bevel final drive.
Chassis: Independent front suspension, torsion bars and wishbones. Rack-and-pinion steering. Rear suspension by half-elliptic leaf springs and Panhard rod. Front and rear drum brakes. 5.25-15in tyres.
Dimensions: Wheelbase 8ft 1in; front track 4ft 5in; rear track 4ft 5in; length 13ft 10in; width 5ft 4.5in; height 5ft 2in. Unladen weight (approx) 2,210lb.
Typical performance: Maximum speed 71mph; 0-60mph 31.0sec; standing ¼-mile 24.5sec: overall fuel consumption 31mpg.
Distinguishing features from previous model: Entirely different from previous cars bearing the Oxford name. General styling family resemblance to Morris Minor MM announced at same time.
Derivatives: 4-door saloon (1948-54), Traveller estate car (1952-54), plus van and pick-up versions (1950-56).
Fate: Discontinued in 1954 and replaced by Series II models, which had B-Series ohv engines and completely new monocoque style.

Morris Oxford Series MO (1948 to 1954)

Once the Second World War was over, Morris urgently needed a whole range of new models for their 1939-variety offerings were very old-fashioned. It was only because world markets were anxious to buy *anything* that these cars sold so well in the 1945-48 period.

In that time, Morris virtually ignored the medium saloon

From 1952 to 1954, Morris Oxford MOs had a more rounded grille style than the original cars. All the saloons had four doors.

The Morris Oxford MO Traveller was a larger lookalike to the Minor Traveller with the same style of estate car back end. This was the final early-1950s derivative.

When BMC was formed in 1952, this was the facia style of the Morris Oxford MO, complete with a clock. The radio was not standard, of course. Export markets consumed a large proportion of car output in the early postwar years.

category, for their largest model was the Ten Series M, which had an overhead-valve 1,140cc engine (of the same basic design and closely related to that used in the MG Y-Series and the T-Series sports cars). The styling was classic 1930s, and although there was a unit-construction bodyshell, there was no independent suspension. Any postwar design of medium-size Morris, therefore, would have a warm reception.

The all-new car, known as the Oxford MO, was launched in October 1948 and was one of a complex family sharing the same passenger cabin and centre-rear style and engineering, which also included the new Morris Six, the Wolseley 4/50 and the Wolseley 6/80 cars. Although it was quite clearly a major new design, it exhibited a strange mixture of advanced and old-fashioned engineering. Its unit-construction four-door bodyshell was larger, but otherwise looked very much like the new Morris Minor, it had torsion-bar independent front suspension and it featured that fashionable fitting, a steering-column gear-change – yet it was fitted with a newly-designed, very cheap and cheerful side-valve 1½-litre engine.

The new Series MO Oxford was an unexciting car, and was frankly never meant to be anything else, for it had a stodgy performance and character which could not match the chassis. The gear-change, like most other British offerings of the period, was a disappointment, and few could see the point of having a bench front seat when the width between the front doors was only 50 inches.

In nearly six years in production, few important changes or improvements were made to the car and (unlike the Morris Minor) no attempt was made to re-engine it after the BMC merger was formalized. From October 1951, development changes included the option of a 3½kW heater and better seats, while from the autumn of 1952 there was a new two-door Traveller station wagon featuring timber in the rear section; both cars were treated to a polished stainless-steel radiator grille. One should also mention that there were van and pick-up versions from 1950 to 1956.

The Series MO gave way to a new Series II Oxford during 1954.

Morris' first new large-engined postwar model was the Six, which shared its body and style (except for the grille) with the Wolseley 6/80.

Morris Six (1948 to 1953)

After the Second World War, Morris abandoned the large-car field entirely for three years, allowing its stable-partner, Wolseley, to pick up a few sales wtih its 14/60 and 18/85 saloons and 25hp limousine models. However, the re-equipment programme which Sir Miles Thomas laid down before he was ousted by Lord Nuffield in 1947 included commonized medium and large Morris and Wolseley models,

and this included a new six-cylinder car called the Morris Six.

From this period, the Wolseley 6/80 was the more famous model, so perhaps it is fair to describe the Morris Six as a detuned 6/80 with different grille and interior appointments. The two cars shared the same 9ft 2in-wheelbase monocoque and different versions of the new Morris-designed (but Wolseley- influenced) overhead-camshaft straight six-cylinder engine. From the windscreen backwards, these cars were also the same as the Morris Oxford Series MO and Wolseley 4/50 four-cylinder models, this being the sort of sensible product planning which the Nuffield Organisation needed to embrace.

The Six's engine was a 2.2-litre unit producing 70bhp, and it used a single SU carburettor (whereas the Wolseley 6/80 had 72bhp and twin SUs), and although it had the same gearbox as that used in the Oxford Series MO, along with a steering-column gear-change, the overall gearing was much higher. A rather anonymous, traditional type of radiator grille was offered, this apparently having been specified at Lord Nuffield's insistence.

Like the Oxford MO, the Six was not an exciting car, and since only 12,400 of these cars were sold in five years (7,000 of them being exported), it must be judged as a commercial failure. The engine made a nice noise (but suffered from exhaust valve burning) and the long-nosed styling was dignified, if not exactly beautiful, but although the car had a creditable top speed it was never actually known as a high-performance machine. Its sister car, the Wolseley 6/80, not only had its 'police car' image to bolster it up, but was also much more tastefully trimmed and furnished. Development changes in the autumn of 1951 included the fitting of a pressurized cooling system, with an oil-bath air cleaner for UK cars from the autumn of 1952.

Although the 6/80's career prospered, therefore, that of the Six languished, and it was quietly dropped from production, at Cowley, in March 1953. It would be more than two years before its replacement, the Isis, came on to the scene.

Morris Six specification

Produced: Cowley, 1948-53, 12,400 cars built.
General layout: Pressed-steel unit-construction body-chassis structure in 4-seater, 4-door body style. Front-mounted engine driving rear wheels.
Engine and transmission: Nuffield-designed Type VC22M engine, 6-cylinder, ohc, in-line. 2,215cc, 73.5 x 87mm, 70bhp at 4,800rpm; 98lb ft at 1,800rpm; 4-speed gearbox, no synchromesh on 1st gear; steering-column gear-change; live (beam) rear axle with hypoid-bevel final drive.
Chassis: Independent front suspension, torsion bars and wishbones. Cam-gear steering. Rear suspension by half-elliptic leaf springs and Panhard rod. Front and rear drum brakes. 6.00-15in tyres.
Dimensions: Wheelbase 9ft 2in; front track 4ft 5in; rear track 4ft 5in; length 14ft 9in; width 5ft 5.0in; height 5ft 3in. Unladen weight (approx) 2,690lb.
Typical performance: Maximum speed 83mph; 0-60mph 22.4sec; standing ¼-mile 22.4sec: overall fuel consumption 20mpg.
Derivatives: Wolseley 6/80 saloon was basically the same car with different nose and trim; Oxford Series MO used same centre section, but short wheelbase and different engine.
Fate: Discontinued in 1953 and replaced in 1955 by Isis model, which had C-Series ohv engine and completely new monocoque style.

The first 'BMC' Morris Oxford was the Series II of 1954, though this was entirely designed at Cowley. The style was bulbous, and hid the new BMC B-Series engine and transmission.

The Oxford SII's facia layout was a long way from the driver's hands, and the gear-change was on the steering column, which was considerably offset. Cowley facias were similar, but without a horn ring, temperature gauge, or clock.

Morris Oxford Series II (1954 to 1956)

Although an engines and transmissions rationalization policy was applied almost as soon as BMC was founded, Austin and Nuffield were both encouraged to produce their own distinctly different new cars for some years after that. In 1952, therefore, Austin set about preparing its own successor to the A40 Somerset, while Morris started to design a new Oxford. The result was that the Morris Oxford Series II of May 1954 had unique styling and body-chassis engineering. As with the previous model, the cabin and rear end of the new Oxford was also intended for use in a new six-cylinder-engined car, in this case the Isis of 1955.

Nuffield, which retained its own engineering and styling teams for the time being, picked up the new corporate B-Series engine, gearbox and beam back axle assemblies, but clothed them in a bulbous, but quite unmistakable, new four-door bodyshell. Alec Issigonis had produced a scheme for an updated Morris Minor in 1951, and the latest Oxford was definitely influenced by that style. Since Issigonis also inspired the front-wheel-drive Mini, it was not surprising that some of the front end and other proportions of the Oxford SII were also reflected in the tiny new front-wheel-drive car. This was the first use of the new B-Series drive-line in a BMC *mass-production* car – although its original use, in a car only now going into series production, had been in the MG Magnette ZA sports saloon.

Compared with the Series MO Oxford which it replaced, the new SII was a fatter, squatter and altogether more spacious saloon, though the new car also used an independent suspension system by longitudinal torsion bars, allied to rack-and-pinion steering. There was a steering-column gear-change, and the column itself was somewhat offset so that on right-hand-drive models the driver's right arm had to reach considerably further than the left to get a grip on the steering

wheel rim. A front bench seat was standard, and the handbrake lever was tucked down the outside of that seat, close to the (UK) driver's right hand and to the door trim panel.

Naturally, Morris hoped to sell this car very strongly in export markets, and one odd feature of the original cars was

---

Morris Oxford Series II specification

Produced: Cowley, 1954-56, 87,341 cars built.
General layout: Unit-construction, pressed-steel body-chassis structure in 4-seater, 4-door style. Front-mounted engine driving rear wheels.
Engine and transmission: BMC B-Series engine, 4-cylinder, ohv, in-line. 1,489cc, 73.02 x 88.9mm, 50bhp at 4,800rpm; 78lb ft at 2,400rpm; 4-speed gearbox, no synchromesh on 1st gear; steering-column gear-change; live (beam) rear axle with hypoid-bevel final drive.
Chassis: Independent front suspension, torsion bars and wishbones. Rack-and-pinion steering. Rear suspension by half-elliptic leaf springs. Front and rear drum brakes. 5.50-15in tyres.
Dimensions: Wheelbase 8ft 1in; front track 4ft 5.5in; rear track 4ft 5in; length 14ft 2in; width 5ft 5in; height 5ft 3in. Unladen weight (approx) 2,464lb.
Distinguishing features from previous model: Entirely different car compared with earlier Morris Oxfords, with more bulbous style not shared with any other marque.
Typical performance: Maximum speed 73mph; 0-60mph 29.0sec; standing ¼-mile 24.2sec: overall fuel consumption 26mpg.
Derivatives: The Morris Isis, which followed, used the same basic monocoque and centre style. Estate Traveller, also built 1954-56. Series III and (estate) Series IV were derived from the original Series II.
Fate: Discontinued in 1956 in favour of the slightly updated facelift model.

---

that right-hand-drive models had semaphore indicators, while left-hand-drive cars had the flashing variety. There was a four-door saloon, and a typically Olde English half-timbered type of two-door Traveller estate car. As with its predecessor, the Oxford SII was not an exciting car, the very ordinary chassis engineering and performance being matched by what can only be called 'plain Jane' styling, particularly from the rear aspect. Nevertheless, getting on for 1,000 cars a week were normally built before it was displaced from the Cowley scene by the considerably facelifted Oxford Series III in 1956.

Morris Cowley (1954 to 1956)

Perhaps Morris Motors would never have produced this car if its BMC masters had not insisted on matching whatever Austin had on offer. However, since the rival Austin Cambridge was to be built as an A40 and an A50, the new medium-size Morris had to be produced as both an Oxford and a Cowley.

The Cowley of 1954 revived a famous name, which had originally appeared on a 'Bullnose' model and had been used on several small or medium-sized Morris models between the wars. All these cars had been built at Cowley, too, so there was never any doubt of their origins!

The 1954 Cowley was launched a couple of months after the Oxford Series II, and it shared the same bodyshell, chassis and mechanical layout. For the Cowley, however, the 1.2-litre version of the new BMC B-Series engine was used (which had 42bhp instead of the 50bhp of the Oxford), and the trim and furnishing was a stripped-out version of the Oxford's equipment. Certain parts plated on the Oxford were painted on the Cowley, and there was a general lack of chrome items and embellishment.

As with many other 'bargain basement' cars built over the years, the public did not really take to the Cowley and only

---

Morris Cowley specification

Produced: Cowley, 1954-56, 17,413 cars built.
General layout: Unit-construction, pressed-steel body-chassis structure, in 4-seater, 4-door saloon style. Front-mounted engine driving rear wheels.
Engine and transmission: BMC B-Series engine, 4-cylinder, ohv, in-line. 1,200cc, 65.48 x 88.9mm, 42bhp at 4,500rpm; 58lb ft at 2,400rpm; 4-speed gearbox, no synchromesh on 1st gear; steering-column gear-change; live (beam) rear axle with hypoid-bevel final drive.
Chassis: Independent front suspension, torsion bars and wishbones. Rack-and-pinion steering. Rear suspension by half-elliptic leaf springs. Front and rear drum brakes. 5.60-15in tyres.
Dimensions: Wheelbase 8ft 1in; front track 4ft 5.5in; rear track 4ft 5in; length 14ft 2in; width 5ft 5in; height 5ft 3in. Unladen weight (approx) 2,464lb.
Distinguishing features from previous model: Entirely different car compared with earlier Morris Cowleys, with more bulbous style, not shared with any other marque. Compared with Oxford Series II, had slightly less exterior brightwork.
Typical performance: Maximum speed 65mph; 0-60mph 37.5sec; standing ¼-mile 25.7sec; overall fuel consumption 29mpg.
Derivatives: The Morris Cowley 1500 which followed used the same basic monocoque style with enlarged engine.
Fate: Discontinued in 1956 in favour of the Cowley 1500.

17,413 were sold, as compared with 87,341 Oxfords over the same period. Not even the larger-engined Cowley 1500 which followed could rescue this 'poor-man's Oxford' reputation.

The Morris Cowley of 1954 was really a stripped-out Oxford with a 1.2-litre B-Series engine.

The Morris Oxford became a Series III in late 1956, with a facelifted body style, including rear fins and this very contrived optional duo-tone colour scheme.

Morris Oxford Series III (1956 to 1959)

BMC scheduled a comprehensive facelift for most of its existing cars for the autumn of 1956, and one result was that the Oxford Series II became the Oxford Series III after only two and a half years. Although the latest car was still recognizably the same design as before, it had received a thorough 'spring clean' in many respects.

The two mechanical innovations were the use of a higher-compression engine (55bhp instead of the Series II's 50bhp), and the offer of two-pedal semi-automatic Manumatic transmission as an option, but most of the work had gone into freshening up the styling and the equipment.

To counter criticism of the rather plain looks of the Series II, the SIII was given a deeply fluted bonnet pressing, together with longer rear wings incorporating embryo fins and revised tail-lamp treatment. Inside the car there was a new facia layout, where not only the styling was different, but the controls were brought several inches closer to the driver's hands; on the SII it had sometimes been easier to operate switches with a spare foot than with a spare hand!

Saloon and estate car derivatives carried on as before, but in mid-1957 the wood-battened Series III estate was displaced by the new Series IV; don't be confused by the fact that no Series IV saloon was ever marketed. Like other medium-sized BMC cars of the period, the Oxford also benefited from the use of a centre-floor gear-lever after spring 1958, but there were few other technical changes before the model was dropped and replaced by the Farina-styled Oxford Series V. A ½-ton van version was also produced, from 1956 to 1960.

Morris Oxford Series III specification

As for Morris Oxford Series II except for:
Produced: Cowley, 1956-59, 58,117 cars built (including Series IV estate Travellers).
Engine and transmission: 1,489cc, 73.02 x 88.9mm. 55bhp at 4,400rpm; 78lb ft at 2,400rpm. 4-speed gearbox, no synchromesh on 1st gear; optional Manumatic transmission. Centre-floor gear-change from spring 1958.
Chassis: 5.60-15in tyres.
Distinguishing features from previous model: Fins on rear quarters, duo-tone colour schemes, restyled bonnet.
Typical performance: Maximum speed 73mph; 0-60mph 27.1sec; standing ¼-mile 23.9sec: overall fuel consumption 29mpg.
Derivatives: Series III estate (Traveller) until 1957, when replaced by Series IV estate. Cowley 1500 was mechanically identical. ½-ton van and pick-up produced 1956-60.
Fate: Discontinued in 1959 in favour of new Farina-style Oxford Series V range.

Morris Cowley 1500 (1956 to 1959)

The original Cowley of 1954 not only suffered from a lack of 'glamour' compared with the Oxford from which it was derived, but it also suffered from a lack of performance.

When the Oxford was restyled for 1957 as the Oxford Series III, the original Cowley model was dropped altogether and the similarly restyled Cowley 1500 became the only Cowley model in the price lists. However, it sold even less well than the original 1.2-litre model, and was a forgotten car by the time the last example was built in 1959.

From late 1956, the Morris Cowley became the Cowley 1500 and had the same facelifted bodyshell as the Oxford SIII.

Morris Cowley 1500 specification

As for Morris Cowley except for:
Produced: 1956-59, 4,623 cars built.
Engine and transmission: 1,489cc, 73.02 x 88.9mm. 55bhp at 4,400rpm; 78lb ft at 2,400rpm. 4-speed gearbox, no synchromesh on 1st gear; optional Manumatic transmission.
Chassis: 5.60-15in tyres.
Distinguishing features from previous model: Fins on rear quarters and restyled bonnet.
Typical performance: Maximum speed 73mph; 0-60mph 27.1sec; standing ¼-mile 23.9sec; overall fuel consumption 29mpg.
Fate: Discontinued in 1959 and not replaced.

Morris Oxford Series IV Traveller specification

As for Morris Oxford Series III estate except for:
Produced: Cowley, 1957-60. Production included in Oxford Series III figures.
Distinguishing features from previous model: 4 doors instead of 2, and all-steel body.
Typical performance: Maximum speed 76mph; 0-60mph 29.9sec; standing ¼-mile 24.2sec: overall fuel consumption 26mpg.
Fate: Discontinued in 1960 in favour of new Farina-style Series V estate type.

Morris Oxford Series IV Traveller (1957 to 1960)

The Morris Oxford Series IV was only ever built as a Traveller estate car, and the use of the Series IV title was only justified because it was a completely different type and construction of body structure from the Series III which it replaced.

Although the same basic front end, underpan and running gear was carried over from Series III to Series IV, the Series III had the traditional half-timbered construction of the 'greenhouse', whereas the Series IV had an all-steel shell. Not only that, but the Series III had two passenger doors whereas the Series IV had four. Also, for the first time the Traveller bodyshell was entirely produced from the Cowley assembly plant by the Pressed Steel Company, across the road.

As with the saloon, this latest Traveller had a very contrived wing-line of chrome striping, so that an optional two-tone colour scheme could be applied, and a centre-floor gear-change was made available from the spring of 1958.

Even though the Series III saloon was dropped early in 1959 to make way for the new Farina-styled Series V, the Series IV Traveller carried on for some time, the last not being produced until April 1960.

The only Morris Oxford Series IV was an estate car, with four passenger doors and an all-steel shell. Dumpy, but practical.

Morris Isis (1955 to 1956)

In the years after the Second World War, Morris had little success with large-engined cars. The Six of 1948-53 had been rather overshadowed by the more interesting Wolseley 6/80, and the Isis which followed it fared no better.

The Morris Six was killed off in the spring of 1953, and it was not until July 1955 that its replacement, the Isis, was launched. The Isis, a rather ungainly relative of the Series II

The Morris Isis was really the successor to the Six, and was a long-wheelbase version of the Oxford SII's monocoque with a C-Series engine.

The Isis facia and instrument panel resembled that of the Oxford SII, except that the steering column was realigned and less offset.

Morris Isis specification

Produced: Cowley, 1955-56, 8,541 cars built.
General layout: Unit-construction, pressed-steel body-chassis structure in 4-seater, 4-door saloon style. Front-mounted engine driving rear wheels.
Engine and transmission: BMC C-Series engine, 6-cylinder, ohv, in-line. 2,639cc, 79.38 x 88.9mm, 86bhp at 4,250rpm; 124lb ft at 2,000rpm; 4-speed gearbox, no synchromesh on 1st gear; steering-column gear-change; live (beam) rear axle with hypoid-bevel final drive. Optional Borg-Warner overdrive from early 1956.
Chassis: Independent front suspension, torsion bars and wishbones. Bishop cam-gear steering. Rear suspension by half-elliptic leaf springs. Front and rear drum brakes. 6.00-15in tyres.
Dimensions: Wheelbase 8ft 11.5in; front track 4ft 5.5in; rear track 4ft 5in; length 14ft 10in; width 5ft 5in; height 5ft 3.75in. Unladen weight (approx) 2,960lb.
Distinguishing features from previous model: Entirely different car compared with earlier six-cylinder Morris Six, with more bulbous style not shared with any other marque.
Typical performance: Maximum speed 86mph; 0-60mph 17.8sec; standing ¼-mile 21.1sec; overall fuel consumption 23mpg.
Derivatives: Saloon and 2-door estate Traveller models built.
Fate: Discontinued in 1956 in favour of Isis Series II.

Morris Oxford, was only built for three years and it sold no better than the Six had done. Compared with the Austin Westminsters, with which it shared so much of the running gear, it was a commercial failure.

Like the Six compared with the Oxford MO, the Isis was really a longer-wheelbase version of the Oxford Series II with a six-cylinder engine. In the case of the Isis, the wheelbase stretch of the monocoque was 10.5 inches (and 8 inches on the overall length), while the engine was an 86bhp version of the new 2.6-litre C-Series design allied to a four-speed gearbox with a steering-column gear-change. The torsion-bar independent front suspension was like that of the Oxford SII,

As with the Oxford, so with the Isis, there was a Traveller estate car, the two cars sharing the same body aft of the windscreen.

but in the case of the Isis there was Bishop cam-gear steering ahead of the front suspension, rather than the Oxford's rack-and-pinion behind it. One result of this was that the steering column of the Isis was not offset as much as that of the Oxford, which gave a more satisfactory driving position.

Except that the bonnet was considerably longer than that of the Oxford (from certain angles it even seemed that the Isis shell was bending slightly at the scuttle!) the styling and general proportions of the two cars were virtually the same. As with the Oxford Series II, an estate car version with only two passenger doors (and complete with Ye Olde English Cottage timbering around the hind-quarters) was also produced, this going on sale at the same time as the saloon. Like the other C-Series engine/transmission BMC models of the period, too, from early 1956 the Isis also gained an optional Borg-Warner overdrive.

Reading between the lines of *The Autocar* road test, we can soon decide about the character of the Isis, for the analysis included these words:

'. . . the Isis appeals to the businessman, active or retired, who enjoys effortless travel with economy, and who does not place rapid acceleration and high-speed handling among a car's most important characteristics . . . . . Unobtrusive, it assumed the role of willing horse in our thoughts . . . . . The combination of suspension and steering would not appeal to the driver who likes to take his corners fast, for although the Isis will get round bends quickly and safely on a dry road, there is more roll than a driver likes, and the general softness and mild degree of spring damping detracts from the accuracy of the steering. The mild damping . . . . . contributes to the car's tendency to hop around at the rear . . . . . The Isis must be driven with care when the road surface is wet and not entirely smooth . . .'

No wonder it didn't sell all that well! After a showroom life of only 16 months, the original Isis was replaced by the Isis Series II in October 1956.

Morris Isis Series II (1956 to 1958)

Since production of the Isis, which was mechanically related to the Oxford Series II, was so limited, its specification was subservient to that of the Oxford. Accordingly, when the Oxford's styling was changed, so too was that of the Isis, and when the Oxford's timber-decorated Traveller estate car was dropped, so was the equivalent Isis Traveller. In the Isis' case, however, no all-steel four-door Traveller was ever put on sale.

The Isis Series II was introduced in October at the same time as the Oxford Series III and shared this car's improvements. There was a new fluted bonnet pressing, longer rear wings with small fins and different tail-lamps, a new facia style and a deeply dished steering wheel.

For the Isis Series II, there was also a floor-mounted manual gear-change, the lever being positioned on the right side of the driving position on right-hand-drive cars (the layout was very similar to that of the Nuffield-designed Riley Pathfinder installation), and there were also the options of Borg-Warner overdrive or Borg-Warner automatic transmission. At the same time the engine was given a higher compression ratio, and peak power went up from 86bhp to 90bhp.

Although the Isis Series II was a better car than before, it sold even less well, for only 3,614 were built. The Traveller disappeared in October 1957 and the saloon was dropped in April 1958. This was the last large-engined Morris motor car, for the front-wheel-drive Morris 2200 of 1972 was only a 2.2-litre machine, and in any case was a badge-engineered British Leyland Austin.

Morris Isis Series II specification

As for Morris Isis except for:
Produced: Cowley, 1956-58, 3,614 cars built.
Engine and transmission: 90bhp at 4,500rpm; 124lb ft at 2,000rpm. Optional Borg-Warner automatic transmission. Side-floor gear-change.
Distinguishing features from previous model: Fluted bonnet style, and fins at rear quarters.
Derivatives: Saloon and estate car as before, estate car discontinued in autumn 1957.
Fate: Discontinued in 1958 and not directly replaced. Effectively replaced in 1959 by new C-Series Farina Austin and Wolseley saloons.

The Isis became Series II in late 1956, complete with a fluted bonnet; the new grille had already appeared on Series Is in 1956. The Traveller was continued.

This Isis II had a facelifted tail, including fins – the Oxford SIII and the Cowley 1500 shared the same sheet metal.

The first of the BMC B-Series Farina-styled Morris cars was the Oxford Series V, introduced in 1959. In almost every way it was identical to the Austin A55 Cambridge Mk II.

152

The Farina-styled Morris Oxford Series V had prominent tail-fins, but very little body decoration on its flanks.

The Series V Morris Oxford had a well-equipped facia. This version had the centre-floor gear-change, but a steering-column change was optional, too.

Compared with the superseded Series III and Series IV models, there was a floor gear-change as standard (though a steering-column change was still optional), and there was no sign of the Manumatic transmission which had been available on the previous models.

Only a four-door saloon style was available at first, but a Traveller estate was announced in the autumn of 1960. Both of these cars had a short, but commercially successful life before, in another restyling and re-engineering orgy, BMC were to improve all their B-Series *and* C-Series family cars in the autumn of 1961.

Morris Oxford Series V (1959 to 1961)

The simple way to describe the life and times of the Oxford Series V is to say 'see Austin A55 Cambridge Mk II', for the two cars were almost identical. Purely because there were Austin and Morris dealer chains to be serviced all round the world, BMC decided to produce two differently badge-engineered versions of the same car. The other important difference, of course, was that the Cambridge was assembled at Longbridge and the Oxford at Cowley.

The B-Series Farina range, when completed, comprised five models – Austin, Morris, MG, Riley and Wolseley – and in fact the Morris Oxford was the fourth of these types to be launched, in March 1959. Compared with the Austin Cambridge, the differences were confined to facia and steering wheel styles, the front grille and the badging, plus different seating arrangements and a different paint job when duo-tone paintwork was ordered. As far as the customer was concerned, the UK price of the Morris was £14 more than that of the equivalent Austin.

Morris Oxford Series V specification

Produced: Cowley, 1959-61, 87,432 cars built.
Engine layout: Unit-construction pressed-steel body-chassis structure in 4-seater, 4-door saloon style. Front-mounted engine driving rear wheels.
Engine and transmission: BMC B-Series engine, 4-cylinder, ohv, in-line. 1,489cc, 73.02 x 88.9mm, 52bhp at 4,350rpm; 82lb ft at 2,100rpm; 4-speed gearbox, no synchromesh on 1st gear; centre-floor gear-change; live (beam) rear axle with hypoid-bevel final drive.
Chassis: Independent front suspension, coil springs and wishbones. Cam-and-lever steering. Rear suspension by half-elliptic leaf springs. Front and rear drum brakes. 5.90-14in tyres.
Dimensions: Wheelbase 8ft 3.25in; front track 4ft 0.87in; rear track 4ft 1.87in; length 14ft 10in; width 5ft 3.5in; height 4ft 11.75in. Unladen weight (approx) 2,473lb.
Distinguishing features from previous model: Entirely different car compared with earlier Nuffield-styled Oxford Series III, bearing family resemblance to other related Farina models.
Typical performance: Maximum speed 78mph; 0-60mph 23.6sec; standing ¼-mile 22.5sec; overall fuel consumption 28mpg.
Derivatives: Estate car from late 1960. The Oxford Series VI of 1961 was a further developed version of the Oxford Series V. All other B-Series 'Farinas' were closely related.
Fate: Discontinued in 1961 in favour of the updated Series VI model.

When the Morris Oxford became Series VI, its rear fins were trimmed back, with new tail-lamps, the wheelbase was increased, and the tracks were widened. It also had a 1.6-litre engine.

Morris Oxford Series VI (1961 to 1971)

At the same time as all the other Farina-styled BMC B-Series models were upgraded in the autumn of 1961, the Morris Oxford Series V became the Series VI. In almost every respect, the improvements made were the same as those applied to the Austin Cambridge when it progressed from being A55 to A60. The obvious visual change was that the rear fins, which had been rather obvious on the Series V, were cut down into an altogether more graceful shape, and of course this meant that the tail-lamps were also new.

Compared with the Oxford Series V, the Series VI had a slightly longer wheelbase and wider tracks, and anti-roll bars on front and rear suspensions to firm up the roadholding, the result being a car which felt more stable and handled better.

The important mechanical change, however, was that the B-Series engine was enlarged to 1,622cc, this making the Oxford a genuine 80mph car for the first time. At the same time, BMC made Borg-Warner Type 35 automatic transmission optional, though the take-up was very limited in the first few years.

Once it had been introduced, the Oxford was virtually ignored by BMC's product planners and engineers, for although it sold successfully, if not spectacularly, for 10 years, the 1971 model was almost the same as the 1961 variety. Even after British Leyland was formed, the Oxford soldiered on until the Traveller was dropped in February 1969 and the saloon finally disappeared in April 1971. It was immediately replaced on the Cowley scene by the new British Leyland-designed Morris Marina.

Morris Oxford Series VI Diesel (1961 to 1971)

Exactly as for the Austin A60 Cambridge, BMC also put a diesel-engined Morris Oxford Series VI on sale from the end of 1961. At first this slow, rattly and rather smoky model was only available on the export market, but it was introduced into the UK from the spring of 1962.

Frankly, its only merit was its fuel consumption (up to

Morris Oxford Series VI specification

As for Oxford Series V except for:
Produced: Cowley, 1961-71, 208,823 cars built.
Engine and transmission: 1,622cc, 76.2 x 88.9mm. 61bhp at 4,500rpm; 90lb ft at 2,100rpm. 4-speed gearbox, no synchromesh on 1st gear; centre-floor gear-change; optional automatic transmission.
Dimensions: Wheelbase 8ft 4.35in; front track 4ft 2.6in; rear track 4ft 3.4in; length 14ft 6.5in.
Distinguishing features from previous model:
Different front and rear bumpers, changed profile to rear fins, new grille and facia, new waistline mouldings.
Typical performance: Maximum speed 81mph; 0-60mph 21.4sec; standing ¼-mile 21.8sec; overall fuel consumption 26mpg.
Derivatives: Estate car version also available. Close mechanical and family resemblance to all other B-Series Farina models.
Fate: Discontinued in 1971 (estate car in 1969) in favour of the forthcoming and entirely different Morris Marina.

Morris Oxford Series VI Diesel specification

As for petrol-engined Morris Oxford Series VI except for:
Engine and transmission: BMC B-Series diesel engine, 1,489cc. 40bhp at 4,000rpm; 64lb ft at 1,900rpm.
Dimensions: Unladen weight 2,520lb.
Typical performance: Maximum speed 66mph; 0-60mph 39.4sec; standing ¼-mile 25.9sec; overall fuel consumption 37mpg.
Distinguishing features from previous models: Diesel engine, and obvious diesel 'knock' when being driven.
Fate: Discontinued in 1971 and not replaced.

154

The early 1960s Morris Oxford Series VI range comprised a four-door saloon and a useful Traveller derivative.

40mpg if driven appropriately), for with a 66mph top speed, reached after much leisurely acceleration, and that rather obtrusive engine, there was little else to attract the customer. For that reason, nearly every Oxford Diesel was sold as a hire car.

Morris Mini Minor (later called Mini) (1959 to 1967)

The tiny front-wheel-drive Mini range was designed by Alec Issigonis' team at Longbridge, but it was always intended that it should be built in various guises with different badges. Thus, at the time the Austin Seven was announced, the Morris Mini Minor was also put on sale. The public did not like either of these names, took up the 'Mini' part of the title as a proper name, and eventually forced BMC to fall in with this convention.

Although the Austins were made at Longbridge at first and the Morris Minis at Cowley, the two cars were structurally and mechanically identical and were priced at exactly the same level. As far as the customer was concerned, there was no real reason to choose one make or the other, his choice mainly being influenced by how near was his appropriate BMC dealer.

Like the Austin Minis, the Morris versions had a transverse engine, front-wheel drive, a very compact seating package and the most amazingly nimble roadholding behaviour. Like the Austins, too, they suffered from teething troubles which have now passed into motoring folklore, and they attracted all manner of music hall-style jokes because of their small size and low stance.

Publicity pictures of the 1959 Mini Minor showed it swallowing mountains of luggage. There seems to be a bit of a problem, here . . .

155

First of the front-wheel-drive Morris cars was the Mini Minor, which was introduced in 1959.

Early Mini Minors had a single instrument binnacle and a wide parcel shelf, plus door bins to add to stowage capacity.

Like the Austin Mini, the Morris Mini soon grew from merely being a two-door saloon model into a veritable family, with the longer-wheelbase estate car (Traveller) arriving on the scene in 1960, along with van and pick-up versions. The interesting feature of Morris Mini production was that only the saloons were built at Cowley, around the basis of Pressed Steel Company bodyshells; *all* other types were assembled at Longbridge, intermingled with Austin, Riley and Wolseley derivatives. It was also a measure of BMC's flexibility (some would call it disorganization) that from time to time Austin Mini saloons were built at Cowley and Morris Minis at Longbridge!

Morris Mini development proceeded hand-in-hand with

The Traveller version of the Morris Mini Minor had a 4in longer wheelbase, but the same type of independent rear suspension.

Morris Mini Minor specification

Produced: Saloons at Cowley, other styles at Longbridge, 1959-67, 5,000,000 of *all* types of Mini built by early 1986.

General layout: Pressed-steel unit-construction body-chassis structure, in 4-seater, 2-door saloon or estate body styles, plus vans and pick-ups. Transversely and front-mounted engine driving front wheels.

Engine and transmission: BMC A-Series engine, 4-cylinder, ohv, in-line. 848cc, 62.9 x 68.26mm, 34bhp at 5,500rpm; 44lb ft at 2,900rpm; 4-speed gearbox, no synchromesh on 1st gear; centre-floor gear-change; spur-gear final drive. Optional automatic transmission from late 1965.

Chassis: Independent front suspension, rubber cones and wishbones. Rack-and-pinion steering. Independent rear suspension by rubber cone springs and trailing arms. Front and rear drum brakes. 5.20-10in tyres. Hydrolastic suspension units, interconnected front and rear, from late 1964.

Dimensions: Wheelbase 6ft 8in; front track 3ft 11.75in; rear track 3ft 9.9in; length 10ft 0.25in; width 4ft 5in; height 4ft 7in. Unladen weight (approx) 1,290lb.

Typical performance: Maximum speed 72mph; 0-60mph 27.1sec; standing ¼-mile 23.6sec: overall fuel consumption 40mpg.

Distinguishing features from previous models: Totally different in every way from any previous Austin or other BMC models, with front-wheel drive and tiny 10in wheels.

Derivatives: Austin and Morris Mini Minors were identical in all but badging. Mini-Cooper, Mini-Cooper S and Mini-Moke followed (see separate entries). 2-door saloon from 1959, longer-wheelbase estate car from 1960, plus van and pick-up light commercial vehicles.

Fate: Discontinued in 1967 in favour of Mk II models.

that of the Austin models, which meant that better-trimmed Super models were announced in September 1961 and Super de Luxe types in October 1962. The original wood-decorated Traveller body style of 1960 was joined by an alternative all-steel Traveller in October 1962.

Baulk-ring synchromesh was gradually applied from late 1962, Hydrolastic suspension on the saloons replaced rubber cones from late 1964, and there was an AP four-speed automatic transmission option from late 1965.

Within two years of announcement, the BMC Mini had become something of a classless British institution, so there never seemed to be an urgent need to restyle it, or dramatically improve its specification. After eight years, therefore, the original type merely gave way to the Mk II models, which came on the scene in October 1967.

Morris Mini Mk II (1967 to 1969)

In the autumn of 1967 the entire Mini range was freshened up, for by this time it had been on the market for eight years. Even though it was still selling very well indeed, it was time to make improvements, short of changing the car completely. Then, as earlier, the Morris Mini was exactly the same car as the Austin Mini (except for its badging), so it is really only necessary to refer the reader to the Austin Mini Mk II section.

The cars had a new and slightly larger front grille, an enlarged rear window and different tail-lamps, while the Super de Luxe had the three-instrument facia panel of the Mini-Cooper type.

There was now a choice of engines – 848cc or 998cc – the latter being the same as that already fitted to Riley Elf and Wolseley Hornet versions of the Mini; 998cc-engined cars were also treated to the Mini-Cooper type of remote-control gear-change. AP automatic transmission was optional with

When the Morris Mini became 'Mk II' in October 1967 there was a 998cc engine option, and a revised grille and tail-lamps.

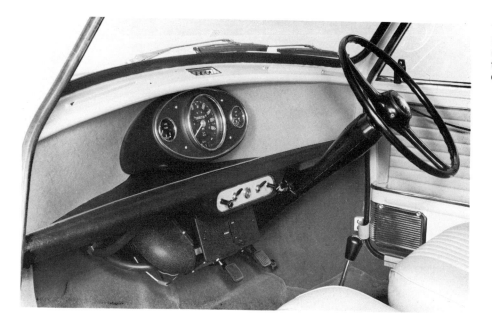

The Mk II Super de Luxe version of the Morris Mini had this oval three-instrument facia nacelle, and the 998cc engine had a transmission with a remote-control gearchange.

Morris Mini Mk II specification

Produced: Cowley and Longbridge, 1967-69, more than 5,000,000 Minis of all types built by early 1986.
General layout: Pressed-steel unit-construction body-chassis structure, in 4-seater, 2-door body styles. Front and transversely-mounted engine driving front wheels.
Engine and transmission: BMC A-Series engine, 4-cylinder, ohv, in-line. 848cc, 62.9 x 68.26mm, 34bhp at 5,500rpm; 44lb ft at 2,900rpm. Alternative engine (for Mini 1000), 998cc, 64.58 x 76.2mm, 38bhp at 5,250rpm; 52lb ft at 2,700rpm. 4-speed gearbox, no synchromesh on 1st gear at first, but all-synchro from autumn 1968; optional automatic transmission; centre-floor gear-change; spur-gear final drive.
Chassis: Independent front suspension, Hydrolastic units and wishbones. Rack-and-pinion steering. Independent rear suspension by Hydrolastic units and trailing arms. Interconnection between front and rear suspensions. Front and rear drum brakes. 5.20-10in tyres.
Dimensions: (Saloon) Wheelbase 6ft 8in; front track 3ft 11.4in; rear track 3ft 9.8in; length 10ft 0.25in; width 4ft 7.5in; height 4ft 5in. Unladen weight (approx) 1,400lb.
Typical performance: 850 as original Mini. (1000) Maximum speed 75mph; 0-60mph 26.2sec; standing ¼-mile 22.7sec; overall fuel consumption 34mpg.
Distinguishing features from previous models: Enlarged rear window, different front grille, tail-lamps, remote-control gear-change and trim changes, plus 998cc option.
Derivatives: As with early Minis, sold as saloon, or longer-wheelbase (7ft 0.1in) estate (Traveller), plus vans and pick-ups. Also see Mini-Coopers and Mini-Cooper S. Austin Mini was same car with different badges.
Fate: Discontinued in 1969 as marque badges were dropped; all Minis became, simply, BL Minis.

both engines, and an all-synchromesh manual transmission was phased-in during 1968.

This type of Mini only lived for two years, for after British Leyland was formed a rationalization process was begun. Accordingly, from the autumn of 1969, the Austin and Morris Minis were de-badged and the cars thereafter took on the marque name of 'Mini'.

[Those Minis are, strictly speaking, British Leyland products, so they must be considered in a separate section. Coded ADO 20 in BMC's design hierarchy, these cars had wind-up door windows and a reversion to the original rubber-cone suspension springs.]

Morris Cooper (later known as Morris Mini-Cooper) (1961 to 1967)

Like the Mini range from which this type was derived, the Mini-Cooper was an Issigonis-BMC design from Longbridge, with virtually no input from the rump of the Morris company. Like other Minis, however, the Mini-Cooper was sold as an Austin or a Morris through appropriate dealers, at the same price and with the same specification and list of extras. Assembly was always at Longbridge, the two marques being built on the same production lines, and the only distinguishing features were in different grilles and badging.

To keep the peace, as it were, the works Mini-Coopers were sometimes raced or rallied as Austins and sometimes as Morris cars. On at least one occasion, a team rally car turned up with different identification at the front and rear of the car!

Like the Austin equivalent (see the Austin section), the Morris Mini-Cooper received 'wet' Hydrolastic suspension from late 1964 and a reclining front seat option from the end of 1965. It was replaced by the improved Mk II version in the autumn of 1967.

In 1961, the official name was Morris Mini-Cooper, but most people just called it Mini-Cooper. The 997cc engine produced 55bhp and a sparkling performance. This was a splendid little sports saloon.

Morris Mini-Cooper specification

Produced: Longbridge, 1961-67, 101,242 Mini-Coopers of all types (Austin and Morris, Mk I and Mk II) built.
General layout: Pressed-steel unit-construction body-chassis structure, in 4-seater, 2-door saloon style. Front and transversely-mounted engine driving front wheels.
Engine and transmission: BMC A-Series engine, 4-cylinder, ohv, in-line. Original engine, 997cc, 62.43 x 81.28mm, 55bhp at 6,000rpm; 54lb ft at 3,600rpm; from 1964, 998cc, 64.58 x 76.2mm, 55bhp at 5,800rpm; 57lb ft at 3,000rpm. 4-speed gearbox, no synchromesh on 1st gear; centre-floor gear-change; spur-gear final drive.
Chassis: Independent front suspension, rubber cones and wishbones. Rack-and-pinion steering. Independent rear suspension by rubber cone springs and trailing arms. Front disc and rear drum brakes. 5.20-10in tyres. 145-10in tyres from 1964. Hydrolastic suspension units, interconnected front to rear, from late 1964.
Dimensions: Wheelbase 6ft 8in; front track 3ft 11.75in; rear track 3ft 9.9in; length 10ft 0.25in; width 4ft 5in; height 4ft 7in. Unladen weight (approx) 1,400lb.
Typical performance: Maximum speed 85mph; 0-60mph 18.0sec; standing ¼-mile 20.9sec: overall fuel consumption 27mpg.
Distinguishing features from previous models: Larger, tuned, engine and remote-control gear-change, plus front disc brakes, different grille, facia and badging.
Derivatives: Austin Mini-Cooper was identical in every way but for badges and grille. Mk II models (see separate entries) followed. Mini-Cooper S had specialized engine and transmission components.
Fate: Discontinued in 1967 in favour of Mk II model.

Morris Mini-Cooper S (1963 to 1967)

As with all other Minis, the Morris Mini-Cooper S was merely a badge-engineered version of the Austin, and was always built next to it on the assembly lines at Longbridge. Bodyshells, engines and transmissions were all from the same source, the two cars had exactly the same specification, and were always the same price. New engine sizes and performance options

Morris Mini-Cooper S specification

As for Morris Mini-Cooper Mk I except for:
Produced: Longbridge, 1963-67, 4,017 1071S, 972 970S and 40,449 1275S of all types (Austin and Morris, Mk I and Mk II) built.
Engine and transmission: A-Series engine, three types: 970S: 970cc, 70.6 x 61.91mm, 65bhp at 6,500rpm; 55lb ft at 3,500rpm. 1071S: 1,071cc, 70.6 x 68.26mm, 70bhp at 6,000rpm; 62lb ft at 4,500rpm. 1275S: 1,275cc, 70.6 x 81.28mm, 76bhp at 5,800rpm; 79lb ft at 3,000rpm.
Chassis: 145-10in tyres.
Dimensions: Front track 4ft 0.6in; rear track 3ft 11.3in; unladen weight (approx) 1,410lb.
Distinguishing features from previous models: Wider-rim wheels, radial-ply tyres and different badging.
Typical performance: (1071S) Maximum speed 95mph; 0-60mph 12.9sec; standing ¼-mile 18.9sec; overall fuel consumption 27mpg. (1275S) Maximum speed 97mph; 0-60mph 10.9sec; standing ¼-mile 18.2sec; overall fuel consumption 30mpg. (970S) No authentic independent figures available.
Derivatives: Austin and Morris models were identical in every way. Mk II models followed (see separate entry).
Fate: Discontinued in 1967 in favour of Mk II models.

From 1963, there was the Morris Mini-Cooper S, at first only with a 1,071cc engine. Recognition points included the 'S' badges at front and rear and the radial-ply tyres.

were always made at the same time.

The first in this family, therefore, was the 1071S, built only in 1963 and 1964, after which it was replaced by the 970S 'homologation special' of 1964 and 1965, along with the very successful 1275S of 1964 to 1967. For all further details, see the Austin entries.

Morris Mini-Cooper Mk II (1967 to 1969)

The upgrading of the Mini-Cooper to Mk II specification was all part of the general improvement in Minis which was undertaken in the autumn of 1967. Technically there were no immediate changes, though a new grille and the enlarged rear window and new tail-lamps were all adopted. From the summer-autumn of 1968 an all-synchromesh gearbox was progressively phased in to the specification.

However, once British Leyland was formed and it became known that the new management team was determined to get out of all the existing royalty and consultancy agreements, the

The Morris Mini-Cooper Mk II had appropriate rear badging to identify it from other Mk II models showing the larger rear screen and revised tail-lamps. It was introduced in 1967.

days of the Mini-Cooper were clearly numbered. When the mass-production car became the (ADO 20) Mini for 1970, the opportunity was taken to get rid of the Riley Elf and Wolseley Hornet Minis, and at the same time the Mini-Cooper (but *not* the Mini-Cooper S) was dropped completely.

Even though there was a Morris Mini-Cooper, it was always built at Longbridge, alongside the Austin equivalent.

Morris Mini-Cooper Mk II specification

As for Morris Mini-Cooper Mk I except for:
Produced: Longbridge, 1967-69.
Engine and transmission: All-synchromesh gearbox from autumn 1968.
Typical performance: (also for 998cc-engined Mk I model) Maximum speed 90mph; 0-60mph 16.8sec; standing ¼-mile 20.1sec; overall fuel consumption 33mpg.
Distinguishing features from previous models: Different front grille and enlarged rear window, plus new badging.
Derivatives: Morris was identical to Austin of the period except for badging.
Fate: Discontinued in 1969 and not replaced

Morris Mini-Cooper S Mk II (1967 to 1969)

The Mk II version of this very deep-breathing, long-legged and successful little sports saloon was the same in every respect as its Austin equivalent. Even though drivers using these cars in competition disliked the installation, all Mk IIs had Hydrolastic suspension, which did not give as firm or precise a ride-handling combination as the original rubber-cone spring system.

For all details, see the Austin Mini-Cooper S Mk II description.

Morris Mini-Cooper S Mk II specification

As for Morris Mini-Cooper S Mk I except for:
Produced: Longbridge, 1967-69.
Engine and transmission: Only 1,275cc engine available; all-synchromesh transmission fitted during summer 1968.
Distinguishing features from previous models: Different front grille and enlarged rear window, plus new badging.
Derivatives: Morris was identical to Austin of the period except for badging. From spring 1970, Mk II became Mini (*not* Morris) Mk III, with wind-up windows.
Fate: Discontinued in 1970 in favour of Mk III, itself discontinued in 1971 and not replaced.

The Morris Mini-Cooper S Mk II was distinguished by the use of a 120mph speedometer. Simple, but complete equipment – competition cars tended to get a lot more added!

Morris Mini-Moke (1964 to 1968 in UK, to date overseas)

Although the Mini-Moke was badged as an Austin *and* a Morris, it was really a Longbridge (Austin) invention, and was always built on the Austin assembly lines at Longbridge.

For details of this interesting 'fun machine', consult the Austin Mini-Moke entry.

Morris Mini-Moke specification

Produced: Longbridge, 1964-68 (then in Australia and latterly in Portugal). 14,518 Mokes of all types built in UK, and overseas production continues (approx 40,000 in total by end of 1985).
General layout: Pressed-steel unit-construction body-chassis structure, in 4-seater, no-door open body style. Front and transversely-mounted engine driving front wheels.
Engine and transmission: BMC A-Series engine, 4-cylinder, ohv, in-line. 848cc, 62.9 x 68.26mm, 34bhp at 5,500rpm; 44lb ft at 2,900rpm. 4-speed gearbox, no synchromesh on 1st gear; centre-floor gear-change; spur-gear final drive.
Chassis: Independent front suspension, rubber cone springs and wishbones. Rack-and-pinion steering. Independent rear suspension by rubber cone springs and trailing arms. Front and rear drum brakes. 5.20-10in tyres.
Dimensions: Wheelbase 6ft 8in; front track 3ft 11.4in; rear track 3ft 9.8in; length 10ft 0in; width 4ft 3.5in; height 4ft 8in. Unladen weight (approx) 1,430lb.
Typical performance: Maximum speed 84mph; 0-60mph 27.9sec; standing ¼-mile 23.5sec; overall fuel consumption 40mpg.
Distinguishing features from previous models: Mini-Mokes were utterly different from all other Minis, with stark open four-seater bodies, sometimes with hood and skimpy weather protection.
Derivatives: None except for prototype twin-engined versions and Austin or Morris-badged versions.
Fate: Discontinued in UK in 1968, but production transferred to BMC Australia and eventually Portugal.

The Farina-styled Morris 1100 was announced in 1962, the first of the new transverse-engined, Hydrolastic-suspended range.

The Morris 1100 had this unique style of facia and instrumentation, which was dropped at the end of 1967.

Morris 1100 (1962 to 1967)

By the late 1950s the Nuffield section of the BMC combine was beginning to feel rather neglected. After an early flurry of new-model activity (with cars such as the Oxford Series II, the Riley Pathfinder, the MG Magnette ZA and the MGA being authorized) it found itself frozen out while the Longbridge end of BMC began to produce a series of corporate cars, all thoroughly badge-engineered and mostly with a Morris version included.

It must have been a real boost to Nuffield's morale, therefore, not only that its team was given the job of starting the design and development of the new ADO 16 front-wheel-drive

project, which was to have Farina styling, but that the first version of this car to be put on sale, from August 1962, would be called a Morris – the new Morris 1100.

Perhaps it was over-optimistic for one British magazine to call the new 1100 a 'world car', but there was no doubt that it was a very sensibly engineered machine which, *if* it could be built and serviced properly, would appeal to drivers in many countries.

Much of the detail design has already been analyzed in the Austin 1100 section, so it is only necessary to recall that in many ways the ADO 16 1100 design was a 'grown-up' Mini in many respects, for it used an enlarged, long-stroke, 1,098cc version of the same transversely-mounted A-Series engine, the same gearbox-in-sump transmission design and the same type of front-wheel-drive installation.

The important step forward from the Mini was that the all-independent suspension was by Hydrolastic units, interconnected front-to-rear, which gave a much softer ride, though one which could become quite bouncy as the units' settings and condition deteriorated. The 1100, however, was still a very good-handling car, though its steering and response was never as immediate or as crisp as that of the Mini.

The original car was only to be sold as a four-door saloon in the UK (though two-door shells were also available for the Morris, and its sister car, the MG 1100, to use in some export markets), but it had very crisp styling and, like the Mini, was extraordinarily roomy inside. Distinguishing features of the Morris, as opposed to the Austin, model were the horizontal-barred grille and the instrument panel binnacle.

In the next five years, the Morris 1100 was so successful that few important changes had to be made to keep it in the best-selling list. However, from the autumn of 1965 the AP four-speed automatic transmission became optional, and from March 1966 a useful two-door Traveller estate car was also made available; similar changes were made to the Austin 1100 at the same time. On the Traveller, reclining front seats were optional (as they also were on the saloons by this time), and the rear seats could also be folded so that there was a large (but somewhat uneven) potential bed for emergency use.

When the time came for BMC to undertake a mid-term facelift to their smaller front-wheel-drive cars, the 1100s became Mk II in the autumn of 1967.

The first Morris 1100s coming off the assembly line at Cowley, identified by the distinctive horizontal grille style.

Morris 1100 specification

Produced: Cowley (and some cars at Longbridge), 1962-67, 703,000 saloons, plus combined total of 41,000 Austin/Morris estates of all types built 1962-74.
General layout: Pressed-steel unit-construction body-chassis structure, in 4-seater, 2-door and 4-door saloon styles. Front and transversely-mounted engine driving front wheels.
Engine and transmission: BMC A-Series engine, 4-cylinder, ohv, in-line. 1,098cc, 64.58 x 83.72mm, 48bhp at 5,100rpm; 60lb ft at 2,500rpm. 4-speed gearbox, no synchromesh on 1st gear; from 1965 optional AP automatic gearbox, 4 forward gears; centre-floor gear-change; spur-gear final drive.
Chassis: Independent front suspension, Hydrolastic units and wishbones. Rack-and-pinion steering. Independent rear suspension by Hydrolastic units, trailing arms and anti-roll bar. Interconnection between front and rear suspensions. Front disc and rear drum brakes. 5.50-12in tyres.
Dimensions: Wheelbase 7ft 9.5in; front track 4ft 3.5in; rear track 4ft 2.9in; length 12ft 2.7in; width 5ft 0.4in; height 4ft 4.7in. Unladen weight (approx) 1,800lb.
Typical performance: Maximum speed 78mph; 0-60mph 22.2sec; standing ¼-mile 22.7sec: overall fuel consumption 33mpg.
Distinguishing features from previous models: Entirely new type of Morris model with Pininfarina styling.
Derivatives: Austin 1100 was the same car, with different badges and details. MG 1100, Riley Kestrel and Wolseley 1100 models were all slightly modified versions, too. Estate Traveller for 1966 and 1967. Mk II (see separate entry) was same car with minor changes.
Fate: Discontinued in 1967 and replaced by Mk II models.

This was the compact engine bay of the Morris 1100, with a transversely-mounted A-Series engine, the gearbox beneath it 'in the sump' and the radiator to the left (top of this picture).

Along with other front-wheel-drive 1100s, the Morris became a Mk II in the autumn of 1967. There was a two-door version – this being the de Luxe variety.

Morris 1100 Mk II (1967 to 1971)

In the autumn of 1967 the reshuffle to the Morris 1100 range was rather more comprehensive and thoughtful than might have been expected of BMC, for by this time they were becoming known for their vacillation and lack of incisive thinking in so many new-model programmes. Basically, the 1100's style and specification was not only freshened-up, but a choice of engines was made available *and* a choice of specifications.

The original 1100, therefore, was replaced by the 1100 Mk II and the 1300. The 1100 Mk II was now officially available in

two-door and four-door saloon guise and was also built as a de Luxe and a Super de Luxe type.

Compared with the original car, there was a new front grille, commonized with the Austin, except that the actual badges were different, and the rear fins had been cropped back and now had a new type of tail-lamp. Perforated wheel discs completed the exterior retouching.

Inside the car, the original Morris 1100 type of instrument panel had been abandoned, for Austins and Morrises were now to share the same installation. The de Luxe models (the cheaper variety) had simple central instrument clusters, with a parcel shelf to either side, while the Super de Luxe types had a strip speedometer, with switch gear on each side of a similar type to the original Austin 1100.

All the existing options (automatic transmission, reclining front seats and other details) of the Mk I were carried on to the Mk II models, and the Traveller estate car was offered for the first six months only. By this time there had been something of a pruning of types, for the two-door Super de Luxe and four-door de Luxe types also disappeared from the price lists.

An all-synchromesh gearbox cluster, which had been announced for the 1300s in October 1967, was standardized in the 1100s from the autumn of 1968, after which the model carried on, virtually unchanged, until the summer of 1971.

At this point the 1100/1300 range became Mk III, but as the new British Leyland-designed Morris Marina had been launched and was beginning to fill up the available assembly line space at Cowley, the Morris-badged 1100 was quietly allowed to die.

Morris 1100 Mk II specification

As for Morris 1100 Mk I except for:
Produced: 1967-71.
General layout: 2-door and 4-door saloon bodies always available, estate Traveller only for 1967 and 1968.
Engine and transmission: All-synchromesh manual gearbox from mid-1968.
Distinguishing features from previous models: Different front grille, chopped-off tail-fins with different tail-lamps, different trim and details.
Derivatives: 1100 Mk II was itself a derivative of original 1100. Also 1300 (see separate entry). Austin 1100/1300 was same car; also MG, Riley, Wolseley and Vanden Plas all used same basic design.
Fate: Discontinued in 1971 and not replaced.

From late 1967, the Morris 1300 became available, with a productionized 1,275cc engine and a distinctive grille.

Below left, Morris 1300s (1967 to 1971) were available with two or four doors. The grille was standardized with the Austin equivalent.

The Morris 1300's facia and instruments were the same as those found in the badge-engineered Austin 1300s of the period.

Morris 1300 specification

As for original 1100 model except for:
Produced: Cowley, 1967-71, for production totals, see original 1100 entry.
General layout: 2-door and 4-door and estate car types available.
Engine and transmission: 1,275cc, 70.6 x 81.28mm, 58bhp at 5,250rpm; 69lb ft at 3,000rpm. All-synchromesh manual transmission from mid-1968.
Dimensions: Unladen weight (approx) 1,780lb.
Typical performance: Maximum speed 88mph; 0-60mph 17.3sec; standing ¼-mile 20.7sec; overall fuel consumption 30mpg.
Distinguishing features from previous models: Different grille, chopped-off fins, different tail-lamps and trim.
Derivatives: Austin and Morris models were identical in every way.
Fate: Discontinued in 1971 in favour of Morris Marina models.

Morris 1300 (1967 to 1971)

At the same time as BMC turned the Mini into a Mini Mk II, with the option of an enlarged engine, they carried out the same improvement process on the larger 1100 models. A few of the more up-market MG/Riley/Wolseley/Vanden Plas 1100s had been fitted with 58bhp 1,275cc A-Series engines during the summer of 1967, so it was no surprise that this became the regular option for the revised Mk II models for 1968.

The Mk II 1300 picked up all the styling and equipment changes already described for the 1100 Mk IIs, while the new engine was henceforth to be matched by a new all-synchromesh gearbox. As with the 1100 Mk II, there was a slimming-down of the model range in the spring of 1968, but the 1300 remained as a very important and very successful member of the Morris range until the autumn of 1971, when the British Leyland management reshuffled the trim and styling once again into the final Mk III specification.

The Morris 1300GT was announced in the autumn of 1969, and was really an MG 1300 Mk II with a different nose, a four-door style and rather different trim. Some people thought it was also a better bargain. This car was identical to the Austin 1300GT.

Side view of the Morris 1300GT of 1969, with contrasting trim stripe and special wheel trims for identification.

Morris 1300GT (1969 to 1971)

In every respect except its badging, the Morris 1300GT was the same car as the Austin 1300GT, and was built for two years as a very successful cheaper version of the MG 1300 Mk II, for it shared that car's mechanical specification and instrument layout. For all details, see the Austin 1300GT entry.

Morris 1300GT specification

Produced: Cowley, 1969-71, 19,304 cars built.
General layout: Pressed-steel unit-construction body-chassis structure, in 4-seater, 4-door saloon style. Front and transversely-mounted engine driving front wheels.
Engine and transmission: BMC A-Series engine, 4-cylinder, ohv, in-line. 1,275cc, 70.6 x 81.28mm, 70bhp at 6,000rpm; 74lb ft at 3,250rpm. 4-speed gearbox, all-synchromesh; centre-floor gear-change; spur-gear final drive.
Chassis: Independent front suspension, Hydrolastic units and wishbones. Rack-and-pinion steering. Independent rear suspension by Hydrolastic units and trailing arms. Interconnection between front and rear suspension. Front disc and rear drum brakes. 145-12in tyres.
Dimensions: Wheelbase 7ft 9.5in; front track 4ft 3.5in; rear track 4ft 2.9in; length 12ft 2.7in; width 5ft 0.4in; height 4ft 4.7in. Unladen weight (approx) 1,900lb.
Typical performance: Maximum speed 93mph; 0-60mph 15.6sec; standing ¼-mile 20.0sec: overall fuel consumption 27mpg.
Distinguishing features from previous models: Compared with other 1300s, GT had different grille, wheel trims, badging and interior, plus twin-carb engine.
Derivatives: MG 1300 Mk II and near-identical Austin 1300GT were to the same design.
Fate: Discontinued in UK in 1971, effectively (but not directly) in favour of larger-engined Morris Marina models.

The Morris 1300GT's facia and instruments were shared with the Austin, MG and Riley equivalents of the period. The differences were minor, notably the panel finish being less glossy than the MG and Riley models.

The Morris 1300 Traveller had the same two-door body style as the Austin 1300 Countryman. This was the Mk III of 1971 – there was no Mk III saloon in UK markets.

Morris 1300 Mk III (1971 to 1973)

When the time came for British Leyland to reshuffle the 1100/1300 models which they had inherited from BMC, they had to take account of the fact that the Morris Marina had arrived and was dominating the scene at Cowley. Accordingly, when the Morris 1300 was upgraded from Mk II to Mk III, the saloon car was dropped from the UK market (but some Morris 1300 saloons were built at Longbridge for export), and only the Traveller (also built at Longbridge) was available in the UK.

All 1300 Mk IIIs had a new matt-black grille with three horizontal brightwork bars, new seat styling and a new facia panel, and although there was now water splash protection over the transversely-mounted engine, there were no significant improvements to the power unit itself. The last of the 1300 Mk III Travellers was built in April 1973.

Morris 1300 Mk III specification

As for 1300 Mk II model except for:
Produced: Longbridge, 1971-73. Some saloons for export, but only Traveller estate cars available in UK.
Distinguishing features from previous models: New grille with matt-black finish and 3 horizontal bars, plus badging, facia and seat style revisions
Fate: Discontinued in 1973 and not replaced.

The Morris 1300 Mk III, sold only as a Traveller estate car in the UK, had a simple facia style, shared with the Austin 1300 Mk III.

Like other transverse-engined BMC cars of the period, the Morris 1300 Mk III Traveller's engine had a plastic cowl to protect the ignition elements from water and debris.

167

Morris 1800 specification

Produced: Cowley (later Longbridge), 1966-68, 373,356 1800s and 2200s of *all* types, badges and years built.
General layout: Pressed-steel unit-construction body-chassis structure, in 5-seater, 4-door saloon style. Front and transversely-mounted engine driving front wheels.
Engine and transmission: BMC B-Series engine, 4-cylinder, ohv, in-line. 1,798cc, 80.26 x 88.9mm, 80bhp at 5,000 rpm; 100lb ft at 2,100rpm. 4-speed gearbox, all-synchromesh; centre-floor gear-change; spur-gear final drive.
Chassis: Independent front suspension, Hydrolastic units and wishbones. Rack-and-pinion steering (optional power assistance from late 1967). Independent rear suspension by Hydrolastic units and trailing arms and anti-roll bar. Interconnection between front and rear suspensions. Front disc and rear drum brakes. 175-13in tyres.
Dimensions: Wheelbase 8ft 10in; front track 4ft 8in; rear track 4ft 7.5in; length 13ft 8.2in; width 5ft 7in; height 4ft 7.5in. Unladen weight (approx) 2,645lb.
Typical performance: Maximum speed 90mph; 0-60mph 17.1sec; standing ¼-mile 20.5sec: overall fuel consumption 24mpg.
Distinguishing features from previous models: Entirely new type of front-wheel-drive BMC model without ancestors.
Derivatives: Austin 1800/Morris 1800 was the same car, with different badges and details. Wolseley 18/85 model was slightly modified version, too. Mk II (see separate entry) was same car with minor changes.
Fate: Discontinued in 1968 and replaced by Mk II models.

The Morris 1800 was announced in 1966 and was the same car in every way, except for its badging, as the Austin 1800.

Morris 1800 (1966 to 1968)

By the mid-1960s, BMC were completely wedded to their 'badge-engineer everything' philosophy, so after the new B-Series-engined Austin 1800 was put on sale in 1964, it was really only a matter of time before a Morris equivalent was announced. The only surprise was that it took so long for this move to be enacted.

The Morris 1800 was launched in March 1966, and was identical to the Austin 1800 in every way except for a different front grille and badging; the price was the same, too. For further details, see the Austin 1800 entry.

The Morris 1800 Mk II's engine was a 1.8-litre B-Series, transversely mounted and driving the front wheels.

The Morris 1800 became Mk II in 1968 and was completely commonized with the Austin 1800 Mk II, with the same grille and details, but different badges.

The Morris 1800 Mk II's tail style incorporated vertical tail-lamp units and clipped-back fins.

Morris 1800 Mk II specification

As for Morris 1800 Mk I except for:
Produced: 1968-72. Approximately 46,000 Mk II models built.
Engine and transmission: 86bhp at 5,300 rpm; 101lb ft at 3,000rpm. Optional AP 4-speed automatic transmission.
Chassis: 165-14in tyres.
Typical performance: Maximum speed 93mph; 0-60mph 16.3sec; standing ¼-mile 19.9sec: overall fuel consumption 27mpg.
Distinguishing features from previous models: New front grille (common with Austin), different rear wings and vertical tail-lamp clusters, trim, facia equipment and other details.
Derivatives: 1800 Mk II was itself a derivative of the original 1800. Austin 1800/Morris 1800 was effectively the same car; Wolseley 18/85 used same basic design. Mk III (see separate entry) followed on.
Fate: Discontinued in 1972 in favour of Mk III derivative.

Morris 1800 Mk II (1968 to 1972)

The Morris 1800 became Mk II in May 1968, just as BMC was formally being submerged into the new British Leyland combine. The changes were relatively minor and, as before, the car was almost identical in every way to the Austin 1800.

See Austin 1800 Mk II entry for further details.

Morris 1800 Mk II 'S' (1968 to 1972)

Here was an oddity. For some years, BMC had tended to phase-in Austin and Morris cars at the same time, so that none of their dealers could complain that one marque was gaining an advantage over the other. However, when the time came to introduce an upgraded, faster and more sporty version of the front-wheel-drive 1800, only the Morris version was introduced at first. The Morris made its bow in October 1968, whereas the launch of the equivalent Austin was delayed for a year.

Although the new car was launched after British Leyland was founded, it was very definitely a BMC design. The basic engineering layout of the 1800 Mk II was not changed, but a

The Morris 1800 Mk II 'S' had an MGB-type engine tune and near 100mph top speed. The contrasting colour strip was a means of identification.

Notice the 'S' on the boot-lid, which identifies this Morris 1800 as a Mk II 'S' version.

great deal of work had gone into developing the engine. In place of the basic 1800's single-carburettor engine, the 'S' had twin SUs and a revised camshaft profile (that of the MGB), together with a higher compression ratio and a three-branch tubular exhaust manifold. The result was a more powerful and torquey unit which provided the 1800 with near-100mph performance, and this was kept in check by the provision of Girling four-spot front brake calipers.

Visually the only identifying feature, compared with the ordinary 1800, was the new rear badge at first, though a

contrasting-colour stripe was later added along the car's flanks. Like the Austin 1800 Mk II 'S', this car was dropped by British Leyland in 1972 in favour of the six-cylinder-engined 2200 model.

Morris 1800 Mk III (1972 to 1975)

Four years after British Leyland had taken over the existing BMC product range, they continued to milk it to the profitable limit. At the same time, therefore, as they produced the six-cylinder-engined front-wheel-drive 2200 models, they also produced the final Mk III versions of the long-running 1800s.

The Morris and Austin models were identical in every way – see the Austin entry for details.

Morris 1800 Mk III specification

As for Morris 1800 Mk II except for:
Produced: 1972-75, approx 23,000 Mk IIIs built.
Distinguishing features from previous models: New grille style (commonized with Austin) and slightly revised facia, with handbrake between seats.
Derivatives: 1800 Mk III was itself a derivative of the Mk II. Austin 1800/Morris 1800 was the same basic car.
Fate: Discontinued in 1975 in favour of new British Leyland-designed ADO 71 18/22 range.

Morris 1800 Mk II 'S' specification

As for Morris 1800 Mk II except for:
Produced: 1968-72.
Engine and transmission: 96bhp at 5,700 rpm; 106lb ft at 3,000rpm; automatic transmission not available.
Typical performance: Maximum speed 99mph; 0-60mph 13.7sec; standing ¼-mile 19.4sec: overall fuel consumption 22mpg.
Distinguishing features from previous models: No external changes except for 'S' badging on tail, plus twin-carb engine.
Derivatives: 1800 Mk II 'S' was itself a derivative of original 1800 Mk II. Austin 1800/Morris 1800 was the same basic car.
Fate: Discontinued in 1972 in favour of 2200 model.

The Morris 1800 Mk II 'S' had a twin-carburettor B-Series engine. It was identical in every way with the Austin 1800 Mk II 'S' of the same period.

Chapter 8

MG

Throughout the BMC period, MG cars sold very well indeed, whether as sports cars or saloon models. Almost every MG of the period relied heavily on an Austin or a Morris car for its running gear, but somehow there was usually a goodly dose of the 'Abingdon touch' in the design which helped give all the cars a great deal of character.

In broad terms, however, it is fair to describe all MGs built, or newly introduced, up until 1953 as 'Morris Specials', whereas all those built thereafter were 'BMC Specials' – the ZA Magnette saloon being the first to use modified BMC engine and transmission assemblies.

MG entered the BMC period with two models, which shared many common chassis parts and were distinctly traditional in style and engineering; the sports car was the TD and the saloon was the YB. Both were built at the Abingdon factory, a few miles south of Cowley and Oxford. Although the YB was dropped in 1953, in the same year the TD was facelifted and became the TF, this being further uprated into the TF1500 in the summer of 1954.

Thereafter, the BMC influence spread rapidly. The next generation of MG saloons was the ZA Magnette of 1953, which combined a modified version of the Nuffield-designed Wolseley 4/44 unit-construction bodyshell with the brand-new BMC B-Series engine and transmission. This was a very pretty sports saloon, which was much more successful than the obsolete YB, and it became the ZB series (with a Varitone derivative) from late 1956.

To replace the TF1500 there was the MGA, the first-ever sleek and streamlined MG sports car. This was also fitted with a BMC B-Series engine and transmission, all these parts being almost the same as those used in the ZA Magnette saloon. The MGA appeared in 1955, and was built in one of several different versions until 1962, by which time more than 100,000 had been assembled. The one truly exciting version of this car was the Twin-Cam, with a twin-ohc engine specially developed and manufactured by the Morris Engines Branch; this engine was never used in any other MG model.

It was around this time that the MG marque began to lose some of its identity. In 1959, not only was the Z-Series Magnette saloon displaced by the Magnette Mark III, which was effectively a badge-engineered Austin/Morris B-Series Farina model, but this car was actually assembled at Cowley. This was the first MG since 1929 to have been produced outside Abingdon. The Mark III, and its improved derivative the Mark IV, were not as successful as the Z-Series Magnettes, and were dropped in 1968 as BMC itself was about to disappear.

By this time there were four other MG model ranges to be considered – three new sports cars and one new saloon. The sports car was the Midget, a name reborn, but the design itself was identical in almost every way with the Austin-Healey Sprite. The first new-generation Midgets were produced in 1961 and the last in 1979, the cars produced during the last five years having disfiguring energy-absorbing bumpers at front and rear and Triumph Spitfire 1500 engines and transmissions.

The other mass-market sports car was the MGB, which was announced in 1962, needs no introduction, was built until the end of 1980, and sold more than half a million examples. When the MGB died, so did Abingdon – but that was 12 years after BMC itself had also gone. The MGC of 1967 appeared just before the end of the BMC period, was really a replacement for the Austin-Healey 3000 Mk III, and combined MGB styling with a reworked version of the Austin (ADO 61) 3-litre's engine and torsion-bar front suspension – it only lasted for two years. The MGB GT V8 of 1973-76 was a British Leyland invention.

Finally, we come to the MG 1100/1300 range. The MG 1100 was a tuned-up version of the transverse-engined front-wheel-drive Morris 1100 saloon, made its bow in 1962, and was always assembled at Cowley. It was built in various forms until 1971.

The MG marque still exists, of course, but *all* the modern products are developed versions of Austin models, for there have been no new-design MG sports cars.

Postscript
In 1968, the SMM & T *Register of Model Titles* had the following MG model names listed, but not used on BMC cars to that date:
Magister
Maxi
Mogul
Midgette

The MG TD was the first sports car from Abingdon to have independent front suspension. Surprisingly, though, it was not available with wire-spoke wheels until the end of its run.

The MG TD, like previous MG sports cars, had a slab tank and an exposed spare wheel.

MG TD (1950 to 1953)

MG was already a very successful part of the Nuffield empire before BMC was formed, and in the years to come it would expand even further. In 1952, however, its only sports car was the TD, which was traditional in its engineering and old-fashioned in its looks. Nevertheless, in less than four years, the TD sold faster than *any* previous MG motor car.

In essence, the TD, which had been launched in January 1950, was a mixture of modified MG YA (saloon) running gear and the basic styling lines of the TC which it replaced. Although it was to be a car which sold very well, particularly in the United States, the TD was really a late-1930s type of sports car, built for the 1950s.

Tradition and continuity, however, were facets of the MG character which had always served the company well; these features, and a great deal of character, made the TD very appealing.

It had been designed in 1949, in a great hurry, by shortening the chassis of a YA saloon and cobbling-up a new bodyshell along the 1930s-style lines of the TC, but wider and altogether more squat. The production chassis-frame, in fact, was very different again, for its side members swept up and over the back axle line, whereas those in the YA had been underslung.

The TD, therefore, used the 1,250cc Type XPAG engine which had been in production since 1939, along with the gearbox which had always backed it. However, it was the first MG sports car to use a hypoid-bevel back axle (this was related to the Morris Minor component), and the first to have independent suspension and rack-and-pinion steering (both of which had been 'lifted' from the YA saloon). One major disappointment, however, was that it was fitted with steel disc wheels – wire wheels not being available, even as an option, until the very end of the production run. The bodyshell,

---

MG TD specification

Produced: Abingdon, 1949-53, 29,664 cars built.
General layout: Separate chassis-frame with wooden-framed, steel-skinned body structure, in 2-seater sports car style. Front-mounted engine driving rear wheels.
Engine and transmission: Nuffield XPAG-type, 4-cylinder, ohv, in-line. 1,250cc, 66.5 x 90mm, 54bhp at 5,200rpm; 64lb ft at 2,600rpm. 4-speed gearbox; no synchromesh on 1st gear; live (beam) rear axle with hypoid-bevel final drive.
Chassis: Independent front suspension, coil springs and wishbones. Rack-and-pinion steering. Rear suspension by half-elliptic leaf springs. Front and rear drum brakes. 5.50-15in tyres.
Dimensions: Wheelbase 7ft 10in; front track 3ft 11.4in; rear track 4ft 2in; length 12ft 1in; width 4ft 10.6in; height 4ft 5in. Unladen weight (approx) 1,930lb.
Typical performance: Maximum speed 80mph; 0-60mph 19.4sec; standing ¼-mile 21.3sec; overall fuel consumption 30mpg.
Derivatives: TD was original type, TDII followed (slightly changed) from summer 1951. TD Mk II was tuned-up version (rare) with 60bhp at 5,500rpm. Typical performance – 81mph top speed, 0-60mph 16.5sec, standing ¼-mile 20.8sec, overall fuel consumption 25mpg.
Fate: Dropped in favour of MG TF model in 1953.

---

produced at the Morris Bodies Branch, in Coventry, had a wooden skeleton frame and pressed-steel skin panels – the door sides were cutaway, there were removable sidescreens and a build-up soft top, and the no-nonsense specification included a large slab fuel tank facing the tail, a bench-type seat

This is the facia and instrument panel of the MG TD, which was available in left-hand-drive form.

backrest, and no provision for a fresh-air heater, radio, or indicators.

There *was*, however, provision for right-hand or left-hand drive (the TD was the first left-hand-drive MG ever to be built), which made the car more readily saleable overseas, and the new chassis gave the car a much more supple ride than the TC had ever had. The TD, indeed, behaved like a thoroughly modern little sports car, while looking like an older model – this being a combination which many traditionalists found irresistible.

In four selling seasons, very few important changes were made to the TD. By 1952, when BMC was founded, it was already in TDII specification, and a limited number were eventually sold with tuned-up engines and stiffened-up suspension, being called TD Mk II. The TD was nimble, but it was neither fast, nor economical, and by 1952 it was already beginning to look obsolete. Its replacement, the TF, was really a great disappointment.

MG TF (1250) (1953 to 1954)

In 1952, a new MG sports car design was already on the way, but when it was put up to BMC for project approval this was refused. As a stop-gap, therefore, MG had to produce a face-lift for the TD, to keep it going for two more years. This stop-gap was the TF, much derided at the time, but now looked on as the prettiest of all the T-Series cars.

Even MG enthusiasts admit that the TF was not really designed, but just 'happened'. On to an almost unchanged TDII chassis (except that wire-spoke wheels were to become freely available), MG developed a facelifted bodyshell which retained the same centre-section as the TD, but had a lowered nose with partly-faired headlamps, a more swept tail and a new facia panel with all its instruments grouped in the centre of the car.

MG TF specification

As for MG TD except for:
Produced: Abingdon, 1953-54, 6,200 TF1250 cars built.
Engine and transmission: 57bhp at 5,500rpm; 65lb ft at 3,000rpm.
Chassis: Front anti-roll bar fitted. 145-13in radial-ply tyres.
Dimensions: Length 12ft 3in; width 4ft 11.7in; height 4ft 5in; unladen weight (approx) 1,930lb.
Typical performance: Maximum speed 80mph; 0-60mph 19.0sec; standing ¼-mile 21.5sec; overall fuel consumption 25mpg.
Distinguishing features from previous model:
Lowered nose, sloping grille and headlamps partly faired in; more sloping tail and different facia style.
Derivatives: TF1500 took over from TF (1250) in summer 1954, with 1,466cc engine, 72 x 90mm, 63 bhp at 5,000rpm; 76lb ft at 3,000rpm. Typical performance – 85mph top speed, 0-60mph 16sec, standing ¼-mile 20.5sec, overall fuel consumption 30mpg. 3,200 TF1500s built.
Fate: Discontinued in spring 1955 and replaced by all-new MGA sports car.

The TF was not what MG enthusiasts were expecting of a 1954-model car, and it must be admitted that it was only marginally better than the TD in looks, appointments and performance. Perhaps this explains why MG made haste to improve it in the only way they were allowed – which was to produce a larger engine and develop the TF1500 model.

In more recent years, the original TF has become known as the TF1250. Whatever people thought about the styling at the time, it clearly has great 'classic' appeal these days, for a replica, the Naylor, was put on sale in the mid-1980s, using modern BL running gear and a newly-designed chassis.

Compared with the TD, the MG TF had a slightly lowered front and a more rakishly styled tail.

The MG TF was the first MG sports car to have headlamps partly faired in to the bodywork.

were built, but it helped plug the gap at Abingdon.

Quite simply, the TF1500 was the TF with a larger engine. By using a re-cored cylinder block and an enlarged cylinder bore, the XP-Series engine was enlarged from 1,250cc to 1,466cc. In the process, the engine type changed from XPAG to XPEG (E = Enlarged, perhaps?), an extra 6bhp was found, and peak torque rose from 65lb ft to 76lb ft.

The only visual change to the car was the use of 'TF1500' badges on the sides of the bonnet (even then, not all TF1500s seemed to have such badges). There was no change to overall gearing, and the car was only marginally quicker than before.

Such is the perversity of fashion, however, that the TF1500 is now thought to be the most desirable of the T-Series family. At the time, however, it was dropped from production when it stopped selling, several months before the MGA could be made ready, and for a time the production lines at Abingdon were very quiet indeed.

The MG TF had an instrument panel with octagonal-shaped dials.

MG TF1500 (1954 to 1955)

To provide the TF model with one last spark of life, and to keep it selling until an all-new model, the MGA, could be made ready, MG designers produced the TF1500. This was only in production from July 1954 to April 1955, and only 3,400 cars

MG MGA 1500 (1955 to 1959)

Even before the TF was developed, MG's chief designer, Syd Enever, had produced an all-new layout for an MG sports model. This car, which carried an Abingdon project code of EX175 and used TF running gear, was shown to, but rejected

The MGA of 1955 had sleek full-width styling and a 100mph top speed to go with this exceptionally strong chassis.

The MGA 1500 had an unmistakable rear style, with enclosed boot space.

by, BMC in the autumn of 1952 – they went ahead with the Austin-Healey 100 project instead. However, it was hastily given approval and committed for production in 1954, when it became obvious that the TF was not selling at all well.

The original car had been designed around a massively rigid new chassis-frame which used TF-type suspension and rack-and-pinion steering, and this was retained for the production car. By this time, however, BMC's rationalization plans were proceeding apace, and the planners commanded that B-Series running gear should be used. The old XPEG engine, plus the related transmission and back axle components, were therefore taken out of the design, and what were in effect modified versions of the MG ZA Magnette engine and transmission were used instead.

The body style was sleek, full-width and beautiful. It bore no resemblance to any previous production MG style, but was very close indeed to the special shape developed at Abingdon for an MG TD which had been raced by George Phillips at Le Mans in 1951. Unlike previous MG sports car bodies, there was no structural wood in it, the whole shell being a

conventional (by current standards) pressed-steel assembly. At first there was only an open two-seater roadster version, this having removable sidescreens and a rather tiny luggage boot. There was, however, provision for a fresh-air heater (not standard on these early cars) and there were separate seats, proper indicators and a spacious cockpit.

Not only that, but this was an MG sports car with real up-to-date performance. The first cars' top speed was nearly 100mph, this being a real quantum leap forward from the TF1500, which had very poor aerodynamics.

MGA prototypes with light-alloy bodies raced at Le Mans and in the Tourist Trophy race before the production car was ready. In fact there was *no* MG sports car in production at Abingdon in the May-to-August 1955 period, which was the point at which MGA assembly began, the car officially being launched in September 1955.

For the next four years the cars sold as rapidly as they could be made at Abingdon. After a year, a second body derivative, the coupe, was introduced, this combining the chassis and general lines of the original car with a bubble-top hardtop, a

From the autumn of 1956, there was a permanent hardtop coupe alternative to the MGA roadster, with wind-up windows.

The MGA's engine bay was very roomy, and there was ample space around the power unit for service to be carried out.

wraparound windscreen, and wind-up windows in the doors; it was a very pretty and very practical closed two-seater.

The MGA was everything that an MG sports car should be, for it handled very well indeed, it looked magnificent, it was fast and it felt (and was) safe to drive fast. Although it was rather too heavy to be truly successful as a competition car, it also performed with honour in races and rallies all round the world.

To make it better, more performance was needed, and this explains the appearance of the MGA 1600 in 1959.

MG MGA specification

Produced: Abingdon, 1955-59, 58,750 cars built.
General layout: Separate chassis-frame with pressed-steel body structure, in 2-seater sports car style, open tourer or closed coupe. Front-mounted engine driving rear wheels.
Engine and transmission: BMC B-Series, 4-cylinder, ohv, in-line. 1,489cc, 73.02 x 88.9mm, 68bhp (raised to 72bhp soon after launch) at 5,500rpm; 77lb ft at 3,500rpm. 4-speed gearbox; no synchromesh on 1st gear; live (beam) rear axle with hypoid-bevel final drive.
Chassis: Independent front suspension, coil springs and wishbones. Rack-and-pinion steering. Rear suspension by half-elliptic leaf springs. Front and rear drum brakes. 5.50-15in tyres.
Dimensions: Wheelbase 7ft 10in; front track 3ft 11.5in; rear track 4ft 0.75in; length 13ft 0in; width 4ft 9.25in; height 4ft 2in. Unladen weight (approx) 1,988lb (tourer), 2,105lb (coupe).
Typical performance: Maximum speed 100mph; 0-60mph 15.0sec; standing ¼-mile 19.3sec; overall fuel consumption 28mpg.
Derivatives: Original MGA was open tourer, with closed coupe following from late 1956.
Fate: Discontinued in favour of MGA 1600 model in 1959.

The MGA 1500 of 1955 had this facia and instrument style, including obvious provision for a radio to be fitted.

The MGA 1600 Coupe (note the new side/indicator lamps) had beautiful lines and the driver sat very low inside the bubble top.

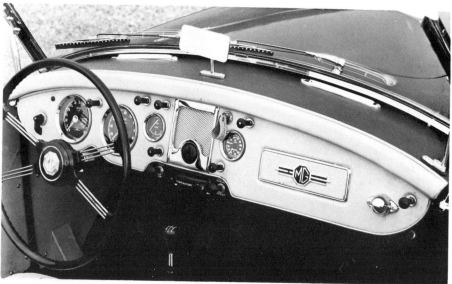

The MGA 1600s of both types had this style of facia. Note the kph speedometer on this export-market car.

MG MGA 1600 (1959 to 1961)

The first major change to the MGA's specification was made in the summer of 1959, which was also the year in which the Abingdon factory oversaw the upgrading of the Austin-Healey 100-Six to the 3000 specification. Since the original MGA was a very successful car, there were no shortcomings to be overcome; quite simply, the MGA 1600 was an even better car than before.

Apart from minor visual changes made to separate the car from its predecessors, the styling was unchanged. There were two important mechanical improvements – one to the engine,

the other to the brakes. The engine was enlarged from 1,489cc to 1,588cc, a process which allowed the power to be boosted by 7bhp. This made the cubic capacity the same as that of the MGA Twin-Cam, which was also in production at that time, but it is interesting to note that *no* other pushrod B-Series-powered BMC model built in the UK ever shared this engine size, which must have made the production of cylinder blocks somewhat awkward at times. The MGA 1600 was also equipped with Lockheed disc brakes at the front wheels, this making it a match for its deadly sales rival, the Triumph TR3A.

As before, there were open roadster and closed coupe

derivatives and, also as before, the vast majority of these cars were sold in the North American continent. The MGA 1600 was replaced by the MGA 1600 Mk II in 1961.

MG MGA 1600 specification

As for MGA 1500 except for:
Produced: Abingdon, 1959-61, 31,501 cars built.
Engine and transmission: 1,588cc, 75.39 x 88.9mm, 79bhp at 5,600rpm; 87lb ft at 3,800rpm.
Chassis: Front disc brakes, rear drums.
Dimensions: Weight 2,015lb (tourer), 2,075lb (coupe).
Typical performance: Maximum speed 101mph; 0-60mph 14.2sec; standing ¼-mile 19.3sec; overall fuel consumption 24mpg.
Distinguishing features from previous model:
Different front and rear indicator lamps, badges and sliding side windows.
Derivatives: As before, the MGA 1600 was available as an open tourer or a closed coupe. The 1600 De Luxe (see Twin-Cam) used the same running gear in a Twin-Cam chassis.
Fate: Discontinued in favour of MG MGA 1600 Mk II in 1961.

MG MGA Twin-Cam (1958 to 1960)

Even before the MGA went on sale, twin-cam engines had been produced and raced by the factory. It took three years to choose between rival Austin and Morris designs, to refine the Morris Motors version of the B-Series engine and to make it ready for sale. The result was the MGA Twin-Cam model,

which was technically interesting, but not always properly built and adjusted, and was very definitely a commercial failure.

The Twin-Cam, as its name implies, was built around a twin-overhead-camshaft engine, which started life as a B-Series conversion on the existing cylinder block, but ended up as a special engine in almost every way. Although it followed classic Jaguar and Coventry Climax lines, with inverted bucket tappets and lines of valves opposed at 80 degrees, BMC had trouble in making it reliable, and there was a history of piston burning and heavy oil consumption which eventually killed off the model *after* the problems had been solved. The capacity chosen was 1,588cc – unique at the time, eventually applied to the MGA 1600 pushrod engine, but never found on any other BMC family car. Neither was the Twin-Cam engine used in any other production car, though BMC flirted with the idea of Twin-Cam Magnettes at one period.

To match the much increased power – 108bhp, compared with the 72bhp of the MGA 1500 – the Twin-Cam was given four-wheel Dunlop disc brakes and centre-lock disc wheels of the type found on Jaguar D-Type and BRM F1 competition cars, and the steering gear had to be modified to clear the rather more bulky engine.

On the other hand, there were no other styling changes except for the use of discreet 'Twin-Cam' badges, and this chassis was available in open roadster or closed coupe styles.

If only it had been reliable, the Twin-Cam was a car which ought to have outsold anything which Alfa Romeo, Fiat or Porsche could offer in the United States, but it never achieved such status. Competition appearances were few and far between, the price was too high, and the engine seemed to have an extremely high petrol octane requirement. The result was

Between 1958 and 1960, MG built the MGA Twin-Cam, whose exterior styling included centre-lock disc wheels.

MG MGA 1600 Twin-Cam specification

Produced: Abingdon, 1958-60, 2,111 cars built.
General layout: Separate chassis-frame with pressed-steel body structure, in 2-seater sports car style, open tourer or closed coupe. Front-mounted engine driving rear wheels.
Engine and transmission: Special twin-ohc version of BMC B-Series, 4-cylinder, in-line. 1,588cc, 75.39 x 88.9mm,108bhp at 6,700rpm; 104lb ft at 4,500rpm. 4-speed gearbox; no synchromesh on 1st gear; live (beam) rear axle with hypoid-bevel final drive.
Chassis: Independent front suspension, coil springs and wishbones. Rack-and-pinion steering. Rear suspension by half-elliptic leaf springs. Front and rear disc brakes. 5.90-15in tyres.
Dimensions: Wheelbase 7ft 10in; front track 3ft 11.9in; rear track 4ft 0.9in; length 13ft 0in; width 4ft 9.25in; height 4ft 2in. Unladen weight (approx) 2,185lb (tourer), 2,245lb (coupe).
Typical performance: Maximum speed 113mph; 0-60mph 9.1sec; standing ¼-mile 18.1sec; overall fuel consumption 22mpg.
Derivatives: Twin-Cam was available as an open tourer or a closed coupe.
   Also sold were the 1600 De Luxe (82 cars in all) and 1600 Mk II De Luxe (313 cars), which used Twin-Cam rolling chassis, but pushrod-engined 1600, or 1600 Mk II engines and transmissions.
Fate: Discontinued in 1960 and never replaced by any other model.

that production was really all over by the beginning of 1960, only 18 months after launch, and the car was officially dropped in the spring of that year.

However, there was an intriguing offshoot of this design, which was the MGA 1600 De Luxe (see separate entry).

MG MGA 1600 Mk II (1961 to 1962)

The second MGA facelift was introduced in June 1961, and cars of the type known as MGA 1600 Mk II were built for just over a year before the assembly lines were cleared to make way for the monocoque MGB model. It was in 1962 that MG proudly built their 100,000th MGA (in less than seven years), which was a left-hand-drive MGA 1600 Mk II roadster.

Compared with the MGA 1600 which it displaced, the Mk II had an enlarged engine, higher overall gearing and minor styling changes to make the rejuvenation of the design obvious. Apart from the use of new-type horizontal tail-lamp clusters, the most obvious styling change was to the radiator grille, where the vertical bars were now somewhat recessed, making the front of the car look a bit 'undershot', like a British bulldog.

The engine had been enlarged to 1,622cc, this being the first use of this B-Series engine size, and something of a proving run for BMC's planners as engines of this size were due to be

MG MGA 1600 Mk II specification

As for MGA 1600 except for:
Produced: Abingdon, 1961-62, 8,719 cars built.
Engine and transmission: 1,622cc, 76.2 x 88.9mm, 86bhp at 5,500rpm; 97lb ft at 4,000rpm.
Dimensions: Weight 1,985lb (tourer), 2,045lb (coupe).
Typical performance: Maximum speed 101mph; 0-60mph 13.7sec; standing ¼-mile 19.1sec; overall fuel consumption 22mpg.
Distinguishing features from previous model: Different front grille and tail-indicator lights.
Derivatives: As before, the MGA 1600 Mk II was available as an open tourer or a closed coupe. The 1600 Mk II De Luxe (see Twin-Cam) used the same running gear in a Twin-Cam chassis.
Fate: Discontinued in favour of the new MG MGB in 1962.

The 100,000th MGA, built in 1962, was a 1600 Mk II, with the characteristic recessed-bar radiator grille.

The MGA 1600 Mk II had horizontal-motif tail-lamps.

fitted to several of the medium-sized family saloons from the autumn of 1961.

As with the 1600, there were roadster and coupe types, many cars had wire wheels, and all stayed faithful to the original MGA's tradition of providing good looks with high performance and 'Safety Fast' characteristics.

MGA 1600 De Luxe (Mk I 1960 to 1961, Mk II 1961 to 1962)

De Luxe, in this case, had nothing to do with body equipment, but everything to do with the chassis and fittings. In fact, this was an interesting and resourceful way to get out of a production problem following the abandonment of the MGA Twin-Cam project.

The story went like this. After the MGA Twin-Cam had been withdrawn, there were hundreds of special chassis, suspensions, wheels, steering and other items in stock from the original buying sanction of 2,500 sets of parts. Accordingly, in an interesting and little-publicized move, BMC decided to offer De Luxe versions of the MGA, which were really Twin-Cams fitted with existing pushrod engines!

There were two types. The 1600 De Luxe was fitted with the 1,588cc pushrod overhead-valve engine (82 of these cars were built), while the 1600 Mk II De Luxe had the Mk II styling revisions, plus the 1,622cc pushrod engine (313 of these cars were built). All had the Twin-Cam chassis, suspension, four-wheel disc brakes and special Dunlop wheels, but *not* the Twin-Cam bodyshell (which included wheelarch cutouts inside the arches), and the Mk IIs in particular were often loaded up with optional equipment that the production planners were trying to move before MGB production began.

In many ways, the De Luxe offered the best of both worlds – Twin-Cam chassis, handling and braking with ordinary pushrod-engine reliability. Such cars had a limited, but honourable, career in motor sport in the early 1960s.

MG Midget Mk I (1961 to 1964)

The original 'frog-eye' Austin-Healey Sprite was designed by Healey, but finally developed at Abingdon and produced there. When the time came to restyle it, Healey got the job of reshaping the nose, while MG reshaped the tail. It sounds

---

MG Midget specification

Produced: Abingdon, 1961-64, 16,080 cars built with 948cc engine, 9,601 cars with 1,098cc engine.

General layout: Unit-construction body-chassis structure in 2-seater sports car style. Some cars with removable hardtop. Front-mounted engine driving rear wheels. Identical in every way with the equivalent Austin-Healey Sprite Mk II.

Engine and transmission: BMC A-Series, 4-cylinder, ohv, in-line. 948cc, 62.9 x 76.2mm, 46bhp at 5,500rpm; 53lb ft at 3,000rpm. 4-speed gearbox; no synchromesh on 1st gear; live (beam) rear axle with hypoid-bevel final drive.

Chassis: Independent front suspension, coil springs and wishbones. Rack-and-pinion steering. Rear suspension by cantilever quarter-elliptic leaf springs and radius-arms. Front and rear drum brakes. 5.20-13in tyres.

Dimensions: Wheelbase 6ft 8in; front track 3ft 9.75in; rear track 3ft 8.75in; length 11ft 5.9in; width 4ft 5in; height 4ft 1.75in. Unladen weight (approx) 1,525lb.

Typical performance: Maximum speed 86mph; 0-60mph 20.0sec; standing ¼-mile 22.0sec; overall fuel consumption 39mpg.

Derivatives: From autumn 1962 to 1964, 9,601 cars produced with 1,098cc, 64.58 x 83.72mm engine, 56bhp at 5,500rpm, 62lb ft at 3,250rpm. Front disc brakes, and rear drums. Styling unchanged.

Typical performance: 89mph top speed, 0-60mph 16.9sec, standing ¼-mile 21.0sec, overall fuel consumption 30mpg.

Fate: Dropped in favour of Mk II model in 1964.

The original Sprite-based MG Midget Mk I was announced in the summer of 1961.

The Midget Mk II was the same car as the Sprite Mk III, with wind-up windows, deeper windscreen and half-elliptic leaf-spring rear suspension.

illogical, but it worked. Then came another momentous decision – not only would there be a Mk II Sprite, but there would be a badge-engineered version to be called the MG Midget. The two cars were announced in June 1961, but for company political reasons the Sprite came first and the Midget made its bow a couple of weeks later.

I have already described the Sprite's layout, so at this point it is only necessary to say that the MG Midget was mechanically identical, shared the same structure, but had a few distinguishing features in its styling.

Compared with the Sprite, there was an MG grille, chrome strips along the flanks, different rubber floor covering, different instrument faces and seats with contrasting piping. The Midget customer had to pay a total of £38.25 extra (on top of £641, at first) compared with the price of a Sprite; the miracle is that so many thousands chose to do so, even though the cars were identical and built side-by-side, back-to-back, at

the Abingdon factory.

Like the Sprite Mk II, the Midget Mk I received a 1.1-litre engine and front-wheel disc brakes in autumn 1962 and was replaced by a revised model in the spring of 1964.

MG Midget Mk II (1964 to 1966)

Like the Austin-Healey Sprite, the Midget was substantially altered in the spring of 1964. It not only gained a conventional half-elliptic leaf-spring rear suspension, but there was also the larger windscreen, the wind-up windows in the doors, the new facia layout and the better-developed 1,098cc engine.

In all respects except minor decoration and price, the two cars – Sprite Mk III and Midget Mk II – were identical. On announcement in 1964, the Midget Mk II cost £12 more than the Sprite in the UK, but no less than $170 extra in the USA.

The Midget became Mk III in the autumn of 1966.

182

MG Midget Mk II specification

As for Midget Mk I except for:
Produced: Abingdon, 1964-66, 26,601 cars built.
Engine and transmission: 1,098cc engine, 59bhp at 5,750rpm; 65lb ft at 3,500rpm.
Chassis: Rear suspension by half-elliptic leaf springs.
Dimensions: Front track 3ft 9.25in; length 11ft 5.9in; unladen weight 1,566lb.
Typical performance: Maximum speed 92mph; 0-60mph 14.7sec; standing ¼-mile 19.8sec; overall fuel consumption 30mpg.
Distinguishing features from previous model: Wind-up windows in doors, larger screen, new facia and instrument panel.
Fate: Dropped in favour of Mk III model, which was announced in 1966.

MG Midget Mk III (1966 to 1969)

In the autumn of 1966, the MG Midget, like the Austin-Healey Sprite, received an engine transplant which turned it into a much better car. Although it was still recognizably from the little A-Series family, the new unit was a 1,275cc unit, effectively a detuned 'S' engine, with 65bhp and a much more robust feel than the earlier 1,098cc engine.

Along with the Sprite, which became Mk IV at the same time, the latest Midget was also given a neat, lower-profile, fold-away soft-top. Production of this type ran on, very successfully, until the autumn of 1969, when a further facelift was made to what had really become a British Leyland model.

MG Midget Mk III (G-AN5 type) (1969 to 1974)

In the autumn of 1969, the Midget became the G-AN5 type, mechanically unchanged, but with cosmetic differences, which included a commonized grille with the Sprite, Rostyle road wheels and BLMC badges on the wings.

In the next few years, development changes included the standardization of radial-ply tyres, an alternator instead of a dynamo, the fitment of an anti-roll bar and – from 1972 to 1974 – the use of a rounded rear wheelarch style, which was abandoned after only two years due to crash-test safety considerations.

MG Midget Mk III specification

As for Midget Mk II except for:
Produced: Abingdon, 1966-69, 13,722 cars built.
Engine and transmission: 1,275cc engine, 70.6 x 81.28mm, 65bhp at 6,000rpm; 72lb ft at 3,000rpm.
Dimensions: Unladen weight 1,575lb.
Typical performance: Maximum speed 94mph; 0-60mph 14.1sec; standing ¼-mile 19.6sec; overall fuel consumption 30mpg.
Distinguishing features from previous model: Fold-away hood instead of build-up variety.
Derivatives: For 1970 model year, became Midget Mk III (G-AN5 type) with Rostyle wheels, new grille and badging. Carried on to 1974, when replaced by Midget 1500. 86,623 Mk IVs were built.
Fate: Dropped in favour of Midget 1500 model, which was announced in 1974.

For the 1967 model year, MG produced the Midget Mk III, complete with 65bhp 1,275cc engine and a new 'low-line' soft-top.

By 1970, the Midget Mk III had been cosmetically changed, with a black windscreen surround, Rostyle wheels and British Leyland badges on the side of the front wings.

The BMC A-Series engine, with twin-SU carburettors, powered every Sprite and Midget built from 1958 to 1974.

In character, if not in ownership, this Midget was still a BMC car, but the Midget 1500 which took over in late 1974 was most certainly not!

The late-model Midget Mk III cars (1972 to 1974) had rounded, rather than squared-off, rear wheelarch cut-outs, but these disappeared for 1975, when the 'black-bumper' model arrived.

MG MGB (1962 to 1967)

When BMC came to replace the MGA for the 1960s, they had a very difficult task. The MGA had been very successful indeed, and the next MG would be expected to improve on that. Planning for the new car began at the end of the 1950s, but it was not until September 1962 that it was ready to go on sale, as the MGB.

Although modified versions of the MGA's engine, transmission and front suspension were all used, the new car's structure was very different. Whereas the MGA had used a sturdy separate chassis-frame and a separate steel bodyshell, the MGB used a pressed-steel monocoque body-chassis structure. The new car also had a slightly shorter wheelbase than before, but was more roomy in the cockpit and had even sleeker good looks. At first there was only a two-seater open roadster on sale, but from late 1965 a very elegant hatchback GT coupe (the MGB GT) was also made available. These two body styles were to remain on sale until the last of the MGBs was built in 1980.

MG's general manager, John Thornley, said in later years that he realized that the MGB would be MG's last new sports car when he received the tooling bill from Pressed Steel! The

MGB was certainly the most costly sports car, in investment terms, ever to be approved by BMC, and even when it became obsolescent the new controlling company, British Leyland, never found the money to replace it, except by the TR7.

Technical novelties in the MGB's layout, apart from the unit-construction body-chassis, were the first BMC use of the 1.8-litre B-Series engine (and the *only* use of that engine size with a three-bearing crankshaft) and the option of Laycock overdrive, which worked on top and third gears. In all other mechanical respects it was a well-proven car. As to creature comforts, this was the first MG sports roadster to have wind-up windows, though you still had to pay extra for the heater at first, and the soft-top mechanism was still strictly Do-It-Yourself.

The MGB was such a ruggedly pretty car, with safe and predictable handling allied to a 100mph-plus top speed, that it sold very rapidly indeed. In the next three years it was only necessary to improve it in detail, or to bring it more into line with other BMC products. From late 1964, for instance, the engine received a five-bearing crankshaft (to make the block common with that of the new Austin 1800), and soon after the MGB GT was put on sale both types were standardized with the new, more robust, Salisbury type of back axle to replace the original B-Series banjo-type.

Except for these and other development changes, an MGB of 1967 was still recognizably the same car as a 1962 type, so the package of improvements leading to the launch of the Mk II was timely, and welcome.

MG MGB specification

Produced: Abingdon, 1962-67, 115,898 tourers and 21,835 GTs built.
General layout: Unit-construction body-chassis structure, in 2-seater sports car style, open tourer or closed coupe. Front-mounted engine driving rear wheels.
Engine and transmission: BMC B-Series, 4-cylinder, ohv, in-line. 1,798cc, 80.26 x 88.9mm, 95bhp at 5,400rpm; 110lb ft at 3,000rpm. 4-speed gearbox, no synchromesh on 1st gear; optional overdrive on top and 3rd gears; live (beam) rear axle with hypoid-bevel final drive.
Chassis: Independent front suspension, coil springs and wishbones. Rack-and-pinion steering. Rear suspension by half-elliptic leaf springs. Front disc and rear drum brakes. 5.60-14in tyres.
Dimensions: Wheelbase 7ft 7in; front track 4ft 1in; rear track 4ft 1.25in; length 12ft 9.3 in; width 4ft 11.7in; height 4ft 1.4in. Unladen weight (approx) 2,030lb (tourer), 2,190lb (coupe).
Typical performance: Maximum speed 103mph; 0-60mph 12.9sec; standing ¼-mile 18.9sec; overall fuel consumption 22mpg.
Derivatives: The MGB was available as an open tourer from the start, or a closed GT coupe from late 1965.
Fate: Discontinued in 1967 and replaced by the MGB Mk II model.

The MG MGB of 1962 had a monocoque body/chassis unit and this front-end style.

The first series of MGBs had the B-Series engine mounted well back from the nose.

From the autumn of 1965, MG also sold the MGB GT, which had a smart style and a hatchback facility. This is a slightly later (early 1970s) derivative with Rostyle wheels.

MG MGB Mk II (1967 to 1980)

In the autumn of 1967, BMC introduced the MGC (see separate entry) and changes made to the MGB were much influenced by this major launch. Although it was visually unchanged, there were significant MGB changes under the sheet-metal skin.

The most important of these concerned the transmission. Manual-transmission cars received a new all-synchromesh gearbox (the type used in the Austin 3-litre saloon and the MGC sports car), and while overdrive was still optional, there

The Mk II MGB in one of its many facelifted forms, with a black grille and Rostyle wheels, but the same basic sheet metal.

MGB GTs, in Mk II form, had optional automatic transmission, with the selector lever on the transmission tunnel.

was also the option of Borg-Warner automatic transmission. The bodyshell's floorpan was altered to make allowance for this.

Apart from this, the basic specification was not changed and the engine's peak power was unaltered. From this point on, therefore, the MGB began to lose ground against its major competitors, which not only seemed to get faster, but to have restyled bodies in the years which followed.

In spite of all manner of cosmetic changes imposed by the new business masters at British Leyland, including the controversial black plastic bumpers from late 1974, the MGB carried on into the 1980s, at which point the Abingdon factory was completely closed down and the facility sold off. In that time there were suspension changes, facia changes, different grilles, different wheels, but little mechanical improvement. The MGB died off, much lamented by diehards, but with tens of thousands in stock, unsold, in the USA. It has never been replaced.

By 1971, the MGB Mk II had a centre console between the seats, and style modifications (but not a complete rejig) of the facia, seats and door trims.

MG MGB Mk II specification

As for original MGB except for:
Produced: Abingdon, 1967-80, 271,777 tourers and 103,762 GTs built.
Engine and transmission: Less powerful engines for USA sale; all-synchromesh gearbox, overdrive standard on home market cars from 1975. Optional automatic to 1973.
Chassis: Front anti-roll bar standard.
Dimensions: Weight 2,140lb (tourer), 2,260lb (coupe). Length 13ft 2.25in from late 1974.
Distinguishing features from previous model: Different front grille and wheels on some models; black plastic-covered bumpers from late 1974.
Derivatives: As before, MGB Mk II was available as an open tourer or a closed GT coupe.
Fate: Discontinued at end of 1980. No MGB replacement ever developed.

MG MGC (1967 to 1969)

The concept and development of the car which became the MGC was studded with controversy. As early as 1964 BMC began to look for a natural successor for the Austin-Healey 3000, decided to produce a six-cylinder version of the MGB, and to badge it as an MG *and* an Austin-Healey! Donald

Healey himself would have nothing to do with such a proposal, and the result was that the projected Austin-Healey 3000 Mk IV never appeared.

The MGC production car was effectively a new car forward of the windscreen, though the skin styling was nearly the same. Not only had the 2.9-litre six-cylinder engine developed for the

The six-cylinder MGC, announced in 1967 and sold in open or GT forms, had a bonnet bulge and 15in road wheels to identify it from the MGB. Right, a bird's-eye view of the MGC's engine bay, showing how the very long six-cylinder engine helped to push the majority of the weight on to the front wheels.

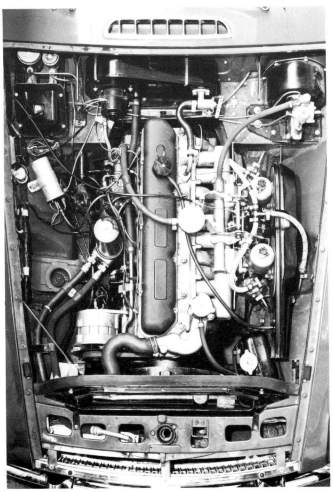

MG MGC specification

Produced: Abingdon, 1967-69, 4,527 tourers and 4,449 GTs built.

General layout: Unit-construction body-chassis structure in 2-seater sports car style, open tourer or closed coupe. Front-mounted engine driving rear wheels.

Engine and transmission: 'New generation' BMC C-Series, 6-cylinder, ohv, in-line. 2,912cc, 83.36 x 88.9mm, 145bhp at 5,250rpm; 170lb ft at 3,400rpm. 4-speed all-synchromesh gearbox; optional overdrive on top and 3rd gears; optional automatic transmission; live (beam) rear axle with hypoid-bevel final drive.

Chassis: Independent front suspension, torsion bars, wishbones and anti-roll bar. Rack-and-pinion steering. Rear suspension by half-elliptic leaf springs. Front disc and rear drum brakes. 165-15in radial-ply tyres.

Dimensions: Wheelbase 7ft 7in; front track 4ft 2in; rear track 4ft 1.25in; length 12ft 9.3in; width 4ft 11.7in; height 4ft 2.25in. Unladen weight (approx) 2,460lb (tourer), 2,610lb (coupe).

Typical performance: Maximum speed 120mph; 0-60mph 10.0sec; standing ¼-mile 17.7sec; overall fuel consumption 18mpg.

Derivatives: The MGC was available as an open tourer or a closed GT coupe.

Fate: Discontinued in 1969 and not replaced.

Austin 3-litre (*not* the old Austin-Healey engine) been modified, and shoehorned into place, but there was new torsion-bar front suspension as well. The all-synchromesh gearbox, apart from internal ratios, was shared with the MGB Mk II and the Austin 3-litre, and as with the four-cylinder car there were overdrive and automatic transmission options. You could buy an MGC as a roadster or a GT, and the only way to pick a six-cylinder car from the 'four' was by spying the bonnet bulges and the larger 15in-diameter wheels.

The MGC was not a success and lasted less than two years, but there were several reasons for this. The most important, mechanically, was that the engine was not at all as zestful as it might have been, and the handling certainly tended towards sluggish understeer, with rather heavy steering. There was also the problem of being asked to pay a lot more for a car which still looked almost the same as an MGB.

Perhaps too many of the pundits gave the car a bad name at first (for there was no doubt that the later cars were much better built and more responsive than the originals), but the sad fact was that the car did not sell well enough. It was an easy decision for British Leyland to kill it off during 1969, and to free more of Abingdon's facilities for enlarged four-cylinder MGB production.

In 1969, a number of MGCs were sold off to University Motors, and these were modified (some more than others) and sold as UM Specials.

There was an optional automatic transmission on the MGC; this was the 1969 model. Note the leather-bound steering wheel.

The YB, built between 1951 and 1953, had a simply equipped, but very dignified facia and driving position.

MG YB (1951 to 1953)

To get at the real design roots of the YB saloon, which was MG's only saloon car offering at the time of the BMC merger, we have to go back to 1938 and the launch of the Morris Eight Series E and the Morris Ten Series M engine, both of which were shown at Earls Court for the first time that year.

The Eight Series E had a separate chassis, but a beam front axle, and the Ten Series M engine was then a modern overhead-valve four-cylinder unit. If the Second World War had not intervened, the Y-Type MG saloon would have been launched in 1940, effectively being an amalgam of Eight Series E passenger cabin and tuned-up Ten Series M engine, all packaged on to a new chassis with coil-spring independent suspension.

That car, as it happens, was launched in 1947, and the YB was a further developed version of it which appeared in the autumn of 1951. I ought to cross-refer, at this point, to the TD sports car, which was developed from a cut-and-shut version of

When BMC was founded in 1952, MG were assembling the separate-chassis YB saloon at Abingdon. Its design dated from 1938, and it was dropped in 1953.

the YA's chassis in 1949.

Compared with the YA saloon, which had a proudly traditional nose style, including vertical MG radiator and free-standing headlamps, the YB used several components developed specially for the TD sports car, including the

hypoid-bevel back axle, the smaller-diameter (15in) road wheels and two-leading-shoe brakes. There was also a front anti-roll bar, though the engine tune remained the same with a mere 46bhp peak power. This, incidentally, was much the same engine as used in the Wolseley 4/44 which followed a year later, but it was not used on any other BMC-period saloon car of the 1950s.

The YB was not at all a fast seller, probably because it had no particular export market appeal, also because it was quite sluggish by 1950s standards. Like the sports cars built alongside it at Abingdon, it was several years behind the times, and by the early 1950s this was showing rather badly. The handling was good, the appointments pleasing, but the rest of the car out-of-date.

It must have been a relief to BMC when they could withdraw the comatose YB saloon and replace it by the much more modern and stylish looking ZA Magnette.

There had been, incidentally, an open tourer version of the YA chassis, called the YT, but this was an export-only product and was not made available on the YB chassis at all.

MG Magnette ZA (1953 to 1956)

Gerald Palmer, who had been responsible for the design of the Jowett Javelin, joined Nuffield in 1949 with a simple brief – to design new Riley, MG and Wolseley models for the 1950s. He proposed two different ranges, the smaller of which was a design adapted to become the Wolseley 4/44 (announced in autumn 1952) and the MG Magnette ZA (announced in autumn 1953).

Although the Wolseley and the MG models were *basically*

MG YB specification

Produced: Abingdon, 1951-53, 1,301 saloons built.
General layout: Separate steel chassis, topped by pressed-steel bodyshell, in 4-seater, 4-door saloon style. Front-mounted engine driving rear wheels.
Engine and transmission: Nuffield-manufactured engine, 4-cylinder, ohv, in-line. 1,250cc, 66.5 x 90mm, 46bhp at 4,800rpm; 58lb ft at 2,400rpm. 4-speed gearbox; no synchromesh on 1st gear; live (beam) rear axle with hypoid-bevel final drive.
Chassis: Independent front suspension, coil springs and wishbones. Rack-and-pinion steering. Rear suspension by half-elliptic leaf springs. Front and rear drum brakes. 5.50-15in tyres
Dimensions: Wheelbase 8ft 3in; front track 3ft 11.4in; rear track 4ft 2in; length 13ft 8in; width 4ft 11in; height 4ft 9in. Unladen weight (approx) 2,341lb.
Typical performance: Maximum speed 71mph; 0-60mph 30.4sec; standing ¼-mile 24.5sec; overall fuel consumption 27mpg.
Derivatives: The YB was an evolution of the original Y-Type produced between 1947 and 1951.
Fate: Discontinued in 1953 and replaced by the Magnette ZA saloon model.

The MG Magnette ZA was launched in October 1953. This was a *very* early example, maybe even a prototype, for the front doors have no quarter-windows.

The rear end of the Magnette ZA was smoothly contoured and had a rectangular-shape rear window.

the same design, there were many important differences. Some of these were caused by the BMC merger (the Wolseley had Nuffield running gear, the Magnette BMC power unit and transmission), but some were deliberate. Although the cars shared the same basic unit-construction monocoque, the MG was an altogether lower car, with turned-under sills and an MG-type grille.

If the BMC merger had not taken place, the MG might have used tuned-up (TD/TF-type) Nuffield engine and transmission, but in the event it became the very first BMC new model to use the B-Series engine, gearbox and hypoid axle which were being developed for all the other medium-sized

family cars. The Magnette, in turn, donated these units to the MGA sports car, which followed it a couple of years later.

Although the Magnette (an historic MG name, of course, but with no technical connection with 1930s-style Magnettes) had the same basic suspension as the 4/44, it also had a torque-arm linking the axle casing forward to the bodyshell, which helped to locate the axle even more precisely.

It was a very pretty car, in all the proper MG traditions, even though there was not an ounce of actual MG componentry in it at the time it was introduced. The interior was smartly furnished (though it was a pity that the so-called wooden facia turned out to be rather poorly-matched painted metal at first.

The Magnette ZA's facia had metal panels finished to look like wood at first, but real wood veneer was soon fitted to improve the feel and the quality.

MG Magnette ZA specification

Produced: Abingdon, 1953-56, 18,076 saloons built.
General layout: Unit-construction pressed-steel body-chassis structure in 4-seater, 4-door saloon style. Front-mounted engine driving rear wheels.
Engine and transmission: BMC B-Series engine, 4-cylinder, ohv, in-line. 1,489cc, 73.02 x 88.9mm, 60bhp at 4,600rpm; 78lb ft at 3,000rpm. 4-speed gearbox; no synchromesh on 1st gear; live (beam) rear axle with hypoid-bevel final drive.
Chassis: Independent front suspension, coil springs and wishbones. Rack-and-pinion steering. Rear suspension by half-elliptic leaf springs and torque-arm. Front and rear drum brakes. 5.50-15in tyres
Dimensions: Wheelbase 8ft 6in; front track 4ft 3in; rear track 4ft 3in; length 13ft 11.5in; width 5ft 1in; height 4ft 10.25in. Unladen weight (approx) 2,465lb.
Typical performance: Maximum speed 80mph; 0-60mph 22.6sec; standing 1/4-mile 22.4sec; overall fuel consumption 25mpg.
Derivatives: The Magnette ZB (see below) evolved directly from the ZA Magnette.
Fate: Discontinued in 1956 and replaced by the Magnette ZB saloon model.

For the 1955 model year, a proper wood facia was fitted), the steering was very precise and the roadholding was quite outstanding for a car of this type.

It was no wonder that it immediately began to sell at a rate 10 times as fast as that of the old-style YB, and that within three years BMC decided to make it even better. The ZB of 1956 was the result.

MG Magnette ZB (1956 to 1958)

At the Earls Court motor show of October 1956, BMC introduced the ZB version of the Magnette, and this sold even faster than the ZA had done. Yet the mechanical changes were insignificant and the styling improvements minor.

On the standard saloon, the changes were confined to the use of a slightly more powerful (64bhp instead of the ZA's 60bhp) engine, and the offer of two-pedal Manumatic transmission as an option.

There was also the more expensive Varitone model, in which the rear window was enlarged, to almost get rid of the blind rear quarter behind the doors, and in which a two-tone colour scheme was standardized. This looked ever so slightly over-

MG Magnette ZB specification

As for Magnette ZA except for:
Produced: Abingdon, 1956-58, 18,574 cars built.
Engine and transmission: 64bhp at 5,400rpm; 83lb ft at 3,000rpm. Optional two-pedal-control Manumatic transmission.
Dimensions: Length 14ft 1in.
Distinguishing features from previous model:
Different chrome strip on front wing, more wood trim in passenger cabin and enlarged rear window on Varitone models.
Typical performance: Maximum speed 86mph; 0-60mph 18.5sec; standing 1/4-mile 21.2sec; overall fuel consumption 25mpg.
Fate: Discontinued in the winter of 1958-59 in favour of the BMC Farina-type Magnette Mk III.

The ZB Magnette, introduced in October 1956, had an enlarged window. The Varitone derivative had a duo-tone colour scheme as shown here.

the-top, but it sold well to the colour-conscious trendies of the period and kept MG saloon sales bubbling along well for another two years and more. Some Varitones, incidentally, were supplied with monotone paintwork . . .

This breed of Magnette, incidentally, was good for between 85 and 90mph and was a proper sports saloon in all respects. If only the MGA Twin-Cam's engine had been reliable, and if only it had been made available in this bodyshell . . .

However, after a peak, there is always a trough. To replace the ZB, BMC produced the Magnette Mk III. Need I say more?

The MG Magnette Mk III was one of five versions of the Farina-styled B-Series saloon family and was announced in the spring of 1959.

MG Magnette Mk III (1959 to 1961)

I wish I could be more charitable about this MG model, but it was really not one of BMC's better late-1950s efforts and has rather deservedly been pushed into the background of the MG heritage. And well it should, for unlike the ZB Magnette (which was at least assembled at Abingdon), the Mk III had almost no MG connections at all. The Magnette Mk III, in

---

MG Magnette Mk III specification

Produced: Cowley, 1959-61, 16,676 cars built.
General layout: Unit-construction, pressed-steel body-chassis structure in 4-seater, 4-door saloon car style. Front-mounted engine driving rear wheels.
Engine and transmission: BMC B-Series engine, 4-cylinder, ohv, in-line. 1,489cc, 73.02 x 88.9mm, 64bhp at 4,800rpm; 85lb ft at 3,300rpm; 4-speed gearbox, no synchromesh on 1st gear; centre-floor gear-change; live (beam) rear axle with hypoid-bevel final drive.
Chassis: Independent front suspension, coil springs and wishbones. Cam-and-lever steering. Rear suspension by half-elliptic leaf springs. Front and rear drum brakes. 5.90-14in tyres.
Dimensions: Wheelbase 8ft 3.25in; front track 4ft 0.87in; rear track 4ft 1.87in; length 14ft 10in; width 5ft 3.5in; height 4ft 11.75in. Unladen weight (approx) 2,507lb.
Distinguishing features from previous model: Entirely different car from earlier Magnette ZA/ZB model, bearing family resemblance to other related Farina models.
Typical performance: Maximum speed 84mph; 0-60mph 20.6sec; standing ¼-mile 21.9sec; overall fuel consumption 27mpg.
Derivatives: The Magnette Mk IV of 1961 was a further developed version of the Mk III. All other B-Series 'Farinas' were closely related, the Riley 4/Sixty Eight being mechanically identical.
Fate: Discontinued in 1961 in favour of the updated Magnette Mk IV model.

From the three-quarter rear, you can recognize an MG Magnette Mk III by the cut-back tail-fins, the colour scheme and the boot-lid badging.

This was the well-equipped facia of the MG Magnette Mk III of 1959. Pity there was no rev-counter, though.

fact, was merely a jazzed-up and tuned-up version of the Austin/Morris/Wolseley B-Series Farina range, which was launched by BMC in 1958-59.

There was no Nuffield and no MG involvement in the Mk III's design, which had been conceived at Longbridge. In addition, although the well-known B-Series engine, gearbox and back axle were used, there was no other chassis connection with the nice-handling ZA/ZB family. Nor was there any sense of occasion when the Mk III was launched, as it was merely the third (after the Wolseley and the Austin derivatives) of five different versions to appear.

Like all the other B-Series 'Farinas', the Mk III had a be-finned four-door saloon bodyshell in which the tracks looked (and were) rather narrow and on which a squat MG-type grille was grafted. There was more space inside than in the displaced ZB, but the surroundings were not as elegant. The 1.5-litre engine had slightly less peak power, but more peak torque, than the ZB.

The big let-down was the suspension, and the car's general stance. The ZA/ZB had always looked squat and handled well, whereas the Mk III looked a bit high and boxy and did not behave in the same sort of way. Not only was the springing softer than that of the old ZB, but the steering was by cam and lever and not at all as precise. The final insult was that it was not even assembled at Abingdon by MG workmen, but at Cowley on the same production lines as the Morris Oxford, Wolseley 15/60 and Riley 4/Sixty Eight types, which all shared the same body.

Predictably, it was not at all successful, and it needed a major rethink, prior to the Mk IV which followed in late 1961, before the Magnette could approach the standard of being a proper sports saloon again.

Like the other BMC B-Series Farina-styled saloons, the Magnette was much improved for 1962, with a longer wheelbase, wider tracks, a 1,622cc engine and better roadholding. The styling, though, was unchanged.

MG Magnette Mk IV (1961 to 1968)

The Farina-styled Magnette had only been on sale for three summers when BMC announced a comprehensive redesign of all this family of B-Series cars. In the process, the Magnette moved from Mk III to Mk IV and became a much better car than before. The problem for the sales force was that it looked almost exactly the same, and its reputation never recovered from the early pasting it had received from the critics.

The Mk IV had a slightly longer wheelbase and wider wheel tracks, which was bound to give it more stability, but it also had anti-roll bars on the front *and* rear suspension. Not only that, but this was the time when BMC enlarged the standard B-Series engine size to 1,622cc, which meant that the Mk IV also had more power and torque than the Mk III.

The fact is that the Mk IV was a much better-developed car than the original, though even in this form it lacked the steering capabilities and the sheer sports saloon character of the well-loved ZA/ZB family.

It struggled on, unloved and mostly ignored by the public – as did its Riley clone, the 4/Seventy Two – for several years. By the end of the BMC era, sales were down to less than 1,000 cars a year, so its death in April 1968, just as BMC was also being killed off, was a merciful release.

MG Magnette Mk IV specification

As for MG Magnette Mk III except for:
Produced: Cowley, 1961-68, 14,320 cars built.
Engine and transmission: 1,622cc, 76.2 x 88.9mm. 68bhp at 5,000rpm; 89lb ft at 2,500rpm. 4-speed gearbox, no synchromesh on 1st gear; centre-floor gear-change; optional automatic transmission.
Chassis: Anti-roll bars at front and rear.
Dimensions: Wheelbase 8ft 4.35in; front track 4ft 2.6in; rear track 4ft 3.4in.
Distinguishing features from previous model: Different 2-tone colour scheme (optional).
Typical performance: Maximum speed 86mph; 0-60mph 19.5sec; standing ¼-mile 21.5sec; overall fuel consumption 25mpg.
Derivatives: Close mechanical and family resemblance to all other B-Series Farina models; Riley 4/Seventy Two was mechanically identical.
Fate: Discontinued in 1968 and never replaced by another MG.

The MG 1100 of 1962 was the first-ever front-wheel-drive MG, and was a tuned-up version of the Morris 1100.

MG 1100 (1962 to 1967)

After the Mini, BMC's next major front-wheel-drive family of cars was the 1100 series. The first of these cars to be launched, from Cowley, was the Morris 1100, and within weeks it was joined by the upmarket, rather faster version, badged as an MG. Although the MG 1100 was no more of an MG than the Farina Magnette which was also a current model, it *was* a fast, relatively interesting and significantly different motor car.

Like all the 1100/1300 models, the MG version had a transversely-mounted A-Series engine driving the front wheels, and the crisply-styled body was suspended on liquid Hydrolastic units, interconnected front to rear. Certainly this gave a more supple ride than most rival conventional systems,

The MG 1100's instrument display included a strip speedometer, but at least there was a remote-control gear-change.

MG 1100 specification

Produced: Cowley, 1962-67, 124,860 MG 1100s of Mk I *and* Mk II types built.

General layout: Pressed-steel unit construction body-chassis structure, in 4-seater, 2-door or 4-door saloon style. Front and transversely-mounted engine driving front wheels.

Engine and transmission: BMC A-Series engine, 4-cylinder, ohv, in-line. 1,098cc, 64.58 x 83.72mm, 55bhp at 5,500 rpm; 61lb ft at 2,500rpm. During summer-autumn 1967, some cars sold with 1,275cc engine, 70.6 x 81.28mm, 58bhp at 5,250rpm; 69lb ft at 3,500rpm. 4-speed gearbox, no synchromesh on 1st gear; centre-floor gear-change; spur-gear final drive.

Chassis: Independent front suspension, Hydrolastic units and wishbones. Rack-and-pinion steering. Independent rear suspension by Hydrolastic units, trailing arms and anti-roll bar. Interconnection between front and rear suspensions. Front disc and rear drum brakes. 5.50-12in tyres.

Dimensions: Wheelbase 7ft 9.5in; front track 4ft 3.5in; rear track 4ft 2.9in; length 12ft 2.7in; width 5ft 0.4in; height 4ft 4.7in. Unladen weight (approx) 1,820lb.

Typical performance: (1,098cc version) Maximum speed 85mph; 0-60mph 18.4sec; standing ¼-mile 21.3sec; overall fuel consumption 29mpg.

Distinguishing features from previous models: Entirely new type of MG model with Pininfarina styling.

Derivatives: Austin/Morris 1100 was the same car, with different badges, details and engine tune. Riley Kestrel and Wolseley 1100 models were all slightly modified versions. Mk II (see separate entry) was same car with minor changes.

Fate: Discontinued in 1967 and replaced by Mk II models.

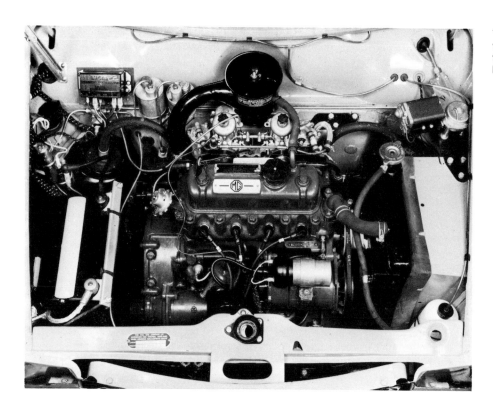

The MG 1100 had a 1,098cc A-Series engine with SU carburettors and 55bhp. Like the Minis, the radiator was at the far left side of the engine bay.

but it could also be very bouncy and floaty. There was no self-levelling, which meant that the tail sat well down when the car was heavily loaded, and many older cars developed fluid leaks and sagged to one side!

Compared to the Austin/Morris models which were the core of this range, the MG version had a characteristic MG front grille and the long-stroke 1,098cc engine had twin SU carburettors and a fabricated three-branch exhaust manifold. These, and a higher compression ratio, allowed the MG engine to develop 55bhp (compared with 48bhp), and although the engines were rather different in detail, it is worth noting that the current Midget had almost exactly the same rating.

The MG 1100 was let down by its interior at first, for the Austin type of strip speedometer was used, but surrounded by a Formica-like 'wood' facia board. Better trimmed seats could not really make up for this. All UK-market cars had four passenger doors, but there was a two-door version for North American export markets.

Because it was not too expensive (£812 for the four-door, compared with £695 for the equivalent Morris 1100, at first), and because it was a briskly-performing little car, it sold well. The feeling remained among customers, however, that it *could* be quite a lot better if BMC's engineers could be bothered to try. With the Mk II versions which followed in 1967, this was eventually achieved.

In the meantime, the facia became real tree wood from the beginning of 1963, there was a reclining seat option from spring 1966, and in the last few months of its life the car was also made available with a single-SU version of the 1,275cc engine which was about to become standard equipment on several other BMC front-wheel-drive cars.

MG 1100 Mk II (1967 to 1968)

When the 1100 corporate design was updated in the autumn of 1967, the MG 1100 received all the detail changes, including the chopped-off tail-fins. However, in this process, the standard MG version became the 1300 (see separate entry) and the 1100 Mk II was merely an interim car which was built for a few months in the winter of 1967-68.

In all respects except engine size, it was the same car as the MG 1300, and although AP automatic transmission became optional, it is doubtful if more than a handful were ever built in this form.

MG 1100 Mk II specification

As for MG 1100 except for:
Produced: 1967-68.
Engine and transmission: Optional AP 4-speed automatic transmission.
Distinguishing features from previous models: Chopped-off tail-fins with different tail-lamps, different trim and details.
Derivatives: The 1100 Mk II was itself a derivative of the original 1100. Also 1300 (see separate entry). The Austin 1100/1300 was the same car; also Riley, Wolseley and Vanden Plas all used the same basic design.
Fate: Discontinued in 1968 and not replaced.

MG 1300 (1967 to 1968)

In 1967 and 1968, BMC went through a very confusing period when they changed several of their cars in detail, then had another go at them within months. In the case of the MG version of the 1100/1300 front-wheel-drive range, not only did it become Mk II in October 1967, but a 1.3-litre engine was then offered, significantly changed within months, after which the model was changed yet again for 1969!

This needs a bit of careful sorting out. In October 1967, all the 1100/1300 models were updated, and all had chopped-off rear fins with different tail-lamps; there were other detail changes, but visually the rest of the MG body and its equipment were left alone.

The 1100 became Mk II, but lasted only for a few months, then was dropped early in 1968. The mainstream model, therefore, was the MG with the 58bhp version of the 1,275cc engine, which was known as the MG 1300 (*not* the Mk II, please note – that came later!). There was an AP automatic transmission option, and a choice of two-door or four-door coachwork in all markets until April 1968, when the four-door version was discontinued.

Only months later, from April 1968, the engine was substantially revised, with twin SU carburettors once again being standardized, and the peak power output rose. From the 1100, therefore, at 55bhp, to the original 1300 at 58bhp, the latest cars were given 65bhp! Confused? Hold tight, for there was yet more to come.

An all-synchromesh manual transmission was phased-in during the summer of 1968, which means that none of the single-carb, and by no means all of the twin-carb, 1300s were so equipped.

In any case, it was all a temporary jumble-up, for the definitive MG 1300 – the Mk II – was announced in the autumn of 1968.

MG 1300 specification

As for original 1100 except for:
Produced: Cowley, 1967-68, 32,549 1300s of all types (Mk I and Mk II) built.
General layout: 2-door and 4-door saloon types available.
Engine and transmission: 1,275cc, 70.6 x 81.28mm. Original cars, 58bhp at 5,250rpm; 69lb ft at 3,000rpm; from April 1968, with twin-carb engine, 65bhp at 5,750rpm; 71lb ft at 3,000rpm. All-synchromesh manual transmission from mid-1968; optional automatic transmission.
Dimensions: Unladen weight (approx) 1,850lb.
Typical performance: (58bhp version) Maximum speed 88mph; 0-60mph 17.3sec; standing ¼-mile 20.7sec; overall fuel consumption 30mpg.
Distinguishing features from previous models: Cropped-off fins, different tail-lamps and trim.
Derivatives: MG 1300 Mk II followed in autumn 1968.
Fate: Discontinued in autumn 1968 in favour of MG 1300 Mk II model.

For 1968, the MG 1100 became 'Mk II', with chopped back tail-fins, and there was also the MG 1300, with a bigger and more torquey engine; this was the 1300.

MG 1300 Mk II (1968 to 1973)

As I have already explained, the MG 1100/1300 design went through a very confused, ever-changing, period in 1967-68. It was only with the launch of the 1300 Mk II that stability was achieved.

From October 1968, the car was made faster than ever and better equipped. The twin-carb engine was power-tuned with the aid of a higher compression ratio and a more robust crankshaft, the result being a peak of 70bhp and substantially higher torque. To match this, the gearbox internal ratios were also made closer, and radial-ply tyres were standardized.

Visually, the most satisfying improvement was to the facia, which was finally made more special (for the moment – see Austin/Morris 1300 GT!) for the MG, and given neat circular

200

The MG 1300 Mk II, built from late 1968, had a much improved display of instruments including, at last, a rev-counter. This display was also to be found in the Riley 1300 and, later, the Austin/Morris 1300GT models.

Externally, there was little obvious difference between the MG 1300 Mk II's engine for 1969 models (this picture) and the original MG 1100 engine of 1962. An output of 70bhp was a lot better than 55bhp, though!

MG 1300 Mk II specification

As for original 1300 model except for:
Produced: Cowley, 1968-73, 32,549 1300s of all types (Mk I and Mk II) built.
General layout: Only 2-door saloon type available.
Engine and transmission: 70bhp at 6,000rpm; 77lb ft at 3,000rpm. All-synchromesh manual transmission; optional automatic transmission available until summer 1969.
Chassis: 145-12in radial-ply tyres.
Dimensions: Unladen weight (approx) 1,850lb.
Typical performance: Maximum speed 97mph; 0-60mph 14.1sec; standing ¼-mile 19.6sec; overall fuel consumption 27mpg.
Distinguishing features from previous model: 2-door style only available, with revised facia display.
Fate: Discontinued in autumn 1971 and not replaced.

instruments and relocated controls. It had originally been used in the Riley Kestrel. There was also a leather-rimmed steering wheel.

As you might expect, this was much the best MG 1300 of all three types built in such a short time, and the performance figures showed that it was now a near-100mph car, with equipment and handling to match. Even so, compared with the original 1100 version it did not sell at all well – probably because the Austin and Morris 1300GTs (which were its mechanical clones) were just as fast and quite noticeably cheaper. British Leyland, who had taken control while this last type was being finalized, needed little excuse to drop it from the UK market in 1971. CKD production continued until 1973.

Chapter 9

RILEY

As a separate marque, Riley kept its independence for quite a few years, but in the end it descended to the same rather tacky level of badge engineering. After the formation of British Leyland, too, it was the first of those 'badges' to be killed off.

Nuffield had absorbed Riley in 1938 after that famous Coventry firm had finally run into serious financial trouble, yet little was done to rationalize it before the outbreak of war in 1939. The first postwar Rileys – the famous RM-Series models – were complete Riley-Coventry designs, and were still being built in 1952 when BMC was founded; these cars had virtually nothing in common with any other Nuffield model of the period. Assembly of Rileys, however, was moved out of Coventry into the MG plant at Abingdon during 1949.

Of these RM-Series cars, the 1½-litre and 2½-litre models were facelifted in 1951 and then received chassis improvements and more style changes in 1952; the 1½-litre was changed yet again in 1953 and ran on until 1955, while the unchanged 2½-litre was dropped in 1953.

There was no immediate 1½-litre replacement, but the next big Riley was the Pathfinder, which was a Nuffield-Cowley design, a separate-chassis model which shared much of that chassis and some of its body style and panelling with that of the forthcoming Wolseley 6/90, but used the famous old-design Riley twin-high-cam engine. This car lasted for four years before it was replaced by a car known as the Two-Point-Six, which was almost pure Wolseley 6/90 with a Riley grille and badges; it was only on the market for two years. A few of these later cars were produced at Abingdon, but to make way for expanded sports car production on that site Riley assembly was then moved to Cowley, were the cars were built alongside the Wolseley 6/90s.

The next 1½-litre Riley was the One-Point-Five of 1957, which was produced with hardly any significant changes until 1965. This model was developed from a design originally to have been a 1.2-litre-engined Morris 1200 to replace the Morris Minor, and was an enterprising amalgam of Morris Minor 1000 floorpan and suspension, a B-Series power train and a new superstructure and style, all shared to a greater or lesser degree with the Wolseley 1500 of the day. The basic body style was also to be found in various Australian-built BMC cars of the late 1950s/early 1960s. As with the Two-Point-Six, the first cars were built at Abingdon, but assembly moved to Longbridge thereafter and shared a production line with the Wolseley 1500.

From 1959 on, all Rileys were badge-engineered Austin-Morris cars. First there was the 4/Sixty Eight saloon of that year (which became the 4/Seventy Two in 1961), which used the same design as all the other B-Series 'Farinas'; it was always built at Cowley. Next there was the Elf, which was virtually a Mini with a long tail and larger boot, allied to a Riley grille and assembled at Longbridge; to all intents and purposes, too, this was the same car as the Wolseley Hornet. Finally, there was the Kestrel, made from 1965, which was really a badge-engineered Austin-Morris 1100/1300 and almost exactly the same car as the Wolseley 1100/1300 too; early examples were assembled at Longbridge, but most were assembled at Cowley.

The Riley marque was killed off by British Leyland in the autumn of 1969, but it had really been moribund since the early 1960s.

Postscript

The model names registered for Riley use, but not taken up, in the 1968 SMM & T list were as follows:

Adelphi	Nimrod
Merlin	Maxi

The original type of Riley 1½-litre (Series RMA) was designed in Coventry; it had been assembled at Abingdon since 1949, when BMC was founded.

Riley 1½-litre Series RMA (1946 to 1952)

In the 1930s, Riley had produced far too many models for the number of cars they were selling. This, together with heavy expenditure on sports car racing, resulted in substantial financial losses, and the marque was rescued by Lord Nuffield, who almost immediately resold his 'investment', at a heavy loss, to the Nuffield Organisation. The Riley-Coventry design team led by Harry Rush, however, remained intact, and during and immediately after the Second World War they produced a new family of cars which have always been known as the RM-Series models. The same basic coachbuilt style was used for both cars, but two different Riley twin-high-camshaft four-cylinder engines were employed, and the larger 2½-litre car had a longer wheelbase than the 1½-litre.

Riley assembly had been moved from Coventry to the MG factory at Abingdon in 1949, and in the same year the original

facia style had been modified. The first cars had a 1930s-style instrument panel with rather scattered dials and switches, but from late 1949 a new and more integrated layout was used, with two large circular instruments and four rectangular auxiliary instruments, all on a wooden panel.

The 1½-litre style was a classic of its type, for the 9ft 4.5in wheelbase and the transitional lines, still with running-boards under the doors and with headlamps only partly faired in to the wings, were graceful. There was a split windscreen, a fabric covering to the roof panel, and a great deal of middle-class 'clubby' furnishing of the interior. Riley enthusiasts loved it.

They also loved the chassis, which had torsion-bar independent suspension, inspired by the *traction avant* Citroen, the traditional Riley torque-tube type of transmission, and the well-known 1.5-litre 12/4 engine which had first been seen in 1934. The only problem was that it was a heavy car, so the

This was the original facia style for the Riley 1½-litre/2½-litre models, as built until 1949, then superseded by . . .

. . . the facia of the 1½-litre/2½-litre cars built thereafter. This was a 1½-litre – 2½-litre cars were more likely to have a rev-counter instead of a clock.

Riley 1½-litre Series RMA specification

Produced: Coventry, 1946-49, Abingdon 1949-52, 10,504 RMA models built.

General layout: Separate box-section steel chassis-frame with wooden-framed and steel-skinned bodyshell, in 4-seater, 4-door body style. Front-mounted engine driving rear wheels.

Engine and transmission: Riley-designed Type 12/4 engine, 4-cylinder, twin-high-camshaft, ohv, in-line. 1,496cc, 69 x 100mm, 55bhp at 4,500rpm; 78lb ft at 2,500rpm; 4-speed gearbox, no synchomesh on 1st gear; centre-floor gear-change; live (beam) rear axle with spiral-bevel final drive.

Chassis: Independent front suspension, torsion bars and wishbones. Rack-and-pinion steering. Rear suspension by half-elliptic leaf springs, anti-roll bar and torque-tube location. Front and rear drum brakes. 5.75-16in tyres.

Dimensions: Wheelbase 9ft 4.5in; front track 4ft.25in; rear track 4ft 4.25in; length 14ft 10in; width 5ft 2.5in; height 4ft 9in. Unladen weight (approx) 2,745lb.

Typical performance: Maximum speed 78mph; 0-60mph 32.6sec; standing ¼-mile 24.8sec; overall fuel consumption 28mpg.

Distinguishing features from previous models:
Different in every structural way from previous 'Coventry' Riley models, but using same engine as 1930s-style 1½-litre cars.

Derivatives: Riley 2½-litre used basically the same chassis and bodyshell with different engine and longer wheelbase. Before the formation of BMC, a drophead coupe, basically the same style, was also produced.

Fate: Discontinued in 1952 in favour of revised RME version built from 1952 to 1955.

---

performance (a 78mph top speed was matched by 0-60mph acceleration in more than 30 seconds) was slightly disappointing.

Before the BMC merger took place, saloon and a few drophead coupe models had been produced, but by the end of 1951 only the saloon was still being made. Immediately before the merger, the 1½-litre had been treated to larger and more substantial bumpers (two horizontal bars surrounding the rear number-plate), and this time the rear suspension incorporated telescopic as opposed to lever-arm dampers, and this was the form in which the Series RMA model was built for the first year of the BMC era.

From the autumn of 1953, Riley 1½-litre saloons had modified styling, with helmet-type front wings and no running-boards under the doors.

Riley 1½-litre Series RME (1952 to 1955)

Nuffield had already planned to make substantial changes to the RM-Series Rileys before the BMC merger took shape, but these were not ready until 1952 and 1953. Two dates are quoted, in this case, because the mechanical changes were made in October 1952, and body style improvements followed in October 1953.

In 1952, the chassis layout of the Riley was extensively changed, and in the process one of the bench-marks of Riley design was lost. The original design had featured a torque tube (complete with universal-joint location up near the transmission) to locate the Riley spiral-bevel back axle, but for 1953 there was a conventional open-propeller-shaft transmission layout and a Nuffield hypoid-bevel back axle. At the same time an all-hydraulic Girling braking system took over from the original hydro-mechanical layout. Engine changes were confined to a repositioning of dynamo and water pump components, plus their drive belt runs.

There were no style changes at that point, but a year later the body came in for attention. In place of the flowing wing-lines which had been a feature of the car for seven years, shorter and more rounded front wing pressings were used, new sill pressings took over from the original running-boards, and rear quarter changes included the use of extra pressings which partly covered the wheels. Assembly in this guise went on gently until mid-1955, when the RME-Series 1½-litre was dropped and not replaced.

Riley 1½-litre Series RME specification

As for original Riley 1½-litre model except for:
Produced: Abingdon 1952-55, 3,446 cars built.
Engine and transmission: Hypoid-bevel final drive.
Chassis: Rear suspension by half-elliptic springs, no torque tube location, no anti-roll bar.
Dimensions: Unladen weight 3,105lb.
Typical performance: Maximum speed 75mph; 0-60mph 29.5sec; standing ¼-mile 24.1sec; overall fuel consumption 24mpg.
Distinguishing features from previous models: Conventional half-elliptic rear suspension, then from late 1953, facelift style including different front wings and no running-boards.
Fate: Discontinued in 1955 and not replaced. Riley 1.5 of 1957 was an entirely different type of car with Morris Minor 1000 underpan and B-Series engine

---

The Series RME version of the Riley 1½-litre was the last surviving RM saloon, outlasting the 2½-litre model by two years and being the only one to be given the styling facelift.

The Riley 2½-litre (Series RMB) saloon was similar to the 1½-litre, but had a longer bonnet and wheelbase.

Riley 2½-litre Series RMB (1946 to 1952)

The 2½-litre RM-Series Riley was the sister car, in every way, of the 1½-litre models, for it shared the same basic body style, the two cars being identical from the windscreen backwards in a longer-wheelbase (by 6.5 inches) version of the independent-suspension chassis. The 2½-litre model, however, used the 90bhp (later 100bhp) 2,443cc 'Big Four' Riley engine, which was entirely different in detail from the 1½-litre 12/4 unit, although it shared the same type of twin-high-camshaft valve gear and cross-flow breathing. Like the 1½-litre model, the 2½-litre had been built in Coventry until 1949 and at Abingdon thereafter.

In its original form, the 2½-litre was the RMB-Series, and it had once been built in four-door saloon, drophead coupe and 2/3-seater roadster guise, all on the same chassis, but by 1951-52 only the saloon car was still being made. In 1949, the more modern type of instrument panel had been fitted (though 2½-litre cars usually had rev-counters, whereas 1½-litres had clocks), and for 1952, just before the BMC merger was formalized, the RMB also inherited the more substantial bumpers.

Riley 2½-litre Series RMF (1952 to 1953)

In October 1952, the 2½-litre Riley received the same chassis changes as the 1½-litre, which is to say that the torque-tube transmission and spiral-bevel back axle were dropped in favour of a conventional open propeller shaft, a hypoid-bevel axle and conventional location of that axle by the half-elliptic leaf springs.

However, the revised car, which was known as the RMF, was only built for one year, and never came in for the body facelift made to the 1½-litre models at the end of 1953. The reason was that it was replaced by the new Nuffield-designed Pathfinder model, which made its debut in October 1953.

Riley 2½-litre Series RMB to RMF specification

Produced: Coventry, 1946-49, Abingdon 1949-53, 6,900 RMB, 507 RMC, 502 RMD, 1,050 RMF models built.
General layout: Separate box-section steel chassis-frame with wooden-framed and steel-skinned bodyshell, in 4-seater, 4-door body style. Front-mounted engine driving rear wheels.
Engine and transmission: Riley-designed 'Big Four' type engine, 4-cylinder, twin-high-camshaft, ohv, in-line. 2,443cc, 80.5 x 120mm, 100bhp at 4,500rpm; 134lb ft at 3,000rpm; 4-speed gearbox, no synchromesh on 1st gear; centre-floor gear-change; live (beam) rear axle with spiral-bevel final drive.
Chassis: Independent front suspension, torsion bars and wishbones. Rack-and-pinion steering. Rear suspension by half-elliptic leaf springs, anti-roll bar and torque-tube location. Front and rear drum brakes. 6.00-16in tyres.
Dimensions: Wheelbase 9ft 11in; front track 4ft 4.25in; rear track 4ft 4.25in; length 15ft 6in; width 5ft 3.5in; height 4ft 11.5in. Unladen weight (approx) 3,135lb.
Typical performance: Maximum speed 94mph; 0-60mph 16.4sec; standing ¼-mile 20.8sec; overall fuel consumption 21mpg.
Distinguishing features from previous models: Different in every structural way from previous 'Coventry' Riley models, but using same engine as 1930s-style 'Big Four'-engined cars.
Derivatives: Riley 1½-litre used basically the same chassis and bodyshell with different engine and shorter wheelbase. Before the formation of BMC, a drophead coupe (Type RMD) and a 2/3-seater roadster (Type RMC) had also been built, basically to the same style. From late 1952, torque-tube back axle location was abandoned along with the rear anti-roll bar, and a hypoid-bevel final drive fitted.
Fate: Discontinued in 1953 in favour of new Riley Pathfinder, which used the same engine, but a newly-designed chassis, body and running gear.

The late-model (1952 and 1953) Riley 2½-litre (Type RMF) had more substantial bumpers and open propeller shaft drive to the back axle.

Riley Pathfinder (1953 to 1957)

Although the RM-Series models of 1946 to 1955 had a proper Riley-Coventry pedigree, the Pathfinder and its successor, the Two-Point-Six, were designed at Cowley. As already mentioned in the MG section of this book, Gerald Palmer had arrived from Jowett in 1949 to take charge of Riley and Wolseley family car design. His MG responsibilities were added later. One of his first projects for the Nuffield Organisation was formed quite independently of any old Riley-Coventry or Wolseley-Birmingham influence and resulted in two related large cars, the Riley Pathfinder launched in 1953 and the Wolseley 6/90 of 1954.

The new Riley project was well on the way before BMC was founded, which probably explains why it was allowed to go into production with a *real* Riley engine as opposed to a BMC unit; the Wolseley, which followed a year later, was to use the new BMC C-Series six-cylinder unit.

When designing the new Pathfinder (whose nickname, need I say, immediately became 'Ditchfinder'. . .), the Nuffield team looked carefully at the RM-Series models in case there were any points in which tradition should be upheld, but eventually restricted these touches to the use of the Riley 'Big Four' 2½-litre engine, torsion-bar independent front suspension, and a traditional Riley radiator grille style.

The basis of the car was a completely new box-section chassis-frame, which accepted the IFS and the Nuffield-type Bishop-cam gear steering, and to which a novel type of rear suspension was fixed. In place of the RM-Series car's torque-tube transmission (which was, in any case, to be dropped in 1952), there was open propeller-shaft drive to the hypoid-bevel back axle; this was located by semi-trailing torque-arms,

Riley Pathfinder specification

Produced: Abingdon, 1953-57, 5,536 cars built.
General layout: Separate box-section steel chassis-frame with pressed-steel bodyshell, in 5/6-seater, 4-door saloon car style. Front-mounted engine driving rear wheels.
Engine and transmission: Riley 'Big Four' engine, 4-cylinder, twin-high-camshaft, ohv, in-line. 2,443cc, 80.5 x 120mm, 110bhp at 4,400rpm; 134lb ft at 3,000rpm; 4-speed gearbox, and (on RHD cars) gear-lever on right side of driver's seat; no synchromesh on 1st gear; Borg-Warner overdrive optional from late 1955; live (beam) rear axle with hypoid-bevel final drive.
Chassis: Independent front suspension, torsion bars and wishbones. Bishop cam-and-peg steering. Rear suspension by coil springs, radius arms and Panhard rod. Front and rear drum brakes. 6.70-16in (later 6.00-16in) tyres. From late 1956, rear suspension by half-elliptic leaf springs, no Panhard rod.
Dimensions: Wheelbase 9ft 5.5in; front track 4ft 6in; rear track 4ft 6.5in; length 15ft 3in; width 5ft 7in; height 5ft 0in. Unladen weight (approx) 3,450lb.
Typical performance: Maximum speed 98mph; 0-60mph 16.7sec; standing ¼-mile 20.6sec; overall fuel consumption 21mpg.
Derivatives: The Wolseley 6/90 was broadly based on the chassis design of the Riley Pathfinder, but had a higher body and a BMC C-Series engine (see Wolseley).
Fate: Discontinued in 1957 in favour of the Riley Two-Point-Six, which was a lightly-modified Wolseley 6/90 Series III saloon model.

whose forward fulcrum was in the centre of the car, under the prop-shaft, along with a Panhard rod, and suspension was by concentric coil springs and telescopic dampers, which were mounted on to the torque arms, just ahead of the line of the

The Riley Pathfinder, Nuffield-designed rather than Riley-designed, was introduced in 1953, but first deliveries began in 1954. The traditional twin-high-cam Riley engine was retained.

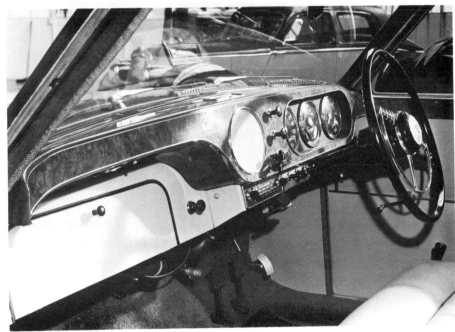

The Riley Pathfinder had three types of facia – this was the original style. Note the right-hand location of the gear-lever.

back axle.

One interesting mechanical feature was that a new BMC gearbox was used. This was designed with side-mounted selectors so that a steering-column change could be used, but this was not acceptable to Riley, so a complex linkage was arranged to a stubby remote-control lever on the floor, outside the driver's seat and close to the door trim panel.

The body style was a smooth and low (by the standards of the day) four-door, five or even six-seater, which had been personally influenced by Palmer himself. A three-abreast front bench seat was standard, though buckets were optional, as was a radio.

It took ages to get the Pathfinder into the showrooms (deliveries did not begin until mid-1954), and after that there

was a steady stream of important modifications to the mechanical design.

The Borg-Warner overdrive, as used on other large-engined BMC cars of the day, became optional towards the end of 1955, and this meant that the chassis had to be modified. An extra 'cross-over' Panhard rod was added to improve back axle location at about the same time. The third chassis derivative came along towards the end of 1956 when (at the same time as the Wolseley 6/90 became Mk II) the coil-spring rear suspension was ditched in favour of conventional half-elliptics, and there was also a revised facia style for the last few months. The last of these unsuccessful cars, however, was built in January 1957, and was not replaced by the Two-Point-Six until the autumn of that year.

209

To replace the Pathfinder, BMC introduced the Riley 2.6 in the autumn of 1957. This was a badge-engineered version of the current Wolseley 6/90 and had a C-Series engine. The enlarged rear window and the duo-tone colour scheme, plus hooded headlamps, are all recognition points.

Riley Two-Point-Six (1957 to 1959)

Although the Two-Point-Six took over from the Pathfinder in 1957, and looked similar to it, it was a very different car indeed. Whereas the Pathfinder had used a Riley twin-high-camshaft engine and a significantly lower body than its relative, the Wolseley 6/90, the Two-Point-Six was really no more than a badge-engineered Wolseley.

The heritage of the 6/90 is covered in detail in the Wolseley section. However, by 1957 it had already become Series III, by which time the body had been slightly restyled, with an enlarged rear window, the Pathfinder's right-hand gear-change had been adopted, and the rear suspension had reverted to half-elliptic leaf springs. Throughout this short but eventful career, the 6/90 had used the BMC C-Series six-cylinder engine, a rather higher version of the Pathfinder's bodyshell and 15in road wheels; when the time came to announce the car called Riley Two-Point-Six, all these features were carried over without change.

Compared with the 6/90 Series III, the only features unique to the Riley Two-Point-Six were the distinctive Riley radiator grille, the special facia and instrument layout and the two-tone colour scheme. The headlamps were slightly hooded, Lockheed Brakemaster servo-assisted brakes were used, and there was now the choice of Borg-Warner overdrive or fully automatic transmission. Compared with the Pathfinder, the Two-Point-Six had 13bhp *less* peak power, and a 5mph lower top speed. It was no wonder that no-one, not even Riley fanatics, liked the car, which was quietly dropped in May 1959, ahead of the launch of the new Farina-styled BMC C-Series cars. It was never replaced.

Riley Two-Point-Six specification

Produced: Abingdon, 1957-58, Cowley 1958-59, 2,000 cars built.

General layout: Separate box-section steel chassis-frame with pressed-steel bodyshell, in 4-seater, 4-door saloon car style. Front-mounted engine driving rear wheels.

Engine and transmission: BMC C-Series engine, 6-cylinder, ohv, in-line. 2,639cc, 79.37 x 88.9mm, 97bhp at 4,750rpm; 135lb ft at 2,000rpm; 4-speed gearbox, and (on RHD cars) gear-lever on right side of driver's seat; no synchromesh on 1st gear; optional Borg-Warner overdrive; optional Borg-Warner automatic transmission; live (beam) rear axle with hypoid-bevel final drive.

Chassis: Independent front suspension, torsion bars and wishbones. Bishop cam-and-peg steering. Rear suspension by half-elliptic leaf springs. Front and rear drum brakes. 6.70-15in tyres.

Dimensions: Wheelbase 9ft 5.5in; front track 4ft 6in; rear track 4ft 6.5in; length 15ft 5.5in; width 5ft 7in; height 5ft 1in. Unladen weight (approx) 3,610lb.

Distinguishing features from previous model:
Higher body overall, wrapround rear window, more upright grille, free-standing auxiliary lamps and extra chrome strips along flanks.

Typical performance: Maximum speed 93mph; 0-60mph 17.4sec; standing ¼-mile 20.6sec; overall fuel consumption 19mpg.

Derivatives: The Wolseley 6/90 Mk III was closely related to this Riley model, which actually evolved from it.

Fate: Discontinued in 1959 and never replaced. This was the last of the large-engined Rileys.

The Riley 1.5 of 1957 used a Morris Minor 1000 floorpan, a B-Series engine and transmission, and the same superstructure as the Wolseley 1500.

Riley One-Point-Five (1957 to 1960)

Here is a car which had a very complicated beginning, a rather muted launch and a somewhat uninspired career. The car called the Riley One-Point-Five was, in any case, a tuned-up and better-equipped version of the Wolseley 1500, but both of these cars were developed from a rejected Morris project.

In the beginning, at Nuffield in 1951, there was a proposed Morris Minor restyle by Alec Issigonis, which had lines rather like those of the Morris Oxford Series II of 1954. This was reshaped by Gerald Palmer, then cancelled in favour of a different Austin design which was to use a 1.2-litre B-Series engine. That project grew and grew, but was eventually cancelled as a Morris project. Instead, in its final form it was given a pair of new noses, rebadged, and given the larger and more powerful 1½-litre B-Series engine.

The Wolseley 1500 was launched in the spring of 1957, and the Riley One-Point-Five version came along in November 1957. Both cars used a modified version of the Morris Minor 1000's floorpan, torsion-bar front suspension, 14in road wheels and rack-and-pinion steering, but the superstructure was a neat but understated four-door saloon layout. The B-Series engine, gearbox and final drive were all familiar corporate units, and in the case of the Riley the engine had 62bhp and a high final-drive ratio of 3.73:1.

The Riley, unlike the Wolseley, was intended to be a desirable little sports saloon, and not only had smart duo-tone colour schemes – the roof, the boot-lid and the body panels down to the base of the windows being in the contrasting colour – but neat separate front seats, a remote-control gear-change (the box was closely related to that of the MGA sports car) and

Riley One-Point-Five specification

Produced: Abingdon, 1957 only, Longbridge, 1957-60. 150 built at Abingdon, then 39,418 of all Riley One-Point-Five types at Longbridge.
General layout: Unit-construction, pressed-steel body-chassis structure in 4-seater, 4-door saloon car style. Front-mounted engine driving rear wheels.
Engine and transmission: BMC B-Series engine, 4-cylinder, ohv, in-line. 1,489cc, 73.02 x 88.9mm; 62bhp at 4,500rpm; 83lb ft at 3,000rpm; 4-speed gearbox, no synchromesh on 1st gear; centre-floor gear-change; live (beam) rear axle with hypoid-bevel final drive.
Chassis: Independent front suspension, torsion bars and wishbones. Rack-and-pinion steering. Rear suspension by half-elliptic leaf springs. Front and rear drum brakes. 5.00-14in tyres.
Dimensions: Wheelbase 7ft 2in; front track 4ft 2.9in; rear track 4ft 2.3in; length 12ft 9in; width 5ft 1in; height 4ft 11.75in. Unladen weight (approx) 2,060lb.
Distinguishing features from previous model: Entirely different car compared with earlier Rileys, based on floorpan of Morris Minor 1000, bearing very close resemblance to Wolseley 1500 model.
Typical performance: Maximum speed 84mph; 0-60mph 17.4sec; standing ¼-mile 20.5sec; overall fuel consumption 28mpg.
Derivatives: The Wolseley 1500, also introduced in 1957, was a less-highly-developed version of the Riley One-Point-Five.
Fate: Discontinued in 1960 in favour of the slightly updated 'facelift' model.

211

a fully-equipped facia. An engine rev-counter was standard.

Compared with the Wolseley, the Riley was easily recognized by its traditional-style front grille and by the badging on the front wings and the tail. It was disappointing to see that it was quite a heavy car, and the constraints of the Minor's floorpan meant that it was only a four-seater, not a five-seater, in the passenger cabin.

By the standards of the day, the Riley had a brisk, if not sensational performance. Some people thought that it should have approached MGA performance, for it was a much more compact car with only 10bhp less, and the BMC Competitions Department soon dropped it from their fleet in favour of more suitable machines. Even so, Riley One-Point-Fives performed well in British saloon car racing for some years.

It did not sell as well as the Wolseley, one reason undoubtedly being that it cost a little bit more – £864 instead of £796 at 1957 prices – and another that there were fewer Riley dealers in the BMC chain. It was, however, very profitable for BMC to produce, as so much of the shell and all the running gear was shared with other BMC models. There were downmarket versions of the car, called Austin Lancer and Morris Major, with a different nose, trim and power output, which were built in Australia from the spring of 1958.

The original One-Point-Five gave way to the (unofficially-named) Mk II in May 1960.

Riley One-Point-Five Mk II (1960 to 1961)

In May 1960 there were minor changes to the Riley One-Point-Five (and Wolseley 1500) specification, sufficient for the revised car to be known as the Mk II model. The obvious structural changes were that the bonnet and boot hinges were hidden away instead of being on top, while there were minor changes to the engine.

The performance and general style of the car was not changed.

Riley One-Point-Five Mk II specification

As for original Riley One-Point-Five except for:
Produced: Longbridge, 1960-61, 39,568 of all Riley One-Point-Five types built.
Chassis: 5.60-14in tyres (since 1959 on Mk I).
Distinguishing features from previous model:
Hidden bonnet and boot-lid hinges and minor engine changes.
Fate: Discontinued in 1961 in favour of slightly changed Mk III type.

Riley One-Point-Five Mk III (1961 to 1965)

Although the change from Riley One-Point-Five Mk I to Mk II had been very minor indeed, that from Mk II to Mk III was a little more noticeable. In October of 1961, almost every BMC family saloon received a facelift of one sort or another, and the Riley One-Point-Five/Wolseley 1500 models joined in with that.

There was no change to the engine of these cars (which was a surprise, really, as most other cars using B-Series engines benefited from an increase in size to 1,622cc), though there were several important detail improvements to the gearbox.

A new front grille style was specified – though you had to stand the new and the old One-Point-Fives alongside each other to see the difference – and the whole car was slightly lowered to improve the roadholding capabilities. This was achieved by resetting the front torsion bars and by adding packing blocks between the axle and the rear leaf springs. There were new tail-lamp clusters, actually those already specified for the latest Austin A40 Farina.

In this final form, the Riley One-Point-Five stayed in production until April 1965, when both it and the Wolseley 1500 were quietly discontinued.

Riley One-Point-Five Mk III specification

As for Riley One-Point-Five Mk II except for:
Produced: Longbridge, 1961-65, 39,568 of all Riley One-Point-Five types built.
Dimensions: Height 4ft 11in.
Distinguishing features from previous model:
Revised grille, new colour and trim schemes, lowered suspension.
Fate: Discontinued in 1965 and not replaced.

The facelifted Riley 1.5 used the same sheet-metal bodywork, but the grille had more horizontal bars than before.

This was the 'facelift' Riley 1.5 saloon, with the more prominent tail-lamps. Note the duo-tone colour scheme.

Riley 4/Sixty Eight (1959 to 1961)

Nuffield and BMC took more than 20 years to squeeze all individuality out of the Riley marque, but with the new 4/Sixty Eight of 1959 they finally achieved it. To produce a One-Point-Five, which was little more than a tuned-up Wolseley 1500, which *itself* used a lot of Morris Minor and BMC engine in its make-up, was one thing – but the 4/Sixty Eight was even less distinguished. The miracle of it all is that the new car sold quite well – better in two years than the 1½-litre RM-Series models had achieved in the first six years!

The new 4/Sixty Eight, in fact, was merely the fifth and last of the new wave of Farina-styled B-Series saloons which were introduced in 1958-59. I have already described the basic engineering of this car in the Austin A55 Mk II section, and the Riley complied with this in almost every respect. The first of the five cars (the Wolseley 15/60) had appeared in December 1958, and the Riley was revealed in April 1959.

In almost every respect the Riley was a clone of the MG Magnette Mk III (announced in February and built on the same assembly lines at Cowley), for it shared with this car the same chopped-back rear wing-line derivative of the basic body style, and the same 64bhp B-Series engine tune. Compared with the MG, however, there was a different nose style, with a special grille, and the Riley badge actually mounted on the bonnet panel above it, and there was also a unique instrument layout, complete with a rev-counter and walnut veneer backing. This meant that, by mid-1959, the same production lines at Cowley were churning out four different types of BMC B-Series Farina saloon, all with different grilles, badging, facias, seating and other details; but then, in those days, BMC was *like* that, and no-one was surprised!

Like the other early B-Series Farina-styled saloons, the Riley's wheel tracks were too narrow, and its handling was not at all reassuring, yet because it sold at the very competitive price of £1,028 there was no shortage of customers. On the one hand, the tragedy was that it was not at all the same sort of car as the traditional Riley – not even the Nuffield-inspired RM-Series Rileys – but on the other hand Riley dealers sold quite enough of the cars to keep themselves and BMC's accountants happy.

Perhaps *The Autocar* got it right when, in their first description of the car, they wrote:

'In addition to having more power than its predecessor, the 4/Sixty Eight, which has an integral body-and-chassis structure, is nearly 4cwt lighter, and its maximum speed should be faster by nearly 10mph. Despite this added performance, however, the 4/Sixty Eight is, perhaps, less sporting in character.'

The 4/Sixty Eight was only in production for 2½ years before the BMC B-Series family was substantially revised. At the same time as cars like the Austin A55 and the Morris Oxford Series V became A60 and Oxford Series VI, respectively, the Riley progressed from being 4/Sixty Eight to 4/Seventy Two.

Riley's version of the B-Series Farina-styled theme was the Riley 4/68, which was mechanically identical to the MG Magnette Mk III.

Riley 4/Sixty Eight specification

Produced: Cowley, 1959-61, 10,940 cars built.
General layout: Unit-construction, pressed-steel body-chassis structure in 4-seater, 4-door saloon car style. Front-mounted engine driving rear wheels.
Engine and transmission: BMC B-Series engine, 4-cylinder, ohv, in-line. 1,489cc, 73.02 x 88.9mm, 64bhp at 4,800rpm; 85lb ft at 3,300rpm; 4-speed gearbox, no synchromesh on 1st gear; centre-floor gear-change; live (beam) rear axle with hypoid-bevel final drive.
Chassis: Independent front suspension, coil springs and wishbones. Cam-and-lever steering. Rear suspension by half-elliptic leaf springs. Front and rear drum brakes. 5.90-14in tyres.
Dimensions: Wheelbase 8ft 3.25in; front track 4ft 0.87in; rear track 4ft 1.87in; length 14ft 10in; width 5ft 3.5in; height 4ft 11.75in. Unladen weight (approx) 2,507lb.
Distinguishing features from previous models: Entirely different car compared with earlier Rileys, bearing family resemblance to other related Farina-styled models.
Typical performance: Maximum speed 84mph; 0-60mph 20.6sec; standing ¼-mile 21.9sec; overall fuel consumption 27mpg.
Derivatives: The Riley 4/Seventy Two of 1961 was a further developed version of the 4/Sixty Eight. All other B-Series 'Farinas' were closely related, the MG Magnette Mk III being mechanically identical.
Fate: Discontinued in 1961 in favour of the updated 4/Seventy Two model.

The Riley 4/68 may be identified by the badging, and the cut-back tail-fins which it shared with the MG Magnette Mk III.

The Riley 4/68's B-Series engine used twin SU carburettors, and an air-cleaner which lived on top of the tappet cover.

The Riley 4/68's instrument panel was not shared with any other B-Series Farina-styled saloon. It had a rev-counter and a wood veneer finish.

The Riley 4/72 was announced in October 1961, taking over from the 4/68. Improvements included a 1.6-litre B-Series engine and better handling, but no significant styling changes.

Spot the difference? This is the Riley 4/72 – distinguished from the 4/68 by its new badging, wider tracks and longer wheelbase.

Riley 4/Seventy Two (1961 to 1969)

When the B-Series saloon family was updated and substantially re-engineered for the 1962 model year, the Riley version inherited all the changes and was a substantially better car because of them. Like the other four saloons in this family, the principal chassis changes were the slightly longer wheelbase (the rear axle was actually moved rearwards under the modified monocoque), wider wheel tracks, plus anti-roll bars front *and* rear – all of which meant that it handled significantly better than the 4/Sixty Eight which it displaced.

Not only that, but the engine size was increased to 1,622cc (which meant more power and significantly more torque) and Borg-Warner Type 35 automatic transmission became optional.

Unlike other cars in this range, however, there were absolutely no changes to the exterior styling, for the Riley (like its sister car, the MG Magnette) retained the same chopped-back fins and unique tail-lamps. Nevertheless, BMC did little to promote its sale from 1962 onwards, for they were far too busy with the new generation of front-wheel-drive cars. Production was at a peak in the first year (2,877 in the financial year 1961-62), after which it dropped away to less than 1,000 a year in the late 1960s.

Although the MG Magnette was dropped in 1968, the Riley equivalent soldiered on after the death of BMC until October 1969, at which point the Riley marque was killed off completely by British Leyland.

Riley 4/Seventy Two specification

As for Riley 4/Sixty Eight except for:
Produced: Cowley, 1961-69, 14,151 cars built.
Engine and transmission: 1,622cc, 76.2 x 88.9mm, 68bhp at 5,000rpm; 89lb ft at 2,500rpm. 4-speed gearbox, no synchromesh on 1st gear; centre-floor gear-change; optional automatic transmission.
Chassis: Anti-roll bars at front and rear.
Dimensions: Wheelbase 8ft 4.35in; front track 4ft 2.6in; rear track 4ft 3.4in.
Distinguishing features from previous model: Minor details and badges.
Typical performance: Maximum speed 86mph; 0-60mph 19.5sec; standing ¼-mile 21.5sec; overall fuel consumption 25mpg.
Derivatives: Close mechanical and family resemblance to all other B-Series Farina models; MG Magnette Mk IV was mechanically identical.
Fate: Discontinued in 1969 and never replaced by another Riley.

Riley Elf (1961 to 1963)

October 1961 was a very busy month for BMC's production facilities and the sales and dealer chains. Not only were the B-Series *and* C-Series Farina-styled saloons considerably updated, but new body derivatives of the ubiquitous front-wheel-drive Minis were introduced at the same time. The two new 'booted Minis' to make their bow were the near-identical Riley Elf and Wolseley Hornet models.

For either application, here was almost, but not quite, a perfect example of badge-engineering, for there was a bit more involved than that. The basis of the new cars was a standard Mini structure and front-wheel-drive power pack, with one significant difference – instead of the ordinary Mini's small boot and downward-folding boot-lid, there was a 'bustle' extended rearwards, with a much increased stowage capacity and an *upward* opening boot-lid. The larger boot had a wooden floor, carpet-covered, with the battery position unchanged.

Compared with the ordinary Mini, therefore, the car's overall length (and rear overhang) was increased by 8.5 inches, and the luggage boot could absorb an extra 2.5cu ft of material. There was an inevitable, but small, weight increase, and naturally (BMC *always* did this) there was a unique Riley front grille.

Apart from changes to seat trim styling, the only real improvement to the interior was that the Riley had a new square instrument panel, burr walnut-covered, which supported a speedometer, fuel contents gauge and water temperature gauge. When the car was launched the publicity pictures showed open parcel shelves on each side of this panel, but by the time road tests appeared early in 1962 it was seen that the wood panel stretched from side to side of the car, with glove lockers on each side.

Like other Minis, the Elf had rubber cone springs, a hard ride and a cheeky and endearing manner. Except that acceleration was slightly down on that of the ordinary Mini, the performance was much the same. One benefit of this new car (which cost £694 when a basic Mini cost £526) was that there was a great deal more sound-deadening equipment hidden out of sight, so the car was considerably quieter than the Mini on which it was based.

The original Elf had a production life of no more than 1½ years, and on its first anniversary it was treated to a baulk-ring synchromesh gearbox. Then, in March 1963, the Mk II version was revealed.

Riley Elf specification

Produced: Longbridge, 1961-63, 30,912 Elf cars of all types built.

General layout: Pressed-steel unit-construction body-chassis structure, in 4-seater, 2-door saloon body style. Front and transversely-mounted engine driving front wheels.

Engine and transmission: BMC A-Series engine, 4-cylinder, ohv, in-line. 848cc, 62.9 x 68.26mm, 34bhp at 5,500rpm; 44lb ft at 2,900rpm; 4-speed gearbox, no synchromesh on 1st gear; centre-floor gear-change; spur-gear final drive.

Chassis: Independent front suspension, rubber cones and wishbones. Rack-and-pinion steering. Independent rear suspension by rubber cone springs and trailing arms. Front and rear drum brakes. 5.20-10in tyres.

Dimensions: Wheelbase 6ft 8in; front track 3ft 11.75in; rear track 3ft 9.9in; length 10ft 8.75in; width 4ft 5in; height 4ft 7in. Unladen weight (approx) 1,435lb.

Typical performance: Maximum speed 71mph; 0-60mph 32.3sec; standing ¼-mile 23.7sec: overall fuel consumption 33mpg.

Distinguishing features from previous models: Totally different in every way from any previous Riley model, with front-wheel drive and tiny 10in wheels; based on Austin-Morris Mini layout, with lengthened tail and different grille and trim.

Derivatives: Wolseley Hornet was identical in every way but for badges, grille and minor details. Mk II and Mk III models (see separate entries) followed.

Fate: Discontinued in 1963 in favour of Mk II model.

The Riley Elf Mk I of 1961-63 had its own, unique, instrument panel, with wood veneer and two glove lockers. The gear-lever was chrome-plated.

The Riley Elf Mk II looked just like the Mk I, but used a 998cc instead of an 848cc engine.

Riley Elf Mk II (1963 to 1966)

Very simply, the Elf Mk II (and its sister car, the Wolseley Hornet Mk II) was the original car fitted with a larger and more powerful engine. This, in fact, was the first use of the 998cc A-Series engine, which soon became a very important part of BMC's strategy – 20 years on it was still an engine size used on Austin-Rover Metro models.

The engine actually combined the original 850cc Mini's cylinder block and bore dimension, and was allied to the crankshaft stroke of the old 948cc A-Series engine. Confused? So were many pundits in 1963!

For the customer, the benefit was a 12 per cent increase in peak power – from 34bhp to 38bhp – while peak torque went up from 44lb ft to 52lb ft. This helped produce a substantially livelier performance and even better fuel consumption.

After 1½ years, the Mk II was further updated, along with other cars in the Mini range, and fitted with Hydrolastic suspension units in place of the original rubber cone springs. This resulted in a softer ride, but at the cost of a tendency to squat down at the tail when heavily loaded.

The Mk II Elf was then made for another two years before being displaced by the Mk III of 1966.

Riley Elf Mk II specification

As for Riley Elf except for:

Produced: Longbridge, 1963-66.

Engine and transmission: 998cc; 64.6 x 76.2mm, 38bhp at 5,250rpm; 52lb ft at 2,700rpm.

Chassis: Hydrolastic suspension units, interconnected front to rear, from late 1964.

Dimensions: Unladen weight 1,395lb.

Typical performance: Maximum speed 77mph; 0-60mph 24.1sec; standing ¼-mile 22.4sec: overall fuel consumption 35mpg.

Distinguishing features from previous model: 998cc engine and improved trim.

Derivatives: Mk III version followed in 1966. Elf was near-identical to Hornet of the period.

Fate: Discontinued in 1966 in favour of Mk III model.

The final Riley Elf was the Mk III, announced in 1966, which had wind-up windows and (by this time) Hydrolastic suspension.

Riley Elf Mk III (1966 to 1969)

In October 1966, five years after the original Elf had been launched, the smallest Riley became Mk III. There were no mechanical changes at first, for all the improvements were cosmetic.

The important change to the Elf bodyshell was that the old-style sliding windows were abandoned in favour of a more usual wind-up window installation. The detail styling, of course, was sleeker, but the space needed for window-drop mechanism meant that the Mini's very practical door bins had to be modified, and somewhat reduced in size.

At the same time the ventilation system was modified so that there were swivelling fresh-air 'eyeballs' at waist level on each side of the facia panel.

A welcome improvement to the transmission was that Mk III Elf models were given the remote-control gear-change of the Mini-Coopers, and from mid-1968 there was a further improvement when an all-synchromesh manual gearbox was standardized. Surprisingly enough, the new AP automatic

transmission was not offered on the Elf until the autumn of 1967.

The latest Elf continued to sell steadily, even after BMC gave way to British Leyland in 1968, but the new owners were soon determined to simplify their inherited model range and they killed off the Riley marque in the autumn of 1969. The Elf died at that time – and detail features from it, such as the wind-up windows, were to be found on the unbadged Minis of the 1970s.

Riley Kestrel (1965 to 1967)

As with other Farina-styled saloon cars, BMC were determined to squeeze every possible sale out of the front-wheel-drive 1100 type. This explains why the first one to be launched was a Morris, the second an MG, and so on. The Morris 1100 was announced in 1962, but it was not until October 1965 that the last pair of derivatives – the Riley Kestrel and the Wolseley 1100 – were produced. The use of the 'Riley' name did not infer any proper Riley heritage in the car's background – it was just a handy badge and marque name to be used to keep the Riley dealers happy and the profit margins up. These cars were not introduced earlier, by the way, so that they would not clash with the final Riley One-Point-Five and Wolseley 1500 saloons, which eventually ran out of production in the spring of 1965.

The new front-wheel-drive Riley and Wolseley models were mechanical twins, which also happened to use precisely the same running gear as the MG 1100, which had already been on sale for three years. This was logical, not only to cut down the number of different types which the engine/transmission factories had to produce, but so that these cars could be built at Cowley, in and among the MGs and the rather different Morris 1100s.

The Riley features which distinguished the Kestrel from any of its fellows included a characteristic front grille style (rather

---

Riley Elf Mk III specification

As for Riley Elf Mk II except for:
Produced: Longbridge, 1966-69.
Engine and transmission: Optional AP automatic transmission from autumn 1967. All-synchromesh gearbox from mid-1968.
Dimensions: Unladen weight 1,456lb.
Distinguishing features from previous models: Wind-up windows, face-level ventilation on facia, plus remote-control gear-change.
Derivatives: Elf was near-identical to Wolseley Hornet of the period.
Fate: Discontinued in 1969 and not replaced.

The Riley Kestrel was announced in 1965, at the same time as the Wolseley 1100. Both cars were mechanically identical with the MG 1100 and had front-wheel drive with Hydrolastic suspension.

like that of the current 4/Seventy Two) and a comprehensive instrument panel layout, which included a rev-counter and a circular-pattern speedometer; in this respect, at least, the Riley was an advance over the MG 1100 and the Wolseley 1100, both of which still had strip speedometers and no rev-counter. The Kestrel facia layout was later 'borrowed' by the MG 1300 Mk II and the Austin/Morris 1300 GT models.

As with all the other 1100s, there was Hydrolastic suspension at front and rear, front-wheel-drive and front-wheel disc brakes. For the Kestrel, the four-door saloon style was standard – there were never any two-doors or other body derivatives.

In the summer and autumn of 1967, too, the Kestrel became one of the very first BMC cars to be offered with the productionized 1,275cc engine as an option. This only raised peak power by 3bhp, but there was a more noticeable increase in torque. Cars of this type are more properly known as Riley 1275s, and their boot-lids were badged accordingly.

All in all, the Riley was trimmed and advertised as an up-market model, which explains why its price, on announcement in 1965, was £781 at a time when the Morris equivalent cost £644 and the MG 1100 £742. It was a little strange that the new AP automatic transmission was never offered as an extra, though this omission would be rectified on the derivatives which followed. Like the other upmarket 1100s, there was a great deal of extra sound-deadening to help keep the cabin quiet, but there was exactly the same amount of interior space as in other 1100s of the day.

This car was supplanted by the Mk II models, which were launched in the autumn of 1967.

Riley Kestrel 1300 (1967 to 1968)

Because the specification of the Riley Kestrel was so closely linked to that of the equivalent MG, its running gear changed at the same time. Thus, when the MG 1100 became 1300 in the autumn of 1967, so did the Riley Kestrel, and when the MG inherited its more powerful (65bhp) twin-carb engine in April 1968, so did the Riley.

Like all other 1100/1300 models, the 1300 of 1967-68 took the slightly-modified bodyshell, which had the chopped-back tail-fins and different badges, though in almost all other respects it looked the same as before. Now that a more robust automatic transmission was available, this was put on offer for the Kestrel, and the latest corporate all-synchromesh gearbox was also phased in during 1968.

This particular Kestrel, however, was strictly an interim model (as was the MG 1300), as it was supplanted by the Mk II version after only one year. In almost all respects, therefore, it was the same sort of car as its predecessor, except that it was faster and more flexible, as its performance figures prove.

Riley Kestrel 1100 Mk II (1967 to 1968)

For a very brief period, and purely as an interim model, there was an 1100 version of the new Kestrel 1300, complete with its chopped-back tail-fin body style. Only the different badging gave the game away. A very few of these cars, incidentally, had automatic transmission, but none seem to have had the new all-synchromesh transmission. Production lasted only from October 1967 to January 1968.

Riley Kestrel 1300 specification

As for original 1100 model except for:
Produced: Cowley, 1967-68.
Engine and transmission: 1,275cc, original cars 58bhp at 5,250rpm; 69lb ft at 3,000rpm; from April 1968, with twin-carb engine, 65bhp at 5,750rpm; 71lb ft at 3,000rpm. All-synchromesh manual transmission fitted during 1968; optional automatic transmission available.
Dimensions: Unladen weight (approx) 1,850lb.
Typical performance: 58bhp version, as for 1.3-litre version of original Kestrel.
Distinguishing features from previous model: Changes as for Kestrel 1100 Mk II model.
Fate: Discontinued in autumn 1968 in favour of Mk II model.

Riley Kestrel 1100 Mk II specification

As for Riley Kestrel except for:
Produced: 1967-68.
Engine and transmission: Optional AP 4-speed automatic transmission.
Distinguishing features from previous model: Chopped-off tail-fins with different tail-lamps, trim and details.
Derivatives: Kestrel 1100 Mk II was itself a derivative of original Kestrel 1100. Also 1300 (see separate entry). Austin 1100/1300 was same car; also MG, Wolseley and Vanden Plas all used same basic design.
Fate: Discontinued in 1968 and not replaced.

This was the Riley Kestrel Mk II – sold either as an 1100 or a 1300 in 1967 and 1968 only. Thereafter it became the Riley 1300 Mk II, with single rather than duo-tone colour scheme.

All Riley Kestrels and Riley 1300s had this well-equipped facia. The instruments, but not the wood trim, were later adopted for Austin/Morris 1300GTs and the MG 1300 Mk II.

Riley 1300 Mk II (1968 to 1969)

In October 1968, the Riley Kestrel was given a more powerful engine (at the same time as the MG 1100 was similarly up-gunned), and was also renamed plain '1300' instead of 'Kestrel'. However, this was the time at which Riley and Wolseley specifications began to diverge, as the Wolseley was *not* upgraded at this point.

The Riley's engine, henceforth, produced 70bhp instead of 65bhp, which meant that it had a top speed of nearly 100mph in favourable conditions, and this better engine was matched by close-ratio all-synchromesh gears. Radial-ply tyres were also standardized on an otherwise unchanged chassis.

There were no styling changes of any sort (it was almost impossible to tell the difference, externally, between this car and – say – an 1100 Mk II), but in any case this car had only one year to run, for in the autumn of 1969 the new owners, British

Leyland, killed off the Riley marque completely. There was no doubt that in its short life the last of these front-wheel-drive Rileys was also the *best* of the modern Rileys.

Riley 1300 Mk II specification

As for Kestrel 1300 except for:
Produced: 1968-69.
Engine and transmission: 70bhp at 6,000rpm; 77lb ft at 3,000rpm.
Typical performance: Maximum speed 97mph; 0-60mph 14.1sec; standing ¼-mile 19.6sec; overall fuel consumption 27mpg.
Fate: Discontinued in July 1969 when Riley marque dropped.

Chapter 10

WOLSELEY

Wolseley, like Riley, had all its old character ruthlessly expunged by the BMC product planners during the 1950s and 1960s. No Wolseley enthusiast will enjoy reading this section, even though it covers several commercially-successful models.

Even by 1939, Wolseley had been well-integrated into the Nuffield Organisation's design and development network, and in the late 1940s and early 1950s this process was accentuated. At the time of the BMC merger there were two Wolseleys in production at Cowley and another was on the way.

Like prewar Wolseleys, the 1952 4/50 and 6/80 cars were based on Morris designs – in this case the Oxford MO and Six models. In its chassis engineering and general style, the 6/80 was almost pure Morris Six except for its front grille, trim, an extra carburettor and a bit more horsepower. The 4/50, however, not only had an overhead-cam engine (whereas the Oxford MO was side-valve), it also had a longer-wheelbase version of the monocoque and the higher-standard trim and furnishing.

Then, in the autumn of 1952, came another Nuffield-designed car, the 4/44, which had a new monocoque (soon to be shared, in part, with the MG ZA Magnette) allied to the use of MG Y-Series (or detuned MG TD) engine and transmission. This was rationalized by the use of a BMC B-Series transplant in 1956, at which point it became the 15/50 and ran on to 1958.

Next on the scene was the 6/90 of 1954, which shared much of its chassis engineering and some of its bodyshell with the Riley Pathfinder, but had a BMC C-Series six-cylinder engine. This car, also built at Cowley, ran until the summer of 1959, in various Series.

From the spring of 1957 to the middle of 1965 there was also the Wolseley 1500, really a detuned Riley One-Point-Five, using a B-Series power train in conjunction with Morris Minor 1000 underpan and suspensions and with a new four-door style. It sold much better than the Riley, though – 100,000 to 40,000 in round figures.

Then, as with Riley, the Wolseleys for the 1960s and 1970s were all virtually badge-engineered Austin-Morris products, built where the planners found most convenient. In order of announcement these were the 15/60 (later 16/60) saloons, which were B-Series Farina cars and built at Cowley, and the 6/99 (later 6/110) saloons, which were C-Series 'Farinas' like the Austin A99/A110s and also built at Cowley.

Next there was the Wolseley Hornet of 1961, a Riley Elf clone and a long-tailed Mini, and after that the Wolseley 1100 range of 1965 were transverse-engined front-wheel-drive cars like the MG 1100s and Riley Kestrels. Hornets were also built at Longbridge, as were the early 1100s, but later versions were produced at Cowley.

Confused? – there is more to come. Following up the transverse-engined theme came the Longbridge-built Wolseley 18/85 of 1967, which was an upmarket version of the B-Series-powered Morris 1800. A higher-powered 'S' version followed in 1969 after BMC had been killed off, and both these cars were displaced by the six-cylinder 2200 from 1972 until 1975, when the short-lived ADO 71 'wedgie' Wolseley Six appeared. There were no Wolseleys after the end of 1975, and the name has never been revived.

Postscript
The unused model names registered to Wolseley in the 1968 SMM & T list were as follows:

County	Wasp
Cygnet	Maxi
Messenger	

The Wolseley 6/80 was a handsome long-wheelbase car, closely related to the Morris Six of the same period. It had a six-cylinder overhead-camshaft engine.

The Wolseley 6/80's instrument panel was like that of the 4/50, except for the speedometer calibrations.

Wolseley Six-Eighty (1948 to 1954)

In October 1948, the Nuffield Organisation unveiled a whole new family of saloon cars based on the same monocoque passenger cabin. A variety of front ends and wheelbase lengths were used, and with a choice of four-cylinder or six-cylinder engines these cars became the Morris Oxford and Six (already described), the Wolseley Four-Fifty and the Wolseley Six-Eighty.

In all its principal technical features, the Wolseley Six-Eighty (a title which was often shortened to 6/80, for obvious reasons) was the same car as the Morris Six, which is to say that

it had a 9ft 2in version of the new unit-construction body/chassis structure, a long and dignified nose, independent front suspension by longitudinal torsion bars, an overhead-camshaft six-cylinder engine, and a new transmission with a steering-column gear-change.

Compared with the Morris-badged car, however, there was that distinctive Wolseley front grille, a more powerful 2.2-litre engine (which had twin SU carburettors, whereas the Morris only had one SU) and a much more plush interior. The facia had centrally-grouped instruments – main dials round, auxiliary instruments oblong-shaped – over a full-width parcel shelf, there were leather seats and there was a built-in heating/demisting system as standard equipment.

Although the engine had been designed and was built by Morris Engines Branch, in Coventry, Wolseley enthusiasts didn't seem to mind as it was a welcome return to the traditional type of overhead-camshaft layout which Wolseley cars had used until 1936, when the Nuffield Organisation had become involved.

The 6/80 sold very well indeed, and must have made a great deal of money for Nuffield. It was a more distinctive and altogether more classy car than the Morris Six which it so closely resembled, and with such an enterprising performance the owner could also enjoy that distinctive engine and exhaust note, which was immortalized on numerous BBC radio plays and in films, for *this* was the car which was used by so many British police forces as a high-speed patrol car in the late 1940s and throughout the 1950s.

No styling changes were made to this car during its six-year career at Nuffield, though from time to time the mechanical specification was upgraded. Telescopic dampers were added from January 1950 (rear end) and May 1950 (twins at the front end), while the engine's compression ratio inched down from 7.0:1 to 6.6:1 and a larger-capacity heater was fitted from the autumn of 1951. The front seat style was changed from separate 'buckets' to a divided bench style in the spring of 1952.

Only 19 such cars were built at the old Ward End factory in Birmingham before assembly of all Wolseleys was transferred to Cowley at the beginning of 1949. The 6/80 was phased out in the autumn of 1954, to be replaced by the Palmer-inspired new-generation 6/90.

Wolseley Four-Fifty (1948 to 1953)

Although the 6/80 was a very similar car to the Morris Six, the closely related 4/50 was rather different from the Morris Oxford. The paradox, for Nuffield, was that the new 'small' Wolseley did not sell at all well – the 6/80 took most of the headlines – and it disappeared without a murmur in January 1953.

The Four-Fifty (or, as it was so often called, the 4/50) was the fourth of the new monocoque family introduced by Nuffield in 1948, the other three derivatives of this design being the Morris Oxford, the 6/80 and the Morris Six. However, it is easier to describe the 4/50 as a four-cylinder

The Nuffield-designed Wolseley 4/50 had the same basic monocoque as the 6/80 and the Morris Oxford MO, but with an intermediate-length wheelbase and an overhead-cam four-cylinder engine.

The earlier Wolseley 4/50 and 6/80 models had this style of facia – this being a 4/50, with 80mph speedometer. Note the steering-column gear-change.

version of the 6/80 than as an upmarket version of the Morris Oxford MO.

Compared with the 6/80, which it resembled so closely, the 4/50 had a shorter wheelbase (8ft 6in instead of 9ft 2in) and a rather more snub nose, because its front end only had to accommodate a four-cylinder version of the 6/80's overhead-

---

Wolseley 4/50 specification

Produced: Ward End, Birmingham, 1948-49 and Cowley, 1949-53, 8,925 cars built.
General layout: Unit-construction pressed-steel body/chassis structure in 4-seater, 4-door saloon car style. Front-mounted engine driving rear wheels.
Engine and transmission: Nuffield-type engine, 4-cylinder, ohc, in-line. 1,476cc, 73.5 x 87.0mm, 51bhp at 4,400rpm; 72lb ft at 2,900rpm; 4-speed gearbox with steering-column change; no synchromesh on 1st gear; live (beam) rear axle with hypoid-bevel final drive.
Chassis: Independent front suspension, torsion bars and wishbones. Bishop-cam steering. Rear suspension by half-elliptic leaf springs and Panhard rod. Front and rear drum brakes. 5.50-15in tyres.
Dimensions: Wheelbase 8ft 6in; front track 4ft 5in; rear track 4ft 5in; length 14ft 1in; width 5ft 6in; height 5ft 3in. Unladen weight (approx) 2,575lb.
Typical performance: Maximum speed 74mph; 0-60mph 31.6sec; standing ¼-mile 24.3sec; overall fuel consumption 26mpg.
Derivatives: The 4/50 was a modified longer-wheelbase version of the Morris Oxford MO, but with overhead-cam instead of side-valve engine. The Wolseley 6/80 was a longer-wheelbase version of the 4/50, with a six-cylinder engine.
Fate: Discontinued in 1953 and replaced by the Wolseley 4/44 saloon model.

---

cam engine design. Strangely enough, the Oxford, whose engine was no shorter than that of the 4/50, though side-valve, made do with an even shorter wheelbase of 8ft 1in.

The 4/50 was almost identically trimmed and furnished to the standards of the 6/80, but naturally it was a rather slower car, and perhaps it was the rather pedestrian gait (top speed was only 74mph) in conjunction with a relatively high price – £703 compared with the £767 asked for a 6/80 in 1948 – which damaged its chances.

The same basic trim and mechanical changes were made to the 4/50 as to the 6/80 (except that telescopic front dampers did not arrive until September 1950), but as soon as the much more attractive-looking 4/44 arrived on the scene in the autumn of 1952 its days were numbered. Like the 6/80, too, its production base moved, for only 99 cars were built at Ward End before the assembly of all Wolseleys was centred at Cowley.

Wolseley Four Forty-Four (1952 to 1956)
As far as BMC's planners were concerned, the Wolseley Four Forty-Four (like the Riley Pathfinder) was 'one that got away'. Its design and its production planning were too far advanced at the beginning of 1952 for the new rationalization policy to take effect. The new Wolseley, therefore, went into production with an old-style Nuffield engine a full year after the decision had been made to phase it out!

In effect, but not in fact, the Four Forty-Four (which will henceforth be called 4/44) was a very close relative of the MG Magnette ZA sports saloon which followed it into production less than a year later. The design was laid out by Gerald Palmer as soon as he arrived from Jowett – and at this time, in 1949-50, it was intended that the same type of Morris/MG XP-Series overhead-valve engine (but in different stages of tune) should be used in both cars.

The Wolseley 4/44 was announced in 1952, and was really an MG YB successor as it had the same MG type of engine and gearbox.

Wolseley 4/44s originally had this style of facia, though from 1954 glove box lids and wooden veneer facings would be added.

A good deal of the unit-construction monocoque of these two cars was shared, as the general lines make clear, but compared with the MG Magnette, the Wolseley sat up higher from the road, had more pronounced outswept sills under the doors, and of course it had the traditional type of Wolseley radiator grille at the front. Coil-spring-and-wishbone independent front suspension, plus rack-and-pinion steering, were shared, but the 4/44 made do with simple half-elliptic leaf-spring rear suspension and no extra location.

The 4/44's engine was very similar indeed to that of the MG

YB saloon (which was, in any case, soon to go out of production), for the 1,250cc unit produced 46bhp; for this application, however, it was married to a Nuffield gearbox with steering-column gear-change; there was a YB/TD type of hypoid-bevel back axle.

The car's interior, naturally, was what one might expect of a middle-class Wolseley, and was clearly related to the style of the 4/50 which was about to be made obsolete; the facia panel, in fact, had the same combination of large round instruments

---

Wolseley 4/44 specification

Produced: Cowley, 1952-56, 29,845 cars built.
General layout: Unit-construction pressed-steel body-chassis structure in 4-seater, 4-door saloon car style. Front-mounted engine driving rear wheels.
Engine and transmission: Nuffield-built engine, 4-cylinder, ohv, in-line. 1,250cc, 66.5 x 90mm, 46bhp at 4,800rpm; 58lb ft at 2,400rpm; 4-speed gearbox, no synchromesh on 1st gear; steering-column gear-change; live (beam) rear axle with hypoid-bevel final drive.
Chassis: Independent front suspension, coil springs and wishbones. Rack-and-pinion steering. Rear suspension by half-elliptic leaf springs. Front and rear drum brakes. 5.50-15in tyres.
Dimensions: Wheelbase 8ft 6in; front track 4ft 2.7in; rear track 4ft 3in; length 14ft 5in; width 5ft 1in; height 5ft 0in. Unladen weight (approx) 2,445lb.
Distinguishing features from previous model: Entirely different car compared with 4/50 model, bearing family resemblance to forthcoming MG Magnette ZA model.
Typical performance: Maximum speed 73mph; 0-60mph 29.9sec; standing ¼-mile 24.2sec; overall fuel consumption 22mpg.
Derivatives: The MG Magnette ZA of 1953 used the same basic monocoque and suspensions, but had different running gear. The 15/50 model of 1956 was really the 4/44 with BMC engine and transmission substituted for Nuffield units.
Fate: Discontinued in 1956 in favour of the updated 15/50 model.

and oblong auxiliary units.

The launch of this car was several months premature (perhaps Nuffield executives did it to make sure that BMC's planners could not force the Austin-designed B-Series engine on to them!), for production did not begin until March 1953. It was not a cheap car (£997 at launch, compared with £1,020 for the 4/50 and £989 for the MG YB saloon), nor was it very fast (73mph), but it was, above all, an elegant little machine, well-trimmed and with good road manners, which made it a sure-fire seller. In three years no fewer than 29,845 cars left the line at Cowley.

In that period, however, it was always living on borrowed time, and BMC rationalization caught up with it in 1956 when the 15/50 took over.

Wolseley 15/50 (1956 to 1958)

The birth of the 15/50 and its *raison d'etre* are easily explained. By the mid-1950s, BMC was well on the way to rationalizing all its engine/gearbox combinations and getting rid of low-volume units. The XP type of Nuffield engine, once used in so many cars, was on its way out, for the MG YB saloon had died in 1953 and the MG TF sports car followed early in 1955. The Wolseley 4/44 was the last user of all, so it soon had to fall into line. In addition, the 4/44's close relative, the MG Magnette ZA, had gone into production at the end of 1953 with the new BMC B-Series engine and gearbox.

Accordingly, the 4/44 was discontinued in June 1956, and the 15/50, which looked almost exactly the same except for the use of droopy instead of straight chrome side flashes and twin instead of one auxiliary fog lamp, took over. The new 15/50, in effect, was a lower-powered version of the Magnette ZA/ZB,

The Wolseley 15/50's driving position and facia were different from that of the 4/44 because of the dished steering wheel, the floor gear-change and the padded strip across the top rail.

Compared with the Wolseley 4/44, this car, the 15/50, had a BMC B-Series engine and transmission and very slightly different body decorations.

for it used a 50bhp single-carb version of the same 1,489cc B-Series engine, and it had the same gearbox with a very crisp centre-floor change. The facia layout, improved by fitting a full-width wood-veneer panel and glove boxes at each side for the 1954-model 4/44, was not altered.

In the next two years, the only important change was that Manumatic two-pedal-control transmission became optional from the end of 1956, though it was so unpopular that it was dropped in the autumn of 1958, just two months before the last 15/50 was produced at Cowley.

The 15/50 did not sell as well as the 4/44 had done, partly because the MG Magnette was on sale throughout the period, and partly due to the way that other BMC models came along to divert the customers' attention. But it was still a good, roadworthy and somehow very pleasant medium-sized car of which Gerald Palmer and the Nuffield team could be proud.

The 15/50 and the MG Magnette were discontinued at the same time, at the end of 1958, for both were about to be replaced by the new Farina-styled B-Series saloons, which were neither as graceful, as good handling, nor as memorable. What a shame . . .

Wolseley 15/50 specification

As for Wolseley 4/44 except for:
Produced: Cowley, 1956-58, 12,352 cars built.
Engine and transmission: BMC B-Series engine and transmission. 50bhp at 4,200rpm; 78lb ft at 2,400rpm. 4-speed gearbox, no synchromesh on 1st gear; centre-floor gear-change; optional Manumatic transmission.
Chassis: 5.60-15in tyres.
Dimensions: Weight 2,490lb.
Distinguishing features from previous model: Different model name badges, and twin fog lamps as standard.
Typical performance: Maximum speed 78mph; 0-60mph 24.3sec; standing ¼-mile 23.4sec; overall fuel consumption 25mpg.
Derivatives: MG Magnette ZB was mechanically similar, but with lowered body style, different appointments and higher engine tune.
Fate: Discontinued at end of 1958 in favour of the entirely different Wolseley 15/60 model.

The Wolseley 6/90 was revealed in 1954, and had a similar (but not identical) body style to the Riley Pathfinder, with which it shared the chassis and suspension. The engine was BMC C-Series.

Wolseley Six-Ninety (1954 to 1956)

In the same way that the 6/80 was derived from the Morris Six in 1948, the new 6/90 of 1954 was derived from the basic design of the Riley Pathfinder, which had been announced a year earlier. The two cars had the same sort of relationship, too, as the 4/44 and the MG Magnette ZA – they were inspired by the same design leader (Gerald Palmer), detailed and assembled at Cowley, and had very similar body styling, but substantially different body constructional details and very different running gear.

The 6/90 ran on the same basic chassis and suspensions as the Riley Pathfinder, which is to say that there was a separate

The Wolseley 6/90 Series I facia, 1954 to 1956 style, looked like this.

frame with a 9ft 5.5in wheelbase, torsion-bar independent front suspension and back axle location by combined coil-spring/damper units, semi-trailing radius-arms and a Panhard

---

Wolseley 6/90 specification

Produced: Cowley, 1954-56, 5,776 cars built.
General layout: Separate box-section steel chassis-frame with pressed-steel bodyshell, in 4-seater, 4-door saloon car style. Front-mounted engine driving rear wheels.
Engine and transmission: BMC C-Series engine, 6-cylinder, ohv, in-line. 2,639cc, 79.37 x 88.9mm, 95bhp at 4,500rpm; 133lb ft at 2,000rpm; 4-speed gearbox with steering-column gear-change; no synchromesh on 1st gear; live (beam) rear axle with hypoid-bevel final drive.
Chassis: Independent front suspension, torsion bars and wishbones. Cam-type steering. Rear suspension by coil springs, radius arms and Panhard rod. Front and rear drum brakes. 6.00-15in tyres.
Dimensions: Wheelbase 9ft 5.5in; front track 4ft 6.4in; rear track 4ft 6.5in; length 15ft 8in; width 5ft 7in; height 5ft 2in. Unladen weight (approx) 3,220lb.
Typical performance: Maximum speed 94mph; 0-60mph 18.1sec; standing ¼-mile 21.2sec; overall fuel consumption 21mpg.
Derivatives: The 6/90 was broadly based on the chassis design of the Riley Pathfinder, which had a lowered body and a Riley engine (see Riley).
Fate: Discontinued in 1956 in favour of the modified Wolseley 6/90 Series II saloon model.

---

rod. The smart four-door saloon body looked like that of the Pathfinder, but was 2 inches higher overall even though it rode on smaller (15in) wheels than the Pathfinder. This was because there was a more substantial sill under the doors, with front and rear wings also being deeper to match.

Unlike the Pathfinder, however, the 6/90 did not retain its own running gear, for the obsolete 6/80's overhead-camshaft engine had been allowed to die after only six years' use. Instead, the brand-new BMC C-Series driveline was used – 2,639cc overhead-valve engine, four-speed gearbox with steering-column gear-change and a new hypoid back axle. With twin SU carburettors and 95bhp, it was an impressive new unit, which was bound to make it much faster than the superseded 6/80.

Unlike the Pathfinder, which was months late in getting from announcement to the showrooms, the 6/90 was available for sale right away, where it took over smoothly from the 6/80. It was not, however, a big seller, even though it was considerably cheaper than the Pathfinder and many were sold to British police forces to take over from the previous 6/80 model.

One reason, undoubtedly, was that it soon got a reputation for rather uncertain handling (and not even the duplicating of the Panhard rod locations could solve the back-end problem completely), and perhaps another was that the public did not warm to the idea of a steering-column gear-change (which, by this time, was becoming an unpopular feature in British cars), or the idea of a divided bench front seat in what was supposed to be a 'quality' middle-class British car.

After two years, therefore, the original type was dropped and the revised Series II model took its place.

The Wolseley 6/90 Series II looked like the original, but the Series III of 1957 had an enlarged rear window.

The Wolseley 6/90 Series II and Series III cars shared the same facia layout, which was completely different from that of the Series I. There was also a right-hand gear-change (just visible here), which was actually that of the Riley Pathfinder.

Wolseley Six-Ninety Series II (1956 to 1957) and Series III (1957 to 1959)

The Six-Ninety (or 6/90) became Series II in October 1956, but this visually unchanged car was only built in that form for eight months, whereupon it was superseded by the facelifted model, which therefore became known as the Series III. Perhaps we shall never know the real reason for this rapid double-change (if we are not to blame it on BMC's much-vaunted inefficiency of the period!), unless it was that BMC wanted to phase-in the chassis improvements as rapidly as possible, then allow the restyling to follow later.

The move to Series II was timed to coincide with similar changes to the Riley Pathfinder and to bring the two cars' chassis specification closer together. On both cars the use of a coil-spring rear end had not been a success, so the principal improvement which turned the 6/90 into the Series II was its use of a straightforward half-elliptic leaf-spring rear suspension. At the same time the floor gear-change of the Riley

Pathfinder (with the lever on the right of the driver's seat on right-hand-drive cars) was also specified, which naturally meant that changes were also needed to the front seat cushion. The late-model Series I cars had already been given a restyled facia, complete with a wood (instead of the original plastic) panel, and this was carried forward for the Series II.

This car, however, did not last long, and a Series III type was put into production in May 1957, although the public announcement was delayed until August. Not only was the latest car given Lockheed Brakemaster servo-assisted brakes, with 11in diameter drums, but there was slightly lower-geared steering and the rear window was considerably enlarged – all without raising the price.

The Series III then ran on successfully until the middle of 1959 at Cowley (though it was still only built at the rate of about 2,500 cars a year during that time), a period in which the Riley Pathfinder had also been dropped and replaced by the Two-Point-Six, which was a clone of the latest 6/90 in every respect. The Wolseley was finally dropped, at that time, to make way for the new unit-construction Farina-styled 6/99 model, which was a badge-engineered Austin A99.

Wolseley 6/90 Series II specification

As for original 6/90 except for:
Produced: Cowley, 1956-57, 1,024 Series II and 5,052 Series III cars built.
Engine and transmission: 97bhp at 4,750rpm; 135lb ft at 2,000rpm. Optional Borg-Warner automatic transmission.
Chassis: Rear suspension by half-elliptic leaf springs.
Distinguishing features from previous model: Restyled facia, and manual gear-change on right of RHD driver's seat, plus half-elliptic leaf-spring rear suspension.
Derivatives: Series III model took over in summer 1957, with enlarged rear window, larger brakes and servo assistance.
Fate: Discontinued in the summer of 1959 in favour of the BMC Farina-type Wolseley 6/99.

The Wolseley 1500 was announced in the spring of 1957. It had a Morris Minor floorplan and suspension, but B-Series running gear. The basic design was shared with that of the Riley 1.5 of the same period.

Wolseley 1500 (1957 to 1960)

As has already been made clear in the Riley 1.5 section of this book, the Wolseley 1500 was not *originally* conceived as such, but rather evolved from a more humble BMC project which outgrew itself. Specifically, the new car was once to have been a Morris Minor replacement, then a rather different Morris model fitted with a 1.2-litre BMC B-Series engine, but finally a much more upmarket version of the latter concept.

The new BMC car, which was called a Wolseley, even though it had a modified Morris Minor 1000 floorpan and suspension, corporate B-Series engine and transmission and was built at the erstwhile Austin factory at Longbridge, was an interesting, though rather timid, first step to what we might now call a sports saloon. In its more powerful form, and badged as a Riley, this design *was* a sports saloon, though it never quite achieved the same status as cars such as the RM-Series had enjoyed.

Because it shared the Minor's floorpan and suspension, the Wolseley 1500 was a compact little car, with a 7ft 2in wheelbase and an overall length of only 12ft 7.7in. The superstructure was exactly the same as would be used on the Riley 1.5 model, and was also very similar to that of BMC cars to be built in Australia with Austin and Morris badges in the next few years.

The BMC B-Series engine was in absolutely conventional single (SU) carburettor form for the period, though with a low (7.2:1) compression ratio and a mild camshaft profile it only produced 43bhp at 4,200rpm. By comparison, the Austin A55, which was being built at Longbridge at the same time, had 51bhp from the same engine size.

Behind the engine there was the usual B-Series

Wolseley 1500 specification

Produced: Longbridge, 1957-60, 46,438 cars built.
General layout: Unit-construction, pressed-steel body-chassis structure in 4-seater, 4-door saloon car style. Front-mounted engine driving rear wheels.
Engine and transmission: BMC B-Series engine, 4-cylinder, ohv, in-line. 1,489cc, 73.02 x 88.9mm, 43bhp at 4,200rpm; 71lb ft at 2,600rpm; 4-speed gearbox, no synchromesh on 1st gear; centre-floor gear-change; live (beam) rear axle with hypoid-bevel final drive. Note: For the Republic of Ireland market, a total of 110 cars were produced with the 1.2-litre B-Series engine.
Chassis: Independent front suspension, torsion bars and wishbones. Rack-and-pinion steering. Rear suspension by half-elliptic leaf springs. Front and rear drum brakes. 5.00-14in tyres.
Dimensions: Wheelbase 7ft 2in; front track 4ft 2.9in; rear track 4ft 2.3in; length 12ft 7.75in; width 5ft 1in; height 4ft 11.75in. Unladen weight (approx) 2,060lb.
Distinguishing features from previous model: Entirely different car compared with earlier Wolseleys, based on floorpan of Morris Minor 1000 and bearing very close resemblance to Riley 1.5 model.
Typical performance: Maximum speed 78mph; 0-60mph 24.4sec; standing ¼-mile 22.1sec; overall fuel consumption 35mpg.
Derivatives: The Riley 1.5, also introduced in 1957, was a further developed version of the Wolseley 1500.
Fate: Discontinued in 1960 in favour of the slightly updated facelift model.

transmission, and the back axle carried the surprisingly high final-drive ratio of 3.73:1, so along with the usual Morris Minor type of 14in wheels this gave the car a pleasant, high-geared feeling. However, except that it had a neat and understated style, with four seats and adequate luggage space, the Wolseley was a strictly conventional type of BMC car, with little special character. On the one hand it had rather basic seating (the front seats were adjustable on roller slides), but on the other it had a neat walnut veneer facia, and the remote-control gear-change gave a nice feel to it. Nevertheless, it sold well – for in 1957 its UK price was £759, compared with £772 for the Austin A55 Cambridge.

Apart from an increase in tyre size, the car was little changed in the three years before it was supplanted by the Mk II version in May 1960.

Wolseley 1500 Mk II (1960 to 1961)

Although very few changes indeed were made to the Wolseley 1500 in the spring of 1960, BMC felt able to call it the Mk II model. The overall style and layout was not altered, and the most noticeable development was that the boot and bonnet hinges were now to be hidden away under the skin instead of being on top of the panels.

There were minor engine changes, which did not affect the peak power or torque outputs.

Wolseley 1500s (this was the Mk III version) all had the same close-coupled four-door body style.

'Facelift' Wolseley 1500 Mk IIIs had a more prominent radiator grille, but the same basic body and engineering as before.

233

Wolseley 1500 Mk III (1961 to 1965)

After only a year and a half's life, the Wolseley 1500 Mk II was displaced by another slightly improved version, this time called the Mk III. Thus modified, it was to carry on until 1965, when it was dropped to make way for a new generation of small-medium Wolseleys, the front-wheel-drive 1100.

It was at the 1961 Earls Court motor show that BMC's family cars were all given a facelift, or mid-life freshen-up. At this time, therefore, certain changes were made to the neat, four-door Wolseley 1500.

The engine was not changed (which was surprising, as all the B-Series Farina-styled saloons had *their* engines enlarged to 1,622cc), though there were important minor changes inside the gearbox. There was a new front grille, and the whole car rode slightly lower on its suspension, as did the Riley 1.5, in an attempt to make it look more sporty and to improve the roadholding capabilities. New tail-lamp clusters, of Austin A40 Farina type, were also fitted.

```
Wolseley 1500 Mk III specification

As for original Wolseley 1500 Mk II except for:
Produced: Longbridge, 1961-65, 31,989 cars built.
Distinguishing features from previous models:
Revised grille, new colour and trim schemes, lowered
suspension.
Fate: Discontinued in 1965 and not replaced.
```

Wolseley 15/60 (1958 to 1961)

As already described in the Austin, Morris, MG and Riley sections, there were five saloon derivatives of the Farina-styled BMC B-Series saloons, all of which were carefully badge-engineered and had their equipment aligned to suit the dealer

```
Wolseley 15/60 specification

Produced: Cowley, 1958-61, 24,579 cars built.
General layout: Unit-construction, pressed-steel
body-chassis structure in 4-seater, 4-door saloon car style.
Front-mounted engine driving rear wheels.
Engine and transmission: BMC B-Series engine,
4-cylinder, ohv, in-line. 1,489cc, 73.02 x 88.9mm, 52bhp at
4,350rpm; 82lb ft at 2,100rpm; 4-speed gearbox, no
synchromesh on 1st gear; centre-floor gear-change; live
(beam) rear axle with hypoid-bevel final drive.
Chassis: Independent front suspension, coil springs and
wishbones. Cam-and-lever steering. Rear suspension by
half-elliptic leaf springs. Front and rear drum brakes.
5.90-14in tyres.
Dimensions: Wheelbase 8ft 3.25in; front track 4ft 0.87in;
rear track 4ft 1.87in; length 14ft 10in; width 5ft 3.5in; height
4ft 11in. Unladen weight (approx) 2,473lb.
Distinguishing features from previous model: Entirely
different car compared with 15/50 model, bearing family
resemblance to other related Farina-styled models.
Typical performance: Maximum speed 77mph;
0-60mph 24.3sec; standing ¼-mile 22.6sec; overall fuel
consumption 28mpg.
Derivatives: The 16/60 of 1961 was a further developed
version of the 15/60. All other B-Series 'Farinas' were
closely related.
Fate: Discontinued in 1961 in favour of the updated 16/60
model.
```

chains in question. Paradoxically, although the Wolseley version, called the 15/60, is the fifth to be described in this book, it was the first to be launched, in December 1958.

Because the chassis details of the Wolseley were exactly like those of the other B-Series 'Farinas', in this case it is only necessary to list its distinctive mechanical and equipment features. The engine of this Wolseley was the same 52bhp

The Farina-styled Wolseley 15/60 was the first of five badge-engineered B-Series saloons to be announced, in December 1958.

The Wolseley 15/60 had traditional interior styling, with wood, leather and pile carpets well in evidence.

single-SU carburettor version of the 1,489cc unit as used in the Austin and Morris models.

The body style incorporated the prominent tail-fins of the

The Wolseley 15/60 used a single-carburettor 1.5-litre BMC B-Series engine, but it was replaced with this 1.6-litre version for the 16/60.

Austin and Morris (as opposed to the cut-back fins of the MG and Riley types), and there was a characteristic Wolseley front grille with the illuminated name badge. Two-tone paintwork was optional, but many cars had this feature, while front and rear bumper overriders were standard.

The individual feature of the interior was the facia style, which had a burr walnut face, in which the heater installation was standard and where the instruments were in a raised cowl ahead of the driver's eyes. There was a lockable glove box on the passenger's side. Front seats were arranged in the form of a divided bench, and the handbrake was tucked down at the outside of the driver's side.

The 15/60 was built at Cowley for three years, in and among the Magnettes, 4/68s and Morris Oxfords, and had the same rather stodgy character as all those cars. It was displaced by the 16/60 model in the autumn of 1961.

Wolseley 16/60 (1961 to 1971)
When BMC upgraded and considerably improved the B-Series Farina-styled cars in the autumn of 1961, the Wolseley derivative received all those benefits. As already described in

Compared with the 15/60, the Wolseley 16/60 had the pared-down tail-fins and different tail-lights, the 1.6-litre engine and the chassis improvements given to all this family from late 1961.

The Wolseley 16/60's interior had a deeply-dished steering wheel and a nicely-detailed facia panel.

the Austin, Morris, MG and Riley sections, this involved lengthening the wheelbase, widening the wheel tracks and stiffening up the suspension to turn a rather narrow-tracked and 'topply' car into a much more stable machine. There was also the increase in engine capacity from 1,489cc to 1,622cc, and the arrival of the Borg-Warner automatic transmission option.

There were minor exterior sheet metal changes for the Wolseley version, which inherited the reduced-height rear tail-fins and the new tail-lamps to go with them; the rear overriders were moved outboard to line up neatly with the rear lamp clusters. In addition there were new waistline brightwork mouldings, which extended forward to the headlamp rims.

Like the Morris Oxford Series VI, which it resembled very closely, once the 16/60 was launched, it continued to sell and was virtually ignored by the planners for the rest of its long life. Like the Morris, it was dropped in the spring of 1971.

Wolseley 6/99 (1959 to 1961)

In 1959, the new Wolseley 6/99 took over from the well-known 6/90, which meant a complete change of design direction for the big-Wolseley model range. For more than 25 years, from the mid-1930s, all large-engined Wolseleys had been based on Nuffield Organisation designs (sometimes being no more than badge-engineered Morris cars), but the new 6/99 was actually a badge-engineered Austin instead.

The basis of the Wolseley 6/99 was the Austin A99, which has already been described in the appropriate Austin section – this car itself being a replacement for the A95/A105 Westminster of the 1950s. In all major respects except for front styling, trim and equipment, the Wolseley 6/99 was identical with the Austin A99. The odd thing was that the Wolseley was assembled at Cowley, while the Austin was built at Longbridge! Austin production was later moved to Cowley.

Whereas the superseded 6/90 had been a close relation of the Riley Pathfinder/Two-Point-Six model, with which it shared the same separate chassis-frame, torsion bar front suspension and smoothly-styled four-door shell, the new 6/99 had a unit-construction monocoque four-door body/chassis unit, with styling credited to the Farina organization. Compared with the old car, the 6/99 was much squarer, bulkier and more spacious in the passenger cabin, and

---

Wolseley 16/60 specification

As for Wolseley 15/60 except for:
Produced: Cowley, 1961-71, 63,082 cars built.
Engine and transmission: 1,622cc, 76.2 x 88.9mm. 61bhp at 4,500rpm; 90lb ft at 2,100rpm. 4-speed gearbox, no synchromesh on 1st gear; centre-floor gear-change; optional automatic transmission.
Dimensions: Wheelbase 8ft 4.35in; front track 4ft 2.6in; rear track 4ft 3.4in; length 14ft 6.5in.
Distinguishing features from previous model: Different front and rear bumpers, changed profile to rear fins and new waistline mouldings.
Typical performance: Maximum speed 81mph; 0-60mph 21.4sec; standing ¼-mile 21.8sec; overall fuel consumption 26mpg.
Derivatives: Close mechanical and family resemblance to all other contemporary B-Series Farina-styled models.
Fate: Discontinued in 1971 in favour of the already established and entirely different front-wheel-drive Wolseley 18/85 model.

This was the original Farina-styled Wolseley, the 6/99 of 1959, which was a mechanical clone of the Austin A99 and used a 2.9-litre BMC C-Series engine.

naturally (for the period) there were tail-fins to give the same 'Farina' identity as was to be found on the smaller-bodied B-Series Farina-styled saloons.

Like the Austin A99 version, therefore, the Wolseley had coil-spring independent front suspension, half-elliptic springs at the rear, with front *and* rear anti-roll bars to provide handling stability. There were Lockheed front disc brakes (the 6/90 had always had drums) and rather vague cam-and-lever steering. The entire driveline was corporate BMC C-Series equipment, including the 2.9-litre overhead-valve six-cylinder engine (which was noticeably more powerful than the 2.6-litre unit used in the 6/90), and there was Borg-Warner automatic transmission as an option, but the principal mechanical innovation was a new manual transmission.

For the Austin A99 and the Wolseley 6/99 BMC had developed a new all-Porsche-type-synchromesh *three*-speed gearbox, which was backed by a Borg-Warner overdrive which worked on top and second gears. The overdrive was brought into operation by pulling on a lever which was centrally mounted under the front parcel shelf; it could be brought into operation above 30mph, once engaged, by releasing the throttle momentarily, and could be 'kicked out' by fully depressing the throttle pedal.

The Wolseley cost £1,255 in 1959, compared with £1,149 for the Austin, and the extra price was justified by the fitment of a special Wolseley front grille, flanked by auxiliary lamps (but without bonnet scoop, unlike the Austin) and by distinctive colour schemes, a wooden veneer facia (with differerent instruments and controls from the Austin), plus more plushly constructed and trimmed seats (leather-covered) and other furnishings. There was a deeply dished steering wheel, and the gear-change was on the steering column for manual *or* automatic transmission cars. In just over two years the Wolseley sold as well as the Austin until replaced by the improved 6/110 for 1962.

Wolseley 6/110 (1961 to 1964)

BMC gave their Farina-styled cars a comprehensive series of chassis improvements in the autumn of 1961, and although the 1962 models looked virtually the same as before, they were very different and altogether better under the skin. Both the B-Series and C-Series Farina saloons benefited from this treatment. In the process, the Austin A99 became the Austin A110, and to match it, the Wolseley 6/99 became the 6/110.

The Wolseley 6/110 received all the improvements applied to the Austin (see the appropriate Austin section), which included the use of a longer wheelbase, modified rear suspension linkage and (after a few months) the option of power-assisted steering. The engine became more powerful, there was a floor gear-change instead of the unpopular column change, and during 1962 air-conditioning became optional.

Except for the use of the floor gear-change, there was no visual way of identifying the 6/110 from the 6/99 model. In this form the 6/110 was produced from the autumn of 1961 until the spring of 1964 before being displaced by the further-improved Mk II model.

Wolseley 6/110 specification

As for original 6/99 except for:
Produced: Cowley, 1961-64, 10,800 6/110 Mk I types built.
Engine and transmission: 120bhp at 4,750rpm; 163lb ft at 2,750rpm. Optional Borg-Warner automatic transmission.
Chassis: Rear suspension with transverse anti-sway hydraulic damper, no anti-roll bar. Optional power-assisted steering from summer 1962.
Dimensions: Wheelbase 9ft 2in; height 5ft 0.5in. Weight 3,470lb.
Distinguishing features from previous model: Restyled facia, manual gear-change on centre floor and twin exhaust system.
Typical performance: Maximum speed 102mph; 0-60mph 13.3sec; standing ¼-mile 19.4sec; overall fuel consumption 19mpg.
Derivatives: Mk II model took over in spring 1964. Austin A110 was mechanically identical, but with different nose style and interior trim.
Fate: Discontinued in the spring of 1964 in favour of Mk II models.

Wolseley 6/110 Mk II (1964 to 1968)

The big Wolseley 6/110 became the 6/110 Mk II in May 1964 and, like the Austin equivalent, was the best of the three derivatives of this model range. The mechanical changes made to upgrade the Wolseley – of which the most important were the fitment of a new four-speed manual transmission and the rejigging of the suspension settings – were identical to those

The Wolseley 6/110 was a developed version of the 6/99, and was introduced in the autumn of 1961.

The third version of the C-Series saloons was the Wolseley 6/110 Mk II, announced in 1964, using 13in road wheels.

made for the Austin, and are fully described in the appropriate Austin section. Borg-Warner overdrive, incidentally, was no longer standard, but a £51 extra.

For the Wolseley, there were reclining front seats (whose backrests also had picnic tables for rear seat passengers to use) but no exterior styling changes. For eagle-eyed observers, the use of smaller-diameter (13in) road wheels gave the game away, and there was also a distinctive boot-lid badge. In 1964,

on announcement, the Wolseley sold for £1,179, the Austin 6/110 Super de Luxe for £1,112 and the basic A110 for £997.

When the Austin A110 Mk II was dropped in favour of the new Austin 3-litre, the Wolseley was obviously on borrowed time, and production ended in March 1968, between the announcement of the British Leyland merger and the actual inauguration of that company.

Wolseley Hornet (1961 to 1963)

Except in minor details of trim, equipment and price, the Wolseley Hornet was the twin of the Riley Elf of the day, which has already been described. It was, in other words, a Mini with a longer tail and enlarged boot, with an appropriate Wolseley grille and rather better-equipped interior. The name 'Hornet', of course, was an old Wolseley model name which had been used on a variety of sporting (some say, pseudo-sporting) Wolseleys in the early 1930s; there was nothing remotely sporting about *this* car.

Compared with the Riley Elf, the Hornet had a different facia layout, in this case the oval nacelle and three circular instruments as used in the Mini-Cooper. The gear-lever was painted instead of chrome-plated as in the Riley. The Hornet's seats had plastic covers simulating cloth, whereas the Riley's seats were of heavily-textured cloth.

Like all the other Minis of the period, the Hornet had the rubber-cone suspension, and in its original form it also had the same 848cc engine. There was more sound-deadening material than in normal Minis. On its first anniversary, in the autumn of 1962, the Hornet was given a baulk-ring synchromesh gearbox.

A price comparison is interesting. In October 1961, when

Wolseley 6/110 Mk II specification

As for original 6/110 except for:

Produced: Cowley, 1964-68, 13,301 6/110 Mk II types built.

Engine and transmission: 120bhp at 4,750rpm; 163lb ft at 2,750rpm. 4-speed gearbox, no synchromesh on 1st gear; optional Borg-Warner overdrive; optional Borg-Warner automatic transmission.

Chassis: Rear suspension without transverse anti-sway hydraulic damper, no anti-roll bar. 7.50-13in tyres.

Dimensions: Wheelbase 9ft 2in; height 5ft 0.5in. Weight 3,470lb.

Distinguishing features from previous model: Restyled facia and interior, smaller road wheels and different front grille.

Typical performance: Maximum speed 102mph; 0-60mph 13.3sec; standing ¼-mile 19.4sec; overall fuel consumption 19mpg.

Derivatives: Austin A110 Mk II was mechanically identical, but with different nose style and interior trim.

Fate: Discontinued early in 1968 and not replaced by any other large-engined Wolseley.

---

launched, the Hornet was priced at £672, the Riley Elf at £694, the Mini-Cooper at £679, and the Mini de Luxe at £568. Many people, however, preferred the upmarket image of the Wolseley to the sports-saloon aura of the Mini-Cooper, so the car sold very well in its short life. It was replaced by the Mk II model in March 1963.

The Wolseley Hornet of 1961 revived a famous old Wolseley name, but this car was identical to the Riley Elf, except for grille and badging details. Underneath it was pure Mini.

Wolseley Hornet specification

Produced: Longbridge, 1961-63, 28,455 Hornets of all types built.

General layout: Pressed-steel unit-construction body-chassis structure in 4-seater, 2-door saloon body style. Transversely and front-mounted engine driving front wheels.

Engine and transmission: BMC A-Series engine, 4-cylinder, ohv, in-line. 848cc, 62.9 x 68.26mm, 34bhp at 5,500rpm; 44lb ft at 2,900rpm; 4-speed gearbox, no synchromesh on 1st gear; centre-floor gear-change; spur-gear final drive.

Chassis: Independent front suspension, rubber cones and wishbones. Rack-and-pinion steering. Independent rear suspension by rubber cone springs and trailing arms. Front and rear drum brakes. 5.20-10in tyres.

Dimensions: Wheelbase 6ft 8in; front track 3ft 11.75in; rear track 3ft 9.9in; length 10ft 8.75in; width 4ft 5in; height 4ft 7in. Unladen weight (approx) 1,435lb.

Typical performance: Maximum speed 71mph; 0-60mph 32.3sec; standing ¼-mile 23.7sec; overall fuel consumption 33mpg.

Distinguishing features from previous models: Totally different in every way from any previous Wolseley model, with front-wheel drive and tiny 10in wheels; based on Austin-Morris Mini layout, with lengthened tail and different grille/trim.

Derivatives: Riley Elf was identical in every way but for badges, grille and minor details. Mk II and Mk III models (see separate entries) followed.

Fate: Discontinued in 1963 in favour of Mk II model.

The Wolseley Hornet of 1961, though Mini-based, was distinguished by a lengthened tail and enlarged boot.

Wolseley Hornets progressed to Mk II specification early in 1963, with a 998cc instead of an 848cc engine.

Wolseley Hornet Mk II specification

As for Wolseley Hornet Mk I except for:
Produced: Longbridge, 1963-66.
Engine and transmission: 998cc; 64.6 x 76.2mm, 38bhp at 5,250rpm; 52lb ft at 2,700rpm.
Chassis: Hydrolastic suspension units, interconnected front to rear, from late 1964.
Dimensions: Unladen weight 1,395lb.
Typical performance: Maximum speed 77mph; 0-60mph 24.1sec; standing ¼-mile 22.4sec; overall fuel consumption 35mpg.
Distinguishing features from previous model: 998cc engine and improved trim.
Derivatives: Mk III version followed in 1966. Hornet was near-identical to Riley Elf of the period.
Fate: Discontinued in 1966 in favour of Mk III model.

Wolseley Hornet Mk II (1963 to 1966)

The Wolseley Hornet became Mk II in March 1963 at exactly the same time and in precisely the same way as its sister car, the Riley Elf. In summary, this meant that the 848cc engine was ditched in favour of a more powerful 998cc unit.

For all other details, please consult the Riley Elf Mk II entry.

Wolseley Hornet Mk III (1966 to 1969)

As with the Mk I and Mk II models, the Wolseley Hornet Mk III was a badge-engineered twin of the Riley Elf of the period. Both cars became Mk IIIs at the same time, in October 1966, after which they were built for three years, at Longbridge. When the Riley Elf was killed off, as British Leyland ditched the Riley marque, the Wolseley Hornet also died, for it was the only other BMC car to share the long-tail derivative of the Mini's body.

Like the Riley Elf, the Mk III Hornet inherited face-level

The Wolseley Hornet Mk III was announced in 1966 and had wind-up windows. Hydrolastic suspension had featured on these cars since late 1964.

ventilation outlets, but the Hornet kept its familiar oval instrument nacelle, which had a wooden veneer face.

For all other details, please consult the Riley Elf Mk III entry.

Wolseley Hornet Mk III specification

As for Wolseley Hornet Mk II except for:
Produced: Longbridge, 1966-69.
Engine and transmission: All-synchromesh gearbox from mid-1968.
Dimensions: Unladen weight 1,456lb.
Distinguishing features from previous models: Wind-up windows and face-level ventilation on facia, plus remote-control gear-change.
Derivatives: Hornet was near-identical to Riley Elf of the period.
Fate: Discontinued in 1969 and not replaced.

Wolseley 1100 (1965 to 1967)

By the mid-1960s, BMC had squeezed all signs of originality out of their upmarket Riley and Wolseley marques. When new models appeared, there would usually be a Riley *and* a Wolseley version, the two types inevitably having the same running gear. The only surprise, as far as the front-wheel-drive BMC 1100 range was concerned, was that it took so long for the Riley and Wolseley versions to appear. This event was delayed until the autumn of 1965 because the old-model Riley 1.5 and Wolseley 1500 cars were still selling.

The Wolseley 1100 of October 1965, therefore, used the same running gear as the new Riley Kestrel – and, for that matter, the MG 1100, which had already been on the market for three years. The Wolseley's instrument display was the same as that of the MG 1100, along with a wood veneer facia panel, and there were individual touches to the exterior decoration (including the Wolseley grille at the front) and distinctive duo-tone paintwork and brightwork as an option.

At launch, the Wolseley slotted into the BMC range as the

The Wolseley 1100 of 1965-67 was mechanically identical with the MG 1100 and Riley Kestrels of the same period.

Wolseley 1100 specification

Produced: Longbridge, then Cowley, 1965-67, 17,397 1100s of Mk I *and* Mk II types built.

General layout: Pressed-steel unit-construction body-chassis structure in 4-seater 4-door saloon body style. Front and transversely-mounted engine driving front wheels.

Engine and transmission: BMC A-Series engine, 4-cylinder, ohv, in-line. 1,098cc, 64.58 x 83.72mm, 55bhp at 5,500rpm; 61lb ft at 2,500rpm. During summer-autumn 1967, some cars sold with 1,275cc engine, 70.6 x 81.28mm, 58bhp at 5,250rpm; 69lb ft at 3,500rpm. 4-speed gearbox, no synchromesh on 1st gear; centre-floor gear-change; spur-gear final drive.

Chassis: Independent front suspension, Hydrolastic units and wishbones. Rack-and-pinion steering. Independent rear suspension by Hydrolastic units, trailing arms and anti-roll bar. Interconnection between front and rear suspensions. Front disc and rear drum brakes. 5.50-12in tyres.

Dimensions: Wheelbase 7ft 9.5in; front track 4ft 3.5in; rear track 4ft 2.9in; length 12ft 2.7in; width 5ft 0.4in; height 4ft 4.7in. Unladen weight (approx) 1,820lb.

Typical performance: (1,098cc version) Maximum speed 85mph; 0-60mph 18.4sec; standing ¼-mile 21.3sec: overall fuel consumption 29mpg. (1,275cc version) Maximum speed 88mph; 0-60mph 17.3sec; standing ¼-mile 20.7sec; overall fuel consumption 30mpg.

Distinguishing features from previous models: Entirely new type of Wolseley model with Pininfarina styling.

Derivatives: Austin/Morris 1100 was the same car with different badges, details and engine tune. MG 1100 and Riley Kestrel models were slightly modified versions, too. Mk II (see separate entry) was same car with minor changes.

Fate: Discontinued in 1967 and replaced by Mk II models.

The Wolseley 1100 of 1965-67 had an identical facia and instrument display to the MG 1100.

middle-priced version of this group of cars – the MG 1100 cost £742, the Wolseley 1100 £754 and the Riley Kestrel £781.

Like the MG and Riley, the Wolseley 1100 was also available, very briefly during the summer of 1967, as a Wolseley 1275, this being a foretaste of what was to come from BMC in the next few months.

Wolseley 1300 (1967 to 1968)

Like all the front-wheel-drive BMC models, the Wolseley versions were treated to a facelift and a power boost for 1968.

At the same time as the Riley Kestrel became the Kestrel 1300, the Wolseley became a Wolseley 1300. Body style and mechanical changes were the same – for further details see the Riley Kestrel 1300 section.

In the autumn of 1967, BMC upgraded the transverse-engined Hydrolastically-sprung Wolseley into the 1300. This style then remained until 1971 – note the British Leyland badges on the wings of this later model.

The Wolseley 1300 may be identified from the rear by its badging.

Wolseley 1300 specification

As for original 1100 model except for:
Produced: Cowley, 1967-68, 27,470 1300s of Mk I *and* Mk II types built.
Engine and transmission: 1,275cc, original cars 58bhp at 5,250rpm; 69lb ft at 3,000rpm; from April 1968, with twin-carb engine, 65bhp at 5,750rpm; 71lb ft at 3,000rpm. All-synchromesh manual transmission fitted during 1968; optional automatic transmission available.
Dimensions: Unladen weight (approx) 1,850lb.
Typical performance: 58bhp version, as for 1.3-litre version of original 1100.
Distinguishing features from previous model: Changes as for Wolseley 1100 Mk II model.
Fate: Discontinued in autumn 1968 in favour of Mk II model.

Wolseley 1100 Mk II specification

As for Wolseley 1100 except for:
Produced: 1967-68.
Engine and transmission: Optional AP 4-speed automatic transmission.
Distinguishing features from previous model: Chopped-off tail-fins with different tail-lamps, trim and details.
Derivatives: 1100 Mk II was itself a derivative of original 1100. Also 1300 (see separate entry). Austin 1100/1300 was same car; also MG, Riley and Vanden Plas all used same basic design.
Fate: Discontinued in 1968 and not replaced.

Wolseley 1300 Mk II specification

As for 1300 except for:
Produced: 1968-73.
Engine and transmission: 65bhp at 5,750rpm; 71lb ft at 3,000rpm. With automatic transmission, 60bhp at 5,250rpm; 69lb ft at 2,500rpm.
Typical performance: No authentic independent figures published.
Fate: Discontinued in spring 1973 and not replaced.

Wolseley 1100 Mk II (1967 to 1968)

For a very short time, BMC produced an 1100 version of the facelifted Wolseley 1300, which used the original 1,098cc engine. A handful of these cars, too, were built with AP automatic transmission.

The car was only available between October 1967 and February 1968 and was mechanically identical in every way with the Riley Kestrel 1100 Mk II.

Wolseley 1300 Mk II (1968 to 1973)

From the autumn of 1968 to 1973, British Leyland allowed the old BMC car, the Wolseley 1300, a bit of individuality. Not only was it mechanically just that important bit different from

the Riley 1300 (whose Kestrel name was dropped at this time), but it outlived it by three and a half years.

In the autumn of 1968 there was something of a reshuffle among the higher-powered/higher-specification 1300s – the MG, Riley, Vanden Plas and Wolseley varieties – although there were no exterior styling changes. Engines, transmissions and options all came in for attention, and all these cars were slightly distanced from each other. The details of this process have already been described in the appropriate MG and Riley sections.

For 1969, therefore, the Wolseley retained its 65bhp twin-carb engine for manual transmission cars, while it also took up a single-carburettor 60bhp engine where automatic transmission was specified. The all-synchromesh gearbox which had been phased in to the 1300 during 1968 was retained, but it was *not* the close-ratio variety which MG and Riley 1300s were given at this time. Similarly, the Wolseley retained cross-ply tyres at a time when MGs and Rileys were given radials.

Mechanically, in other words, the Wolseley was not to be the same as the even more upmarket Vanden Plas Princess 1300 model, and British Leyland certainly intended that it should be seen as a gentleman's carriage, rather than the sporty type of saloon which the Riley 1300 was becoming.

The Wolseley 1300 Mk II, introduced in the autumn of 1968, had this 65bhp twin-SU carburettor engine as standard, for manual transmission cars only.

Apart from the use of nicer seats, and a T-handle selector for the automatic transmission (where fitted), there were no other important changes, and the Wolseley 1300 carried on until the entire 1300 range was dropped in favour of the new Austin Allegro of 1973. If BMC had still been in charge, no doubt there would have been a Wolseley Allegro, but – in spite of their many faults – British Leyland were made of sterner stuff and were rationalizing dealer networks, so this was the end of the small Wolseley. Henceforth, all surviving Wolseleys would be 1800/2200-based cars and the marque name would disappear completely before the end of 1975.

Wolseley 18/85 (1967 to 1969)

Because BMC's management was so committed to the philosophy of badge-engineering by the mid-1960s, it was almost inevitable that a Wolseley version of the front-wheel-drive 1800 model would arrive one day. There was, after all, a Wolseley Mini, a Wolseley 1100, a Wolseley B-Series Farina saloon and a Wolseley C-Series Farina saloon. Even so, although the first of the 1800s, badged as an Austin, was launched in October 1964, the Wolseley derivative did not reach the public until March 1967. There were two reasons for calling the car 18/85 – one was that it was a 1.8-litre car with

The Wolseley 18/85 was a better-trimmed, distinctively-nosed version of the Austin/Morris 1800. This was the first transverse-engined B-Series car to have optional automatic transmission.

an 85bhp (net) power output, and the other was that there had been a much-respected Morris-based Wolseley 18/85 model built immediately before and after the Second World War.

In this case, however, a genuine and determined attempt had been made to produce a different version of the design, which would justify the use of a distinctive badge. Not only were the expected front styling, interior trim and facia features included, but this was the first of the 1.8-litre front-wheel-drive cars to have automatic transmission as an optional extra, and power-assisted steering was standard equipment.

The general layout of the new Wolseley was that of the Austin/Morris 1800, which is to say that there was a bulky and massively strong four-door saloon car body which used a transverse-engined front-wheel-drive power pack and rode on all-independent Hydrolastic suspension. This was arguably the most spacious of all modern series-production British cars, and although the styling was, shall we say, an acquired taste, it was very practical in every way. The engine was in single-SU-carburettor trim, exactly the same as that fitted to the Austin and Morris versions, as was the transmission if the manual type was chosen.

The Borg-Warner automatic transmission was tucked into the sump space vacated by the manual cluster, but the system was so arranged that the engine and transmission oils were not shared. One interesting detail was that the drive from the crankshaft to the transmission was by a Morse Hy-Vo chain, rather than by a train of gears. The gear selector lever was on the facia, to the right of the instruments (on RHD cars), and behind the steering wheel.

To justify the 1967 price of £1,040 (plus £95 for the optional

Wolseley 18/85 specification

Produced: Longbridge, 1967-69, 35,597 18/85s and 18/85Ss of all types built
General layout: Pressed-steel unit-construction body-chassis structure in 5-seater 4-door saloon body style. Front and transversely-mounted engine driving front wheels.
Engine and transmission: BMC B-Series engine, 4-cylinder, ohv, in-line. 1,798cc, 80.26 x 88.9mm, 85bhp at 5,300 rpm; 99lb ft at 2,100rpm. 4-speed gearbox, all synchromesh; centre-floor gear-change; optional 3-speed Borg-Warner automatic transmission; spur-gear final drive.
Chassis: Independent front suspension, Hydrolastic units and wishbones. Rack-and-pinion steering with power assistance. Independent rear suspension by Hydrolastic units, trailing arms and anti-roll bar. Interconnection between front and rear suspensions. Front disc and rear drum brakes. 175-13in tyres.
Dimensions: Wheelbase 8ft 10in; front track 4ft 8in; rear track 4ft 7.5in; length 13ft 10.1in; width 5ft 7in; height 4ft 7.5in. Unladen weight (approx) 2,576lb.
Typical performance: (with automatic transmission) Maximum speed 90mph; 0-60mph 18.0sec; standing 1/4-mile 21.2sec; overall fuel consumption 22mpg.
Distinguishing features from previous models: Entirely new type of front-wheel-drive Wolseley model without ancestors.
Derivatives: Austin/Morris 1800 was the same car with different badges and details. Mk II (see separate entry) was same car with minor changes.
Fate: Discontinued in 1969 and replaced by Mk II model.

The Wolseley 18/85 had its own distinctive type of tail-lamps in what was basically an Austin/Morris 1800 body structure.

The Wolseley 18/85 of 1967 followed the usual Wolseley traditions, with leather seating and a special instrument layout. This was the optional automatic transmission version.

automatic transmission) – which compared with £883 for the Austin 1800 – BMC gave the Wolseley a traditional type of nose style and unique vertical tail-lamps, along with a wooden facia panel and circular instruments, optional reclining front seats, pile carpet on the floor and leather seat coverings. This was, it seemed, exactly what the middle-class clientele wanted, for the Wolseley was a quieter, better-equipped and somehow more dignified machine than the Austin and Morris models, while it retained all that interior space and the sure-footed, if not at all sporting, handling and roadholding.

The original 18/85 was displaced by the updated Mk II version in the summer of 1969, rather more than two years after the original launch.

Wolseley 18/85 Mk II (1969 to 1972)

Although the Austin and Morris 1800s became Mk II in the spring of 1968, the same development changes were not applied to the Wolseley 18/85 until the high summer of 1969. At that time, not only were all the 1800's chassis changes standardized across the range, but a series of improvements, special to the Wolseley, were also added to the specification.

There were no exterior styling changes except for the addition of a 'II' to the boot-lid badging, but the interior came in for a great deal of attention. Not only did the fitment of reclining seats become standard equipment (instead of an optional extra on the original cars), but the seats had been reshaped and made more comfortable.

The Wolseley 18/85 became 'Mk II' in 1969, to re-align it with the modified Austin/Morris 1800s.

247

Door trim had also been restyled, and wood fillets appeared on the door sills below the windows. There was revised switchgear on the facia panel, which retained its polished walnut veneer. In the process the price went up to £1,224, and the optional automatic transmission (which had been added to the Austin and Morris options list by that time) was priced at £101.

As with the original type, the 18/85 Mk II continued to sell steadily and helped to keep the Longbridge production lines busy for another two and a half years before it was dropped in favour of the British Leyland-developed six-cylinder Wolseley Six in 1972.

Wolseley 18/85 Mk II 'S' (1969 to 1972)

At the same time as the Wolseley 18/85 progressed from Mk I to Mk II, the new corporate owners, British Leyland, announced the 18/85 Mk II 'S'.

This car, in a nutshell, was the Mk II derivative of the 18/85, allied to the 96bhp twin-SU carburettor engine tune of the Austin and Morris 1800 'S' types, all of which have been described earlier in this book.

The 18/85 Mk II 'S' was dropped in 1972 in favour of the smoother and silkier (though not much quicker) Six.

Wolseley 18/85 Mk II specification

As for 18/85 except for:
Produced: 1969-72.
Engine and transmission: 86bhp at 5,300rpm; 101lb ft at 3,000rpm.
Chassis: 165-14in tyres.
Typical performance: Maximum speed 97mph; 0-60mph 15.2sec; standing ¼-mile 20.4sec; overall fuel consumption 24mpg.
Distinguishing features from previous model: No external changes, but different trim, new seats and details.
Derivatives: The 18/85 Mk II was itself a derivative of the original 18/85. Austin 1800/Morris 1800 was same basic car; Six of 1972 followed on, with different engine (see separate entry).
Fate: Discontinued in 1972 in favour of Six model.

Wolseley 18/85 Mk II 'S' specification

As for 18/85 Mk II except for:
Produced: 1969-72.
Engine and transmission: 96bhp at 5,700rpm; 106lb ft at 3,000rpm automatic transmission available as option.
Typical performance: Maximum speed 99mph; 0-60mph 13.7sec; standing ¼-mile 19.4sec; overall fuel consumption 22mpg.
Distinguishing features from previous models: No external changes except for contrast colour paint stripe on sides and 'S' badging on tail, plus twin-carb engine.
Derivatives: The 18/85 Mk II 'S' was itself a derivative of the original 18/85 Mk II. Austin 1800/Morris 1800 was same basic car.
Fate: Discontinued in 1972 in favour of 2200 model.

Wolseley produced this 18/85 Mk II 'S', mechanically identical to the Austin and Morris 'S' models, and fitted with a contrasting colour stripe.

Chapter 11

BMH and British Leyland

BMC's successors and the cars they inherited

Although the BMC era ended in 1968, the cars designed and built by the Corporation did not die off immediately. Many BMC cars continued in production for another five years or more – and one of them, the Mini, was *still* being made in the mid-1980s, when this book was first planned. To make it truly comprehensive, therefore, I must complete the story of all existing BMC cars which were being assembled in 1968, and show how many BMC components and how much design work was used by British Leyland in the years which followed.

BMC began talks with Sir William Lyons and Jaguar in 1966, agreement was speedily reached and a merger was announced in July. The main result of this was that a new parent company, British Motor Holdings, came into existence, with Sir George Harriman as chairman. Pressed Steel Fisher was hived off from BMC, which otherwise continued to operate unchanged, and Jaguar Cars was the third of the main businesses in the new group.

The only rationalization which followed this move was that the new Daimler limousine of 1968 was really a stretched Jaguar 420G floorpan and running gear topped by a bodyshell which was painted, trimmed and completed by Vanden Plas, at Kingsbury. BMC and Jaguar engineers began to co-operate on such matters as exhaust emissions and safety research, but at no time in the next few years were any BMC components used in a Jaguar car – or *vice versa*.

Leyland began merger talks with BMC as early as 1966, even before the Jaguar deal took place, but serious discussions with BMH did not start again until October 1967, when the Prime Minister, Harold Wilson, invited Sir George Harriman and Sir Donald Stokes to dinner at Chequers. The story of the negotiations which followed in the next three months has been told elsewhere (notably by Graham Turner in *The Leyland Papers*), so need only be summarized here.

Originally it looked as if there would be a genuine merger of equals, but as more details were tabled by the two management teams it became clear that BMH was not at all financially strong, while Leyland was booming. From this very moment, it seems, Leyland bosses began to mistrust the calibre of their opposite numbers at BMH and to worry about the prospects for the newly merged company, which they determined to dominate right from the start.

The merger, which was announced on January 17, 1968, was effectively a takeover of BMH by Leyland (in management terms and philosophy, if not in share-dealing terms), and within months Leyland personalities were in charge of the group's destiny. Although BMC's Sir George Harriman became the first chairman of British Leyland, he had already agreed to retire, in favour of Sir Donald Stokes, *before the merger was formalized*. The new British Leyland Motor Corporation began to operate in May 1968, and BMC/BMH then ceased to exist. A purge of top management took place at the old BMC headquarters at Longbridge, with Sir Donald Stokes himself running what was to be called Austin-Morris for the first six months, after which ex-Leyland-Triumph men George Turnbull (as managing director) and Harry Webster (technical director) took over.

By 1967-68 BMC knew (but perhaps would not admit) that it was now building far too many derivatives of far too many models, in too many places, but it was not until the merger with Leyland was being negotiated that the company began to do something about it. In the next few months, therefore, there was something of an old-model/slow-sellers clear-out, and only then did a new British Leyland model policy begin to take shape.

Weeding out the old models

The following cars disappeared in the period between October 1967 and May 1968:

Austin A40 Farina Mk II
Austin A110 Westminster Mk II – to make way for the new ADO 61 Austin 3-litre
[Austin Gipsy 4x4 off-road vehicle – not covered in this book]
Austin-Healey 3000 – to make way for the new MG MGC
MG Magnette Mk IV Farina saloon
Riley Kestrel 1100 Mk II
Vanden Plas Princess 1100 Mk II
Vanden Plas 4-litre R
Vanden Plas 4-litre Limousine
Wolseley 1100 Mk II
Wolseley 6/110 Mk II

– and the Austin/Morris Mini-Moke production facility would be transferred from Longbridge to the satellite factory in Australia a few months later.

BMC's last major new model – the Austin Maxi

Alec Issigonis' design team had already started work on the fourth of their transverse-engined front-wheel-drive cars, the ADO 14, in 1964-1965, and this eventually reached the public in April 1969, badged as the Austin Maxi, but assembled at the old Nuffield factory at Cowley. Maxi, incidentally, was one of those registered trademarks which are listed at the end of each marque section.

There was no danger of it ever being identified as a new British Leyland design concept – not only because it had become something of an open secret in the motor industry well before the merger took place, but principally because British Leyland managers let it be known that they were rather stuck with it, as all the tooling had been ordered, and partly commissioned, before they took control.

In general terms, ADO 14 was meant to slot in to a carefully graduated range of front-wheel-drive cars, halfway between the Farina-styled A-Series-engined 1100/1300 models and the B-Series-engined 1800 models. BMC, in fact, found it rather awkward to provide a suitable power unit for the new project at first, as the A-Series could not comfortably stretch any further, while the B-Series was too heavy and old-fashioned, even though it had once been a 1.5-litre design.

Sir George Harriman and his fellow directors therefore took the very bold decision to design, develop and tool-up for an entirely new car – new body/chassis unit, new engine, new transmission and even a new layout – for they had decided to produce it as a hatchback. The only compromise, and the only touch of rationalization, was that ADO 14 used the same door assemblies as the Austin/Morris 1800 – a cost-saving exercise which rather compromised the styling.

The basic layout of ADO 14, which henceforth I will call the Maxi, was the same as the other current BMC front-drive cars, which is to say that there was a rigid unit-construction pressed-steel body-chassis unit and a transversely-positioned engine at the front of the car, driving to a gearbox in the sump and on to the front wheels. All-independent suspension, wishbone front and trailing-arm rear, by Hydrolastic suspension units, along with front-wheel disc brakes and rack-and-pinion steering, all looked very familiar, and differed only in detail from the other BMC products. It was, in other words, a typical BMC car, which must certainly be described here:

Austin Maxi (later called Maxi 1500) (1969 to 1979)

Because the Austin Maxi was announced in April 1969, as the first major new model from the British Leyland combine, that unlucky corporation had to suffer all the press complaints as if the car had been their own idea! In fact the Maxi was a pure BMC (or, should I say, Issigonis?) design, with body and engine tooling well on the way to completion by 1968, when the corporate upheaval took place. British Leyland's part was merely to facelift the car before it was even announced, then to rejig it yet again after 18 months and allow it to soldier on, unloved, for a further decade!

The Maxi, originally coded ADO14, was developed as the fourth generation of BMC's transverse-engine/front-wheel-drive cars. Work began in about 1964-65, and the car *ought* to have been ready before the British Leyland company formation, but there were many delays (not least because of financial problems in 1966 and 1967). In general layout, the Maxi was like the other BMC front-wheel-drive cars, which is to say that it had a stubby nose, a long wheelbase and a capacious interior, plus all-independent Hydrolastic suspension and front-wheel disc brakes.

The Maxi, however, was new from stem to stern, not only with a new bodyshell, but with a brand new E-Series engine (more properly called E4, as there was a six-cylinder derivative, E6, fitted to the 2200 models of 1972), and a brand-new five-speed gearbox. Not only this, but it was also to be a hatchback, with fold-down rear seats, something which BMC had not properly developed before if we discount the severely-squared-up lines of the A40 Farina. It is not generally known, by the way, that the Maxi used the same passenger doors as fitted to the 1800 bodyshell.

The prototype Maxi, apparently, was even plainer and more sparsely equipped than the car which eventually appeared, but the production car was certainly no sybarite's delight. Mechanically, it was as expected, though the under-square

BMC were developing the new Austin Maxi when absorbed into British Leyland. The result was launched in April 1969.

The Austin Maxi had a five-door hatchback body style.

This was the engine compartment of the first Austin Maxi, with new E-Series overhead-camshaft engine and front-wheel drive.

The original Maxi of 1969 had a very plain facia, not much liked by the critics.

Austin Maxi specification

Produced: Cowley, 1969-1979, 412,161 Maxi 1500 and Maxi 1750 cars of all types built.
General layout: Pressed-steel, unit-construction body-chassis structure, in 5-seater 5-door saloon body style. Front and transversely-mounted engine driving front wheels.
Engine and transmission: BMC E4-Series engine, 4-cylinder, ohc, in-line. 1,485cc, 76.2 x 81.28mm, 74bhp at 5,500 rpm; 84lb ft at 3,500 rpm. 5-speed gearbox, all synchromesh; centre-floor gear-change; spur-gear final drive.
Chassis: Independent front suspension, Hydrolastic units and wishbones. Rack-and-pinion steering with optional power assistance. Independent rear suspension by Hydrolastic units and trailing arms. Interconnection between front and rear suspensions. Front disc and rear drum brakes. 155-13in tyres.
Dimensions: Wheelbase 8ft 8in; front track 4ft 5.8in; rear track 4ft 5.2in; length 13ft 2.3in; width 5ft 4.1in; height 4ft 7.3in. Unladen weight (approx) 2,160lb.
Typical performance: Maximum speed 86mph; 0-60mph 16.6sec; standing ¼-mile 20.6sec; overall fuel consumption 24mpg.
Distinguishing features from previous models: All-new front-drive Austin model with no links with obsolete models, though general layout similar to larger 1800s.
Derivatives: Austin Maxi 1750 (see separate entry) was the same basic car with larger engine. From late 1970 officially became Maxi 1500, with facia, trim and detail improvements.
Fate: Discontinued in 1979 and eventually replaced by British Leyland-designed Austin Maestro range.

proportions of the engine (seemingly without any scope for capacity stretching in future years) took everyone by surprise. The concept of the all-synchromesh five-speed transmission, complete with an overdrive fifth, was fine, but because there was a complex cable linkage between gearbox and gear-lever, the practical result was below standard.

The facia had circular instruments ahead of the driver and was well-equipped, but somehow it fell below the standards expected. This failing, generally low-quality build standards and severe customer reaction against the gear-change, led the designers to rush through the second-guess Maxi by the autumn of 1970, and this was a better, if more conventional, machine.

For 1971 there was a rod gear-change linkage and a wooden facia, plus better trim all round, at which point the car became known as the Maxi 1500. With very few significant changes, except for some cosmetic updates, the car was built until 1979. The Maxi 1750 (see below) which arrived for 1971 was an altogether better car.

Surprisingly, for a car badged as an Austin, Maxi assembly was always carried out at the ex-Nuffield factory at Cowley!

Austin Maxi 1750 (1970 to 1981)

At the same time as British Leyland improved the original Maxi, in time for the 1970 motor show, they also announced the Maxi 1750, which was really the same car with a long-stroke (*not* larger-bore, which was not possible in the confines of a very short cylinder block) engine.

Naturally they called this car the Maxi 1750, for the engine capacity was 1,748cc, and the peak power had been raised from 74bhp (1500) to 84bhp (1750), with an impressive torque boost from 84lb ft to 105lb ft. The gearbox and final-drive ratios were reshuffled to give the same fifth-gear mph/1,000rpm figure, but higher intermediate ratios. There was an appropriate tailgate badge to give the game away, and all the

Austin Maxi 1750 specification

As for Maxi 1500 except for:
Produced: 1970-81.
Engine and transmission: 1,748cc, 76.2 x 95.75mm, 84bhp at 5,500 rpm; 105lb ft at 3,000 rpm. 4-speed automatic transmission available as option from late 1972.
Typical performance: Maximum speed 89mph; 0-60mph 15.8sec; standing ¼-mile 20.2sec; overall fuel consumption 25mpg.
Distinguishing features from previous models: New grille, new badging on tail, plus new wooden facia and enlarged engine.
Derivatives: 1750 was itself a derivative of the original 1500. Maxi 1750HL with 95bhp followed in 1972. A slightly facelifted 'Maxi 2' 1.7-litre car followed in 1979. At this point the HL became the HLS.

changes described for the 1971-model Maxi 1500, including the rod gear-change, were adopted.

The Maxi 1750, in one cosmetic guise or another, was built until the summer of 1981, when it was dropped to make way for the new Maestro range. An automatic transmission option had been available from the end of 1972, and there was also a higher-powered, British Leyland-developed, Highline version from the same time.

All 1750s, like all 1500s, were five-door hatchbacks, and no other body derivative was ever put on sale.

From late 1970 all Maxis had a better facia, and this was the padded-panel version as used in the High Line version.

British Leyland eventually produced a higher-output Maxi 1750, which they called the High Line and gave it HL badges to suit.

The Maxi High Line engine had twin SU carburettors and a tubular exhaust manifold.

One of the later facelifts to the Maxi was as this Maxi 2 HLS.

'Son of Farina' – the Morris Marina

Almost as soon as Leyland had drafted Harry Webster into Longbridge to take over the design offices from Alec Issigonis, Sir Donald Stokes asked him to work up a crash programme of new-model development. Apart from the forthcoming Austin Maxi, and a great deal of work which was then currently going into Alec Issigonis' Mini replacement, the 9X, the Longbridge backlog of new cars was rather limited.

According to Graham Turner's *The Leyland Papers*, Webster: '. . . suggested that the simplest and quickest way of getting started was by taking existing products and improving them . . . The Morris Marina was first conceived as an updated version of the Morris Minor . . . It occurred to Webster that it might be possible to take most of the Minor's mechanical parts (modifying them where necessary), put a new body around them and produce a simple, rugged, low-priced car which could compete very effectively with the Viva and Escort.'

Although that over-simplified what was actually done (for there was to be a two-door fastback and a four-door saloon body style and a choice of BMC A-Series or B-Series engines), the Minor's torsion-bar independent front suspension was used in slightly modified form.

We know, therefore, that the ADO 28 project was a pure British Leyland car, although it was totally conceived at Longbridge and Cowley. The project was detailed in May 1968, immediately after the official start-up of British Leyland, and the styling mock-ups were ready for viewing in August of that year. However, it was not until April 1971, nearly three years after Sir Donald (now Lord) Stokes and Harry Webster had started discussing the matter, that the Morris Marina was launched.

As it was to be produced at Cowley, and as its various models overlapped in so many ways with the Morris Minor and Morris Oxford ranges, this signalled the end for the old BMC Morris models.

The first true British Leyland car, designed by BMC staff at Longbridge, became the Morris Marina of 1971, complete with front-engine/rear-drive A-Series or B-Series running gear.

There were two-door fastback, or four-door saloon versions of the Morris Marina. All were made at Cowley.

Getting rid of the empties – Austin-Healey, Mini-Cooper and Riley

As already explained in the appropriate marque sections, Sir Donald Stokes' policy was to get rid of unwanted marques, and in the first three years he divested his company of some important names:

Austin-Healey

It is *not* true that British Leyland dropped the Austin-Healey 3000 to allow their own Triumph TR5 to prosper. The 'Big Healey' production lines at Abingdon ran down rapidly just before the end of 1967, and one final car was assembled early in 1968, before British Leyland took control.

The 'Big Healey' died off because it would have been profitless to modify it to meet the new USA safety and exhaust emission regulations for 1968 and beyond. Its *true* replacement was not the Triumph TR5, but the MG MGC.

The Austin-Healey Sprite, however, was dropped at the end of 1970, when Donald Healey's royalty agreement with BMC finally expired. The Sprite, as such, continued as a pure 'Austin' in 1971 alone, but its spirit lived on, very successfully indeed, in the badge-engineered MG Midget, until 1979.

Mini-Cooper

The best-selling 998cc Austin and Morris Mini-Coopers were dropped in the autumn of 1969 (British Leyland foolishly thought that the less satisfyingly engineered Mini 1275GT could take over – it couldn't), but the de-badged Mini-Cooper S Mk III model carried on until the summer of 1971. When John Cooper's royalty agreement finally expired, 10 years after he had signed it in 1961, these cars were immediately dropped.

In spirit, if not in cheeky character, the MG Metro and Metro Turbo cars are the descendants of the Mini-Coopers.

Riley

There was really little point in keeping Riley cars in production in the late 1960s, when all brand loyalty and brand distinction had been utterly lost.

When British Leyland was formed, there were three Rileys on the market – the Mini-based Elf, the 1100/1300-based Kestrel and the B-Series Farina saloon, the 4/72. All these cars were dropped at the same time, in the autumn of 1969, and no more Riley cars have been produced since.

Updating the existing BMC cars

Because it was quite impossible for British Leyland to produce a range of 'own-brand' new models in the first few years, it also carried out a programme of updating the cars it had inherited from BMC. In particular, it made many changes to the Mini and 1800 ranges:

Mini

No doubt, when British Leyland was formed, the improvements announced in the autumn of 1969 had already been discussed by BMC's planners, but British Leyland adopted them as its own. At one and the same time, the Austin and Morris Minis were de-badged, given improvements which included wind-up windows, and under the new BMC code of ADO 20 became simply Minis for 1970. Those cars continued, basically

For the 1970s, British Leyland produced the Mini Clubman range, which were being developed at the time of the merger. The principal structural change was to the nose, which was longer and more squared-up than the original Mini had been.

The Mini Clubman, announced in the autumn of 1969, had a different facia/instrument layout from any previous Mini.

The Mini 1275GT used the Clubman body style, allied to a 60bhp 1,275cc A-Series engine, and was supposed to be a replacement for the much-loved Mini-Cooper. However, it didn't work out like that.

By the early 1970s, Minis had lost their marque badges, had gained wind-up windows and British Leyland badges, and looked like this.

unchanged, but with a series of mainly minor improvements (and, at one time, a 1.1-litre limited-edition model), until late 1980, when the BL-designed Austin Metro was introduced. Even then the Mini's long career was not over; a 998cc model carried on in parallel with the Metro, and the five-millionth Mini was produced early in 1986.

In the autumn of 1969, the Mini Clubman was announced as a 998cc (and, later, as a 1,098cc) model, along with the Mini 1275GT (which had the same 1,275cc 60bhp engine as the existing front-wheel-drive 1300 model). The chassis of these cars was really that of the existing Minis, with the new Minis reverting to rubber-cone suspension, while the Clubman was still equipped with Hydrolastic suspension units. The Clubman cars, too, were given a squared-up, long-nose body facelift. The Clubman cars sold well, but not sensationally so, for a decade before being dropped in favour of the Metro.

1800

The four-cylinder, 1,798cc-engined cars became Mk II in 1968 – changes planned by BMC well before the British Leyland takeover was formalized – and then went on to become Mk III in 1972. Both these updates have been detailed in the appropriate Austin, Morris or Wolseley marque sections.

British Leyland, however, made one major contribution to this range. Although BMC had originally planned to produce the new E-Series engine in four-cylinder and six-cylinder forms, the E6 six-cylinder unit was not produced in the UK until 1972, when it was shoehorned into the Mk III version of the front-wheel-drive 1800 saloon. Three different models – Austin, Morris and Wolseley – were announced at the same time, these being identical except for their badges and for the grille and standard of trim and equipment of the Wolseley Six. Here are the details:

Austin 2200 (1972 to 1975)

Although the BMC 1800 series was not selling at all well when British Leyland took over the BMC business, they persevered with it. Because of other, even more pressing commitments, it took time to finalize the last derivatives – but the 2200 of 1972 was very definitely a collection of BMC components which arrived rather late!

The 2200, in effect, was a front-wheel-drive 1800 car fitted with a transversely-mounted six-cylinder engine. This engine, however, was not technically related to the B-Series 'four' which it replaced, but was actually a logical extension of the overhead-camshaft Austin Maxi design, produced by BMC, but not announced until the spring of 1969.

Complicated? Indeed it was – but, then, nothing was simple at BMC or British Leyland during this period, and motoring writers had to come to terms with this. The basic E-Series engine design is described in the Austin Maxi entry, and this, the E6 derivative, was a straightforward six-cylinder version of a transverse 'four', with a large number of common components, including valve gear, pistons, connecting rods, timing gear and, of course, the use of the same machining facilities at Longbridge. The transverse engine fitted surprisingly easily into the spacious engine bay of the 'Land-crab' bodyshell and was mated to a little-altered 1800 gearbox (with rod-operated change) and front-wheel-drive transmission system. With twin SU carburettors tucked behind the overhead-camshaft cylinder head, pointing towards the bulkhead, it was a mechanically elegant design, and its smoothly-delivered 110bhp guaranteed a 104mph top speed.

Naturally, there were Morris and Wolseley equivalents and

The Austin 2200 was really an updated 1800, with the new transversely-mounted six-cylinder E6 engine.

Austin 2200 specification

Produced: Longbridge, 1972-75, 20,865 Austin and Morris 2200s of this type built. 25,214 Wolseley Six of this type also built.
General layout: Pressed-steel, unit-construction body-chassis structure, in 5-seater 4-door saloon body style. Front and transversely-mounted engine driving front wheels.
Engine and transmission: BMC E6-Series engine, 6-cylinder, ohc, in-line. 2,227cc, 76.2 x 81.28mm, 110bhp at 5,250 rpm; 126lb ft at 3,500 rpm. 4-speed gearbox, all-synchromesh; centre-floor gear-change; optional three-speed Borg-Warner automatic transmission; spur-gear final drive.
Chassis: Independent front suspension, Hydrolastic units and wishbones. Rack-and-pinion steering with optional power assistance. Independent rear suspension by Hydrolastic units, trailing arms and anti-roll bar. Interconnection between front and rear suspensions. Front disc and rear drum brakes. 165-14in tyres.
Dimensions: Wheelbase 8ft 10in; front track 4ft 8in; rear track 4ft 7.5in; length 13ft 10.7in; width 5ft 7in; height 4ft 7.5in. Unladen weight (approx) 2,620lb.
Typical performance: Maximum speed 104mph; 0-60mph 13.1sec; standing 1/4-mile 18.7sec; overall fuel consumption 22mpg.
Distinguishing features from previous models: Compared with obsolete 1800 S, had different grille, badging, facia and six-cylinder engine.
Derivatives: Morris 2200 was virtually the same car with different badges and details. Wolseley Six was the same car with different grille, badging and interior.
Fate: Discontinued in 1975 and replaced by British Leyland-designed ADO 71 18/22 range.
Note: Morris and Wolseley specifications were identical.

How to choose an Austin or a Morris 2200? No problem – only the badges were different between 1972 and 1975.

The most distinctive of the E6-engined models was the Wolseley Six of 1972-75. It sold best, too.

The Austin/Morris 2200s had a simple facia style, which they also shared with the 1800 Mk III models.

The Wolseley Six's facia and seating was an improved version of that already found in the Wolseley 18/85, which this car replaced.

The Austin, Morris and Wolseley 2200s all shared this transverse six-cylinder engine, which was related to the four-cylinder Maxi and was an overhead-camshaft design.

an automatic transmission option, though surprisingly enough the power-assisted steering was still an optional extra. Apart from the badging, the 2200's exterior was the same as that of the 1800 Mk III, which was launched at the same time, while the interior featured a plain, but easy-to-read facia with circular instruments and face-level air vents from the heater. The handbrake was between the seats and there was a steering wheel with padded spokes.

The 2200 made the old 1800 Mk II S model redundant, and was built for three years until the entire 'Land-crab' range of cars was swept away by British Leyland, ahead of the launch of the ADO 71 18/22 series. In many ways the 2200 was the best of all the 'Land-crabs' because its engine was silky smooth, and it added performance and refinement to a comfortable and spacious car which had previously been crying out for both. The ADO 71 shape was an even better bet.

Preserving the MG marque

Because British Leyland policy was controlled from the top by ex-Triumph men, it was always likely that the Triumph sports cars would be cosseted, whereas the MGs would be neglected. Although there was once a slight chance that a new mid-engined MG (ADO 21, a Longbridge/Abingdon project) might be taken up, this was soon submerged by corporate enthusiasm for the Triumph TR7 instead.

At Abingdon, therefore, the only product action taken was to keep the Midget and MGB alive, and to produce one new version of the larger car, the MGB GT V8.

The career of the definitive BMC Midget has already been described in the MG marque section. British Leyland kept this car going, selling very well and profitably, until 1974. At this point, with 1975 USA

The MG Midget 1500 of 1975 had a Triumph Spitfire engine and gearbox, along with the big black bumpers and a raised ride height.

The 1,493cc Triumph Spitfire engine was used in the MG Midgets produced between autumn 1974 and 1979.

MG Midget 1500 specification

As for Midget Mk III models except for:
Produced: Abingdon, 1974-79, 73,899 cars built.
Engine and transmission: Triumph Spitfire 1,493cc engine, 73.7 x 87.5mm, 66bhp at 5,500rpm; 77lb ft at 3,000rpm. All-synchromesh 4-speed gearbox.
Chassis: Front anti-roll bar fitted. 145-13in radial-ply tyres.
Dimensions: Length 11ft 9in; unladen weight 1,700lb.
Typical performance: Maximum speed 101mph; 0-60mph 12.3sec; standing ¼-mile 18.5sec; overall fuel consumption 28mpg.
Distinguishing features from previous model: Large black plastic bumpers at front and rear.
Fate: Discontinued in autumn 1979. No replacement BMC/BL sports car was produced.

legislation in view, it was clear that the A-Series engine could not be further 'cleaned up' to meet emissions laws, and that more shock-absorbing bumpers were essential.

Accordingly, British Leyland not only had the Midget restyled, with big, black, soft bumpers (and an increase in ride height), but they also sponsored an engine/transmission transplant. For 1975, therefore, the Midget became the Midget 1500, and was fitted with the same engine/gearbox assembly as the Triumph Spitfire 1500. The details are as follows:

The six-cylinder-engined MGC GT models were dropped in 1969, and it was not until a resourceful private engineer, Ken Costello, started producing MGB conversions with 3.5-litre Rover V8 engines in place of the old 1.8-litre BMC B-Series design that British Leyland decided to produce the same sort of car themselves.

The new car was ready for launch in the summer of 1973, complete with a 137bhp engine and a potential top speed of about 124mph, but its sales prospects were not helped by four factors – its exterior styling was still almost exactly that of the four-cylinder MGB except for the wheels, it was only to be sold as a closed GT type, it was not to be exported to the United States (where the vast majority of all MGB sales had always been made) and it was an expensive car at home.

Two distinctly different types of MG MGB GT V8

MG MGB GT V8 specification

Produced: Abingdon, 1973-76, 2,591 cars, all GT coupes, built.

General layout: Unit-construction body-chassis structure, in 2-seater sports car style, as a closed coupe. Front-mounted engine driving rear wheels.

Engine and transmission: Rover-made light-alloy engine, 90-degree V8-cylinder, ohv, 3,528cc, 88.9 x 71.1mm, 137bhp at 5,000rpm; 193lb ft at 2,900rpm. 4-speed all-synchromesh gearbox and overdrive on top gear; live (beam) rear axle with hypoid-bevel final drive.

Chassis: Independent front suspension, coil springs, wishbones and anti-roll bar. Rack-and-pinion steering. Rear suspension by half-elliptic leaf springs. Front disc and rear drum brakes. 175HR-14in radial-ply tyres.

Dimensions: Wheelbase 7ft 7in; front track 4ft 1in; rear track 4ft 1.25in; length 12ft 10.7in; width 4ft 11.7in; height 4ft 2in. Unladen weight (approx) 2,387lb.

Typical performance: Maximum speed 124mph; 0-60mph 8.6sec; standing ¼-mile 16.4sec; overall fuel consumption 24mpg.

Derivatives: The V8 was available only as a closed GT coupe. From late 1974, black plastic-covered bumpers were fitted and revised dimensions were: length 13ft 2.25in, height 4ft 3in.

Fate: Discontinued in 1976 and not replaced.

The Rover 3½-litre V8 was a snug fit into the engine bay of the MGB. The carburettors were towards the rear for clearance purposes.

BMC's legacy to British Leyland

Quite a number of BMC-designed engines and transmissions, much-modified, live on to this day. Here is what happened to some of them:

Mini/1100/1300

The famous front-wheel-drive A-Series transverse engine/gearbox-in-sump transmission went on to be used in some versions of the Austin Allegro (announced 1973) and the Austin Metro/MG Metro family (announced 1980).

were made – the 'chrome bumper' models of 1973 and 1974 and the 'black bumper' models of the 1975 and the 1976 model years. Although this car has a great deal of classic status nowadays, it was only a slow seller at the time.

The MGB GT was given a Rover V8 engine transplant in 1973 and was sold until 1976. Note the badging. Its full title was MG MGB GT V8.

The engine itself, mated to a different (VW) end-on gearbox, was also used in one version of the Austin Maestro (announced 1983) and the Austin Montego (announced in 1984).

Maxi

The E-Series single-overhead-camshaft engine/gearbox-in-sump transmission went on to be used in some versions of the Austin Allegro (announced 1973) and the Vanden Plas 1500 version of the Allegro (announced 1974).

The E-Series engine was then modified to become R-Series, to mate with a VW end-on gearbox, for some versions of the Austin Maestro (announced 1983), and after a very short life was then further modified to become S-Series, with end-on VW or Honda gearbox, for the Maestro and Montego of 1984.

S-Series engines have also found a home in the so-called Rover 200 Series cars (which are really Honda cars

with a BL engine/transmission transplant), which were first announced in 1984.

1800/2200

The transverse-engined large saloons were built from 1964 to 1975 inclusive, when British Leyland replaced them by cars known as the 18/22 series, which were re-named as Princess towards the end of that year.

For these cars, the 1.8-litre B-Series and 2.2-litre E6-Series engines, complete with gearboxes-in-sump, were carried forward unchanged.

Much later, in 1978, the new overhead-camshaft O-Series engine was introduced to take over from the B-Series engine in the Princess and Morris Marina models. Even this engine had some connection, in terms of general cylinder block dimensions and some of the production-line machinery, with the old B-Series unit!

The E6 engine was dropped in 1981.

British Leyland's replacement for the BMC 1100/1300 models, launched in 1973, was the Austin Allegro, which had A-Series or Maxi-based E-Series transversely-mounted engines and front-wheel-drive transmission.

A contrast in styles – the Princess of 1977 (which was the wedge-shaped successor to the BMC 1800/2200 models) compared with the Morris Oxford MO of the early 1950s BMC period.

Appendix A

BMC's design project numbers

The famous 'ADO' system explained

When developing new products, all companies try to preserve secrecy by using code names or code numbers. It also makes matters simple when staff discussions and planning meetings take place.

As every BMC-watcher knows, each of their new projects was originally allocated an 'ADO . . .' number, and in many cases this became widely known when the car, or engine, was eventually made public. Since major decisions were always made at the old Austin factory at Longbridge under the direction of Sir Leonard Lord or – in later years – Sir George Harriman, it was logical that the project list should be Austin-derived. The letters ADO, therefore, stood for Austin Drawing Office – although there were Morris diehards who sometimes suggested that *Amalgamated* Drawing Office was strictly more correct.

[MG also developed new models with their own 'EX . . .' project codes, and Nuffield had 'DO . . .' models, but I promise not to confuse the reader too much by cross-referring every time!]

The first thing that strikes the eye when reading down the list, which is published below, is that it is neither complete, nor were the numbers allocated in any logical order, either by engine size, or in chronological sequence. ADO 14, for instance, refers to the Austin Maxi, which was conceived in the mid-1960s and announced in 1969, whereas ADO 15 refers to the famous Mini, which was launched in 1959. ADO 16, on the other hand, was the Austin/Morris 1100, first seen in 1962, while ADO 17 was the larger front-wheel-drive Austin/Morris 1800 of 1964.

No definitive table of ADO numbers has been preserved, and although I am told that Charles Griffin kept such a list in his office at Longbridge for many years, the whole system seems to have been a very informal one. Some numbers – ADO 1 to ADO 5, for instance – were certainly allocated in the early BMC years, though no-one seems to know what they were, and others have never been used at all. On several occasions, it seems, a project was given an ADO number at one point, which was then changed, so surviving scraps of archive jumble up the most surprising numbers and cars!

An ADO number, by the way, did not have to be allocated to a complete car, though most *were* used for such major projects.

In some cases it might refer to an engine, a gearbox, or merely a facelift or derivative of an earlier model.

With the diligent help of Ian Elliott, of British Leyland, my first attempt to produce a comprehensive ADO . . . list was published in *Autocar* on March 6, 1976. In the subsequent decade, however, more information has surfaced, and my British Motor Industry Heritage Trust adviser, Anders Clausager, has added considerably to that list for this BMC directory.

Here, then, is the most complete list of BMC projects that records, memories and inspired deduction (but no guessing!) can provide:

ADO Project Number	Allocated to	Project, and production item where applicable
ADO 6	4-door hire car	Austin Taxi – FL2, FL2D, FX4, FX4D
ADO 8	Austin A40 (Farina style)	Austin A40 Farina, announced 1958
ADO 9	4-door saloon and 5-door estate	B-Series Farina models, Austin A55, Morris Oxford SV, MG Magnette Mk III, Wolseley 15/60, Riley 4/68. First announced winter 1958-59
ADO 10	Austin Westminster update	Austin A99/Wolseley 6/99 saloons, announced 1959
ADO 12	Ebert infinitely variable hydrostatic transmission	Fitted experimentally to Austin A35 in 1956
ADO 13	Small 2-seat sports car	Austin-Healey Sprite Mk I, announced 1958
ADO 14	5-door saloon, 1,500cc and 1,750cc engines	Austin Maxi, announced 1969
ADO 15	Small 2-door saloon and derivatives	The Mini range, announced 1959, including all derivatives *until* Clubman models (see ADO 20)

ADO Project Number	Allocated to	Project, and production item where applicable
ADO 16	2-door and 4-door saloon	Austin/Morris 1100/1300 and all badge-engineered MG, Riley, Wolseley and Vanden Plas derivatives, announced 1962
ADO 17	4-door saloon – 1,800cc and 2,200cc engines	Austin/Morris 1800 front-wheel-drive models, including Wolseley, 'S' and 2200 derivatives, announced 1964
ADO 19	Cross-country vehicle	Austin 'Ant', based on chassis of 1100, not put on sale
ADO 20	Facelifted ADO 15	Minis with wind-up door glass, Mini Clubman and all later Mini derivatives, announced 1969
ADO 21	Mid-engined sports car project using ADO 14 ohc engines	To have been MG MGB replacement. Conceived 1968-69, but only styling mock-ups built
ADO 22	Major facelift for ADO 16 1100/1300 front-wheel-drive models	Started 1967, but cancelled by British Leyland. Replaced by ADO 67 (Austin Allegro) model
ADO 23	Replacement for MGA sports car	MG MGB, announced 1962
ADO 24	Revised Austin-Healey 3000	Familiar style and chassis, but fitted with Rolls-Royce 4-cylinder FB60 engine from VDP Princess R and widened structure. Prototypes built in 1966-67, but not put into production
ADO 25	6-cylinder engine	E6 engine, 6-cylinder version of ADO 14 Austin Maxi 4-cylinder overhead-camshaft engine. This number *may* cover the engine itself, the installation in the ADO 14 car, or the Austin/Morris 2200 model; detail is not clear
ADO 26	Revised Austin-Healey 3000	Austin-Healey 3000 Mk III, announced 1964
ADO 27	This project code was definitely used twice!	
	i) Facelift for Wolseley 1500/Riley 1.5 saloons, for which a separate ADO number had apparently never been allocated	Early 1960s, but only styling mock-ups produced
	ii) Australian version of ADO 17 (Austin/Morris 1800/2200 front-wheel-drive models)	The Tasman/Kimberley models, announced in 1970 by British Leyland, but never sold in Europe
	– also known under YDO 19 project code in Australia	
	– number also allocated for major UK facelift of ADO 17, but project cancelled at early stage	
ADO 28	2-door/4-door saloons and all other derivatives, front engine, rear drive	Morris Marina range (also Austin Marina in US), conceived 1968, but announced 1971
ADO 30	Austin-Healey 3000 replacement project	Known as S4 (and, cynically, as 'Fireball XL5'), with new structure and 4-litre RR FB60 engine developed from Princess R unit. Jaguar XK engine also suggested by BMC, but vetoed by Sir William Lyons. A 1966 project, only built as prototype
ADO 31	Revised MGA sports car with 1.6-litre engine	MGA 1600 model, announced 1959
ADO 32	E-Series (overhead-cam Maxi-type) engines, developed from 1968 by British Leyland	Later used in cars like the Allegro and higher-powered Maxis
ADO 34	Front-wheel-drive Mini-based sports car	To have been a small MG model, conceived 1960, only prototype built
ADO 35	Coupe version of ADO 34	To have been MG coupe of above car
ADO 36	Austin-Healey derivative of ADO 34/ADO 35	Never built
ADO 37	Vanden Plas version of ADO 10 (C-Series A99/Wolseley 6/99 saloons)	Became Princess 3-litre (later VDP Princess 3-litre) saloon, announced 1959
ADO 38	Facelifted ADO 9 (B-Series Farina range)	Became Austin A60/Morris Oxford SVI/MG Magnette Mk IV/Riley 4/72/Wolseley 16/60, announced 1961
ADO 39	New taxicab design	To replace long-running ADO 6 Austin Taxi design, only full-size styling mock-up built in 1967, cancelled by British Leyland after 1968 merger
ADO 40	Australian derivative of ADO 8 (Austin A40 Farina)	
ADO 41	Restyled ADO 13 ('frog-eye' Sprite)	Austin-Healey Sprite Mk II, announced 1961
ADO 44	Revised ADO 8 (Austin A40 Farina)	A40 Farina Mk II, announced 1961
ADO 46	Diesel-engined version of ADO 38 (B-Series Farina range)	Austin A60 Diesel and Morris Oxford Diesel, announced 1961
ADO 47	MG version of new ADO 41	MG Midget Mk I – a badge-engineered Austin-Healey Sprite Mk II, announced 1961
ADO 49	Pick-up version of ADO 9/ADO 38 B-Series Farina range	Became the Riley-nosed Siam di Tella 1500 pick-up, built in Argentina

ADO Project Number	Allocated to	Project, and production item where applicable
ADO 50	High-performance versions of ADO 15 (Mini) range	Austin/Morris Mini-Cooper and Mini-Cooper S, first shown in 1961
ADO 51	Austin-Healey version of ADO 52 (MGC)	Car never built and project cancelled at insistence of Donald Healey in 1967
ADO 52	6-cylinder-engined version of ADO 23 (MG MGB)	Became MG MGC, announced 1967
ADO 53	Revised ADO 10 (Austin A99/Wolseley 6/99)	Became Austin A110 and Wolseley 6/110 saloons, announced 1961
ADO 58	Joint project with Rolls-Royce, a short-wheelbase 'Burma' (T-Series Bentley type) shell using a Rolls-Royce F60 6-cyl engine.	Cancelled, after one prototype, registered 225 PLG, was built
ADO 61	Replacement for ADO 10/ ADO 53 3-litre saloons	Austin 3-litre saloon, announced 1967. Proposed Wolseley and Vanden Plas versions of this design were styled and mocked-up, but never put on sale
ADO 66	Rolls-Royce-engined version of ADO 53 (Austin A110/Wolseley 6/110 saloons)	Became Vanden Plas Princess 4-litre R, announced 1964
ADO 67	Replacement for ADO 16 (1100/1300 front-wheel-drive range) with 1.1 to 1.75-litre engines	Became Austin Allegro range, including Vanden Plas 1500 model, announced 1973
ADO 68	2-door coupe to be based on ADO 28 Morris Marina floorpan and running gear	Project dated from 1969 and also called 'Condor' at the time. Might have been badged as an MG, project cancelled
ADO 69	Replacement for ADO 6 Austin taxicab	Conceived in 1970, but soon cancelled
ADO 70	Sports coupe based on ADO 20 (updated Mini) with front-wheel drive	Styled by Michelotti, prototype built in 1970 but project cancelled
ADO 71	4-door saloon to replace ADO 17(Austin/Morris 1800/2200) front-drive range	Became 18/22 'wedge' style Austin/Morris/Wolseley/ Princess range, announced 1975
ADO 73	Revised ADO 28 (Morris Marina) range	Morris Marina II, announced 1975. Also covered Ital project, announced 1980
ADO 74	Proposed new small front-wheel-drive car to replace ADO 20 (Mini range). To have had new K-Series overhead-cam engine	Also known as Ant and Ladybird. Conceived in 1972, cancelled at mock-up stage in 1973. An early ancestor of the Metro.
ADO 75	MG sports car based on ADO 23 (MGB) with Rover V8 engine	Became MG MGB GT V8, announced 1973
ADO 76	Revised MGBs for 1975	MG MGB and MGB GT V8 with black plastic bumpers and other changes to meet USA legis-lation. (Use of Marina back axle also mentioned, but this was never put into production)
ADO 77	Proposed replacement for ADO 28/ADO 73 (Marina) range	Mock-ups produced, but not put into production. Conceived in 1972, only mock-ups built. Cancelled in favour of Rover-Triumph SD2 project, itself dropped in favour of LM11, which became Austin Montego
ADO 88	New small 'Supermini' front-wheel-drive hatch-back to replace the ADO 20 (Mini) range	Several prototypes built, but project superseded by larger and more refined LC8, which became the Metro. ADO 88 conceived in 1974 and active until 1977-78
ADO 99	Replacement for ADO 67 Austin Allegro range on 99in wheelbase	Developed, refined and rational-ized with LM11 project to become LM10 (Austin Maestro) range

Note: Some important cars, such as the cancelled 9X Mini-replacement project, do not seem to have had ADO numbers allocated.

Appendix B

Building the bodies

Pressed Steel, Fisher & Ludlow, Nuffield Bodies and other sources

Even for a corporation as large as BMC, it was not possible to be self-sufficient in all respects, and for many years some of the bodyshells, or combined body-chassis units, had to be bought from independent outside specialists.

Although the largest independent builders of bodies were Pressed Steel, Fisher & Ludlow and Briggs Motor Bodies, Briggs would soon be totally absorbed by Ford (who were its largest single customer, in any case), and in those early postwar years there was also a long queue for tooling facilities at the other companies. In 1952, for instance, Pressed Steel was also supplying bodies to the Rootes Group, Jaguar, Rover and Rolls-Royce, while Fisher & Ludlow also sent supplies to Standard-Triumph.

By the end of the BMC period, however, the Corporation had rectified this situation, first by buying Fisher & Ludlow, and later by taking over the Pressed Steel Company – but it hadn't quite been as straightforward as it sounds!

The body supply situation in 1952
Although there was a large bodybuilding plant at Longbridge (West Works), Austin took supplies from several sources. The A30 was built at Longbridge, the A40 Devon and A70 Hereford by Pressed Steel at Cowley, the A90 and Sheerline bodies at Longbridge, while the Princess was built by Vanden Plas at Kingsbury, North London.

Nuffield took its Morris Minor saloon and tourer bodies from Nuffield Metal Products in Birmingham and the Travellers from Morris Bodies Branch in Coventry, Morris Oxfords, Wolseley 4/50s and the Morris Six/Wolseley 6/80 monocoques from Pressed Steel (which was just across the road), MG YB shells from Nuffield Metal and MG TD and (from 1949) Riley bodies from Bodies Branch, Coventry.

Within months the story had become even more complicated, when BMC agreed to build the Nash Metropolitan on behalf of the American firm and sourced their unit-construction monocoques from Fisher & Ludlow, of Castle Bromwich, in Birmingham. [This F & L factory complex is now owned by Jaguar Cars, after a typically long and complex history in British Leyland ownership . . .]

The Fisher & Ludlow takeover
In his 'Grand Design', Leonard Lord wanted to secure his body supplies for the future, especially as he was determined to make more and more cars as the years progressed. Accordingly, in the summer of 1953 he made a bid for Fisher & Ludlow, offering 56 shillings (£2.80) a unit for the entire shareholding. This was successful, and F & L became a BMC subsidiary from September 30 that year.

One assurance given to F & L by BMC was that 'the company's future trading policy would be materially unaltered . . .', which was a relief to all concerned, not least Standard-Triumph, who obtained its Standard 8/10 monocoques from Tile Hill and Standard Vanguard bodyshells (Castle Bromwich) from this source. Since the small Standard was a direct competitor of the Austin A30, this was obviously an unsatisfactory long-term situation. When Standard replaced the Vanguard with the new Series III model it chose Pressed Steel as the supplier, and when the company asked if the projected Herald could take over from the Standard 8 and 10, it was abruptly told to 'push off' and look for an alternative source of supply.

By that time, in any case, F & L was already building shells for the A40/A50 Cambridge and the Austin/Nash Metropolitan, with the Wolseley 1500/Riley 1.5 monocoque about to join in. The last of the Standard 8 saloon car family (actually a Standard Pennant) was built in the autumn of 1959, after which F & L was totally bound up in the supply of bodies to BMC.

Pressed Steel Company – before BMC
The Pressed Steel Company of Great Britain Ltd – to quote the company's first title – was founded in 1926 to take advantage of the latest methods in building all-steel bodyshells. William Morris had visited the USA on a fact-finding tour in 1925 and had been impressed by the welded all-steel bodies being produced by the Edward G. Budd Manufacturing Company in Philadelphia. The result was that Morris Motors got together with Budd to establish Pressed Steel, a company in which Budd had the controlling financial interest. The ever-cunning William Morris made sure that this was as convenient as possible for his enterprise at Cowley, not only by placing

initial orders for bodies for new-model Oxfords, but by encouraging Pressed Steel to build its new factory just down the road!

There were difficulties at first, not only in getting the right quality from new machinery and a new labour force, but in making the business profitable. As the official biographers of Morris (later Lord Nuffield) pointed out:

'Because of the volume of output which Pressed Steel would require, its commercial freedom to trade elsewhere had been specifically retained, and in fact it was found that Morris work alone would not fill the factory. At the same time, however, two directors of Morris Motors were on the board of the Pressed Steel Company and the latter found it practically impossible to get business from other car firms, who were reluctant to place orders with a supplier who was so closely tied to their major competitor. Similarly, Morris Motors found other manufacturers of stampings unwilling to quote competitive tenders . . .'

It became obvious that the close connection between Morris Motors and Pressed Steel was counterproductive, so the financial links were unscrambled. Morris surrendered its shareholdings in 1930 (and its debentures when they matured in 1949) and the two directors left the board. Almost from that moment, Pressed Steel began to build up business with other companies, such that by the end of the 1930s it was supplying pressings or complete bodies to more than a dozen major car makers, including Austin, Morris, Ford, Rootes, Standard and Vauxhall – all the 'Big Six'.

In the immediate postwar years, up to the early 1950s, its activities continued to expand, and by that time its prestigious customers included Daimler, Jaguar, Rover and Rolls-Royce. Business was booming, profits were on the increase, the Cowley premises were bursting at the seams, and new factories were either open or planned at Swindon and Linwood (near Glasgow).

However, once Fisher & Ludlow had been annexed by BMC, Pressed Steel found that it was the only major independent British bodybuilder, and it seemed that almost every British car company was hammering on its doors, asking for tooling and production facilities. Somehow, to its credit, the company not only kept faith with all its customers, but it actually expanded its business with BMC.

By the early 1960s, not only was Pressed Steel sending bodies all round the industry, but it was building monocoques for BMC cars like the Minis, the 1100s and the B-Series 'Farinas'. BMC certainly did not dominate the scene at Pressed Steel, but it was clear that the balance was gradually tipping in that direction.

A good deal of 'dual-sourcing' was being practised at BMC by this stage, for not only were car families being assembled in more than one factory, so were the body monocoques. A typical example was the Mini which, in one form or another, was based on bodies built at the Pressed Steel, Fisher & Ludlow and Longbridge facilites. Similarly, the B-Series Farina monocoques took shape at Cowley and at Longbridge.

[Since there was a time when some Austins were assembled at the Nuffield factories in Cowley and some Morris models at Longbridge, this was a very confusing period for BMC-watchers. To stand at the side of the road between Oxford and Birmingham, watching loaded – or empty – BMC transporters shuttling one way or another, was a very instructive

occupation . . .]

Pressed Steel's independence finally came to an end when BMC made a takeover offer in July 1965, and the acquisition was formalized in September. BMC's press statement assured the world of the intention to 'maintain the existing goodwill and business relationships that Pressed Steel enjoy with their own customers . . .', which not only reminded younger pundits of what it had said when swallowing up Fisher & Ludlow, but also recalled to older observers the trouble Pressed Steel had encountered in the late 1920s when trying to balance Morris Motors against potential outside customers!

Perhaps these were not meant to be meaningless platitudes, but nevertheless the rationalization process began without delay. The Linwood premises were sold off to the Rootes Group (soon to be Chrysler UK) at the beginning of 1966, after which few important new contracts were accepted from outside customers (the Rolls-Royce Silver Spirit monocoque, revealed in 1980, was an obvious special case).

Nuffield body supplies

In the early postwar years, before the formation of BMC, Nuffield took its bodies from three different sources – Pressed Steel, Nuffield Metal Products and Morris Motors Bodies Branch – the facilities of which had an effect on the way that BMC rationalized itself in the 1960s (and British Leyland in the 1970s . . .):

The Morris Motors Bodies Branch site, with factory premises in Coventry, close to the Coventry-London railway line and backing on to the Armstrong-Siddeley aero-engines and cars complex at Parkside, had enjoyed a long career before (as Hollick & Pratt) it was taken over by Morris in 1922, after a fire had destroyed the buildings; it was to become the Morris Motors Bodies Branch in 1926. Although Morris continued to build his standard bodies at Cowley, the Bodies Branch concentrated on more specialized coachwork, especially those which used wooden frames as their basic structure.

In the BMC days, therefore, estate car derivatives of other cars, such as the Morris Minor and Oxford, and wooden-framed bodies for cars like the RM-Series Rileys and T-Series MGs, were produced at Bodies Branch.

Nuffield Metal Products had originally been set up by the Nuffield Organisation as the Morris Motors Pressing Branch, in 1939, at Common Lane, Washwood Heath, Birmingham, on land owned by Wolseley, and adjoining that factory. Lord Nuffield wanted to minimize his dependance on firms like Pressed Steel, and he used this plant to produce pressed-steel, all-welded bodies in large numbers. It had been renamed Nuffield Metal Products in 1945, had supplied Morris 8 Series E shells in postwar years (these also formed the basis of the MG YA/YB saloon shells) and had concentrated on building Morris Minor monocoques since that car had arrived on the scene in 1948.

Pressed Steel Fisher

The rationalization of body and monocoque supply to BMC's assembly lines took place gradually, and in August 1966 a new subsidiary company, Pressed Steel Fisher Ltd, was set up to take the process a stage further. PSF (as it soon became known) comprised Pressed Steel, Fisher & Ludlow, Nuffield Metal Products, Morris Motors Bodies Branch and other non-automotive businesses including Prestcold, which produced refrigeration equipment. The managing director was Joe Edwards, who had been chief executive of Pressed Steel at takeover time in 1965.

Before BMC was absorbed into British Leyland at the start of 1968, there was no time to make major changes to cut down the number of uneconomic plants. However, the old Nuffield Metal Products and Morris Bodies Branch businesses both closed down in 1971, when production of the Morris Minor came to an end, and this left the Pressed Steel (Cowley and Swindon) and Fisher & Ludlow (Birmingham) factories, allied to Longbridge's own bodybuilding premises at West Works, to supply all the series-production shells. Incidentally, the Nuffield Metal Products factory was eventually converted to commercial vehicle assembly, and in the mid-1980s was the home of the Freight Rover Sherpa van.

Austin's Longbridge body plant

Right from the start, in 1906, Austin had built its own bodies, and as the Longbridge site expanded and was reorganized, so was the supply of bodies. West Works, across the Bristol Road and remote from the main Longbridge site, was built during the First World War as a vast munitions machine-shop, but by 1952, and the BMC merger, it had become Austin's principal in-house body-shop and was producing A30 saloon monocoques. A30 estate car and van monocoques, however, were completed by Fisher & Ludlow, a few miles away on the other outskirts of Birmingham. (These were typical complications of this period in the British motor industry.)

In the years which followed, it was expanded, modernized, modified, reorganized and repeatedly reshuffled to keep up with the demands of the BMC business. Some Mini shells, and possibly some A40 Farina shells (normally supplied from Fisher & Ludlow), were also dual sourced from West Works in the 1960s. Commercially, West Works' big advantage was that it was built alongside a railway spur which led to the main Birmingham-Bristol line, and in later years this meant that train-loads of pressings could be sent from Pressed Steel's Swindon works to Longbridge without ever needing to be transported on public roads.

[Well after BMC had been swallowed by British Leyland, West Works was expanded yet again, so that the ultra-modern robot facilities needed to build Metro monocoques could be produced close to the assembly lines; it is still a vital part of the Austin Rover jigsaw in the late 1980s.]

Vanden Plas – bodies for the 'carriage trade'

The Vanden Plas factory had been in existence for more than 30 years before Austin took over the business in 1946. Its premises at Kingsbury, North London, were ideally sized and equipped to produce limited-production bodies with wooden frames in the true 'coachbuilt' style and for adding that extra touch of luxury to more mundane products.

For some years the Vanden Plas factory concentrated on building Austin Princess bodyshells of various types, on various-wheelbase chassis, but from 1958 they also took up their role as 'improvers', by trimming, upholstering and generally finishing off the 500-off Austin A105 Vanden Plas models of 1958-59.

The obvious progression was for the company to complete, trim and furnish cars carrying the marque badge of Vanden Plas, and large numbers of such cars – based on the Austin A99/A110, 1100/1300 and (in the British Leyland era) Allegro – were built before the Kingsbury plant was closed down and sold at the end of 1979.

Appendix C

BMC overseas

Catering for local needs

Have you ever heard of the Morris Marshal? The Innocenti Coupe C? The Austin Lancer? The Wolseley 24/80? The Morris Nomad? These were all BMC-derived cars, but none of them was ever sold in the UK.

At the height of its power, BMC was a miniaturized version of the British Empire (and Sir Leonard Lord was certainly an empire-builder). Not only did Cowley, Longbridge and Abingdon send hundreds of thousands of new cars to overseas markets every year, but there were assembly facilities in a whole variety of countries.

In 1960, a BMC brochure summed up its worldwide interests as follows:

CKD (Completely Knocked Down) kits of cars or commercial vehicles were being sent to Argentina, Belgium, Ceylon, Colombia, Cuba, Eire, Egypt, Ghana, Holland, Hong Kong, India, Indonesia, Italy, Malaya, Mexico, New Zealand and the Phillipines.

Negotiations over CKD supply were also proceeding with Mauritius, Nigeria, Persia, Spain and Thailand.

Vehicles were manufactured (as opposed to assembled from British-made parts) in Australia, Canada, Rhodesia and South Africa.

In most cases, CKD assembly was of standard, UK-specification, vehicles in either right-hand or left-hand drive to suit particular markets. Unless local regulations made it necessary for a significant proportion of these cars to be manufactured locally, it was usually profitable for BMC to send these out by sea, crated, and in relatively small batches. This particular business only declined in the 1960s as such countries began to establish their own motor industries, and where overseas competition was squeezed out by high import tariffs.

Occasionally, however, one country would be favoured with something special, a most notable case being the Argentinian Di Tella 1500, which was really an Austin A55 'Farina' with a Riley 4/68 front end; there was also a pick-up version of this style, which retained the same styling below the waistline, all the way to the tail.

The cars of particular interest in this section, however, are those machines which were considerably different – in either styling or engineering – from the domestic variety. The two most important nations involved were Italy and Australia.

Italy – the Innocenti operation

In the 1950s, Innocenti of Milan was a major industrial company, producing machine tools and rolling mills for the steel industry, but famous mostly for its Lambretta scooters, those tiny-engined but charismatic little two-wheelers which seemed to appear in every Italian film of the day and to sum up the whole noisy, mobile, world of *La Dolce Vita*. For the 1960s, however, the company decided to expand into cars, and struck a deal with BMC.

There was an Italian connection, right from the start, for it was arranged that the Farina-styled Austin A40 should be built by Innocenti, under licence, but one of the first co-operative deals which involved important design changes also resulted in the prettiest BMC-based car of all. At the Turin motor show of 1960, even the most hard-boiled critics were delighted to see a sleek two-seater sports car on display, which was called the **Innocenti 950 Spider**.

Who would know that under this smart exterior is an Austin-Healey Sprite underpan and all the same running gear? This is the Innocenti S of 1964, complete with Ghia styling.

269

Ghia had produced an attractive style, but under the skin was the inner monocoque and running gear of the Austin-Healey 'frog-eye' Sprite. The Innocenti weighed only 20lb more than the standard Sprite, which was very praiseworthy when one notes that wind-up windows were included in the doors. The OSI concern of Turin (partly funded by Ghia) stamped out and assembled the bodies, using Innocenti-Clearing presses.

Since BMC supplied the assembled floorpans and all the running gear, the Innocenti changed along with the Sprites and Midgets, picking up the enlarged and more powerful engines, the front-wheel disc brakes and the half-elliptic leaf-spring rear suspension as these became available. The Spider evolved into the **C Coupe** in 1967, when OSI grafted a very smart permanent hardtop on to the same basic style as before, and this car was made successfully until 1970.

In the meantime, the Innocenti-BMC link went from strength to strength. The **Innocenti IM3** was announced in the spring of 1963, this being a licence-built Morris 1100 with different front styling, facia and interior furnishings, the MG 1100's twin-carb engine, slightly modified , but a much more raked steering column and steering wheel position, made possible by the insertion of a universal joint part way up the column. IM3 stood for Innocenti-Morris, third project (A40 and Spider having been the first two). Later in the year BMC held a press conference before the Turin show opened, claimed the establishment of 350 dealers in Italy, that 50,000 Innocenti-assembled A40s had so far been delivered, and that Innocenti was now producing 35,000 cars a year.

In the next few years, Innocenti's BMC-based range expanded and became more complex. The **Austin J4** was a licence-built Austin 1100, with the single-carburettor 1,098cc engine, while the **IM3S** was a re-badged version of the IM3, and the **I4S** was a slightly downmarket version of that. In the meantime, licence-building of the Mini had begun from the autumn of 1965 and the Mini t (t = Traveller) soon followed,

as did assembly of the Mini-Cooper.

After BMC had given way to British Leyland, the Mini-Coopers became progressively more special, and British Leyland took complete control in the spring of 1972, with Geoffrey Robinson becoming managing director. Annual production was in the region of 50,000 a year, and the expansionist Robinson was hoping for 100,000 a year before too long. At this time, Innocenti also built a version of the Austin Allegro, called the Regent, which was a complete failure.

But all this came to nought. Robinson moved on to take control of Jaguar (where his expansion plans, likewise, came to nothing when British Leyland's fortunes turned sour), and the only important new car to be launched from this period was the very enterprising **Innocenti Mini**, which was styled by Bertone and produced as the 90 and 120 models. This used the Mini's floorpan and running gear, but had a completely different, crisply-detailed, three-door hatchback superstructure.

Innocenti was taken over by the Argentine-born entrepreneur Alejandro de Tomaso after British Leyland was nationalized and pulled out of their overseas businesses, and

Innocenti hired Bertone to produce this very smart three-door style on the basis of the BMC Mini underpan and running gear, which looked good from every angle. This was the more upmarket 120 variety, complete with bright bumpers.

Innocenti always liked to do their own thing – they produced this facia layout for the Innocenti Regent, which was a British Leyland Allegro under a different name.

The Innocenti Mini of the 1970s was a very practical little car with an opening hatchback, all on the same wheelbase and tracks as the BMC Mini. This is the Innocenti Mini 90 model.

this Bertone-styled car continued to be built for a number of years. At the time of writing the body style is still in evidence from Innocenti, but the Mini's power train is long gone and a Japanese Daihatsu unit has taken its place.

British Leyland asked their consultant stylist Giovanni Michelotti (of Triumph fame) to produce a booted version of the 1100/1300 design. It was called the Austin Apache when built in South Africa, or the Authi Victoria when built in Spain. (Quadrant Picture Library)

Spain – the Pamplona project

By the mid-1960s, BMC had decided that the only way to break in to the Spanish market (whose tariff barriers to imports were already very high), was to build cars locally, so they acquired a site at Pamplona, with the intention of manufacturing front-wheel-drive Morris 1100s in that country. This, the Authi project, did not come on stream until British Leyland were well-and-truly in control.

By the early 1970s, the Italian stylist, Michelotti, had produced a different style for the front-wheel-drive 1100. As with the Riley Elf/Wolseley Hornet models (which had evolved from the Mini), the Victoria (which was also produced by British Leyland South Africa as the Austin Apache), had a lengthened tail and enlarged boot compartment, the effect being not unlike that of the current Triumph 1500 (which Michelotti had also styled for Leyland!). The Authi factory was sold in the mid-1970s, as British Leyland went through its period of contraction.

South African assembly and manufacture

It was the Austin company which originally decided to build a manufacturing, rather than merely an assembly, factory in South Africa, this being opened at Blackheath, near Cape Town, at the beginning of the 1950s. In due course, however, it became known as a BMC manufacturing plant, producing standard-specification cars with an increasing proportion of local content.

Australia – specially-modified BMC products

Before the Second World War, the Nuffield Organisation developed a sizeable export market in Australia and New Zealand, and in 1945 Lord Nuffield decided to develop a manufacturing operation in that continent; his long-term policy, he announced, was to produce a completely Australian car, but the first step was to make bodies in Australia and supply all the other parts from the UK.

Nuffield (Australia) Pty Ltd was founded, and after a considerable planning delay, work began at Victoria Park Racecourse, in Sydney. By the early 1950s, when BMC had started to operate, not only were bodies being built, but gearboxes were also being manufactured in Australia. Over the years the proportion of local content increased, and by 1954 BMC said that up to 1,000 engines a week would also be

This was the Austin Apache, the booted 1100/1300 produced in South Africa by British Leyland in the early 1970s. The Authi Victoria, of Spain, had the same sheet metal, but different decorative details. (Quadrant Picture Library)

At first it might have been a Morris Minor replacement, then it acquired a B-Series engine, and finally it was built in Australia from 1958 as a Morris Major. This, in fact, was a 'Morris 1200' – badged prototype, seen in the Cowley styling studio.

The Morris Major Series I production car of 1958 used a Wolseley 1500-like body structure, but this distinctive nose. (Quadrant Picture Library)

produced. At the same time a 250,000sq ft. factory was acquired at Melbourne for manufacturing and assembly purposes.

The first of a series of specially-modified cars was announced in the autumn of 1957. This was a badge-engineered Austin A95, called a **Morris Marshal**, which had a different bonnet pressing from the domestic product, a different grille, but no mechanical changes. It was the first of several cars which BMC was planning, as they announced, 'to have increasing Australian content'.

All this, in fact, was a prelude to the launch of a pair of new small-medium cars especially developed for Australian motorists – the **Austin Lancer** and the **Morris Major**. The complicated heritage of these cars has already been discussed in the Riley 1.5/Wolseley 1500 sections. Basically, the style had started life as a proposed Morris Minor replacement, then B-Series running gear had been slotted in, in place of the A-Series units, and finally the design was put to use in the UK and, in entirely different marketing slots, in Australia.

Although the basic body style was that of the Wolseley 1500, and the 1.5-litre B-Series engine was in the same state of tune, there were significant differences to the Australian cars. The Austin Lancer version had a curious mixture of Austin grille in Wolseley 1500 grille shape cut-out, and was allied to an A35 type of elliptical instrument panel mounted ahead of the driver's eyes. The Morris Major had a very Plain Jane oval grille, and the instrument nacelle was in the centre of the facia. The Wolseley 1500, incidentally, was also built in Australia in its UK guise. In addition, the Austin A40 Farina joined it on the assembly lines.

The original cars did not last long in Australia, whose motorists were already looking to buy larger cars like their native Holdens. From July 1959, the cars were restyled and re-engineered considerably. The Lancer lost its Wolseley-clone grille in favour of one rather more like the Austin A55, there was a 6-inch longer wheelbase (the back axle being moved that much rearwards) and a new tail which was not only longer, but

The Morris Major Series I used this somewhat austere instrument layout. In the Austin version, the same instruments were mounted ahead of the steering wheel.

The Austin Lancer became a Series II with a longer wheelbase, tail-fins and this A55-like front grille. The basic Wolseley 1500/Riley 1.5 structure, however, is still obvious.

This was the controversially-styled tail of the Series II Austin Lancer/Morris Major models from Australia. This particular car is a Morris, which was later registered in the UK. (*Classic & Sportscar* magazine)

had tail-fins. The fact that the interior of the car was no more spacious than before was not mentioned . . .

This was not a successful car, and the Lancer was dropped in April 1962, at which point the Morris Major became the **Major Elite**, complete with 1,622cc engine and yet more nose and interior restyling. This was a flop, and it finally died away in 1964, when it was replaced by the locally-assembled Morris 1100.

By that time, the Fishermen's Bend, Melbourne, factory had been closed down for some years, and BMC had introduced Australian assembly of the Austin A60 and Morris Oxford Series VI saloons. Their next crack at cars specially developed for Australia came in May 1962, when BMC proudly announced the birth of twins – called the **Austin Freeway** and (a luxury version, this) the **Wolseley 24/80**.

The Freeway and 24/80, were essentially stretched A60-type B-Series Farina-styled cars, still with front engines and rear drive, but now fitted with a straight-six development of the B-Series engine, the capacity of which was 2,433cc.

This was a car intended to compete, head-to-head, with the General Motors Holden, but being seen to be old fashioned,

and a modification of an existing car at that, it was always going to have difficulty in becoming established. Compared with the A60, whose basic Farina-styled passenger box was retained, the MG Magnette/Riley 4/72 type of clipped-back tail-fins were adopted (but only for the Austin version), and there was a 2-inch longer wheelbase (the front wheels being moved forward relative to the windscreen to help balance the longer six-cylinder engine). There was even more of a full-width grille than on the UK-market A60s, with a simple line of horizontal grille bars. The Freeway had a Morris Oxford type of facia style, while the 24/80 had a UK-type Wolseley wooden facia.

Much of the new Blue Streak six-cylinder engine's design was the same as that of the B-Series, for the two units were machined on the same transfer lines in Sydney, and shared the same bore, stroke, pistons, con-rods, valve gear and front timing gear drive arrangements. Above all, this was intended to be a relaxed and torquey engine for Holden lovers, which explains the relatively low compression ratio of 7.7:1 and the peak power output of 80bhp (gross) at 4,350rpm. With this in mind, it was matched by a three-speed, rather than a four-speed gearbox. The upmarket Wolseley version was called 24/

Among many BMC/British Leyland Australian oddities was the Morris Nomad, a 1.5-litre Maxi-engined five-door car based on the basic engineering of the BMC 1100/1300 model. (Michael Allen/Dave Barry)

80, logically enough, because of the 2.4-litre engine and the 80bhp power output.

Regrettably, the six-cylinder engine was just as heavy as one might have expected, there was pronounced understeer on corners which no amount of juggling of springs, dampers and steering gear could rectify, and these cars never made any sort of impact on the Australian market.

For the next few years BMC-Australia gallantly shuffled its options with basically UK-specification cars, and it was not until 1970, after British Leyland had taken control, that two new versions of the Morris 1100/1300 were announced. One was the **Morris 1500 OHC** (work it out for yourselves) which had an Austin Maxi engine but a *four*-speed transmission hiding under a slightly bulgy version of the familiar bonnet, and this was allied to the **Morris Nomad**, which had a hatchback conversion at the rear and three side windows, making it look somewhat like a Maxi from some angles. The **Morris 1500 O/D 5** came along a little later, in which the Maxi's five-speed transmission was featured.

British Leyland also transferred the Mini-Moke production tooling from Longbridge to Sydney and introduced the big Austin 1800 to Australia (and also produced a useful pick-up version of that car, which was never marketed outside Australia); those last-mentioned moves had been planned by BMC before the merger occurred.

Finally, at the end of 1970, the **Austin X6** models, BMC-designed, though British Leyland-introduced, were launched. There were two versions, called **Kimberley** and **Tasman**, both of which were quite clearly developed from the basic Austin 1800 hull, proportions and front-wheel-drive/Hydrolastic suspension design. Nevertheless, these cars were the nearest to an all-Australian design that BMC/British Leyland had produced up to that time.

This was the car for which the six-cylinder version of the E-Series engine (E6) had originally been intended, and it explains designer Eric Bareham's comments of the previous year that the long stroke/narrow bore of the four-cylinder Maxi's unit was due to a 'requirement that a six-cylinder version of the same engine should fit into another car, thus restricting the overall engine length and hence the bore size'. In these Australian cars, in fact, the engine was the same 2,227cc size with which BMC 2200 owners would soon become familiar, but there was a choice of tunes – the Tasman having a single SU and 102bhp, the Kimberley twin SUs and 115bhp. Automatic transmission was optional.

The BMC 1800 heritage was well disguised in the X6 models, for there was an entirely new and squared-up front-end style, a longer and squarer back end (with some similarities to the Austin 3-litre), a different and more squared-up roof, with window frame outline changes to match, and many other details. The wheelbase was quoted at 9ft 0.1in, 2 inches longer than that of the British 1800.

The important furnishing differences, however, placed the Tasman as the cheap version, and the Kimberley as the up-market model. Tasman had two circular headlamps, a bench front seat and rubber mats on the floor, while the Kimberley had four rectangular headlamps and a different grille, separate seats, carpets on the floor and more luxurious trim throughout.

There was still some BMC/BMH influence in the last two new models to be produced by the Australian factory before it was run down rapidly in the wake of British Leyland's financial collapse in 1975. Less than a year after the British Leyland-designed Morris Marina had been launched in the UK, it was also put into production in Australia. Surprisingly, the 'Oz' version of the Marina (*Leyland* Marina, by the way) was not built with A-Series or B-Series engines, but with a choice of

Among the many Australia-only models developed by BMC was this Austin 1800 Mk II utility. It was never sold in the UK, or in Europe.

in-line Maxi-type E-Series engines of 1,485cc or 1,748cc, the latter in 78bhp single-carb or 90bhp twin-carb tunes. In due course, it was also equipped with the 2,623cc six-cylinder E6-Series engine ('one-and-a-half Maxi 1750s', if you see what I mean . . .) which Leyland Australia built, but which was never fitted to a UK model; this produced 123bhp (gross) and was given a three-speed gearbox.

Even the Leyland P76, a last desperate attempt by British Leyland to produce a large Australian Holden-beater, with front engine and rear-wheel drive, had some BMC influence in it, for the project had been started by BMC in Australia before Leyland came on to the scene (though, naturally, the tooling had not been authorized until British Leyland was in charge) – and the lower-priced version used the same E6 2.6-litre engine as the Marina of the same period.

That, however, was the end of the Australian enterprise, and the factory has been sold off for some years.

India – the elephants' graveyard
Here is a rather special case. Before the Second World War there was no indigenous motor industry in India, and when that sub-continent was still a British dominion, almost every car sold there was British. In 1946, however, Hindustan Motors Ltd, of Calcutta, was formed to produce Morris cars for the Indian domestic market.

The first Hindustan was a Morris Ten Series M (as put on sale in 1938), locally called a **Hindustan Ten**, but this was eventually followed by local assembly of a modified Morris Oxford Series MO (**Hindustan Fourteen**), and eventually by the Oxford Series II (**Hindustan Landmaster**), initially with the old side-valve engine of the Series MO instead of the

appropriate B-Series engine.

Then, in 1957, came the Indian version of the Morris Oxford SIII (complete with fluted bonnet and ribbed tail-fins, its own particular type of grille and interior trim), which took the local name of **Hindustan Ambassador**, and this carried on successfully, in the strictly limited scenario of the Indian market, into the mid-1980s. In all that time, a BMC B-Series engine of 1,489cc was standard, along with the Oxford SIII's steering-column gear-change, and to step out on to the taxi rank at Delhi airport after a 747 flight from Europe is like stepping back 30 years in time!

A Riley 4/68 pick-up? Not quite – this was the bodyshell of one version of the Di Tella 1500, which was assembled and sold in Argentina in the early 1960s.

275

Appendix D

BMC model families

Their production life charted

Even in a book as detailed as this has been, it may be difficult for some readers to grasp the twists and turns of BMC's model policy and production planning as the years progress. I hope that this two-part chart will, at least, make everything easier to understand.

The important features of BMC **family-car model development** in the 1950s and 1960s were as follows:

a) When the merger was formalized, in the spring of 1952, there was a great variety of engineering on offer:

Two completely different small cars – Austin A30 and Morris Minor.

Four different medium-sized families – Austin A40, Morris Oxford/Wolseley 4/50, MG YB and Riley 1½-litre.

Three different large car families – Austin A70/A90, Morris Six/Wolseley 6/80 and Riley 2½-litre.

One *very* large passenger car – Austin Princess 4-litre.

Because the two Rileys were basically the same car on different chassis, this meant there were no fewer than *nine* different body types, spread over five marque names.

b) In addition, two new model families, from Nuffield, were already on the way:

Wolseley 4/44 and MG Magnette ZA (launched from autumn of 1952).

Riley Pathfinder/Wolseley 6/90 (launched from autumn of 1953).

c) The most important priority was to rationalize engines and transmissions (this is explained in the next Appendix), after which a start was made on rationalizing chassis and structural design.

However, because Austin and Nuffield continued to exist, side by side, and even to compete with each other in showrooms in the same town or city, there was a general reluctance to rationalize as hard as was really needed. Between 1952 and late 1958, the Austin A40 line was replaced by a new monocoque model, as was the Morris Oxford by an entirely *different* monocoque model. Although the unique Riley chassis and the six-cylinder Morris/Wolseley chassis had been discontinued, three new families (the Nash Metropolitan, the Riley 1.5/Wolseley 1500 monocoque and the Austin A40 Farina) had been

introduced. This was the line-up:

Three small cars – Austin A35, Austin A40 and Morris Minor.

Two small-medium cars – Riley 1.5/Wolseley 1500 and Metropolitan.

Three medium cars – Austin A55, Morris Cowley/Oxford and MG Magnette/Wolseley 15/50.

Two large cars – Austin A95/A105 and Riley 2.6/Wolseley 6/90.

One *very* large car – Austin Princess 4-litre.

In other words, after more than six years of supposed ruthlessly logical business planning, there were 11 different families – two more than there had been originally!

d) By the end of 1961, great strides were being made, not only by the launch of two new badge-engineered and Farina-styled families, but by the arrival of the famous transverse-engined, front-wheel-drive Mini. The Metropolitan, the A55 Cambridge, the Morris Oxford/Cowley, the MG Magnette/Wolseley 15/50, the Riley 2.6/Wolseley 6/90 and the Austin Westminster had all been swept away. The line-up was as follows:

Three small cars – Mini, A40 and Morris Minor (plus A35 van and a few estate cars).

One small-medium car – Riley 1.5/Wolseley 1500.

One medium car – B-Series Farina A60/Morris Oxford range.

One large car – Austin A110/Wolseley 6/110 range.

One *very* large car – Vanden Plas (was Austin) Princess 4-litre.

Since the A35 estate car was about to drop out of production and the Princess 4-litre limousine was a low-production oddity at the Kingsbury factory, in North London, this meant that the entire BMC range had really been reduced to just six different model families.

e) Five years later, in 1966, BMC was in the throes of converting its range to transverse-engined front-wheel-drive cars, but there had still been time to make a bit more sense of the Corporation's resources. This was the situation at the time of the 1966 London motor show:

Three small cars – Mini, A40 and Morris Minor.

One small-medium car – Morris 1100 front-drive range.

One medium car – B-Series Farina A60/Morris Oxford range.

One medium-large car – Austin/Morris 1800 front-drive range.

One large car – Austin A110/Wolseley 6/110 range.

One *very* large car – Vanden Plas Princess 4-litre.

With the A40 Farina due to disappear in 1967, things were *almost* logical at last. More changes, in fact, were planned for the late 1960s, but then the merger with Leyland resulted in the formation of British Leyland, and

the rest, as they say, is history!

It is, however, worth summarizing that in 1971, *after* the formation of British Leyland, and well outside the scope of this book, the Austin-Morris line-up was as follows:

One small car – Mini.

One small-medium car – Austin/Morris 1100 range.

One rear-drive medium car – Morris Marina.

One front-drive medium car – Austin Maxi.

One medium-large car – Austin/Morris 1800 range.

If only the product quality and the styling had been right, *that* was a very logical range indeed.

Year introduced (I) and discontinued (D) with important changes

Model Development – Family Cars

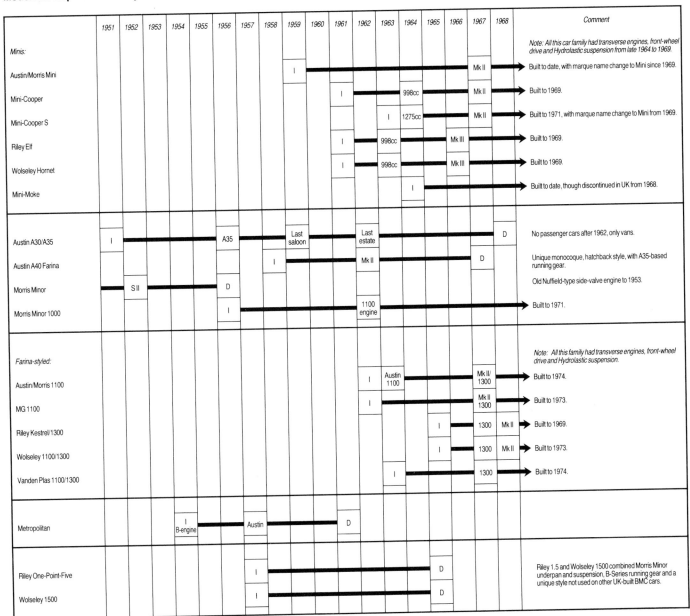

Model Development – Family Cars

	1951	1952	1953	1954	1955	1956	1957	1958	1959	1960	1961	1962	1963	1964	1965	1966	1967	1968	Comment
Austin A40 Devon/Somerset		Somerset		D															Somerset was A40 Devon with a new body style.
Austin A40/A50/A55 Cambridge				I			A55		D										
Morris Oxford MO				D															MO used Nuffield-type side-valve engine.
Morris Oxford S II				I		S III	S IV Traveller		Last saloon	D									S IV was only built as an estate car.
Cowley S II				I		1500			D										
MG YA/YB	YB		D																YA/YB cars used old Nuffield-type XP-series engine and transmission, closely derived from T-Series sport car running gear.
MG Magnette ZA/ZB				I		ZB		D											ZA/ZB style and structure was based on that of Wolseley 4/44, then 15/50.
Riley RM 1½-litre		RME			D														Short-wheelbase/small-engine version of 2½ litre model with unique Riley engine.
Wolseley 4/50			D																Same basic engineering as Morris Oxford MO, but with special ohc engine.
Wolseley 4/44 and 15/50			I			15/50			D										Same basic style and structure as MG Magnette ZA/ZB. 4/44 with engine/running gear like that of MG YA/YB, old Nuffield type. 15/50 with B-Series running gear.
B-Series Farina-styled:																			
Austin A55/A60									I		A60								→ Built to 1969.
Morris Oxford S V/S VI									I		S VI								→ Built to 1971.
MG Magnette Mk III/Mk IV									I		Mk IV							D	
Riley 4/68 and 4/72									I		4/72								→ Built to 1969.
Wolseley 15/60 and 16/60								I			16/60								→ Built to 1971.
Front-wheel-drive:																			
Austin 1800														I				Mk II	→ Built to 1975.
Morris 1800																I		Mk II and S	→ Built to 1975.
Wolseley 18/85																	I		→ Built to 1972.
Austin A70 Hereford				D															Used old early-1940s type of ohv four-cylinder 2.2-litre engine.
Austin A90 Atlantic		D																	Used A70 chassis, enlarged (2.6-litre) version of engine, but unique body style.
Morris Six				D															Same basic car as Wolseley 6/80, with long-nose version of Morris Oxford MO structure and ohc six-cylinder engine.
Morris Isis					I	S II		D											Long-wheelbase version of Morris Oxford SII monocoque using 2.6-litre C-Series engine.

Model Development – Family Cars

	1951	1952	1953	1954	1955	1956	1957	1958	1959	1960	1961	1962	1963	1964	1965	1966	1967	1968	Comment
Riley RM 2½-litre	━	RMF	D																Long-wheelbase chassis/long-nose, 2½-litre version of RM-Series 1½-litre model using unique Riley four-cylinder engine.
Wolseley 6/80	━	━	━	D															Long-nose/long-wheelbase version of 4/50 with ohc six-cylinder engine (see Morris Six).
Riley Pathfinder			I	━	━	S II	D												New style, separate chassis, using old-type Riley 2½-litre four-cylinder engine.
Riley Two-Point-Six							I	━	D										Not just a re-engined Pathfinder, more a rebadged-renosed Wolseley 6/90 using BMC C-Series engine.
Wolseley 6/90				I	━	S II	S III	━	D										Based on Pathfinder chassis and body, but always with BMC C-Series engine.
Austin A90 Westminster				I	━	A95/A105		VDP	D										First big-engined Austin monocoque, really a long-nosed look-alike of the A40/A50 Cambridge. First to use new BMC C-Series engine.
C-Series Farinas:																			
Austin A99/A110									I	━	A110	━	━	Mk II	━	━	━	D	Base car on which Wolseley 6/99 and VDP Princess 3-litres were developed.
Wolseley 6/99 and 6/110									I	━	6/110	━	━	Mk II	━	━	━	D	Mechanically as for A99/A110, but different nose style and trim details.
VDP Princess 3-litre									I	━	Mk II	━	━	D					Mechanically as A99/A110, but different nose style and more luxurious trim.
VDP Princess 4-litre R														I	━	━	━	D	Evolved from VDP Princess 3-litre, but with six-cylinder Rolls-Royce engine and restyled tail.
Austin 3-litre																	I	D Luxe →	Built to 1971 with 'new' six-cylinder engine, loosely based on old C-Series, and same centre-section as Austin 1800 (1964-1975 type).
4-litre Sheerline/Princess family:																			
Sheerline	━	━	━	D															No Sheerline passenger cars from 1950, supplied only as ambulance and hearse.
Princess	━	━	Mk III	━	━	Mk IV	━	━	D										Same basic chassis as Sheerline, but Vanden Plas-built body, with two wheelbases from 1953.
LWB Limousine		I	━	━	━	━	━	━	━	━	━	━	━	━	━	━	━	D	LWB version of S IV, produced as 'mayoral' car, with VDP body.

The important features of BMC **sports car model development** in the 1950s and 1960s were:

a) When the merger was formalized, the only BMC sports car was the MG TD, although within a year the Austin-Healey 100 had been added. It was typical of BMC planning that the TD was built at Abingdon and the Austin-Healey at Longbridge!

b) The next phase was to slot the ubiquitous new BMC engines into the sports car scene. The replacement for the T-Series MG was the MGA, which had a B-Series power train, while the second-generation 'Big Healey' was the 100-Six, which had a C-Series power train.

c) From the end of 1957, BMC centred all their sports car assembly at the MG factory at Abingdon, and from 1958 they also ensured that there would be A-Series, B-Series and C-Series-powered sports cars in the line-up. In 1961 the Sprite was badge-engineered into an MG, and the BMC line-up was as follows:
One small sports car – Austin-Healey/MG Midget.
One medium sports car – MG MGA.
One medium-large sports car – Austin-Healey 3000.

d) The MGA was displaced by the MGB in 1962, and right at the end of the BMC era the 'Big Healey' was dropped in favour of the six-cylinder-engined MGC (which used much of the MGB's styling and structure). Accordingly, in 1968, when BMC was absorbed into British Leyland, the sports car line-up was as follows:
One small sports car – Austin-Healey Sprite/MG Midget.
One medium sports car – MG MGB.
One medium-large sports car – MG MGC.

Except that the unsuccessful MGC was dropped in 1969 and the MGB GT V8 was built from 1973 to 1976, this product range was unchanged, at Abingdon, throughout the 1970s.

Year introduced (I) and discontinued (D) with important changes

Model Development – Sports Cars

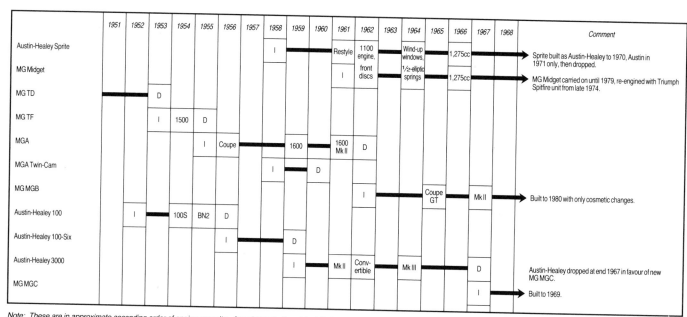

	1951	1952	1953	1954	1955	1956	1957	1958	1959	1960	1961	1962	1963	1964	1965	1966	1967	1968	Comment
Austin-Healey Sprite								I			Restyle	1100 engine, front discs		Wind-up windows, ½-elliptic springs		1,275cc			Sprite built as Austin-Healey to 1970, Austin in 1971 only, then dropped.
MG Midget												I		½-elliptic springs		1,275cc			MG Midget carried on until 1979, re-engined with Triumph Spitfire unit from late 1974.
MG TD			D																
MG TF			I	1500	D														
MGA					I	Coupe			1600		1600 Mk II	D							
MGA Twin-Cam								I		D									
MG MGB												I		Coupe GT		Mk II			Built to 1980 with only cosmetic changes.
Austin-Healey 100		I		100S	BN2	D													
Austin-Healey 100-Six						I			D										
Austin-Healey 3000									I		Mk II	Convertible		Mk III			D		Austin-Healey dropped at end 1967 in favour of new MG MGC.
MG MGC																	I		Built to 1969.

Note: These are in approximate ascending order of engine capacity – from 948cc for the original Sprite to 2,912cc for the Austin-Healey 3000 and MG MGC models.

Appendix E

Engine availability

Before, during and after the BMC years

When Leonard Lord masterminded the formation of BMC, in 1952, he wanted to create a British motoring colossus. He wanted to see BMC take on the largest car-makers in the world, all over the world.

To do that, however, his factories needed to operate efficiently, without waste or duplication, and in 1952 that simply was not likely to happen. By welding Austin and Nuffield together, his immediate achievement was to create a real mishmash of the new and the old, the successful and the unpopular, the modern and the obsolete. No matter where you looked – among the cars, the vans, or the trucks – there was duplication, and direct competition between marques.

One very obvious problem, which would need speedy resolution, was to rationalize the engine production lines. Here is why:

Immediately after the Austin-Nuffield merger, the following different passenger car engines were being used:

Type	Layout	Used in	Introduced
Austin			
A-Series	4-cyl, ohv, 803cc	A30	1951
A40-Series	4-cyl, ohv, 1,200cc	A40	1947
A70-Series	4-cyl, ohv, 2,199cc/ 2,660cc	A70 and A90	1944
D-Series	6-cyl, ohv, 3,993cc	A125 and A135	1939
Nuffield			
UHSM-Type	4-cyl, sv, 918cc	Minor	1934
VS-Type	4-cyl, sv, 1,476cc	Oxford	1948
VC-Type	4-cyl, ohc, 1,476cc	Wolseley 4/50	1948
	6-cyl, ohc, 2,215cc	Wolseley 6/80 and Morris Six	1948
XP-Type	4-cyl, ohv, 1,250cc	MG TD and MG YB	1938
Riley 1½-litre	4-cyl, ohv, 1,496cc	Riley 1½-litre	1934
Riley 'Big Four'	4-cyl, ohv, 2,443cc	Riley 2½-litre	1937

The Austin A70-Series engine was effectively a four-cylinder version of the six-cylinder D-Series. The VC-type engine was really an extensively re-engineered overhead-camshaft conversion of the Morris Oxford VS-Type, this having been done because it was traditional that Wolseley cars had overhead-cam engines! Both types were designed by the Morris Engines Branch. The two Riley engines, though looking superficially similar, and both having the twin-high-camshaft layout, had entirely different castings and details.

All Austin engines were built at Longbridge. Riley engines were produced at the old Riley factory in Coventry, and the other Nuffield engines were produced at the Morris Engines Branch factory in Coventry.

The total, therefore, added up to:

Two small-car engines
Two small-medium-car engines
Three medium-car engines
Three large-car engines
One very-large-car engine

Clearly, the Austin family of engines was much more modern, if conventionally engineered, for although the D-Series was originally a truck engine from 1939, none had been used in a passenger car until *after* the Second World War. The only postwar Nuffield engine was the uninspiring side-valve VS-Type as used in the Oxford, and the ohc VC-Type derived from it.

Strategy and the master plan

In recent years, far too many pundits have suggested that BMC failed because they did not rationalize hard enough, or fast enough. As I have already made clear, earlier in this book, this is only a half-truth, for financial, social and marketing constraints all meant that the process had to be prolonged. Leonard Lord *always* intended to ruthlessly cut down the number of different engine 'building blocks' as soon as it was practical.

Lord was the inspiration behind all such schemes. In every way he was a 'hands-on' chairman, who has often been described as a compulsive designer, and it was his master plan which gradually developed as the 1950s progressed. Lord, and Austin, were the dominant partners, so it was only reasonable that their engines, or their engine designers, should control the destiny of BMC.

Interviews with old Austin and BMC employees (of whom Longbridge designer Eric Bareham provides the most detailed information), suggests that work began on rationalizing the engine line-up as soon as the BMC merger was proposed. The 'bare bones' of a new 'universal' small-medium and medium

The Riley 1½-litre saloons of 1946-55 vintage used this 12/4 type of twin-high-camshaft four-cylinder engine (left), which was completely different from the 2½-litre Riley 'Big Four' engine (above) used in the 2½-litre model of 1946-53 and the Riley Pathfinder of 1953-57. Neither engine figured in BMC's master plan.

In the late 1940s and early 1950s, this twin-carb 2,660cc four-cylinder engine was used in the Austin A90 Atlantic (with a steering-column gear-change), but from 1953 to 1956 it found a home in the Austin-Healey 100, with this floor gear-change.

car engine were sketched before the end of 1951, and work on a new six-cylinder engine began only months later. This is what was proposed:

a) The Austin A-Series engine, newly-launched for the A30 in 1951, would become BMC's only small-car engine as soon as possible. Adaptation to other cars would be simple enough as the A-Series was a physically small unit. This would replace the old side-valve engine in the Morris Minor.

b) A new four-cylinder B-Series engine of 1.2 and 1.5 litres would be designed for use in a large number of vehicles, and would take over from the A40 unit, the side-valve and overhead-camshaft Nuffield engines, the XP-Type MG engine and the Riley 1½-litre unit.

It would be designed by Austin, built at Longbridge, and would be ready by the end of 1953. Incidentally, although it would look superficially like the A40 unit (the same team of designers would be involved in the project work), it would be a physically larger unit, and few parts would be interchangeable.

The old-design Austin D-Series was updated in the mid-1950s and used in the Princess IV and the Princess 4-Litre limousines. It was a much bulkier unit than the C-Series.

[The smaller version would have the same bore, stroke and swept volume as the A40 unit – a coincidence which has led to confusion about interchangeability in the past.]

c) A new six-cylinder C-Series engine of 2.6 litres would be designed, and would take over progressively from the A70/A90 engine, the 2.2-litre overhead-cam Nuffield 'six' and the Riley 'Big Four' 2½-litre unit.

This would be designed by Morris Engines, built at their factory in Coventry, and be ready one year later than the B-Series, before the end of 1954. It was to have nothing in common with the B-Series except for the stroke, some moving parts and valve gear, and nothing in common with any other existing engine.

d) The big D-Series engine (this being something of an unofficial title, by the way), would carry on unchanged, as it was also an essential part of the commercial vehicle scene at Longbridge. However, the Princess IV engine of 1956 was extensively redesigned and had little in common with the truck units thereafter.

History shows that this master plan never had to be altered, except in detail, for the new engine ranges appeared on schedule, and the old units were progressively phased out:

The last Morris Minor side-valve car engine was fitted in 1953.

The B-Series reigned supreme from mid-1956, when the last of the XP-engined Wolseley 4/44s was produced at Cowley.

The C-Series took over completely in cars from the summer of 1957, when the last Riley 'Big-Four'-engined Pathfinder was assembled at Cowley. The old 2.2-litre

A70-type 'four' was retained for years for vehicles like the Taxi and the Gipsy.

Here are summaries and charts of the careers of the A, B and C-Series engines in their 'BMC' years:

A-Series

Until 1956, the A-Series was only built as an 803cc unit, at which point it was enlarged to 948cc. From 1959, this size was joined by the short-stroke 848cc unit (for the transverse-installation Mini), after which the number of derivatives expanded rapidly. Over the years, and in the chronological order in which they were revealed, the following capacities were used:

Capacity	Bore and stroke	Comment
803cc	58.0 x 76.2mm	Original A30 type
948cc	62.9 x 76.2mm	Bored-out version of A30
848cc	62.9 x 68.26mm	Short-stroke version of 948cc engine
997cc	62.43 x 81.28mm	For Mini-Cooper of 1961
1,098cc	64.58 x 83.72mm	Enlarged from 948cc unit
998cc	64.58 x 76.2mm	Juggled capacity – 1100 bore and original stroke
1,071cc	70.6 x 68.26mm	Juggled bore centres, new large bore, 848cc engine's stroke. The first 'S' engine
970cc	70.6 x 61.91mm	'Homologation special' version of 1,071cc 'S' unit, with ultra-short stroke
1,275cc	70.6 x 81.28mm	Long-stroke version of 1,071cc 'S', later productionized

This is where and when they were variously used:

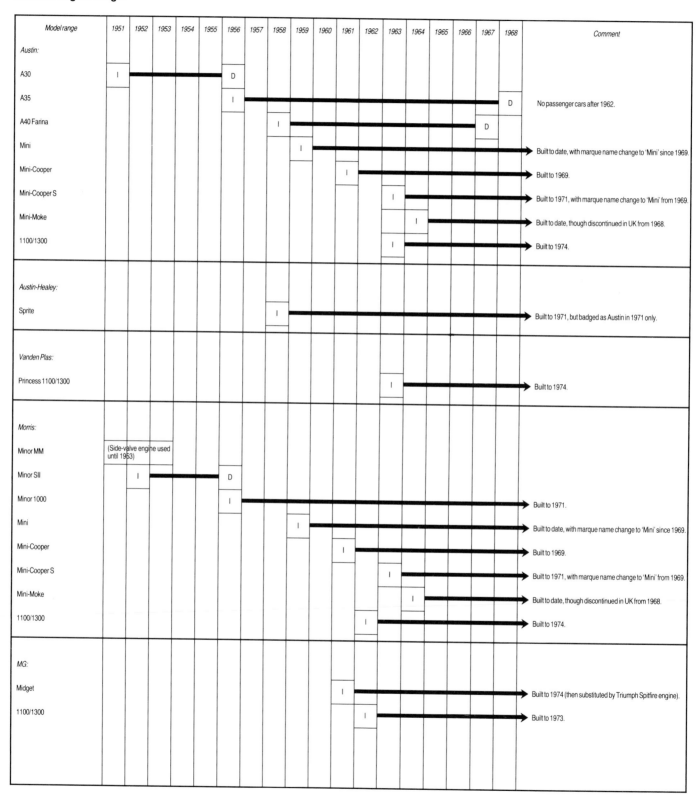

Year introduced (I) and discontinued (D)

A-Series Engine Usage:

Model range	1951	1952	1953	1954	1955	1956	1957	1958	1959	1960	1961	1962	1963	1964	1965	1966	1967	1968	Comment
Austin:																			
A30	I					D													
A35						I											D		No passenger cars after 1962.
A40 Farina							I									D			
Mini								I										→	Built to date, with marque name change to 'Mini' since 1969.
Mini-Cooper										I								→	Built to 1969.
Mini-Cooper S													I					→	Built to 1971, with marque name change to 'Mini' from 1969.
Mini-Moke														I				→	Built to date, though discontinued in UK from 1968.
1100/1300													I					→	Built to 1974.
Austin-Healey:																			
Sprite								I										→	Built to 1971, but badged as Austin in 1971 only.
Vanden Plas:																			
Princess 1100/1300													I					→	Built to 1974.
Morris:																			
Minor MM	(Side-valve engine used until 1953)																		
Minor SII		I			D														
Minor 1000						I												→	Built to 1971.
Mini								I										→	Built to date, with marque name change to 'Mini' since 1969.
Mini-Cooper										I								→	Built to 1969.
Mini-Cooper S													I					→	Built to 1971, with marque name change to 'Mini' from 1969.
Mini-Moke														I				→	Built to date, though discontinued in UK from 1968.
1100/1300													I					→	Built to 1974.
MG:																			
Midget												I						→	Built to 1974 (then substituted by Triumph Spitfire engine).
1100/1300													I					→	Built to 1973.

A-Series Engine Usage:

Model range	1951	1952	1953	1954	1955	1956	1957	1958	1959	1960	1961	1962	1963	1964	1965	1966	1967	1968	Comment
Riley:																			
Elf											I	────────────────────────→							Built to 1969.
Kestrel															I	──────────→			Built to 1969.
Wolseley:																			
Hornet											I	────────────────────────→							Built to 1969.
1100/1300															I	──────────→			Built to 1973.

The long-running A-Series engine eventually became the A-Plus, still a transversely-mounted installation with gearbox-in-sump, for the Austin Metro.

B-Series

From the start, the B-Series engine was built as either a 1,200cc or a 1,489cc unit, but the smaller capacity was discontinued in 1957; the last few were for Eire-only models called the Wolseley 1200 and Austin A45 (which were smaller-engined 1500s and A55s!). In the next few years the capacity was gradually stretched, a diesel-powered version was added, and more than a decade after BMC had been absorbed into British Leyland, the engine was finally ousted by the overhead-camshaft O-Series. In various cars, and at various times, the following capacities have been used:

Capacity	Bore and stroke	Comment
1,200cc	65.48 x 88.9mm	Original type
1,489cc	73.02 x 88.9mm	Original type
1,588cc	75.39 x 88.9mm	Only used in MGA 1600*
1,622cc	76.2 x 88.9mm	From 1961, many models (in Australia, 1,622cc units were built from 1959)
1,798cc	80.26 x 88.9mm	MGB from 1962, 1800 from 1964
1,489cc diesel	73.02 x 88.9mm	Used in some cars and vans from 1961
1,798cc diesel	80.26 x 88.9mm	From 1974, not used in passenger cars
2,433cc 6-cyl version	76.2 x 88.9mm	Used in Australian BMC cars

* Also, from 1958 to 1960, there was the MGA Twin-Cam engine, which was based on, but far removed from, the cylinder block of the B-Series engine. Such engines were assembled at Morris Engines, Coventry, rather than at Longbridge.

These are the passenger cars in which B-Series engines were used:

Year introduced (I) and discontinued (D)

B-Series Engine Usage:

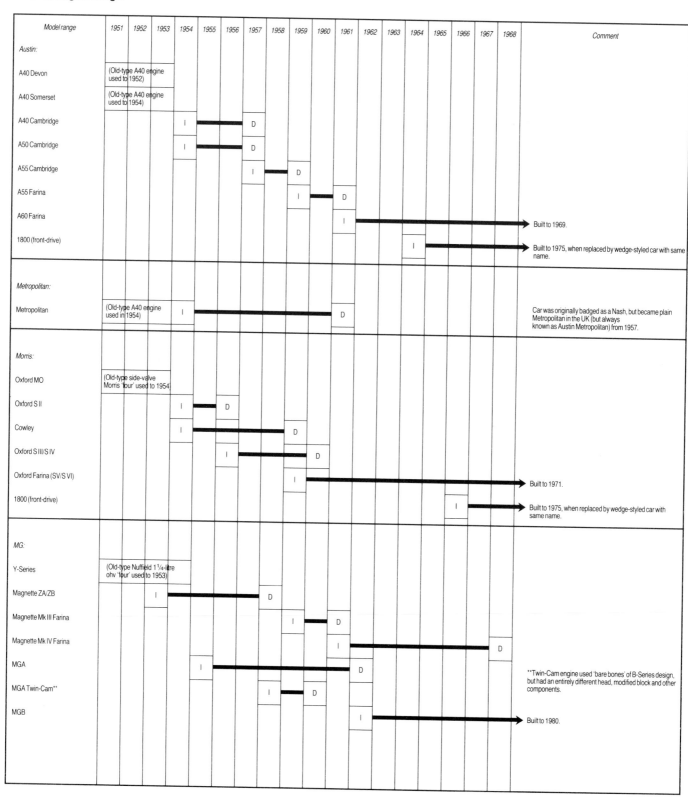

Model range	1951–1968 (I = introduced, D = discontinued)	Comment
Austin:		
A40 Devon	(Old-type A40 engine used to 1952)	
A40 Somerset	(Old-type A40 engine used to 1954)	
A40 Cambridge	I 1954 — D 1957	
A50 Cambridge	I 1954 — D 1957	
A55 Cambridge	I 1957 — D 1959	
A55 Farina	I 1959 — D 1961	
A60 Farina	I 1961 →	Built to 1969.
1800 (front-drive)	I 1964 →	Built to 1975, when replaced by wedge-styled car with same name.
Metropolitan:		
Metropolitan	(Old-type A40 engine used in 1954) I 1954 — D 1961	Car was originally badged as a Nash, but became plain Metropolitan in the UK (but always known as Austin Metropolitan) from 1957.
Morris:		
Oxford MO	(Old-type side-valve Morris 'four' used to 1954)	
Oxford S II	I 1954 — D 1956	
Cowley	I 1954 — D 1959	
Oxford S III/S IV	I 1956 — D 1959	
Oxford Farina (SV/S VI)	I 1959 →	Built to 1971.
1800 (front-drive)	I 1964 →	Built to 1975, when replaced by wedge-styled car with same name.
MG:		
Y-Series	(Old-type Nuffield 1¼-litre ohv 'four' used to 1953)	
Magnette ZA/ZB	I 1953 — D 1957	
Magnette Mk III Farina	I 1959 — D 1960	
Magnette Mk IV Farina	I 1961 — D 1967	
MGA	I 1955 — D 1960	
MGA Twin-Cam**	I 1958 — D 1959	**Twin-Cam engine used 'bare bones' of B-Series design, but had an entirely different head, modified block and other components.
MGB	I 1962 →	Built to 1980.

B-Series Engine Usage:

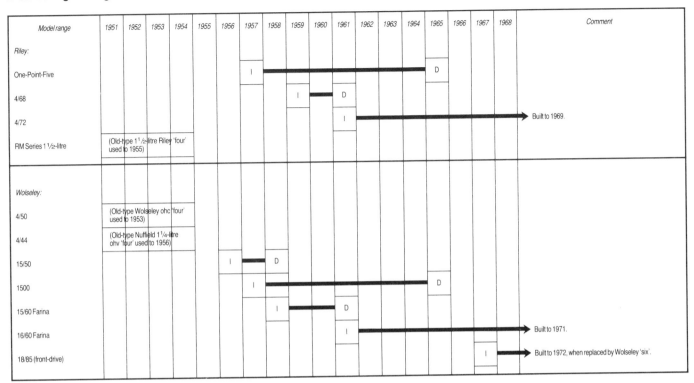

Model range	1951	1952	1953	1954	1955	1956	1957	1958	1959	1960	1961	1962	1963	1964	1965	1966	1967	1968	Comment
Riley:																			
One-Point-Five							I ──────────────────────── D												
4/68								I ─── D											
4/72											I ──────────────────────→								Built to 1969.
RM Series 1½-litre		(Old-type 1½-litre Riley 'four' used to 1955)																	
Wolseley:																			
4/50		(Old-type Wolseley ohc 'four' used to 1953)																	
4/44		(Old-type Nuffield 1¼-litre ohv 'four' used to 1956)																	
15/50						I ── D													
1500							I ────────────────────────────── D											
15/60 Farina								I ─── D											
16/60 Farina											I ──────────────────────→								Built to 1971.
18/85 (front-drive)																	I ──→		Built to 1972, when replaced by Wolseley 'six'.

This MG MGA 1600 application was typical of the way the B-Series engine was used by BMC in the 1950s and 1960s. Attached to it is the corporate B-Series gearbox, with a special remote-control gear-lever extension for the sports car application.

287

. . . or transversely, with front-wheel drive, as in the Austin/Morris 1800. In this case the 'front' of the engine is to the right (radiator) side of the picture.

B-Series engines might find themselves installed lengthways, as in the MG MGA 1600 Mk II (above), or well hidden, as in the Farina-styled saloons such as this Riley 4/68 (below) . . .

There was also a diesel-engined version of the B-Series design, seen here in 1970s display form as a 1.8-litre.

Morris Engines produced a very special twin-overhead-cam conversion on the basis of the B-Series cylinder block for use in the MGA Twin-Cam. It was nearly as wide as it was high, and it almost filled the engine bay of the MGA for which it was developed.

Capacity	Bore and stroke	Comment
2,639cc	79.37 x 88.9mm	Same stroke, but few other similarities, to B-Series
2,912cc	83.36 x 88.9mm	Bored-out version of original engine

C-Series

Compared with the smaller, more mass-market engines, the story of the C-Series is much simpler. The engine was introduced in 1954 as a 2.6-litre unit and used in various cars for the next five years. Then, from mid-1959, the size was increased to 2.9 litres, at which it remained for the next eight years.

These are the details:

Note: From 1967, a new 2,912cc engine was introduced, and was used in the Austin 3-litre saloon and the MG MGC sports car. Although the bore, stroke and capacity of the new engine were exactly the same as before, it was a shorter and lighter unit, with completely new cylinder block and head castings, and very few carry-over components.

Here is a potted history of C-Series usage:

Year introduced (I) and discontinued (D)

C-Series Engine Usage:

Model range	1951	1952	1953	1954	1955	1956	1957	1958	1959	1960	1961	1962	1963	1964	1965	1966	1967	1968	Comment
Austin:																			
A70	(Old 2.2-litre 'four' used until 1954)																		
A90 Atlantic	(Old 2.6-litre 'four' used to 1952)																		
A90 Westminster				I		D													
A95 Westminster						I			D										
A105 Westminster						I			D										
A99 Westminster									I		D								
A110 Westminster											I							D	
Austin 3-litre***																		I	***The engine had the same dimensions (bore and stroke) as the old C-Series, but was considerably different in detail, including different cylinder bore centres and major castings. It was used until 1971.

289

C-Series Engine Usage:

Model range	1951	1952	1953	1954	1955	1956	1957	1958	1959	1960	1961	1962	1963	1964	1965	1966	1967	1968	Comment
Austin-Healey:																			
100/100S	(Old 2.6-litre 'four' used until 1956)																		
100-Six						I	━━	━━	D										
3000									I	━━	━━	━━	━━	━━	━━	━━	D		
Vanden Plas:																			
Princess 3-litre									I	━━	━━	━━	━━	D					Replaced by Princess R model in 1964, which used a Rolls-Royce six-cylinder engine.
Morris:																			
Six	(Old-type 2.2-litre ohc 'six' used until 1954)																		
Isis					I	━━	━━	D											
MG:																			
MGC***																	I	⟶	***This was the same basic engine as the Austin 3-litre (see above), a distant relation of the C-Series, but by no means interchangeable with it. It was used until 1969.
Riley:																			
RM-Series 2½-litre	(Old 2.4-litre Riley 'four' used until 1953)																		
Pathfinder	(Old 2.4-litre Riley 'four' used until 1957)																		
Two-Point-Six							I	━━	D										
Wolseley:																			
6/80	(Old 2.2-litre ohc 'six' used until 1954)																		
6/90				I	━━	━━	━━	━━	D										
6/99									I	━━	D								
6/110											I	━━	━━	━━	━━	━━	D		

There were four-cylinder and six-cylinder versions of the E-Series engine, but none of them appeared until the BMC period was over. This was E6, the six-cylinder 2.2-litre unit used in the Austin/Morris 2200 and Wolseley Six models.

The C-Series engine was extensively used in saloons (as in this Austin A110 Westminster).

The much-modified 2.9-litre engine of the Austin 3-litre and, as shown here, the MG MGC, was no longer a true C-Series unit, but it was still a long and bulky engine.

The C-Series also powered the Austin-Healey 3000. This was the final-tune, 148bhp, variety of the 2,912cc engine in 3000 Mk III form, with the latest BMC C-Series gearbox already attached. The remote-control gear-lever extension was only used in this sports car derivative.

Appendix F

BMC annual production figures

The numbers tell the story

In compiling this section, I have been fortunate. I owe a lot to Anders Clausager, of the British Motor Industry Heritage Trust, for unearthing reams of production figures from the Austin Rover Group's Manufacturing Programming Department.

For the very first time, I believe, it has been possible to present Austin, Nuffield and BMC annual production figures, all according to the financial years starting on August 1, and ending on July 31. [I presume the Nuffield figures had to be reshuffled to comply with Austin and BMC standards.] In some cases these figures include the production of vehicles such as Austin A35 vans and Morris Minor pick-ups.

Year ending	Austin group	Nuffield group	BMC group
July 31, 1945	4,796	6,694	–
July 31, 1946	38,763	50,347	–
July 31, 1947	72,784	70,178	–
July 31, 1948	66,145	68,772	–
July 31, 1949	103,315	80,600	–
July 31, 1950	132,564	117,570	–
July 31, 1951	132,557	110,654	–

Then, in the interim year:

July 31, 1952	124,134	111,643	–

The following are the definitive 'BMC' years, with assembly at Abingdon, Cowley and Longbridge:

July 31, 1953	......	......	240,717
July 31, 1954	......	......	328,226
July 31, 1955	......	......	370,179
July 31, 1956	......	......	385,425
July 31, 1957	......	......	304,882
July 31, 1958	......	......	447,717
July 31, 1959	......	......	431,247
July 31, 1960	......	......	585,096
July 31, 1961	......	......	510,318
July 31, 1962	......	......	525,793
July 31, 1963	......	......	637,803
July 31, 1964	......	......	730,862
July 31, 1965	......	......	727,592
July 31, 1966	......	......	703,576
July 31, 1967	......	......	556,762
Sept 30, 1968*	......	......	719,477

(*14-month period)

Note: Even to the end of the 1967-68 financial year, these production figures are purely for BMC cars. Although BMC joined with Jaguar to form BMH during 1966, there are no Jaguar figures in the above table. Similarly, although BMH joined with Leyland (which included Rover and Triumph) in January 1968, there are no Leyland figures in the above table.

Appendix G

Annual profit figures

The bottom line for Austin, Nuffield, BMC and British Leyland

To stay in business, making cars and trucks, you also have to make money. Austin and Nuffield both performed consistently and well in the postwar period, but the BMC combine had a somewhat roller-coaster financial career.

The tables which follow are instructive, but not quite conclusive, as the Austin/BMC and Nuffield financial years were covered by different periods:

The Austin financial year ran from August 1 to July 31.

The Nuffield financial year ran from January 1 to December 31.

The BMC financial year ran from August 1 to July 31.

Austin		Nuffield	
Year ending	Gross (pre-tax) profit	Year ending	Gross (pre-tax) profit
July 31, 1945	£2,077,400	December 31, 1945	£1,943,000*
July 31, 1946	£2,249,370	December 31, 1946	£2.683,000*
July 31, 1947	£2,262,431	December 31, 1947	£2,856,000*
July 31, 1948	£1,611,903	December 31, 1948	£1,407,000*
July 31, 1949	£2,164,342	December 31, 1949	£2,685,000*
July 31, 1950	£5,080,870	December 31, 1950	£7,229,000*
July 31, 1951	£8,254,142	December 31, 1951	£8,749,000*

*The Nuffield figures are quoted to the nearest £1,000.

The British Motor Corporation officially began operating on March 31, 1952. I have not confused the issue by quoting interim 1951-1952 part-year figures for the Austin and Nuffield companies, but begin again from March 31, 1952 with extra financial information included:

BMC

Year ending	Gross trading (pre-tax)	Profit (after tax)	Dividends paid
July 31, 1952	£6,195,718	£1,854,138	£1,564,000
(4 months only)			

July 31, 1953	£15,001,907	£3,821,012	£1,708,000

The next set of figures include the Fisher & Ludlow contribution for the first time:

July 31, 1954	£21,061,844	£7,284,381	£2,024,000
July 31, 1955	£23,796,806	£11,047,882	£2,480,000
July 31, 1956	£15,825,885	£5,543,792	£2,572,000
July 31, 1957	£12,266,151	£4,127,972	£2,572,000
July 31, 1958	£25,832,404	£9,431,255	£2,572,000
July 31, 1959	£21,488,823	£8,750,242	£5,830,000
July 31, 1960	£32,983,884	£13,431,965	£5,372,000
July 31, 1961	£16,642,604	£5,878,507	£5,372,000
July 31, 1962	£11,573,647	£3,417,429	£5,368,000
July 31, 1963	£23,583,425	£9,357,522	£5,376,000
July 31, 1964	£31,405,496	£11,962,771	£6,010,000

The next set of figures include the Pressed Steel Co contribution for the first time:

July 31, 1965	£33,443,504	£16,254,847	£6,740,000
July 31, 1966	£34,357,187	£15,065,133	£10,381,632

The next set of figures are for British Motor Holdings, and include the Jaguar Group contribution:

July 31, 1967	£12,353,000	£3,869,000	£6,941,000

Following the merger with Leyland, BMH (and its major constituent, BMC) was officially wound up on May 31, 1968. The next set of figures are therefore for the British Leyland Motor Corporation, which was a vastly larger company than even BMH had ever been:

Sept 30, 1968*	£44,385,000	£20,334,000	£15,484,000
(*14 month period)			

Appendix H

Keeping it in shape

Specialist services for the collector, restorer and preserver of BMC cars

The companies whose products or services are featured on these pages offer facilities specifically tailored to the needs of owners of cars manufactured by the British Motor Corporation. They are all regular advertisers in journals specializing in the classic car movement, recent issues of which should be consulted for the most up-to-date information.

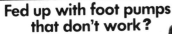

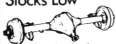

Index of BMC model descriptions